UNMECHANICAL

UNMECHANICAL

RITWIK GHATAK IN 50 FRAGMENTS

EDITED BY
SHAMYA DASGUPTA

WESTLAND
NON·FICTION

WESTLAND
NON·FICTION

Published by Westland Non-Fiction, an imprint of Westland Books, a division of Nasadiya Technologies Private Limited, in 2025

No. 269/2B, First Floor, 'Irai Arul', Vimalraj Street, Nethaji Nagar, Alapakkam Main Road, Maduravoyal, Chennai 600095

Westland, the Westland logo, Westland Non-Fiction and the Westland Non-Fiction logo are the trademarks of Nasadiya Technologies Private Limited, or its affiliates.

ISBN: 9789371971645

10 9 8 7 6 5 4 3 2 1

Typeset by Jojy Philip

Printed at Thomson Press (India) Ltd

Contents

Ritwik and I, Part One: The Collaborators

Discovering Ritwik

Ritwik Ghatak's filmography

1. *Bedeni* (1951), unfinished
2. *Nagarik* (*The Citizen*, 1952), unreleased at the time; released in 1977 after Ghatak's death
3. *Adivasiyon ka Jeevan Srot* (short film, 1955)
4. *Bihar ke Darshaniya Sthan* (short film, 1955)
5. *Oraon* (documentary, 1957)
6. *Ajantrik* (*The Unmechanical/The Mechanical Man/The Pathetic Fallacy*, 1958)
7. *Bari Theke Paliye* (*The Runaway*, 1958)
8. *Koto Ajanare* (1959), unfinished
9. *Meghe Dhaka Tara* (*The Cloud-Capped Star*, 1960)
10. *Komal Gandhar* (*E-Flat*, 1961)
11. *Subarnarekha* (1962), unreleased at the time because of censor-related issues; released three years later in 1965
12. *Scissors* (short film, 1962)
13. *Allauddin Khan* (documentary, 1963)
14. *Bagalar Bangadarshan* (1964), unfinished
15. *Fear* (short film, 1965)
16. *Rendezvous* (short film, 1965)

17. *Scientists of Tomorrow* (short film, 1967)
18. *Ronger Golam* (1968), unfinished
19. *Puruliar Chhau Nritya* (documentary, 1970)
20. *Amar Lenin* (short film, 1970), unreleased
21. *Yeh Kyun?* (short film, 1971)
22. *Durbar Goti Padma* (short film, 1971)
23. *Indira Gandhi* (documentary, 1972), unfinished
24. *Titas Ekti Nodir Naam* (*A River Called Titas*, 1973)
25. *Jukti, Tokko aar Goppo* (*Reason, Debate and a Story*, 1974)
26. *Ramkinkar* (documentary, 1975), unfinished

Editor's Note

To Ritwik Ghatak, with love

Students at Pune's Film and Television Institute of India, where Ritwik Ghatak was the vice principal for a while in the mid-1960s, will tell you about Ghatak's ghost, or spirit, stalking the institute's grounds. Said not as complaint, or in fear, but as a cause for celebration. One-time students, whether the octogenarian Saeed Mirza or the much younger Arjun Gourisaria, remember one of the most popular welcome-to-the-madhouse jokes that greeted newbies on campus: 'Watch it, what do you think you're doing!' 'What, what?!' 'You're walking where Ghatak used to walk—watch it.' Or some variation thereof.

As you walk into the precincts, one of the first wall murals you encounter is of Ghatak. Unkempt hair, more salt than pepper, stubble and thick-rimmed glasses in place, wearing a black coat of possibly questionable provenance (it's a still from *Jukti, Tokko aar Goppo*), chin resting on clasped hands, looking crabby. The mural—with an image of Supriya Choudhury's Nita from *Meghe Dhaka Tara* next to it—is right next to what the students refer to as the Wisdom Tree. Legend has it that Ghatak, never one to be confined, preferred to teach his classes under that tree.

You can't help but feel there, in that space, his presence, keeping an eye on you. Perhaps making sure you deserve to be there. I visited not long ago. I remember thinking that the expression on that piece of art might have been a bit pleasanter when it was made, but turned crabby when Gajendra Chauhan was appointed the institute's chairperson in June

2015. The students at the time certainly asked the venerable Mr Chauhan, though not in these words, 'What do you think you're doing here!'

Ghatak was and remains as much about the mystique and the lores around him—irreverent and eccentric, alcoholic and irresponsible, wastrel and genius—as about his film-making. Not many people watched his films when they were made, sometimes the world conspired to make sure they were not watched, and they made little or no money. This is still true, when many of these films are regulars on the festival circuit, and are being restored by institutions in the West, and are available right there on YouTube and elsewhere, easy to watch. But Ghatak isn't easy to watch. Maybe that's why the cult around him has kept growing. Helped no doubt by the element of mystery around the man. *Who was he? What did he do? What was his cinema about? What did he believe it could do? Why did he do what he did?* I am no expert, on cinema in general or Ghatak in particular, but I suspect few film-makers anywhere in the world are so discussed despite being so unwatched. It's curious.

This is also what makes the journey of discovering Ghatak so rewarding and exciting. Even for me, though I grew up with him, in a manner of speaking.

Ghatak died in a hospital in Calcutta on 6 February 1976, just a couple of months after he turned fifty. I was born five months later. He was my mother's chhotokaka—her father's youngest brother. My father was a great admirer of Ghatak's work and worldview. It was a left-leaning household where the arts, and conversations about the arts, were a thing. Ghatak was a frequent subject of conversation. Possibly more after *Titas Ekti Nodir Naam*, his penultimate and little-watched full-length film, was released in Calcutta for the first time sometime in the early 1990s. He returned to the conversation, and not just in our home, then. And has stayed on since. Thus, this.

Had he lived, Ghatak would have been a hundred years old on 4 November 2025. So, many of the people who knew him—and whom I would have loved to speak to for this book—are now gone. Fortunately, many of his students and some of my older relatives are very much around,

Ritwik, with Supriya Choudhury next to him, on the FTII walls; © Shamya Dasgupta

with memories to share and time to spare. From them, stories of the man emerged. From some of the leading scholars of cinema came ideas and thoughts about, and patterns in, Ghatak's work. From yet others, cinephiles and writers and collaborators, came fresh perspectives. All of these, combined with Ghatak's own articles, and pieces written by now-dead family members and others, painted a picture—warts and all—most engrossing (I hope).

The idea for this anthology came to me fully formed when members of the extended Ghatak clan were thinking of ways to celebrate the birth centenary. The man and his work have fascinated me for many years now, so this seemed a natural fit for the occasion. I reached out to people I knew, and through a ghost-to-ghost hook-up of sorts, managed to connect with pretty much everyone I wanted to. (The acknowledgements section comes at the end.) Almost no one said no. Topics and deadlines were discussed. And everyone was told upfront—in a small voice, with apologies—that I wasn't in a position to pay the honorarium they all deserved, though the publishers would be paying me a modest advance. Still, no one said no.

You see, I wasn't trying to get rich using my granduncle's name. (Get rich using 'Ritwik Ghatak'—that *is* rich!) It's just that Ghatak's son Ritaban, the only surviving member of that family, has been unwell for many years now, and has been living in a government hospital in Kolkata. The government of West Bengal, bless it, has been handling the major medical expenses as part of one of its schemes to care for the families of the state's stalwarts. But there are other expenses, too, which members of the family have been chipping in with. The proceeds of this book—such as they are—will go towards Ritaban's care.

No contributor, many of whom didn't know me when we first spoke, let it come in the way when told why I was looking for freebies. Some of them failed to deliver, but I know it wasn't for lack of trying—I blame it on them having lives.

Maudlin as it sounds, I can only put this enthusiasm down to their love for Ritwik Ghatak. Some of them knew him. All of them know his work.

Hell, one of the contributors went over their piece again and again despite undergoing a pretty serious eye surgery somewhere along the way—'no, I need to do this for Ritwikda,' they said; another had to perform caregiving duties for their partner after an unexpected health scare while juggling their own professional responsibilities, while another had to deal with their mother's poor health; almost all the academics who have contributed here had to make time around their teaching and—in many cases—marking/grading duties; there were people with other, more pressing, deadlines to meet. When I bugged them shamelessly to meet my own rather short deadline, I'd be asked, 'No, I want to do this. Can I get one more week?' One of them once wrote, 'Thank you for your patience with me, and for making me write this essay. I'm so grateful for the things I am noticing now that I hadn't before.' It worked both ways. A writer, whose essay made me rewatch one of the films I had seen countless times already, wrote, 'This is most gratifying. I consider it a great success when research and scholarship, like good art, make us look at our familiar world differently. I am glad that my piece makes you look at that film again. I love it terribly myself.'

And I am in love with everyone who has contributed to this anthology. If there is one thing I am truly happy about at the end of it all—and there are many such things—it's that I made people watch and rewatch and re-rewatch the films. Talk about an inflated and misplaced sense of power.

I mentioned 'rewarding' earlier—another reward while working on this anthology was meeting Ritaban. Babumama to me. We must have met after—what?—thirty years. He was very close to my mother, both he and Mahendra (Kumar), Ritwik's collaborator in many capacities for long years. They were both frequent visitors to our house and were very loved. But I left Calcutta (it wasn't Kolkata yet) in the late nineties and hadn't had occasion to meet Babumama after. Fortunately, thanks to an aunt (Dhriti Bagchi, daughter of one of Ritwik Ghatak's sisters, and someone with a knack for making things happen), I could.

Ritaban has led a scattered sort of life himself. And now, in his sixties, his father, mother and two sisters all gone, should have been leading a quiet sort of existence in the family home in Chetla in south Kolkata, perhaps doing the sort of work this collection is attempting to do: writing, archiving, preserving. Unfortunately, life hasn't been kind to him. And he hasn't been kind to life either. His health is no good. I wanted to do an interview with him around his work with his father's films and memories of their family life and include that here. Unfortunately—the word is so apt for everyone from that family—he answered questions in monosyllables. My takeaways were the brilliant smiles (he was a handsome man once) and the affection he showed, though I suspect he couldn't quite place me.

Ritwik Ghatak didn't get the fame or recognition he deserved when he lived. It's possible—as I realised over the course of reading the essays in this volume—that he actively avoided those things. It's possible that the love he gets in these pages would have made him happy. Feel vindicated. Though it's equally possible that he would have just called all of us 'bloody fakes' (or worse), picked up a bottle and tottered off into the dusk sniggering.

A last bit before I leave the room: the pieces are inconsistent in tone and tenor, and that's entirely deliberate; the attempt was to bring in relevant people from diverse persuasions and backgrounds, and let them speak the way they wanted to, and have something for everyone—the personal and the academic, theories and reminiscences, and whatever falls in between and beyond. I like the mix. Apart from that, there is the occasional contradiction among the writers when it comes to facts. Memories playing tricks, more than anything else. As far as possible, we have tried to correct what was correctable. Some things were not. And the final thing is that there is some overlap among the essays. This is also quite understandable, seeing that there are fifty essays dealing with a man who made only eight full-length films and lived for only fifty years. The overlapping didn't take anything away from the overall yarn for me. I hope you'll feel the same.

Shamya Dasgupta
Bengaluru, August 2025

Introduction

What binds me to Ghatak's cinema

PARAMBRATA CHATTOPADHYAY

Several decades after he's been gone, Ritwik Ghatak is finally acknowledged as one of the greats of Indian, nay world, cinema. But there's something of the underground about his celebrity still. Perhaps his films don't lend themselves to the true mainstream. And he never won a big award, such as an Academy Award, that would make him a household name.

My work takes me across the country, and I see how Ritwik is not as familiar as, say, Satyajit Ray or even Mrinal Sen. The serious film-makers, film watchers and film workers know of Ritwik and his work, of course. Some of them even celebrate him over other film-makers, which invariably leads to pointless Ghatak v. Ray debates. There is another section of people that know his name but have not seen his work. The FTII crowd of course celebrates Ritwik in a very, very big way; he taught there, and the place is rife with legends about him, tales that have become like folklore.

All of this is to say that Ritwik's appeal is limited, even now, to a section of film lovers, film enthusiasts and film workers. Which is why a book on Ritwik in English is important. There are a lot of books on him in Bangla, written both here and in Bangladesh, but those are for the converted, which is also the case with the profusion of academic work on Ritwik. An accessible, engaging book such as this in English will, I hope, open up the man and the work he did to at least a few more people. It will spotlight his groundbreaking work, and tell a new audience how he was different, how he stood out in terms of his cine-language or cine-diction. Whether or not you subscribe to his cinematic language, film-making is—or should be—a democracy of expression, and it's important to understand just how his voice stands out so distinctly. The acknowledgement of his unique outlook to both cinema and society is crucial if we are to form a historical understanding of the Indian film-making tradition.

When I started working in cinema, and my familial connection with Ritwik became known, at least some people have wanted to appraise me in light of that legacy, the fact of me being his grandnephew. But my foray into films has little connection with him or that side of my family. I grew up on Ray rather than Ritwik, to be honest. My appreciation for Ritwik came much later, with my own growth as a more socially and politically conscious individual.

So, what do I, as a film-maker and actor, share with Ritwik? How has his work influenced mine? I get asked this from time to time, and they are not questions I enjoy.

Of course, there are some overlaps in terms of sensibilities. As artists, we all need that ferment that impels us to do something. That churn, you can see it so strongly in Ritwik. It's a turmoil I recognise, even if I am quite a different sort of artist. Of course I have not, as a film director, created anything like his work, least of all a deeply political film that comes from a place of passionate commitment. His churn came from an intensely socio-political place that was, equally, deeply personal.

But it needs to be said that he was also working in a very different time in India. Today, there is a lot of work in the mainstream space in Bengali and in other languages, feature films as well as series on streaming platforms, that can be called political, but the space for jukti, tokko and goppo has diminished in the past few years. Everyone, from producers to financiers to investors to OTT platforms to distributors, is averse to the idea of making films of a certain kind. What you can do is talk about socio-political issues in a somewhat subversive way.

The most stridently political cinema today is a certain kind of agenda or propaganda film. The politics of these productions might not be to my taste, but there is space for them, as there should be for all expression.

As for me, I do have ideas that I hope to work on some day. They come from the same place: wanting to do something, wanting to make a statement about what I see around me, or what affects me or troubles me, things that I feel need to be addressed. There isn't the space for it at the moment—and of course, in a different way, there wasn't the space for Ritwik's films in his day either. But it's also true that I'm a different sort of man. Maybe one day ... when things change, when I am more established, maybe I will have that space, be in a position to make the films I want to make without giving in to market demands. I said I'm a different man, and here's the thing—I do believe in tracking market demands. It's a crushingly difficult industry, and this is essential to its survival. As things stand, I am right inside the market of that industry. I belong to it. Meanwhile, these ideas will remain inside me, dormant but not dead.

And yet ... I'd like to believe that at least some of my choices as an actor as well as in my life have pushed back at those market demands. When I did *Samantaral*, I don't think any other actor in my position would have gone ahead and played the role of an intersex person. That was 2017; today, that sort of thing has much greater acceptance. I am still doing things that I feel I should, doing what is right. Not just for myself, not just morally, but also socially and politically and ideologically. I take pride in my ability to hold to a moral centre.

If I want to make a film as a director about a reality that is very far removed from me, it might turn out to be very superficial. Wannabe. It would be a risk. But should that stop me from exploring something I really desire to say? I don't think so.

I believe Ritwik said that people are best served by making films about what they know best? But I don't know if that is fair. I come from a middle-class background in Calcutta, so that's the milieu that I know best. Does that mean that I should not attempt to make a film set against the backdrop of the Delhi elite? Or the impoverished people living in Purulia

Poster of *Subarnarekha*, the third of Ritwik's films that dealt directly with the theme of Partition

or in the Bastar? If I feel like making something along those lines, I think it's natural on the part of an artist to want to explore, to explore realities that they are not inherently familiar with.

And that is very much there is Ray's work, about situations and people he might not have a direct connect with. I know, for example, that the writer Kamalkumar Majumdar disapproved of Ray's aesthetic and artistic portrayal of rural poverty in *Pather Panchali*. But we have lived in the shadow of that film all these years. I am okay with that.

Now, I always found Ritwik's films, barring the later ones, very entertaining—this is my favourite thing to talk about.

Bengalis have always been attuned to this Victorian sense of aesthetics and morality. The thing about Ray was that he came from that place, and he tried again and again to sort of poke at that sense of morality. With a little pointed sword, so to say, he made holes there. That was the fascinating thing about him. Ritwik came from a very different place. He set his own bar in terms of aesthetics. He was the other voice. One not guided by or defined by the ideas of classical Hollywood film-making, the French new wave, Italian neorealism and so on. He was doing his own thing, which came very organically to him and was, yet, steeped in scholarship and observation.

As a film student, I have studied Ritwik a bit, and have come to understand how various indigenous art forms played a big role in shaping his aesthetics. The other film-makers, all of them great in their own ways, perhaps tried to qualify as Western aesthetes. Ritwik didn't care about that. For him, I think, our indigenous, tribal ways of prayer, of singing, of dance, of theatre were more important and relevant, and that is what shaped his sensibility. Does that mean he didn't study the canons of Western film-making? But of course he did. Maybe more than the others did. But his conscious choice of these indigenous art forms over Western ones set him apart. This is what led to Ritwik experimenting with and establishing melodrama in Indian cinema. Melodrama has, unfortunately, become a derogatory term—when it is, in fact, a vital genre. Almost the entire body of Italian neorealist films belong to the broader category of melodrama. It is a form of expression—neither good nor bad in itself. Melodrama is what our indigenous art forms draw upon.

For me, Ritwik's most influential film has always been *Komal Gandhar*. Of the many, many reasons I could cite, this is one: you see that churning where he tells the story of himself almost. One theatre group is trying to make more pro-people, more direct and political plays, where they talk about workers, labourers, farmers, exploitation, their rights, all just after Independence. And another theatre group is trying to switch to a more 'refined' kind of work—*Abhijnana Shakuntalam*, which is a great piece of art, but is not the requirement of the time. In the course of the film, we see that the members of the theatre groups answer the question themselves. They realise that the new way is not the right way, this is not the time for that. You can't turn your eyes and ears away from the realities of the time.

That's what bhadralok Bengalis have always done, being comfortable in our songs and poetry, and talking about world politics but not what is going on in our backyards. If we had been more politically and socially aware and engaged, we wouldn't have voted the same party to power for thirty-four years or, now, fifteen years at a time. If we had been politically conscious, we would have followed the logic of democracy and voted out the incumbents. Unfortunately, the alternative today is not an alternative, but that's not the point. Bengalis are sensitive people who have lofty thoughts and ideals about serious issues, but we are basically status quoists. That is something that Ritwik challenged constantly through his films, the subjects he chose. *Komal Gandhar* tells you that, no, making *Abhijnana Shakuntalam* is a cop-out. Ritwik didn't care about refined aesthetics. He cared about communicating. To do that, he resorted to home-grown theatre forms: the pala gaan, the jatra, darbeshi gaan, the gambhira and so on.

This is the lens that I look at Ghatak through. People say he made political films. I say, yes, but he was political in terms of his choices—of subjects, of forms—not because he spoke about Partition. He was conscious of how he wanted to tell a story. Going from an extreme long shot to an extreme close-up, it's a political choice, because it shocks. No other film-maker, even the best of them, would dare do something like that because they didn't want to shock the audience like that. He did it because of his understanding of melodrama as a form. So many things are happening all the time in Ritwik's films. *Subarnarekha*, it wrenches you.

I say Ritwik was entertaining—like the word melodrama, the word entertainment is also straitjacketed in our country, evoking only singing and dancing and fighting and comedy. I think entertainment could be something as basic as being able to touch the viewer. A movie as heart-wrenching as *Subarnarekha* can also be entertaining. The drama, chaos, noise is all entertaining. In *Meghe Dhaka Tara*, there are people cursing, they are walking into the frame, quarrelling among themselves—a moment of levity. On the other hand, *Bari Theke Paliye* is one of Ritwik's most intense films, even if it comes across as a lighter work. All of this is entertainment. I'll admit that *Titas Ekti Nodir Naam* or *Jukti, Tokko aar Goppo* may not qualify. But if you are not enjoying yourself watching *Ajantrik* or *Meghe Dhaka Tara* or *Subarnarekha* or *Komal Gandhar*, I don't know what to say. So much is happening there. You smile, you cry, you get angry ...

But most of all, this is what binds me to Ritwik's films: they have given me my sense of identity. Who I am. I am, before everything else, a Bengali. Not Bengali in the way the rest of India sees us: roshogolla, Durga Pujo, ilish maachh. No, I represent a community that was broken into two halves, and the partition of Bengal never did dominate the national imagination as the other one, of Punjab, did. How many cinematic pieces have we seen on the division of the eastern part of the country?

I wasn't born then, but that history lives on in me. Yes, I am Tagore. Yes, I am D.L. Roy. Yes, I am Nazrul Islam. Yes, I am ilish maachh and roshogolla and luchi and dhuti-panjabi and nyakami. But much more than that, I represent a community that was historically wronged. That is who I am. I find my connect as a Bengali there more than in anything else. Cultural identifiers are fun. But they don't define me. What's more important is that I am a product of the largest displacement in human history. I don't mean this in a communal way, and I recognise this pain across the border too. The pain of your roots being torn asunder, that is my greatest takeaway from Ritwik's films. That is why he will always remain important to me, even more than the brave and pioneering cinematic choices he made.

Kolkata
July 2025

Parambrata Chattopadhyay is an actor, director and producer in Bengali and Hindi cinema.

THE LANGUAGE OF CINEMA

Indian cinema didn't have a language before Ritwik Ghatak

SAFDAR HASHMI

On the morning of 7 February 1976, Calcuttans were shocked to learn that Ritwik Ghatak was no more. And as ill news runs apace, Ritwik's death caused an unprecedented commotion among the people of Calcutta, spreading from mouth to mouth like wildfire. By mid-day, hundreds of people from all walks of life—artists and litterateurs, clerks and workers, film technicians and directors, actors and actresses from the stage and the screen, political activists and common people—had thronged the gates of the Presidency General Hospital. Late in the afternoon, the funeral procession started. It was a unique funeral of a unique man. Thousands joined, singing all the way to the burning ghat at Keoratola. The songs he loved most.

Ritwik and Calcutta were inseparable, and by the early seventies, both had aged beyond recognition. The Calcutta that had seen the food movement of 1966, the first United Front government of 1967, the CPI(M)–Naxalite clashes, the rigged elections of 1972. By the mid-seventies, that Calcutta was gasping, and Ritwik's pulse too ran high with the city's. To the world outside, it seemed that Calcuttans were in the wilderness too—especially after the great thaw of 1972. During Ritwik's last days, Calcutta was being reigned over by thugs and terror-masters. Yet, this city rose from under the shadows of terror to pay a heart-rending tribute to her son when he left her for good.

The year 1982 will be the thirtieth anniversary of Ritwik Ghatak's first film, *Nagarik*, described by many as a watershed in the development of Indian cinema. Though many would agree that any one of his films would easily outstrip the Golden and Silver Peacock winners at international film festivals, little has been done to popularise his films or promote them internationally. But wherever they were shown, they were received with the highest honour and admiration. It is high time that this scandalous half-heartedness on the part of the Indian authorities is shed and the needful done not only to open Ritwik's cinematic treasures to the world but also to prove with pride the brilliance and stature of Indian cinema.

In 1955, film-makers and critics around the world sat up suddenly to take notice of a new phenomenon called Satyajit Ray, whose maiden venture, *Pather Panchali*, was welcomed all around as the new wind from the east. He was heralded as the creator, pioneer and acknowledged master of a new aesthetic of cinema. Over a quarter century has elapsed since then and Ray is now universally recognised as one of the greatest masters of cinema. His work has inspired scores of young film-makers in India and abroad, and is regarded by many as having given direction to modern Indian cinema.

Something that went altogether unnoticed, however, thanks to a very efficient commercial-cum-elite mechanism of resisting and suppressing anything of truly revolutionary significance, was the fact that nearly three years before *Pather Panchali* saw the light of day, one of the greatest treasures of cinema was shot and completed by a most startling genius of Indian cinema: Ritwik Ghatak. The film was *Nagarik:* for twenty-five long years after its completion, it lay in damp vaults and was condemned, it seemed, to perpetual obscurity. Only in 1977, a year after the death of its creator, was it restored and a print taken out, thanks to the initiative of the Left Front government of West Bengal. When this film was seen in different cities of India, people began realising the enormity of the damage done to the subsequent career of Ritwik Ghatak, not to talk of the course of the development of Indian cinema, by suppressing this film in 1952.

Ritwik Ghatak went on to complete seven more feature films besides several short ones during his turbulent and disturbed life. He was never free from the hounding of the powers that be. One of his most remarkable films—*Subarnarekha*—lay in cold storage for three years before it could be released. A short film called *Amar Lenin* has not yet been permitted public release, though it was made in 1970 and given a clear censor certificate in 1971. His last film *Jukti, Tokko aar Goppo* ran into a lot of trouble with the censors.[1]

The story of the physical suppression of his work is too long and painful to be recited here. Much more alarming and dangerous is the reaction of the cinema columnists, gloriously called reviewers, to present Ritwik Ghatak as a supreme structuralist and as an enigmatic and contradictory personality. Such views are clearly designed to distort Ritwik's work and its significance. The critics' effort has been to look at his work merely in terms of its contribution to the grammar of cinema, and from there to proceed to disentangle, so to say, the 'brilliant flashes of a superb craftsman' from the more expendable morass of his regimentalised content. An equally sinister school of criticism, which operates via a liberal stance, strives to establish that Ritwik's sensitivity as a film-maker lifted his content out of the constricting pale of regimentalised thought, which his intellectual commitment 'forced' him to adopt.

The second view was reflected in the long-established tendency to project Ritwik as a rebel in the Communist Party, who constantly fought the stranglehold of ideologists and theorists of the progressive cultural movement in the forties and fifties. The drunken and apparently anarchic personal behaviour of Ritwik is seen as a measure of his protest against the discipline, allegedly sought to be imposed upon creative artists by the leaders of the Indian People's Theatre Association, and at his refusal to be bound down by unnatural control of the artists' personality. What such critics fail to understand or refuse to admit is that a lifetime of hounding—and mental torture born out of uncertainties and intense privations at the hands of those who regulate the film market as well as those who man the official bodies ostensibly promoting and patronising new cinema—drove this extremely sensitive individual, poet, scholar and artist to a kind of self-imposed exile from the art world controlled by the commercial monster. An exile that broke him mentally and physically on several occasions.

What these critics also fail to understand or admit is that, in spite of such overbearing torture, Ritwik rose again and again to create films that have become rallying points for those of us who are battling decaying culture in the seventies and the eighties. Far from being a rebel protesting against 'constraints' within the cultural movement, Ritwik, unlike many erstwhile luminaries of the progressive cultural movement, never wavered in his pursuit of a medium and a message that is true to the people and carries on their struggles in the artistic sphere, he never placed his art at the disposal of commercial cinema or fell prey to the attractions of glamour and riches. In his films, he used no populist elements, the shortcuts to popularity resorted to by so many of our so-called 'radical' film-makers these days.

When Ritwik shot his first completed film, *Nagarik,* in 1952, he had very skeletal facilities, a shoestring budget and a cast entirely unused to the film medium. He had the heritage of a medium which had not yet developed in its discipline in India. Yet, propelled by the desire to project the complex nature of his subject, Ritwik brought to bear upon his treatment the accumulated knowledge of the medium from the world over, and produced a work that was as advanced in its technical and grammatical structure as in the conceptual treatment of his story. Gifted as he was with a historical vision, Ritwik made pioneering use of sound as an instrument of structure in his film within a dialectical framework. In his hands, for the first time, sound in Indian cinema graduated from merely amplifying dialogue and 'effect' music to becoming a conscious part of the whole design, serving as much to highlight as to comment, analyse and throw into analytical perspective the immediate dialogical and narrative context.

Another innovation of Ghatak's, which he used in *Nagarik* and which became a characteristic of his later style, was the device of using deep focus to place his characters firmly in their social environment. The first visual introduction of his central character comes only after a panoramic sweep of metropolitan Calcutta, the camera panning over shanties and shops, high-rise buildings and ghettos, webs of electric wires all over the city and streets crowded with common people going about their work. Then, in a long shot taken from a height of at least twenty feet, he introduces his character, one of a crowd, helping an old woman cross the street. He tracks his common-man hero to his house through narrow dirty lanes amidst beggars and street performers. After all this, when the camera closes up on the face of the hero, the audience has already accepted him as one of them—in no way extraordinary, heroic, rich, handsome or promising adventures in a world of fantasy. It is the same with all his characters and all his films. This style is a conscious rejection of the popular and degenerate school, where it is the peculiar predicament or fortune of a unique individual that is subjected to close focus and scrutiny, where only those qualify for such scrutiny who have somehow stepped above or away from ordinary life.

It will not be possible to explore Ritwik Ghatak's entire career in this short introductory article. We will, therefore, very briefly discuss the contribution to the people's cinema as well as to cinema language made by this genius through his films.

Till Ritwik Ghatak appeared on the scene, Indian cinema was at a very primitive stage of development. Though some forceful forms of social protest had been made, cinema as such consisted mainly of a stationary camera or two recording a straight narrative, much like a spectator watching a play unfold on a brightly lit stage. The possibilities of analysis and interpretation, which camera angles, modes of editing, juxtaposition, visual symbolisation, scene arrangement and other techniques offer, were hardly explored by our film-makers. In brief, a distinct cinema language had not emerged. Ritwik showed for the first time that the movie camera was not merely an unobstructive eavesdropper, but a commentator, philosopher, historian, critic and poet. Not a peep-window into the lives of a group of characters but a testament of life as such: narrating, recalling, rejecting, accepting, questioning, protesting, losing and winning. Ritwik thus imparted to Indian cinema a sense of discipline and conscious use of the new language. From *Ajantrik*, through *Bari Theke Paliye*, *Meghe Dhaka Tara* and *Komal Gandhar* to *Subarnarekha*, Ritwik had developed his style sufficiently to create the new structure of cinematic expression his stories demanded. In *Subarnarekha*, we find the film moving at several different planes simultaneously—dialogue, music and the visual image cease to remain mere instruments of carrying the 'story' forward. Each has a life of its own, distinct from the fusion. Each moves on its own as much as it contributes to the totality of the film and is born of that totality. For instance, the dialogue and music at times follow divergent and

Poster of *Nagarik*, Ritwik's first film, made in 1952 but released only in 1977;
© NFDC – National Film Archive of India

contradictory courses; each carries an independent meaning, and a third more profound meaning is born with the collision of the two. He takes ordinary real-life situations with elements even of emotionally charged melodrama, but historicises them in such a way that the sympathies and the antipathies of the audience go beyond the specific pathos of the characters and start reverberating and responding to the pains, sufferings, cruelties and injustices that are factors in the life of our class-related society. Tracing the career of his protagonists through situations of extreme trauma and suffering, he asserts towards the end that life goes on. The essence of the future focused in *Subarnarekha*, for instance, in a little child guiding the tragic hero towards the horizon, which holds the promise of continuing struggles with suffering. 'Man will emerge victorious' is the message driven home inescapably in a tender and poetic manner so different from a sloganised assertion of the same message in the works of the more mediocre of his contemporaries both in theatre and cinema.

The recurrence of the child becomes perhaps the most important 'device' to assert the continuity of life in at least five of his eight films. In the other three, the same thing is done with different symbols. In *Komal Gandhar*, it is signified by marriage; in *Bari Theke Paliye*, by the return home of the runaway child; in *Nagarik*, by the pauperised family moving to live in workers' quarters, leaving behind their middle-class locality and values.[2]

Ritwik Ghatak, though he worked with a medium which promotes individualism, especially when a progressive cinema movement exists, never lost sight of the objective perspective on the role of the artist. He never attempted to assume the voice of a seer or a prophet. Rather, he described his work and achievement in extremely modest terms: 'No film-maker can change the people. The people are too great. They are changing themselves. I am only recording the great changes that are taking place.'

In 1974, in a state of ill-health and near nervous breakdown, he completed his last film, *Jukti, Tokko aar Goppo*, a film so daring in its complete disregard of the very language and grammar of cinema he had mastered and developed that it is difficult to understand how it achieves its intense intimacy with the audience. It is as if the characters step out of the screen to talk to you and you are forced to respond to them, to react very sharply for or against them. The central character, played by Ritwik himself, parodies his real life in such a way that it compels the audience to reflect and criticise him. Perhaps that is just what Ritwik had been struggling to do through cinema all his life. Ironically, perhaps he wanted to see whether it could be achieved only through a conscious rejection of much of what has come to be accepted as the language of cinema.

This great film-maker, neglected all through his life by the bourgeois critics, hounded by the establishment and crushed by those who control the film industry, died on 6 February 1976 at the age of fifty-one.[3] He had several projects in mind, which included Manik Banerjee's great novel, *Padma Nadir Majhi* (The Boatman of the River Padma). These will never be completed now,[4] but the name of Ritwik will live. Five years after his death, Ritwik is beginning to relive. His films are being claimed by the people again. The people are resurrecting what an entire generation of his enemies could not destroy. His work shall soon prove to be a source of inspiration for new film-makers and for cultural activists. His films will be claimed as models of excellence in cinema.

This piece, entitled 'The Genius that Was Ritwik Ghatak', was originally written for Student Struggle *in 1981. It has been published in this collection with permission from Moloyashree Hashmi and SAHMAT. It has been lightly edited for house style. Notes have been added by the editor.*

Safdar Hashmi (12 April 1954–2 January 1989) was a communist and one of the founder members of the Jana Natya Manch (JANAM) in 1973, a revolutionary theatre group that was instrumental in the creation of an all-India street theatre movement. He was also one of the main organisers of the Committee for Communal Harmony. Hashmi was murdered by political goons while performing the play Halla Bol *in Jhandapur, Uttar Pradesh.*

Notes

1. The Indian National Congress was in power in West Bengal in 1952. When *Amar Lenin* was made, it was a turbulent time in West Bengal, with president's rule in place owing to the collapse of successive coalition governments, and that was followed by an Indian National Congress government in mid-1971. Curiously, though the eighteen-minute film has since been shown at some screenings, 'external pressures', understood to be from the Trinamool Congress government in the state, prevented it from being screened at a festival in Kolkata as recently as February 2025. The Indian National Congress was also in power in West Bengal when *Nagarik* was made in the early 1950s.
2 It's likely Safdar Hashmi wanted to include *Ajantrik*, where the 'dead' car is kept 'alive' by a child playing with its horn, which had fallen off the cart when the car was being taken away.
3. He was a few months past fifty.
4. *Padma Nadir Majhi* was made by the director Goutam Ghose in 1993, and was produced, interestingly enough, by Habibur Rahman Khan, who had also produced Ritwik Ghatak's *Titas Ekti Nodir Naam*.

A BIO-SKETCH IN SEVEN PARTS

A daredevil who always got into trouble

MAHASWETA DEVI

Ritwik was my chhotokaka (youngest paternal uncle), but he and his twin sister Pratiti were older than me by just two months. They were called Bhoba and Bhobi at home. We grew up like siblings, all together.

Everyone was a bit cautious around Tutul [Mahasweta's father, the poet and novelist Manish Ghatak]. They all addressed him as 'aapni'. Tutul, despite being the oldest in his family, was 'Mejda' [second-oldest brother] to everyone because he wasn't the eldest among his cousins. Even his brother Sudheesh, just a couple of years younger, used 'aapni' to address him. Bhoba didn't even go where he might fall within Tutul's line of vision. When he was older, and known to everyone as Ritwik Kumar Ghatak, he would refer to my father as 'MG Super'. Not in front of him, in private. My mother was their sister-in-law, and the brothers all used the respectful 'aapni' for her too.

Bhoba and Bhobi were my playmates. We fought, we played, we spent all our time together as we were growing up. If we were separated for long, there was so much crying and shouting. So I often stayed with their parents, my grandparents, and they stayed in our house often too. Tutul thought of Bhoba, Bhobi and me as the same—children, no different.

Like I said, Bhoba stayed as far away from Tutul as he could. But that wasn't always possible.

Ritwik by Marxist painter Bijon Choudhury; © Ghatak family archives

It must have been 1934, Dhaka; we were staying in a house called 'Nalini Kutir'. Both Bhoba and I were reading a Bengali edition of *The Arabian Nights*, or *A Thousand and One Nights*, edited by Ramananda Chattopadhyay, with great interest. One of the stories mentioned a root or tuber of some sort, white in colour, that had been dug up, and the princess who ate it gained eternal youth. Bhoba and I decided that we had to get a hold of that thing, we had to eat it, so we could have eternal youth too. We were too young to know what eternal youth meant, but it sounded like something we should have.

As it happened, maintenance work was on in the garden at the time. Near the wall on one side, there were some maankochu (taro root) plants. The sun never got to those plants, and if you ate maankochu that grew in the shade, your throat itched horribly. The gardener had removed the plants and kept the roots by the side of the wall. They were white. Bhoba and I saw the roots, and it was like touching the moon. We could eat the roots, and voila! Eternal youth! Bhoba, Bhobi and I didn't waste a moment. We picked up the roots and started chomping on them.

Soon, we were making horrible noises, shouting, screeching as we ran back to the house. If anything happened to us, Tutul would panic and start shouting too, usually in English: 'Dangerous! Accident! Poison case? Snakebite?'

Bhoba was so evil. With his swollen throat, he was showing Tutul the roots and saying, 'Khuku, Khuku' [Mahasweta's nickname].

Tutul, still shouting: 'All three of them will die.'

My mother and grandmother were more sensible, practical. They made us lie down on the dining table, and, using their fingers, massaged the inside of our throats with a tamarind-and-mustard-oil paste. Our windpipes had almost closed. When we were in a position to talk, Tutul asked Bhoba, 'What made you eat those roots?'

Scared, Bhoba said, 'Not me, I had nothing to do with it. Khuku said that if we ate the roots, we would have eternal youth.'

'What would you have?' Tutul's roar shook the foundations of the house.

'Eternal youth.'

Tutul was stunned into silence. I was thinking that I needed to just get hold of Bhoba, alone, and then I would show him. Ma never disbelieved Bhoba. My grandmother asked Tutul to leave the room. Things ended there.

Bhoba and I often got into trouble of this sort. The two of us frequently found ways to steal food, and both of us could eat a lot too. In 1937, one of my paternal aunts, Milima (Bratati) got married. Her husband, Anil Bhattacharya, lived next door to us in Bakulbagan Row. Milima and her sister Dollyma used to call me Khukuma when I was a child, so I added the 'ma' to their names too. My brothers and sisters, all younger, followed my example. Everyone in Milima's in-laws' house knew me well.

So, we went to Milima's bou-bhaat [a wedding reception of sorts]. Tutul was outside, welcoming and speaking to everyone. Bhoba came to me and whispered, 'They have kept all the sweets on the floor in the kitchen. The cham-chams are huge. You can't imagine how big they are.' The two of us immediately made our way to the kitchen. No one was there. On massive platters arranged on the floor were the milk-white cham-chams. And they really were very large. Both of us picked up a few of them and stuffed our faces. Our mouths burned! Those were not cham-chams at all. They were mutton chops, not fried yet. Neither could we swallow them, nor could we get rid of them. Finally, we ran to the bathroom. There was a large choubachcha [indoor tanks for storing water] there. We spat out the raw mutton chops, drank water, gargled … shivering in fright all along, scared that Tutul might find out.

I don't know who informed Tutul about it. Bhoba and I could barely eat the wonderful food served at the reception, our mouths were still stinging. The next day, Tutul was speaking to his mother. 'Did Bhoba and Khuku eat well last night? Bhoba, how was the food?'

'Very good,' he mumbled.

'Hmmm, I see. It's not easy to eat after stuffing your face with raw mutton chops, is it?'

Both of us kept absolutely quiet. What could we say?

We had been told that Tutul and his friends used to bring out a hand-written magazine when they were younger. In 1939, when we were living in Earl Street, Bhoba announced that we would do the same, and that he would be the editor. The main writers were Bhoba, my cousin Tushki and I. Tushki's handwriting was the best among us, so she wrote the whole magazine. And Bhoba used to draw well, so he became the illustrator.

Bhoba was always good at drawing. In 1932-33, my grandfather was the district magistrate in Mymensingh, and we used to live in a beautiful house by the Brahmaputra river. Bhoba and I used to fight a lot those days. To make up, Bhoba would draw a series of sketches with a chalk on the floor of the veranda. It would tell a story, like in a comic book. We are playing in one panel. Then we are fighting in the next. Then we are walking away from each other. Then Bhoba is holding out a mango or a banana or a fruit of some sort for me to take. And then we are playing again. Things like that.

Our first code when we put together the magazine was that none of the elders should know about it. It would appear one day and everyone would be stunned. In a house where no one slept in the afternoon, it wasn't easy to do this in secret. Also, Bhoba and I weren't supposed to know what the other was writing. Only Tushki would know, but she had already sworn that she wouldn't tell anyone anything. I seem to remember that Tushki had also written a poem.

Anyway, the magazine made its appearance one fine morning on the drawing-room wall. We peered in from outside, and saw the elders reading it, smiling, laughing. We wanted to know Tutul's opinion most of all. When he finished reading, Tutul guffawed loudly. Some of the others had finished reading it already. He said, 'Why are all of you calling Bhoba precocious? It's quite good. Khuku, well, it's not so original.'

I knew this would happen. I had just read *Pather Panchali* and, severely affected by the story about the grave of a saheb's son or daughter in the Neelkuthi [an indigo factory], had written 'The Autobiography of a Grave'.

But the elders—aside from Tutul—seemed to be quite worried about Bhoba.

I don't remember exactly what he had written, but the gist of it was that many women had come into Bhoba's life already, and all of them had left him confused and disturbed. The only line I remember went: 'The one that came this time wasn't Atoshi or Manoshi, she was …' The first two names were made up. But the third was of a real person. She must have been ten. Very pretty. Thin as a reed. She used to run like the wind. We used to play together at Maddox Square in the evenings.

That evening, Tutul, suppressing a smile, told us, 'Bhoba has written quite well. Khuku too. Tushki might have a poet within her. The drawings are first-class. All of you should keep at it, write about whatever you feel like.'

Bhoba was walking on air after that. But the people that really mattered—Ma, our aunts—decided that there was no need for us to worry about literature, we needed to concentrate on our studies.

While we lived in that house, Bhoba once did something very reckless. Tutul was fond of collecting things, buying fancy things he didn't need. He had a pair of dark blue swimming trunks. Why he bought them, I don't know—we never saw him wear them and go swimming. But he would occasionally say that he wanted Bhoba to learn how to swim—'it's vital'. I don't know if Bhoba ever learnt to swim. But he once told us about the swimming trunks while reminiscing about our childhood.

He had long had an eye on those trunks. Sometime in 1939, Bhoba managed to get his hands on the trunks, and armed with them, went off to the lake at the crack of dawn. He didn't know what to do after that, so he went and stood on a diving board, wearing the trunks, arms crossed in front of him, in the pose that Swami Vivekananda made famous. Just then, someone shouted from behind in Hindi, 'Arre Bachchu, what are you looking at, dive!' And then pushed him into the pool. Bhoba went in the water, and straight under. Somehow, he managed to get to the surface and scream, 'I don't know how to swim, help!'

The gentleman immediately jumped in after Bhoba, rescued him and brought him out of the water. Both of them, drenched, sat there staring at each other. The man was shaking his head and saying that he was a great sinner. He used to bring his little brother to the lake to teach him to swim every morning; the boy had learnt to swim, but was scared of diving. He had mistaken Bhoba for his brother, and so on ...

He dropped Bhoba home in his car after that. Bhoba looked triumphant. He had a lot of sweets and chocolates with him. Tutul, hearing everything, started screaming at Ma. 'Bhoba could have died today. It could have been a disaster.'

Turning to Bhoba, he asked, 'When you don't know how to swim, why did you go to the lake?'

Bhoba had this ability to scrunch up his face and speak in a sobbing voice even when he wasn't crying—something my brother Pholgu also mastered in later years. What Bhoba said was that he thought if he put on the swimming trunks, he'd be able to swim.

Ma pointed to the swimming trunks and told Tutul, calmly, 'If you keep such rubbish at home, young children will naturally be attracted to them. Bhoba is no exception.' After this, Tutul and Ma started arguing about things from ten years ago, how a pair of hunting boots Tutul had bought had never been used and had become home to a family of mice, and so on.

Bhoba, no credit to him, suddenly became a hero to all of us.

That was just one instance. He really had the luck of the devil.

When we were children, we were almost never given any money. In our grandfather's Bakulbagan Row house, there was a room with glass windows all around. Everyone used to go to that room in the evenings and sit and chat. Sometimes, because someone had been careless, an anna would be lying around, and we felt like kings if we found it. With one anna, those days, you could get lots of things. Chocolates packed in golden foil, made to look like gold coins; sugar cigarettes that looked like real cigarettes ... Bhoba would go and buy what he could, and we all sat around and ate them.

Bhoba was the only one who found twenty-five paise coins or other coins of great value. One time, when he found such a coin, it was already dark and the children weren't allowed to go out then. But he told us, 'Don't worry, I will run to the store and come back quickly.' We were so worried. Would the elders get to know? Would Bhoba eat some of the stuff on his way? That sort of thing.

He had stuffed his pockets with whatever he could, and then, dangling a cigarette lozenge from his lips, was walking back.

Those days, it wasn't just the family elders, but even neighbours who disciplined the children. When Bhoba was walking back, a gentleman from the neighbourhood mistook him for his own brother and was so angry—walking around after dark, that too smoking! He caught hold of Bhoba by an ear, and gave it an almighty pull. Then, when he realised it wasn't a real cigarette, he was most contrite. Like the other man, he also took Bhoba to the shop and bought him a huge packet of sweets and chocolates.

When we were young, Tutul had very little time for us; he barely ever spoke to us. In a family of many people, there was a big gap between the seniormost and the youngest members. And when Bhoba became known as Ritwik, the people who spent time with him and knew his stories—like my brothers Anish and Abu and Pholgu—where were they then? All of them had left us one by one. By then, I too was living in Calcutta most of the time, busy with my own life and family.

Bhoba completed his BA from Baharampur, where my parents had built their home. That's where his wedding reception took place too. The stories of that time, with Tutul and a grown-up Bhoba in the same house, must have been fantastic. My sister Konchi or youngest brother Tantu might know more about those days.

I heard about Bhoba's death (in 1976) from my brothers and sisters. Pholgu had been visiting with his wife and infant son from Patna, so there was a festive atmosphere at home. Lots of good food was being cooked. The newspapers used to reach Baharampur late, around 11 a.m., from Calcutta. Tutul got the newspaper first, and hid it in the drawer of his study table. He also picked up the transistor and put it in his almirah. Tutul sat down to eat with a grave expression. He never ate a meal without meat or fish, but said he didn't want any that day.

All day, he sat at his table, silent, doodling on a sheet of paper. In the evening, he called Ma and asked her to sit down beside him, and said, 'Bhoba is gone.' They sat in silence. Tutul had his hand on Ma's back. Both of them were shaking, hands covering their faces, crying. My brothers and sisters who were there told me what had happened.

When *Nagarik* was finally screened the following year, severe diabetes had left Ma blind, and Tutul left the theatre midway. That's how it was.

Excepted from Mahasweta Devi's family memoir Tutul *(published by Swarnakshar Prakasani, Kolkata, in 1994). Translated by the editor with permission from the writer's grandson, Tathagata Bhattacharya.*

Mahasweta Devi (14 January 1926–28 July 2016), a global icon of Indian literature, was a multiple-award-winning writer and a fierce political activist. Her notable literary works include Hajar Churashir Maa, Rudali *and* Aranyer Adhikar.

Ritwik wrote the script of *Titas Ekti Nodir Naam* on my saree

PRATITI DEVI

After my father's retirement, my parents spent a part of the year in Rajshahi and a part of it in Calcutta. Ritwik and I were in a collegiate school in Rajshahi. We didn't know at the time that schools were boys-only and girls-only. But we did know that Ritwik and I couldn't spend a minute apart. The headmaster of the school broke the rules and allowed me to enrol in his boys' school so I could study with Ritwik. I think I was the only girl in that school, though I found out later that my name wasn't in the school register. We wore the same uniform: white shirt and white shorts.

Once, while trying to untie the rope attached to the hand-pulled fan in the school, I fell down and broke my arm—for the second time in my short life thus far. I was more mischievous than Ritwik back then. Over the course of my childhood, I would fracture my arms three times and my legs four times. If anything happened to me, Ritwik would cry very loudly and shout for my mother. So loudly that our neighbours would rush to us.

I was taken to Calcutta that same night, and for the second time, Dr Bidhan Chandra Ray had to pick me up in his arms and take me to his clinic to get an X-ray done.

We returned to Rajshahi after a month-and-a-half. And some days later, I got diphtheria. It is a very contagious disease. No one but Ma was allowed to enter my room. Every morning, Ritwik would sneak into my room, chat with me while finishing off the Horlicks and fruits and whatever else had been placed there for me, and run off to school. When he was caught, Ritwik told Ma that he had just come in to check the clock. Ma caught hold of him, examined his throat, and asked him to stay in the room, the doctor would be coming to see him. Ritwik was most thrilled. He and I could stay together again. We recovered about a month later, and after that, it was back to school, games, putting together small plays and lots of stories.

It was around this time that a strange incident took place in Ritwik's life. Thinking about it later, I realised that it's these sorts of things that can turn a person's life around.

I was studying in a girls' school by then. It was evening. Ritwik had yet to return from his school, and everyone was starting to get worried. Baba said that he would go to the school to check. Just then, we saw two people bringing an unconscious boy in a horse-drawn carriage. From what they said, we gathered that some people had fed Ritwik something, possibly poisonous, and thrown him in the pond behind the school. He was half submerged in the water when they had found him. The doctor arrived soon. He immediately washed Ritwik's stomach, and after some tests, confirmed that the boy had been chloroformed. Ritwik was carrying his school fees that day, and he was wearing a watch on his wrist. The headmaster and the police did their bit but couldn't find the culprits. Maybe they had crossed the Padma and gone off to a village on the other side. Or run away to Murshidabad.

When he regained consciousness, Ritwik told us that some people had taken him to a small room somewhere and given him a very sweet drink in a large glass. He couldn't remember anything else. The doctor said that Ritwik had survived because he had been thrown into water. If not, he would have died that day.

Sometime after that, we returned to Calcutta and lived with Mejda [Manish Ghatak], who was based there at the time. So we didn't return to Rajshahi for a while. Mejda got Ritwik enrolled at Padmapukur

Still of a crucial moment in *Titas Ekti Nodir Naam*;
© NFDC – National Film Archive of India

Institution School. Ritwik had still not entirely recovered from the shock or the physical pain. He couldn't concentrate too well for too long, but he managed his studies. There was an arrangement that either Mejda or Boudi [Manish's wife] would sign a register when they dropped him off at school, and a class teacher would do the same when he left.

Not long after, Mejda decided that it might help Ritwik to study in some sort of a technical education set-up, ideally away from Calcutta. He had travelled to Kanpur on work, and met some people there—at the time, it was mainly an industrial town. Ritwik was in the eighth standard then. Mejda took him and got him enrolled at a school there. I can't remember who Ritwik lived with in Kanpur.

Kanpur changed his life altogether. Remember, it was a town with a lot of labourers and other low-wage workers. Even at that age, Ritwik understood that they were exploited, how they were made to work more than they should have been and how little they were paid for it. That realisation made him—then and in later years—work with people from the poor and working class.

Mejda would keep an eye on Ritwik from a distance. Once, he visited Kanpur and found out that Ritwik had been hanging around with labourers and discussing their excessive working hours. They were made to work eighteen-hour days without being paid overtime. The police commissioner was a British gentleman. He expressed great appreciation for what Ritwik had been up to, but also cautioned Mejda.

After Mejda returned to Calcutta, Boudi suggested that Ritwik should not be so far from home, and that he should be brought back to Calcutta. It must have been 1939, since the war broke out around then. That made the decision easier—he couldn't be kept in faraway Kanpur in such circumstances. He came back, skinny and well over six-feet tall. Calcutta was in complete wartime preparedness at the time; white-faced soldiers were in every nook and cranny.

Ritwik went back to Padmapukur Institution School to complete his matriculation exams. The government had instituted a system of civil guards because of the war. Ritwik joined the guards. Maybe because he wanted to help the most underprivileged people at a time when they would have been forgotten. He used to spend a lot of time with these people, even at night.

Our colonial rulers issued evacuation orders towards the end of 1941. As a result, a heavily populated city like Calcutta became almost empty. We moved back to Rajshahi, though our brothers stayed on in Calcutta for work.

After returning to Rajshahi, Ritwik, then just sixteen, and Mahasweta [his niece, though only two months younger] joined the still fledgling Communist Party of India. The Soviet Union had joined the Allies in the war against Germany. Before we realised it, we had come to 1942, and it was time for the Quit India Movement. Ritwik got very seriously involved with civil society initiatives and started travelling to remote parts of Bengal. Ritwik and Mahasweta travelled to the Dooars, I remember, and met people in the jungles there to spread the anti-British message. A few days after they returned, Ritwik fell seriously ill. He recovered in time to complete his Intermediate Arts exams.

Ritwik didn't spend a minute at home during the daytime. He used to read at night. Mainly literature, and books on politics, cinema and photography. Never his textbooks. He would wake up in the morning at around 9.30, have a pot of tea, pick up a pen or a pencil and go off to write his exams. The principal of Rajshahi College, Dr Snehamoy Dutta, came to Baba later and told him, 'If Ritwik had even glanced at his textbooks before the exams, no one could have stopped him from getting a rank. He would have been the pride of our college.'

I wasn't allowed to go watch a film in the theatre without an elder chaperoning me until I was fourteen or fifteen. *Romeo and Juliet* had just released. I was the only one who could pester Baba, arms around him, and convince him to allow us to go. I succeeded, and we went to a theatre called Aloka. Ma also came with us. The film played in the theatre for eight days, and we went to watch it every day. And each night, some of us built a set of sorts in our bedroom and re-enacted the film. Baba was pleased that all of us were speaking such good English, but we didn't allow anyone in the house to sleep.

Baba asked us for a gist of the film. Ritwik, speaking very stylishly, replied, 'Baba, the only solution is suicide.' When I was asked, I said, 'The scene I liked the most was of Juliet's body floating on the flower-filled lake.' We both looked at it the same way, more or less, but we expressed ourselves differently.

Then we come to August 1946. The time of the communal riots, 'the week of the long knives'. Ritwik and his friends had spread themselves around the sensitive Hindu and Muslim areas, standing guard. Very often, Ritwik wouldn't return home. What he ate, if he ate at all, we didn't know.

Even though some sort of normalcy returned after a few days, the sense of fear didn't go away. What Ritwik did at the time, the enormous resolve and dedication he showed, the strength he demonstrated in helping riot-affected people ... For these people, rehabilitation would only come much later, if it did at all. He ran around, from one place to another, and in all the running around, we arrive in 1947.

We heard that there was a plan to partition the country. Based on religion. In his anger, it seemed Ritwik would lose his mental stability altogether. He never accepted the Partition. He never forgot it. It is the reason he declined the Padma Shri award from the Indian government.[1]

Not long after that, like the waves in an ocean, refugees from East Pakistan arrived in West Bengal and other parts of India, and they filled up most of Sealdah, Dum Dum and the northern parts of the new state. Sealdah held perhaps the largest number of them, maybe because of the railway station. Ritwik ran from pillar to post to help the refugees.

Food shortage, lack of housing, unemployment—everything was a concern at the time. The condition of the refugees was heart-wrenching, shocking, and Ritwik threw himself into his work with them. His experience of the time must have made him want to make films, made him want to talk about what he saw, and he showcased the barbarity of the Partition through his work in the years to come.

His first film was *Nagarik*. Ritwik was quite young at the time and he had no experience in the field. More crucially, he didn't have money. He made the film with whatever money he could scrounge.[2] The cinematographer was our second brother, Sudheesh Ghatak, the only cinematographer in the country at the time to have learnt his craft in England.

It was an outstanding film, but was not released because the West Bengal government found it too controversial and overly political at what was a sensitive time. Ritwik's great work was not allowed to go out to the people he had made the film for. Satyajit Ray has said this on record, and to me personally: 'If *Nagarik* had been allowed to release when it was made, Ritwik would have been spoken of before anyone else in our country.'

Ritwik was studying for his master's in English literature in Calcutta then … he was still a young man!

In the middle of all this, we lost our father in 1951. He was a very gentle, affectionate and simple person. Ritwik, understandably, broke down. Especially when he saw Ma wearing the widow's white attire. Our mother eventually convinced him to return to work. But Baba's death, and my marriage and subsequent relocation to eastern Bengal, hurt Ritwik in a big way. He became closer to Ma than ever before. She became everything to him. In a sense, she completed him. That, however, didn't alleviate his pain or his desperation to fight, protest against all the injustice around him. His concern for the rootless people, whether from the west or from the east, their pain and the uncertainty they lived with ... it was almost as if he couldn't take it anymore. Not to forget, there was the pain of *Nagarik* not being allowed to get a release—the albatross around his neck.

After a few days, or even years, he finally pulled himself together to make *Ajantrik*. That film was received with a lot of love and earned him some recognition. Everyone worked with a lot of love for the film and for Ritwik. A film with that sort of a concept had never been made before; it was an outstanding, beautiful film.

I travelled to Calcutta when the film was being released. He took me to Basusree theatre on the day of the release. I saw that the façade of the theatre was covered in strings of flowers, and the old jalopy—called Jagaddal [an extremely heavy or oppressive weight] in the film—had been raised to the roof of the theatre's portico. They had used a crane to do that. The car had also been covered in flowers.

Ritwik and I got out of the car we had arrived in, he had his arm around me. He called everyone who had come, and said, 'She is my eternal pair, my companion in life and death.'

When my visa ran out, I had to return to Kumilla. He was very upset at me leaving, but he had to let me go.

In 1960, I was back in Calcutta when *Meghe Dhaka Tara* released. Of the theatres it released in, Indira was closest to home, and the two of us went there with Tuntuni (Ritwik's first-born daughter). This was the first time he put the refugees, the rootless and the dispossessed on the screen. There was concern around the release. Calcutta was still severely affected by the refugee crisis—where would they live, what would they do for a living? There was anger on the streets. Anyhow, the film was released.

I saw a strange smile on his face that day. When people started to emerge from the theatre, we were outside, and I saw that everyone had puffy eyes, puffy faces. Ritwik asked them, 'Did you like the film?' As they were answering, the owner or manager of the theatre came, touched Ritwik's feet, and announced to everyone, 'This is Ritwik Ghatak, the creator of the film.' Everyone who had come to watch the film rushed to Ritwik. It was almost like a stampede. They wanted to touch him, touch his feet. He hugged many of the people and said, 'You are my world, you are my god; you are the reason for my being.' Those people left the theatre shouting slogans.

He looked at peace that day. At some point, the theatre management came and asked us to go to an inside room. We went in and saw that a huge spread had been laid out, lots of good food. Ritwik, as was his wont, asked immediately, 'Is this for free?' Then, laughing, he told me, 'Polish it off, polish it off, eat as much as you can.' He introduced me to the people in charge. He ate a little bit—he was never a big eater—but kept asking me to eat more. But I was as small an eater as he was.

We went in for the next show. The hall was silent, but for the occasional sound of someone sobbing. Maybe they saw themselves in the characters. Maybe they just liked the film. The sounds of people sobbing, some crying and some wailing, increased as the film went on, and Ritwik, too, was affected. At one point he told me, 'Reality is so tough, but it can also be so entertaining, you can see the evidence in our audience today.'

When we returned to Ritwik's home, we found Bijonbabu [Bijon Bhattacharya] and Supriya [Choudhury, the lead of the film] standing at the door. Supriya touched our feet, turned to me and said, 'Didi, today I feel complete as an actor.'

Sometime in 1972, late at night, there was a commotion outside our door. The street outside was deserted. Mohan Rozario, the caretaker-cum-cook of the house in Gulshan we were in, asked me if he should open the door.

I went outside and saw a very tall man in an overcoat, felt hat on his head, standing there. Looking like Sherlock Holmes.

As I stepped closer to him, the man said in a loud voice, 'Why is the gate shut? Open it quickly.' Ritwik came inside, and he said, without preamble, 'I have arrived, I want to make *Padma Nadir Majhi*.' I explained to him that everything, including the roads and Hardinge Bridge, had been destroyed, repairs would take months, even years. There was no point thinking about going there. Instead, we should go to Kumilla and think of something we could do there.

We went to Kumilla. At night, we were lying down next to each other and thinking of what to do. Then it struck me, I could give him *Titas Ekti Nodir Naam* to read. He started reading it immediately, and around midnight, he suddenly exclaimed, 'The idea! This is the book I will make. Give me a pen and some paper immediately.' It was late at night. The shops, the few that still existed, were shut.

Finding nothing, he started writing on the palm of my hand. 'It will be washed away when I bathe in the morning,' I told him. Looking helpless, he said, 'Why do you need to bathe? Let me finish, you bathe when you get to Dhaka.' I remembered that I had a washed white saree in the house, ironed and folded. I offered it to him. Like a child who has just been given his favourite toy, Ritwik was overjoyed. He hugged me and said, 'When did you become so intelligent?' And the script of *Titas Ekti Nodir Naam* was written on that saree.

Returning to Dhaka, I dropped him off at Green Hotel in Shahbagh and went to Gulshan. A few days later, when I visited him at the hotel, I found him deep in thought. He was thinking about the actors for the film. He didn't know any of the actors in Bangladesh. He was having to pick from them for the film. He was also going to the FDC [Bangladesh Film Development Corporation] quite often. One evening, he took me there. He showed me rushes of the bits that had been shot. I quite liked what he showed me. That's all I ever saw of the film. I never got a chance to watch *Titas Ekti Nodir Naam*.

Excerpted from Ritwik-ke Shesh Bhalobasha *(published by Oitijjhya, Dhaka, 2023). Translated by the editor with permission from the writer's daughter, Aroma Dutta. Notes have been added by the editor.*

Pratiti Devi was Ritwik Ghatak's twin. She was born in Dhaka and lived in the city until her death in 2020.

Notes

1. This might be incorrect. He is named in the list of awardees in 1970.
2. It would have been a moderate budget, and he did have backers: Bhupati Nandy and the Film Guild were the producers of the film.

From Zeus to Neelkantha: 1960 | 1971

AROMA DUTTA

On the night of 25 March 1971, Operation Searchlight began in East Pakistan. For nine long months, the people of East Pakistan fought their war of liberation, and on 16 December 1971, Bangladesh was born. The story—and history—of my family is deeply entwined with the birth of my nation.

What I am about to write is the story of two nations, India and Pakistan, and the story of a set of twins, their separation and their lives as refugees. The twins were Bhoba (Ritwik Ghatak) and Bhobi (Pratiti Devi), my chhotomama and my mother. It is a story that explains my chhotomama's heartbreaking confession, not long before his death, in April 1971. Hugging me, he had said, 'Bua [my nickname], I can't take the pain I feel in my heart, of losing everything dear to me, the hurt. I have lost the will to live. I have lost everything.'

Chhotomama was a deeply misunderstood person. Not just by the people he worked with and people from the film industry, but also by members of our family, by his friends, by people who were close to him. He came to this world like a cyclone and shook its very foundations before he left it. A mere fifty years after he arrived. With his head held high. In a huff, almost. As Neelkantha, drinking all the poison the churn of the ocean could send his way. Not once did he blame anyone for anything, not once did he complain about anything to anyone.

The people who know more about how we should live, what we should do and what is best for the world decided that India needed to be partitioned in 1947, and then a bloody war of liberation needed to be fought for Bangladesh to be created. All of this meant that I met my chhotomama only three times in all my life. I probably need to say a little bit about my own family to help tell the story better.

The Duttas were originally from the village of Ramrail in the district of Brahmanbaria in Kumilla, now in Bangladesh, then in the princely state of Tripura. They were landowners. Later, they made the legal profession their business. The rebel in the family was Shaheed Dhirendranath Dutta—he devoted his life to fighting the British. He was a champion of equality and was closely associated with the Swadeshi movement. No wonder he spent a lot of his early life in jail, including when Bangladesh was East Pakistan.

After Partition, he chose to stay on in his motherland, East Pakistan, and was a member of Pakistan's Constituent Assembly. On 24 February 1948, Dhirendranath Dutta, now barely remembered, was the first to demand in the Constituent Assembly in Karachi, then the capital of Pakistan, that Bangla be given the status of a state language of Pakistan.

After his fiery speech, the then (first) prime minister of Pakistan, Liaquat Ali Khan, said in Parliament, 'I wish my learned colleague had not come up with this motion. From his speech, I can smell the secession from Pakistan, and for that, he will not be spared.'

The speech ignited something in the people of East Pakistan, especially students, and that's when the language movement started and spread like wildfire, spearheaded by the students of Dhaka University and other educational institutions. The language movement was the first step towards the liberation of Bangladesh in 1971.

Dhirendranath Dutta and his son Dilip Dutta were picked up from their home in Kumilla by the Pakistani army on 29 March 1971, and were brutally tortured and killed, though their bodies were never found. Sanjib Dutta, the eldest son of Dhirendranath Dutta and my father, was a journalist, writer, political analyst and thinker. My mother and he had

Of a time when the writer of this essay recalls thinking of Ritwik as Zeus, the king of gods; © NFDC – National Film Archive of India

an inter-caste marriage in 1948. The Duttas were kayasthas, while my mother, the youngest daughter of Suresh Chandra Ghatak, was a brahmin.

The Ghataks were an important family from the Barind tract, on the banks of the Jamuna river. Suresh Chandra Ghatak was a formidable district magistrate of the British government and a litterateur too. The entire family was, in fact, steeped in the arts. His eldest son Manish Ghatak was a radical writer and poet, among the earliest left-leaning writers of Bengal. Another brother, Sudheesh Ghatak, learnt cinematography in England, was a friend of David Lean, among others, and made documentaries in England before returning to India and joining New Theatres in Calcutta. He was later the chief cameraperson at Indian News Parade (a cinematic newsreel produced between 1943 and 1946). Sudheesh also worked with Bimal Roy and the Films Division of India. Another brother, Lokesh Ghatak, was a high-ranking officer of the Royal Indian Naval Reserve and the first editor of *The Oceanite*, India's first nautical magazine, in 1945.

Ritwik was the youngest brother, Pratiti his twin sister. And their soulmate was Khuku, later the celebrated writer Mahasweta Devi, Manish's eldest daughter, just two months younger than Bhoba and Bhobi.

After Partition, Suresh Ghatak and his wife Indubala Devi had to leave their home in Rajshahi, and move to Calcutta and live in a house their son Sudheesh rented for them. Another mama, Ashish Ghatak, all my maternal aunts and their families, were also rendered homeless at the time, having chosen to move to Calcutta from East Pakistan.

For Bhoba and Bhobi, it was almost like their umbilical cord was cut a second time in 1947. The brother went to India. The sister stayed in Pakistan. Barbed-wire fences separated their lands. To meet, they needed passports, visas, permission, immigration, police verification ...

We did all of that, and went to India to meet Chhotomama, his family and other relatives in June 1960. I was a schoolgoing girl of ten, my brother Rahul was even younger.

It was the first time I saw Chhotomama, a very tall and handsome man, wearing black, thick-rimmed spectacles. In my mind's eye, he looked like a grand peepal tree. He stood there, arms outstretched, a brilliant smile on his face, welcoming us at Dum Dum Airport in Calcutta. When my mother and he hugged, the scene left the people around us stunned. The two grown-ups were hugging each other and crying like children. It took them a while to remember Rahul and me. Wiping away his tears, Chhotomama turned to me, and said, 'Oh, my Bangaal Ma, Bua, come, come to me.' He picked me up. It felt like I was being lifted to the top of the Himalayas.

This was the first time I was meeting any of my mother's siblings. Once, when I was a young child, just about conscious, I had met my grandmother, Indubala Devi. I recall thinking that she was like the goddess Saraswati. I would sit on the floor and stare at her as she sat on a chair with her legs folded under her. She would ask me about Kumilla—*Is the city still like a picture postcard, is the water in the Dharmasagar Lake still clear and beautiful, do the large lotus flowers still bloom?*

I would proudly reply: 'My grandfather's bungalow is on the western bank of the Dharmasagar Lake, so many lotus flowers bloom there even now … I will take you there.'

She would put a hand on my head and say, 'If you take me, I will go for sure.' She was a quiet person, very dignified.

Actually, I need to correct the record here. I had also met Chhotomama on this trip, but I have no memories of him from the time.

At Chhotomama's house on Gangaprasad Road, I met my mamima, Surama Ghatak, and their two daughters (Tuntuni and Bulbuli) for the first time. A happy, well-to-do, healthy family. When we stayed there, Chhotomama would often sit with Ustad Bahadur Khan, both of them on the floor, playing the sarod for hours. I can still picture Chhotomama, calm and meditative as he sat there, sarod in hand. I also remember the musician and singer Jyotirindra Moitra, Batukda to everyone, sitting there and singing for hours. Bahadur Khan, head bowed, would be playing the sarod, while Chhotomama sang with Batukda. Many other people came. I was too young to know who they were. But I remember Supriya Choudhury, she would come with her husband and daughter. Anil Chatterjee, Niranjan Roy … people who were part of *Meghe Dhaka Tara*. They loved my mother, and would ask her questions about East Pakistan.

Those days in Calcutta are among my happiest, most joyful memories. I have vivid memories of playing with my cousins Rakhi, Shakhi, Rana and Dipu, Ashish Ghatak's children, and spending time with all the aunts and uncles and their families, each of them quirky and brilliant in their own ways.

There were happy memories with Chhotomama's family, too. He would take all of us in his car to the banks of the Ganga, and also take us to the popular restaurants of the time, and treat us to chops and cutlets and fish fries, and also sweets like rabri, which he was very fond of. He would always buy us squeaky balloons. His favourite restaurants were Chung Wah and Waldorf. I had a Chinese meal for the first time in my life with Chhotomama. It's still my favourite cuisine. Oh, there are so many memories—going to New Market and buying frocks and shoes, drinking milkshakes at Keventers ... and the love Chhotomama showered on me, on all of us. He would often shout from the other room, 'Where's my Bangaal maiya?' I loved the call.

So many well-known people visited Chhotomama's house. He would introduce us proudly, tell everyone that his sister and niece had come from Kumilla to meet him. They were all understandably curious about East Pakistan. Everyone knew of Dhirendranath Dutta, and asked my mother so many questions about him.

Bijon Bhattacharya, the playwright, was a regular. He was, of course, married to my cousin, Mahasweta, and was therefore my brother-in-law. He would ask me, in Bangaal, 'Have you been to Faridpur? My ancestral home is in Khankhanapur village, I really feel like going. Will you take me there?' Supriya Choudhury, too, had lost her home to Partition. In fact, she was born in Burma, and had moved with her family during World War II to Calcutta. They were all curious about our life in Bangladesh, about the political climate there, about our experiences. I was just ten, but because of the discussions at home, I had some idea of politics already. I'd speak to the grown-ups, and they would all open up to me, talk about their experiences, their lost homes, their lives. I could feel the pain in their hearts as they spoke of undivided Bengal, the people they had lost ... We were all part of one nation, and now that nation didn't exist.

When it was time to leave, Chhotomama and Chhotomaima came to see us off at the airport. I don't know why, I hugged him and cried so much when we left. From the window of the aircraft, I could see Chhotomama waving at us with one hand and wiping his tears away with the other. I think I didn't stop crying till I reached Kumilla and met my father, grandfather and uncle. It was like I had suddenly been given a gift of love, and then I had lost it. Like I would all through my life. What I have is that image: Chhotomama, standing tall at the airport, like Zeus on top of Mount Olympus.

Before moving on, I must mention an incident from that visit in 1960, when Chhotomama took us to the premier show for *Meghe Dhaka Tara*. All the family members were there, and there were Supriya Choudhury, Anil Chatterjee, Bijon Bhattacharya, Gita Dey, Gita Ghatak—who was also my sister-in-law—Niranjan Roy, Gyanesh Mukherjee and many others. We watched the film, and I sobbed through most of it. The characters seemed like people I knew. Then came the famous scene towards the end, where Nita tells her brother, 'Dada, I wanted to live.' I forgot everything, where I was, what I was doing, and started bawling. Chhotomama picked me up and carried me out of the room. I think everyone in the dark theatre was sobbing by that stage, but no one was creating a ruckus like me. We went outside. A lot of reporters were waiting there to speak to Chhotomama. 'I am a success,' he told them. 'My ten-year-old niece can't stop crying, as you can see. She can feel the pain of the refugees. Her tears are proof that my work is a success.'

Maybe I did understand Chhotomama a bit more than others did.

30 March 1971. My mother, my little brother and I, wearing burkhas courtesy our neighbours, left our home—Dhirendranath Dutta's home—and moved to another place in Kumilla. The situation got bad very quickly. On 2 April, and I can no longer remember how, we crossed the Gomoti river from Kumilla and entered Tripura, through the Sonamura border post. At every stage, we felt we wouldn't be able to make it, but we did.

We reached Agartala, the capital of the state of Tripura, and met the chief minister of the state, Sachindralal Singh, and his MLAs. We were asked questions, and we gave them the true picture of how things were in East Pakistan, of the brutality, the torture, the killings. We were connected to Indira Gandhi, then the prime minister of India, over the phone, and I was asked to speak to her. I told her, unflinching, to open the borders so that the innocent, humiliated and tortured people could escape the barbaric armymen from Pakistan, and pleaded that they be given refugee status in India.

It was 1971 that I met Chhotomama in Calcutta again. After eleven years. My mother, my brother and I, this time as asylum-seekers. We met at my paternal aunt Bithika Dhar's flat on Sukiya Street. My father was by then with *Amrita Bazar Patrika*, the Calcutta-based English daily, having been hounded out of Dhaka because of his political activism. He met us there too, having made arrangements for us to fly from Agartala to Calcutta. My mother and I were interviewed by all the newspapers in Calcutta. We hadn't yet been able to speak to Chhotomama, because we didn't have an address or phone number for him, but he read the newspapers and rushed to find us at Sukiya Street.

As he was coming up the stairs, Chhotomama was shouting, 'Bhobi! Bhobi!' As he entered the flat, my mother screamed 'Bhoba!' and rushed into his arms. I don't have the words to explain the scene. It was deeply emotional. After a while, Chhotomama saw me standing some distance away and swept me into his arms. He cried. I wailed. Most people around us stood like stone sculptures, too stunned to react.

But I was having trouble believing my eyes. Chhotomama looked like a broken man. Where was the tall, strong and handsome Zeus from eleven years ago? So much had changed.

After some hours together, Chhotomama told Ma that he wanted to take me to Sainthia (a small town near Calcutta, where Surama Ghatak and the three children—Babu, too, had been born by then—lived at the time). Ma argued with him, saying that my father was in Agartala, trying to speak to the officials there, and trying to find out more about my grandfather and uncle. They had been dragged off by the Pakistani army to Mainamati Senaniwas (the Kumilla Cantonment) and tortured and killed. But Baba wanted to find out more, see what he could do. 'Let him come back, you take Bua after that,' Ma said. Chhotomama was adamant. It was finally agreed that he would take me with him the following day. We had left Kumilla with just the clothes on our backs. Our relatives gave us some clothes. I left with Chhotomama the next afternoon in a taxi he had hired.

Chhotomama told the driver to take us straight to Chung Wah restaurant. We reached, and found some people Chhotomama knew sitting there. He introduced me to them, saying, 'This is my niece, my Bangaal Ma; she is a refugee now, she has escaped from East Pakistan.' He hugged me, and burst into tears. In the middle of the restaurant. The people around us stared at the unkempt man hugging a young girl and crying. The attendants at the restaurant knew Chhotomama, and got us a table. We didn't have to place an order. I stared, dumbfounded, as the waiters brought us all sorts of dishes—they knew what Chhotomama liked. I don't think either of us ate much. So Chhotomama asked the waiters to pack the rest of the food—'I haven't brought Tuni, Buli and Babu here in so long, I'll take the food back for them.'

As we were leaving, Chhotomama realised that I wasn't carrying anything. He asked me if I had another saree. I had, one gifted by the woman of the house we had taken shelter in when we were in Agartala for one night. But I wasn't carrying it. I just had the one I was wearing. I still have it, packed away in my almirah at home in Dhaka. Chhotomama decided to take me to New Market again. 'I will buy you two sarees and buy Lokkhi [his wife] two sarees, and buy some clothes for the children.' We drove from Park Street to New Market—the same route we had taken eleven years ago. It was all familiar. But Chhotomama wasn't familiar. I suppose I had changed a lot too. Between 1960 and 1971, everything had changed. Even the countries had changed.

We ended up in the same shop—Ganga Jamuna, if I remember correctly—we had gone to eleven years ago. We bought sarees, frocks, shirts and pants. Back in the taxi, past Howrah Bridge, then some places I didn't know and, after a while, into the dark of the evening. A few lights here and there, the headlight of the taxi, impenetrable darkness otherwise.

At some point, after crossing Burdwan and reaching Bolpur, Chhotomama asked the taxi to stop, and went off somewhere, leaving me alone in the car. 'Bua, sit here, I will be back soon.' I sat in the taxi for a while, and then stepped out and went to a paan-cigarette shop, which had a light on. The shopkeeper came out and asked me who I was, and what I wanted. I didn't know what to say. I told him that my chhotomama had asked me to wait there, and that he would be back soon. The shopkeeper was an elderly man. He realised that I was scared, so he asked me some questions, and told me that he would shut his shop soon. I requested him to keep his light on for a little while longer: 'Maybe Chhotomama has gone to use the toilet.' As we chatted, I told the shopkeeper my story, how we had escaped from East Pakistan. As I told him that, his expression changed. 'Don't worry, Ma, sit here. We'll wait for your mama to come back.' He also gave me two biscuits and a glass of water. I realised I was very hungry.

Then the taxi driver turned up, very angry, and asked me where Chhotomama was. I didn't know what to say. He was shouting at me when Chhotomama turned up. He came and gave me a hug, and the shopkeeper, having seen who my chhotomama was, asked me, 'Why didn't you say you were with him?' He bent down and touched Chhotomama's feet, but at the same time, started scolding him. After he was pacified, he told us that getting to Sainthia would take a while longer. 'It will get late, please don't leave the girl alone and go off anywhere.' We went back to the taxi, and Chhotomama got another lecture from the taxi driver.

When we sat in the car, there was an unfamiliar, awful smell. The smell got stronger, and I realised that it was coming from Chhotomama. And from his clothes? By then, he was asleep. His head had fallen on my shoulder. The smell was stronger. Chhotomama must have had alcohol, I concluded. And it shocked me. He seemed to have given up on life. And here I was, having just left everything behind and escaped, like a fugitive, from my own country in the dead of night. Maybe, now that I think back, he was taking revenge on life for keeping him alive against his will.

How did a man who was so full of life, playing the flute, the sarod, taking everyone out for a day of fun, making films become like this … like charred wood? In just eleven years.

It was deeply traumatic for me in many ways. Here I was, late at night, in a taxi in an unfamiliar place. With my chhotomama clearly drunk … As I sat there, my mind kept going back to what had happened in Kumilla. Everything that had happened over the past twelve-thirteen days.

At some point, we got close to Sainthia, I could tell by the lights. Chhotomama was awake now, giving the taxi driver directions. At around 11 p.m., the taxi cut across a field and stopped in front of a bungalow. At that hour, it felt like it was unoccupied, but Chhotomama took me by the hand and banged on the door, shouting 'Lokkhi, Lokkhi!' Was it the wrong house, I wondered. After a while, the door opened. A woman on the other side. In that half-light, I could just about make out Chhotomaima's form. 'Why have you come here? What do you want? Get out!' she screamed. I was stunned.

She was clearly furious. When she finally saw me, she asked Chhotomama, 'Who is this! Who have you picked up at this hour of the night?'

'Lokkhi, this is Bua. This is my Bangaal Ma. I have brought Bua to you. Let me in, I will tell you everything.'

Chhotomaima reached out, grabbed me by the arm, pushed me into a room and locked the door. From inside, I could tell that Chhotomama had managed to enter the house with all the gifts and the food he had brought. I was completely frozen. How … how could their relationship have deteriorated to this level?

They were talking outside. After a while, Chhotomaima came in and asked me if I had eaten anything. I had forgotten about my hunger, I hadn't eaten properly in a long time. Tuni and Buli had woken up by then, and they came rushing into the room I was in, they hugged me and kissed me. How much they had grown up! Babu came too. This was the first time I was meeting him. He stood some distance away, gaping.

I realised that, despite everything, Chhotomaima had placed some rice and vegetables in a pressure cooker and put it to boil. 'Eat your food and go to sleep, Bua, I will hear your story in the morning,' she told me.

'Won't Chhotomama eat,' I asked her.

'He doesn't need food,' she snapped.

She filled a plate with food and gave it to me, but I was terribly upset that Chhotomama was not getting any food. I kept telling her that Chhotomama hadn't eaten all day either. 'There's enough rice, we can both eat,' I said.

'He doesn't need rice,' she said again, and shut the door, locking me in.

I managed to eat a little because I was so hungry, and then I hugged Tuni and Buli and fell into deep sleep. All night, I think, I had nightmares. Kumilla. Dhaka. Mainamati Cantonment. Agartala. Calcutta. Like a kaleidoscope.

I remember waking up with the thought that Chhotomama had no semblance of a family left, the tornado, whatever it was, had blown it away. But when the door opened, Tuni, Buli and Babu rushed out and leapt on Chhotomama. He picked them up and hugged them, and sang songs to them, saying, 'Where have all of you been, Tunipakhi, Bulipakhi, see, I have brought you lots of clothes.' I was happy, my pain at his condition receding a little, but still it was all very sad too.

Chhotomama left home after a little while, and then came back with a pile of fish and meat and vegetables for Chhotomaima to cook. Understandably, that made Chhotomaima angry. She shouted at Chhotomama, who just laughed and said, 'Oh Lokkhi, why are you getting angry? If you cook, all of us can have a good meal—it's been so long since I've tasted your cooking.' She did cook, but didn't stop abusing and accusing Chhotomama. Even when we sat down to eat, she was relentless, saying the most hurtful things. The children clung to Chhotomama, not quite sure what was happening.

We had planned to spend five or six days there with everyone, but in the afternoon, suddenly, Chhotomama came to me and said that we would be leaving. He called the children, hugged and kissed them. The taxi was called. I was a little scared. It was already afternoon, even early evening. And it would take a long time to reach Calcutta. And Chhotomama wasn't dependable.

I followed Chhotomama out of the house, touching Chhotomaima's feet and hugging my cousins on the way out. In the taxi, Chhotomama sat with his head bowed, his hand clutching his forehead. Little Babu was shouting for his father. Tuni and Buli stared, crying.

The taxi driver told Chhotomama that there was no chance of reaching Calcutta that night. I asked Chhotomama again if we couldn't spend just one more night in Sainthia. He turned to me and said, 'Aren't you a girl from Bangladesh? What are you scared of? I am here with you.' I felt, yes, that's right. I am just a refugee girl now. I have no address or destination. Why should I worry?

But I couldn't stop thinking. What had Chhotomama done? What had destroyed their lives? There was so much joy and laughter when we had visited in 1960 …

After a point, Chhotomama rested his head on my shoulder and went off to sleep. I stared into the darkness outside. Suddenly, startling me, Chhotomama jumped up and told the driver to turn the taxi towards Santiniketan. It was much closer than Calcutta. We reached Santiniketan quite soon. And Chhotomama asked the driver to stop after a point. It was pitch dark. Chhotomama asked the driver to bring his torch and show us the way. With his long legs, Chhotomama led the way. I had to run to keep up with him. We finally reached a mud hut, with a bamboo fence around it, and lots of plants and flowers—my eyes had become used to the darkness by then. Amazingly, there was beautiful alpona on the walls of the hut. The door was shut. There was just a simple lantern hanging from a hook outside. It was like a dream.

'Ram! Ram! Open the door. It's me, Bhoba. Open the door. See who I have brought with me,' Chhotomama shouted, banging on the door. After a while, a slightly built, ravaged-looking man, wearing a simple dhoti, with unkempt salt-and-pepper hair and a stubble, came out holding a lantern. I wondered how this man, obviously not well-off and certainly much older than my mama, could be his friend.

'Who have you brought at this time of the night, Bhoba,' the man asked.

'Let us come in, I'll tell you,' Chhotomama said, and asked the taxi driver to go sleep in his car.

The house was very bare. There was a simple bed, with a pillow and a blanket that had clearly just been thrown off. One earthen pot for drinking water. And some clothes hanging from a rope that had been tied to two hooks.

'Ma, you sit on the bed,' the man told me gently. I did, feeling confused and upset. He brought me some muri and aakher gur (puffed rice and sugarcane jaggery) on a plate. He placed two mats on the floor, and told Chhotomama that the two of them would sleep on those. I protested a bit, but no one paid attention.

They sat down on their mats, and almost immediately started arguing loudly. The subject seemed to be 'Whose mother is she?' If Chhotomama said, 'She is my Bangaal Ma', the man called Ram shouted back, 'No, she is my mother, Bangabala'. This went on for a while, and then the tiredness caught up with me and I don't know when I fell asleep.

When I woke up, I saw many women, of various ages, sitting all around the bed and staring at me and whispering amongst themselves. *Who is she?* I explained to them that I had escaped from East Pakistan, etc., etc. I don't think they understood what I was saying, but they still stroked me and showered me with affection. When I told them that the man I had come with was my chhotomama, they were even more affectionate towards me.

There was more in store. Chhotomama and Rambabu (which is what I was calling him by then) came to me and said they would take me to see a place I would like very much. We walked a dirt-and-mud road, past woods and bamboo groves, so many beautiful, unfamiliar flowers … until we reached a river. You could see the other bank—it was quite dry, since it was not yet monsoon time. Chhotomama and Rambabu took my arms, and took me down to the river. Since there wasn't much water, one could see the pebbles at the bottom, the water was so clear. As I stepped into the water, all my tiredness seemed to vanish. And—as if I needed to see more strange things—Chhotomama and Rambabu looked up at the sky and started singing at the top of their voices, '*O amar desher maati, tomar pore thekai matha*' (On the soil of my land, I bow to thee). I soon found myself singing loudly with them and crying. When the song was over, we sat down on the bank of the river. Chhotomama splashed water on his face, and kept calling me 'Bangaal Ma, Bangabala …' Sitting there, sobbing, holding Chhotomama and Rambabu's hands, I felt like I had been transported to another land, a land of peace, a land of spirituality. I don't know how long we sat there, and then, still in our wet clothes, we walked back, me in the middle, the two sages on either side.

The women had prepared some rice and spinach and daal for us, and it tasted like heaven. I kept thinking about Kumilla. This must have been the first time since 29 March that I had really enjoyed a meal. Rambabu came to me, stroked my head, and said, 'I don't have the means to give you any other food, Ma.' I remember telling him that the food tasted of heaven. We spent the whole day and night with Rambabu, who had become Ram-mama by then, and spoke of my home, their homes, the two countries, deaths … Every once in a way, I would break down, and they would too. I realised that Ram-mama knew of Dhirendranath Dutta, but had never met him. I didn't get a chance to ask who Ram-mama was. But Chhotomama's friend was god-like, so gentle, so caring.

Later, back in Calcutta, when I met my father, he asked me if I knew who I had spent so much time with. 'Who? Ram-mama?' Baba held my hand and said, 'Bua, you are extremely fortunate, you have been blessed by the maestro, Ramkinkar Baij, the artist and sculptor.' I was dumbfounded.

Anyway, that came later. We left Santiniketan the following morning. On the way, I saw a large sign announcing 'Visva-Bharati University'. So strange. I hadn't even realised I was so close to that historic place. How beautiful it was, surrounded by palash flowers. As we drove, Chhotomama suddenly asked the taxi to stop. I was worried, and told him I wanted to come with him. He said he was just going to use the toilet. I went and sat below a tree, and the taxi driver came and sat with me. We waited. It was starting to be dusk when Chhotomama came back, carrying a satchel, sounding apologetic. 'Did I take too long?' In the taxi, as usual, he put his head on my shoulder and went off to sleep.

When he woke up, I asked, 'Chhotomama, tell me honestly, why are you destroying yourself like this? What has happened to you?'

He said, starting to sob, 'Bua, I have too much pain inside of me. I can't explain this to you. I have nothing left. Just pain, of losing everything. And poison. A lot of poison.'

We were quiet after that, both of us sobbing. The taxi driver the only witness. After a while, Chhotomama seemed to sink into a stupor. He stroked my head and said, as if in a trance, 'You are my mother, you are my real mother, my wretched mother …' And then, 'My Padma river, my sky, my country, my Bangladesh …' Only once, clearly, he said, 'Suffering is my birthright.'

Neelkantha.

I couldn't help crying as I thought of the Zeus from 1960.

Despite everything, there was a stubborn strain of optimism in him. He dreamt of creative possibilities until his last day. I think of that, too, when I think of him.

Let me end this with a song Chhotomama had written for his unreleased film, *Ronger Golam*. It reads like an autobiography to me.

Koto kichhu ashe, koto kichhu jaay;
Daag rekhe jaay na, miliye-miliye jaay.
Tobu akash thake, pakhira thake, phulera thake;
Ghaash-ra dole, hawa boy.
E prithibi ki shundor, manush ki shundor,
Tobu eto dukhkho kyano?
Majhe-majhe emon bNak eshe poDe kyano nodir pothe?

Shegulo to bojha jay na.*
Shegulo ki bojha, na shompod?

So many things come, so many things go;
They leave no mark, just fade away.
Still the sky lives, the birds fly, the flowers bloom;
The grass sways, the breeze blows.
How beautiful the world is, how beautiful its people are;
Why, then, is there so much sorrow?
Why are there so many twists and turns on the path of the river?
It's difficult to understand.
Is this a burden? Or a fortune?

Aroma Dutta is a Bangladeshi social worker, human rights activist and former Parliamentarian.

* The word 'bojha' is used to mean both 'to understand', as used in the penultimate line, as well as 'burden', as used in the last line.

Ritwik's love for the theatre never went away

KUMAR ROY

Ritwik was instrumental in introducing me to the Bohurupee theatre group, as well as to Sombhu Mitra. But that was only at the end of 1948. I had known Ritwik and been friends with him since 1945, when we were both doing our graduation from the University of Rajshahi. He was of course an arts student, and I studied science. His family was in Rajshahi at the time—he lived with his parents and his siblings. I used to live in a missionary students' hostel. But that didn't matter. It didn't take long for students with a cultural bent at the university to become friends.

Our love for the theatre, especially, brought us closer. We looked so different. Me, a man of medium build, and he, tall and thin. He stood out, with his sparkling eyes and the lines, like drawings, on the sides of his lips. The way he spoke, sharply, also set him apart from the rest of us. Ritwik studied English literature (honours). At the time, Dr Subodh Sengupta taught in the English department. He was popular among us for being enthusiastic about the arts, especially Tagore theatre. One time, we were rehearsing Tagore's *Raja* (The King). Subodhbabu was the vice principal at the time. Since the students were producing the play, he gave us permission to stage it in the university auditorium. Ritwik played the grandfather, I the invisible king and Sunil Siddhanta the character of Rani Sudarshana. But we were not able to put up the play. A section of the students forced us to call it off saying that it was communal in nature. It was 1946, and the climate was hardly pleasant. Dr Sengupta got into some trouble over this too. All of us felt bad, but there wasn't much we could do. Ritwik, however, brought together his friends from the area and started rehearsing again, and managed to stage the play in a local theatre.

We mounted a Tagore play again some time later—*Poritraan* (*Salvation*). Ritwik played Dhananjay Bairagi and I played Raja Pratapaditya. A boy called Nripen, Ritwik's friend, played the role of a woman, and another boy, who suddenly appeared among us and became our friend, Kali Dasgupta (Subodhbabu's nephew), also played a woman. Kali Dasgupta and Sunil Siddhanta later became famous as a singer of folk songs and as a professor of chemistry respectively. And Ritwik, with his prodigious talent, became a film-maker of global repute. Clearly, those days in Rajshahi were well spent. The Padma river, the weirs in it, the fish, the boats, the people and the university itself, with its large grounds and the red-brick buildings for each of the disciplines, had left an impression on us.

And then came the Partition, communal riots and Independence. Who knows where everyone went, leaving their homes and their people. The partition of the country, the water of the Padma, all of this never left Ritwik's sensitive mind. To him, it was all the work of a madman. Something that destroyed the centre of his world. And this madness seemed to touch his life and his creations too. People going from this side to that as refugees, staring vacantly at the goings-on, feeling the call of the green from the other side. Perhaps Ritwik's mind was not at rest because of all this. If he had been calm, he wouldn't have been able to make the films he did. It's the restless mind that was reflected in his work.

We went our different ways in 1947. In 1948, after our Pujo holidays, I was standing in front of the University of Calcutta gate when, from College Square across the road, Ritwik called my name. I looked up and saw him standing with a bespectacled man in an orange kurta. I was pleasantly surprised and crossed the street to meet Ritwik. He introduced the man with him as Sombhu Mitra. I had heard Sombhu Mitra's recitation of *Madhubangshir Goli* (the poem by Jyotirindra Moitra) from afar once, and knew that he was a part of the Gananatya Sangha, and had been a part of *Nabanna* (Bijon Bhattacharya's play on the Bengal Famine). I had

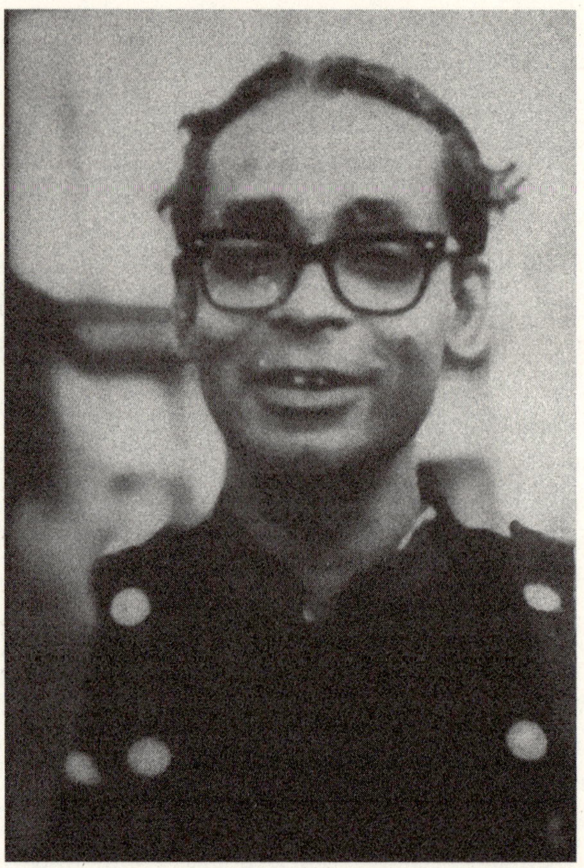

Ritwik at FTII, the happiest and most rewarding period of his life; © NFDC – National Film Archive of India

been intoxicated by his voice already, and, as we spoke, realised that his voice had so many intricate changes of tone. Ritwik told me that they were putting together a new theatre group, which had already performed *Nabanna* on three evenings at Rangmahal theatre. While introducing me, Ritwik spoke highly of my skills in recitation and my acting ability, and Sombhu Mitra asked me to join the group immediately. It was decided that Ritwik would some day soon take me to the house in Park Circus where the group rehearsed. That day, we sat at Basanta Cabin and drank tea. Ritwik excused himself once to quickly go across and register his presence in class.

For a while, I stayed glued to Sombhu Mitra. It was the love of the theatre. It's a sort of glue that had at some point been injected like the poison of a venomous snake. Once bitten, you are never rid of it. Sombhu Mitra had become Sombhuda by then. One day, back at Basanta Cabin, Ritwik read a chunk of his new play, *Dalil.* I knew that he wrote plays. Back in 1945 in Rajshahi, he had read out a story to us that he had written almost like a play, with background narrations and scene descriptions. There were scenes of the Azad Hind Fauj at the border with Burma. He painted a picture with the actors, background narration as well as a sutradhar, lights, sounds, music. It was most exciting. But it was never staged. Maybe Ritwik no longer wanted to work with that story. Subhas Chandra Bose had become a contentious subject by then.

As was true of many of us, this independence of compromise made Ritwik angry. He could go into rants about it without provocation. He never shied away from speaking his mind or making explosive statements. Speaking about our political leaders, especially our prime minister (Jawaharlal Nehru) at the time, he often used the impolite Bengali term for 'son of a pig'. He was pained by the division of the country, and he subscribed to the '*Yeh azaadi jhootha hai*' sentiment.

By this time, Bohurupee had been founded. Ritwik was instrumental in the creation of the group. When he had introduced me to Sombhu Mitra, the group hadn't been christened. I went with Ritwik one day to 11A Nasiruddin Road in Park Circus and was introduced to the other members of the group. I had met Sombhu Mitra already. There was Tripti Mitra. Around this time, Ritwik, or Bhoba, took me to Russa Road to Bijon Bhattacharya's house to introduce us. My first meeting with the creator of *Nabanna*. They were related, of course—Bijonda was married to Ritwik's niece, his eldest brother's daughter Mahasweta. Bijonda (whom I called Gosthoda, his nickname) was also related to Tripti Mitra—he was an older cousin. He called her Moni, so Ritwik called her Monidi, and I did too. But we were all roughly of the same age, a few months here and there.

So, thanks to Ritwik, I became a part of Bohurupee. But Ritwik soon left the group.

I remember that we—Mohammad Israil, Ritwik, the Rabindrasangeet singer Kalim Sharafi and I, among others—had been rehearsing the roles of workers in a colliery for a few days for the play *Pathik*. But Ritwik left, and Kalim Sharafi was forced to move to East Pakistan to find a way to earn a livelihood.

Before they left, while the rehearsals were on, a startling incident took place. Maybe it was nothing, but to my superstitious middle-class mind, it was significant. The outside room in the Mitras' house served as our rehearsal room. Maharshi (Manoranjan Bhattacharya, the legendary theatre actor) was seated at a higher level, wearing a white khadi kurta and a khadi dhoti, as usual scissored in half. We were seated below. Maharshi suddenly said, 'Hey, Ritwik, give me a beedi.' Ritwik, unhesitatingly, put his hand in his pocket and handed Maharshi a rather long beedi. The process of Maharshi asking for the beedi and Ritwik handing it to him left me astounded. I don't know if Maharshi did it to break a taboo of sorts (the younger lot didn't smoke in front of the elders) or to promote camaraderie within the group. I don't think I ever saw Maharshi smoke after that. Maybe he did once in a way.

Ritwik wasn't the sort to be easily cowed; he was just inherently uninhibited.

My life remained entwined with Ritwik's because he was the one who built that bridge between me and those great theatre personalities.

After he left Bohurupee and was busy trying to find a niche in cinema—he had already acted in Nemai Ghosh's *Chhinnamul* and the work for Bimal Roy's *Tathapi* had begun—one day he took me to meet Bimal Roy at his home. Because of that, I got a chance to visit the premises of Bhagyalakshmi Pictures and watch the shooting of *Tathapi*. My first such experience. Ritwik was engrossed in learning the nuances of film-making at the time.

Even though he had left Bohurupee, Ritwik and I continued to share a close personal bond. I watched his play *Bisarjan* at Roxy cinema as well as a production of his play *Dalil*. All this was in the early 1950s. By 1955, his ties with the Indian People's Theatre Association as well as the Communist Party of India were completely severed. Around that time, his relationship with the world of the theatre also became strained. Ritwik was more interested in cinema by then. I remember his words: 'Cinema can impact lakhs of people at the same time.' But he also used to say that he had no great love for the medium; if he found a better one, he would gladly move to it. He had a completely independent mind. That is why, when he sent his response to the Party following his expulsion, he could write without hesitation, 'A Communist group will have to be mobile, and at the same time be capable of maintaining quality in a settled place, a working knowledge of these technical aspects will be helpful. The group must be understood so that the individual may flowerize. The seeming contradiction of collective and individual is non-existent. It is all for one and one for all.'

He was involved with the Gananatya Sangha when he made *Nagarik*. Conflicted by the arguments in his head, between the movement, his own sense of independence, as well as arguments with the realities of the time we were in, he kept returning to the theatre, or at least expressed a desire to. In between, he went off to Bombay to work with Filmistan. I met him after a long gap in 1956. He had married Surama Bhattacharya in 1955, and they were in Bombay. Gangada (the actor Gangapada Basu) and I had been invited to their place. Gangada went, but I couldn't; I was busy with some work for Bohurupee. I think he felt aggrieved, and didn't forgive me for a long time.

Then, in 1970, we met a number of times in quick succession. He was making a couple of short films at the time: *Puruliar Chhau Nritya* and *Amar Lenin*. He had come to the Academy of Fine Arts to watch our plays *Baaki Itihaash* and *Daakghar*. After many, many days, he met us, Sombhuda and me, in the green room. We spoke about many things, about creativity and the life of the creator, about discipline and much else, and I remember that Sombhuda had told Ritwik, somewhat reproachfully, '*Bhule jeo na, amader shamne* Rabindranath-*o achhen*' (Don't forget that we also have the example of Rabindranath in front of us).

I watched his *Sanko*, *Jwala* and *Shei Bishnupriya* around this time, and got a chance to rediscover Ritwik the theatre man. Did he, deep within, always harbour a desire to return to the theatre? Was the call always there? One day, after I had dropped off my son to his school, Patha Bhavan on Palm Avenue, I bumped into Ritwik in front of Bahadur Khan's house. If that call wasn't there, why would he say, 'Let's do *Bisarjan* again. You play Jayasingha and I will play Raghupati'? It felt like we were back in Rajshahi. For a few days after that, I met him at the same place, outside Bahadur Khan's house. Perhaps they were working on the music for a film. I don't know if he was reminded of *Bisarjan* because of the troubles we were seeing at the time. When Sombhuda had made *Bisarjan* with Bohurupee in 1961, it was relevant to the turmoil of the time. Did Ritwik find the play relevant again, in the context of the early 1970s? Here, I am reminded of his statement about being a film-maker: 'I believe that I don't have a right to create anything if I don't create it to tell the truth about the times we are in.'

This essay was first published in Natyaroop. *It has been translated and edited by the editor with permission from the copyright holders, Ritwik Memorial Trust.*

Kumar Roy (2 March 1926–28 February 2010) was a theatre actor, director and writer of Bengali plays, and was closely associated with the theatre group Bohurupee, which he headed for a time. Roy was also president of the Bengali Theatre Academy.

The life of a true artist

NABARUN BHATTACHARYA

Who were the men we saw around Ritwik Ghatak? Bijon Bhattacharya, Jyotirindra Moitra,[1] Hemango Biswas,[2] Chittaprosad,[3] Debabrata Mukhopadhyay,[4] Swarnakamal Bhattacharya?[5] No one knows them anymore. After a few days, they won't know Ritwik either. Which is fair. The invitation card I was sent said 'The modernisation of Bengalis: Ritwik Ghatak'. The speed with which Bengalis have become modern has rendered Ritwik Ghatak superfluous. All the people I mentioned earlier are the same: superfluous.

Now, I have had the chance to see this superfluous person from very close quarters. I used to work in the Soviet Press. Hemango Biswas sat in the room next to mine. He was a 'Pekingist' sitting in the headquarters of the Soviet Union in Calcutta. So no one spoke to him. I had known him since I was child, so I went and chatted with him at times. Ritwik would come by often to ask us for money to buy alcohol. He would take some from Siddheshwar Sen,[6] some from me, some from Hemangoda. He wouldn't hang around, just take the money and leave.

This was the phase before he started making *Jukti, Tokko aar Goppo*. Ritwik used to live on the streets at the time. He would sleep on pavements, sometimes on the steps of a house in front of where I lived. Not just him. There were others, too, all completely superfluous to our society, lumpens. Ritwik considered himself as one with the lumpens. Roaming the streets.

I remember one morning when I had stepped out to buy cigarettes, I had bought a packet of Charminar and had maybe eighteen or twenty-eight paise left. Ritwik turned up, asking me for money. I said I only had those coins. He was happy with it. I asked him what he would get with so little money. He said it was enough. He must have bought the cheapest alcohol available.

After Ritwik died, my father [Bijon Bhattacharya] had said at a memorial meeting that 'Ritwik was murdered'. We mustn't forget this. People can be murdered in various ways. When Jafar Panahi is told that he won't be allowed to make films for twenty years,[7] it is murder. When Dr Binayak Sen is told that he won't be allowed to practice medicine or do anything at all,[8] it is murder. What opportunities did Ritwik get during his time? He was the definition of a struggling, fighting artist.

A part of *Subarnarekha* was filmed in Jagulia, not far from Calcutta. Every night, at 9.30, a train would stop there. And every night, just as it got to that hour, I would see Ritwik getting tense. The cause of the stress was whether the train would come, and if it did, would a familiar person alight or not, and if that person did appear, would they have the raw film with them or not. If the raw stock didn't arrive, there would be no shooting the next day. And, very often, the raw stock didn't arrive as promised. Those were the situations he had to work in.

When Ritwik filmed—of course he had some calculations in his head—he would shoot a lot of extra scenes, which would later be fixed at the editing table. *Subarnarekha* had a lot of such footage, which was later melted in the Tollygunge studios, where they had been stored, to extract silver. If we had an archive, a real archive, in our country, this raw footage would have been so valuable. Sergei Eisenstein did the same. The Russians didn't destroy all the unused footage he left behind. It was all taken to the editing table later, and valuable 'films' were made with it. Ritwik didn't get that either.

As I said, Ritwik had been murdered. One of the people Ritwik loved listening to was Mozart. I had read a biography of Mozart, where it was mentioned that, one time, he had just finished a symphony at a concert

Bijon Bhattacharya, in a still from *Meghe Dhaka Tara*;

and the crowd was giving him an ovation and saying, 'Long live, Mozart'; he heard it as 'Long starve, Mozart'. The people I mentioned at the start all had the same sort of fate. Think of Jyotirindra Moitra. When he didn't have an orchestra or any musical instruments, he found a group of children from a shanty and made an orchestra with them. What were the instruments? Stones in a talcum powder container and things like that. He called the orchestra 'Jogojhompo' [commotion]. Imagine the kind of relationship all these men would have had with each other.

Still, to return to *Subarnarekha*—the script for the following day's shoot was being redone. He was rewriting the dialogues for Haraprasad, the character played by Bijon Bhattacharya. Ritwik was asked why he was rewriting the dialogues that had already been approved. He said, 'He [Bhattacharya] is Asia's greatest artist. Don't I need to project him correctly?' The scene was about similarly superfluous people. Bengalis have no way of knowing about these people now.

An image about Ritwik has been spread, no doubt by politically correct Bengalis, of being wayward and an alcoholic. This is inevitable. Ritwik never spent time cultivating English-speaking film critics. If any of them attempted to act smart with him, Ritwik would have kicked them out of the room. I know very well about many film directors who cultivated these half-sahibs. Because they knew that unless they impressed the English-speaking public, and therefore the Western audiences, they wouldn't get anywhere. Ritwik didn't care for all this. He barely won an award, he was never a part of festivals; now, he is beyond such things. He has reached another level altogether.

Look at his fighting spirit. If he couldn't make films, for whatever reason, he just turned to something else. Like a magazine on theatre. *Abhinaydarpan*. I have seen him work on the magazine with complete sincerity. He told me once that, if he wasn't allowed to make films, he would return to the theatre and act professionally. That project also moved to an extent. For him, it was simple: 'If you don't let me make films, don't. I don't care. I won't beg and plead.' He had plans of making at least three more full-length films, but each of those were scuttled. It was only because Mrs Gandhi[9] favoured Ritwik somewhat that he got the job at the Film and Television Institute of India. It was because of the relationship with Mrs Gandhi that he could return to India in an emergency flight from Bangladesh.[10] Otherwise, he didn't get any help from anyone. No one from the film industry ever came and stood by him. I don't think anyone ever made an effort to understand him, forget his films, which were almost all flops. Empty theatres everywhere.

There's another interesting thing about Ritwik. He was perhaps the only film director of that stature who didn't create film-makers from among his assistants and juniors. It's peculiar. People are expected to learn from someone like Ritwik, but none of these people could. I think it's because they were in awe of Ritwik. Maybe they only learnt to drink from him. Nothing else.

I am familiar with some aspects of Ritwik's way of working, which are curious.

One of them is 'spot improvisation'. Think of the scene with the behrupiya at the airstrip in *Subarnarekha*. It was not in the script at all. We had gone to a haat [market], and saw this behrupiya roaming about there. Ritwik saw him, and immediately took him to the airstrip and shot the scene.

I was very young then, but I recall thinking that I had strolled about the airport for so many days but never seen an aircraft. Even though there was the wreckage of an aircraft in the film. It was much later that I realised that the aircraft had been filmed elsewhere—it was at the old World War II airbase in Dankuni, close to Calcutta. That's the magic of cinema.

But why didn't a 'Ritwik Gharana' take shape in Bengal? In other parts of India, there are many film-makers who loved and respected Ritwik and were inspired by him. John Abraham[11] more than anyone else. But no one in Bengal. Because Bengalis are most modern. They are so modern and so advanced that they had no time for this superfluous person. He was too much trouble for us. Bengalis don't want to have these troublemakers amid them anymore. This is what happens when a society becomes depoliticised.

In *Meghe Dhaka Tara*, Nita had two brothers. The character played by Anil Chatterjee wanted to become a singer, and became one too. The other, played by Dwiju Bhawal, was a footballer. He couldn't make it, and worked in a factory, where he had an accident. In *Subarnarekha*, Abhiram wanted to be a writer, but he had to become a bus driver. After the 1950s, this was a new phenomenon in Bengal, where many young people had to give up their dreams and do unglamorous jobs. This is archived in Ritwik's films.

He was the only director whose politics was clear to see in each and every film he made. His films were filled to the brim with gunpowder. When he showed a humiliated, defeated man, he told us that this humiliation, this hurt, this pain, had to be obliterated. Think of the sense of responsibility. And the culmination of all this was *Jukti, Tokko aar Goppo*. When the film was made, and we watched it, I couldn't understand it at all. In fact, I had a raging row with Ritwik about it. I remember telling him, 'Enough is enough! You think you can do whatever you want and everyone has to sit and watch it? I can't accept that you will walk to the camera lens and pour alcohol on it as a defence of your alcoholism.' He conceded defeat at the time. He said so. He finished by quoting Shakespeare: 'Then mum's the word.'

But I have been astounded each time I have watched the film since, the modernity of it is incredible. Just watch it. See the heights he has reached, see where each image has travelled. And that film talked about every political issue in Bengal, and even in the rest of the world, at the time. This epic quality of Ritwik's framing motivates me every day. Every day some new prostitutes are born, and every other day, their elder brothers reach them at night, drunk. But only Ritwik could have captured this in such a bold sequence.[12]

Great artists are cruel by nature. So was Ritwik. Tremendously cruel. And he whipped people—again and again and again—into consciousness. Well, to be fair, I don't know how much that worked, but he didn't stop trying.

At the end of it, there are the market forces. There is a culture industry at play. That industry looks only at profits. And Ritwik doesn't fit in there. Truth be told, Ritwik's films are being appreciated now, finally, after all these years. But it's true of all artists who are ahead of their time. Their work finds appreciation later. In his time, not many people understood Franz Kafka. But his relevance is increasing every day. I don't know what will happen when the new, still-unpublished manuscripts are read.

Think of Antonio Gramsci.[13] He was thrown in jail with the words, 'For twenty years we must stop this brain from functioning.' But in jail, he managed to get his hands on notebooks and pencils, and wrote his notes. The relevance of what he scribbled was understood much later.

Ritwik will always remain one of the great soldiers in our evolution, and in the philosophy of such change.

I have known this person from up close, as I have mentioned before, and he taught me so much … like the appreciation of music. He had encyclopaedic knowledge about everything, from Hindu religious music to Western classical music to jazz. He taught me to listen to the music of Modest Mussorgsky—'Listen to this,' he said. He would place his glass on the long-playing records, so there would be water rings on them. One day he played 'Night on Bald Mountain' by Mussorgsky for me. When he was working, he used to spend his money on things like that.

But more than all that, it was his knowledge more generally. Once, at Basusree Coffee House, he was talking about cricket. Cricket is a matter of great passion for Bengalis. I can't remember what he said, but he said things that made the others fall silent. The greatest writer on cricket, C.L.R. James, was a Trotskyite and an intellectual giant. Ritwik had read him too.

What Ritwik knew and didn't know is a greatly curious matter. I have heard him recite all of *King Lear*. I have seen him create magic with lights on a theatre stage, despite having no formal knowledge of it. This was for my father's play, and Tapas Sen[14] was handling the lights. Ritwik had gone to watch the performance. He went up to Tapas Sen, sent him packing—'*bero ekhan theke*' (get out of here)—and proceeded to adjust the lights. He was drunk, of course, but the work he did was unimaginable. He turned down a dimmer, increased the intensity of a spotlight, this and that, and changed the entire look of the play. He did know his theatre. He was a good artist. He was a good singer. He knew music. He knew everything without knowing anything. If you look at the credits of his films, you will see the names of cinematographers, but 90 per cent of the camerawork was done by him. As he did the look-through—the act of checking the frame before a shot—he would shout 'action' and the scene would play out. He would sit with Ramesh Joshi[15] on the edits and go through every frame and make his own edits. I have even seen him help with make-up.

So, as I was saying, it's curious what Ritwik knew and what he didn't. On the face of it, he had no formal training in most things. But he could do everything. Bengali critics wrote things like, 'he lacks discipline' and 'there is no grammar in his cinema'. Bloody fools, he was creating the grammar of cinema himself. Try to understand what he is doing. Grammar is not what you are used to, it is not perfection. An ugly, broken object cannot be made perfect. That is not the new aesthetic. The new aesthetic is of montage, which has evolved owing to political reasons. When he films a child on a swing and the camera swirls overhead,[16] it is not meant to be perfect. The child is swinging. He doesn't know where he is going. He doesn't have anyone—a mother, a lover, anything. He is lost. He might fall off the swing at any moment—become a trapeze artist. When Haraprasad tells Iswar,[17] 'Will you take me to Calcutta? It will be fun in Calcutta now.' Iswar says, 'Yes, we'll go.' It's macabre in Calcutta at that time of the year. Scenes from the race course. The horses leap out, start running, the race is on. There is a cut to a nightclub, singing, dancing, drinking. What a scene! Unparalleled in world cinema. People who have been feted in Calcutta, people whose names adorn our institutes and other things, no one has filmed a scene like that. Ritwik did. This man ruthlessly etched his name on all these aspects of global cinema.

It's a matter of pride for us that he was among us, that he was one of us.

At some level, it's so simple. Trust people. Be honest to the downtrodden. There is no need to cosy up to the rich and the powerful, no art is created that way. That is pimping. Be trusting. Be sincere. Be simple. Be politically aligned. 'I stand for a left wing heart, but no, no further than the heart,' he said. Stand up and say it. And, as he owns up to it, he dies at one stage. That is normal. That is the life of a true artist. This is what keeps the artist alive. And no one can point me to a true artist who has lived a happy life, eating and drinking to their heart's content, anywhere in the world. Think of Modigliani. To eat a bread roll, he had to sit in a cafe and draw on the tablecloths. Those works must have sold for millions of dollars later. This is our marketplace.

To conclude, yes, let these politically correct and cultured Bengalis go to hell. Let their modernity go to hell. We, the primitive and old-fashioned, will survive. We have nothing to lose but our (lack of) discipline and our (lack of) political correctness.

This is excerpted from a talk by Nabarun Bhattacharya at Kolkata's Gorky Sadan in February 2003. Translated by the editor and included here with permission from his son, Tathagata Bhattacharya.

Nabarun Bhattacharya (23 June 1948–31 July 2014) was a poet and writer, best known for the novels Harbart *(1994) and* Kangal Malshat *(2003) and the poetry collection* Ei Mrityu Upotyoka Amar Desh Na *(2004), among other works.*

Notes

1. Musician, who also composed the music for *Meghe Dhaka Tara* and *Komal Gandhar*, among other films.
2. Singer, writer, music composer and political activist, also a part of IPTA. He sang in *Meghe Dhaka Tara* and *Komal Gandhar*.
3. Chittaprosad Bhattacharya, political artist and writer, best known, arguably, for his linocuts and woodcuts depicting the horrors of the Bengal Famine of the 1940s.
4. Political artist and activist.
5. Writer, many of whose stories were made into films, including Nemai Ghosh's *Chhinnamul* (1951), which was the first film Ghatak acted in.
6. Poet and journalist.
7. His films have often come under scrutiny in Iran for their political commentary, and in 2010, Panahi was arrested and later sentenced to six years in prison, and was banned from making films or travelling out of Iran for twenty years.
8. Dr Sen, a human rights activist and public health specialist, was sentenced to life imprisonment on charges of sedition in 2010, but was later granted bail by the Supreme Court of India.
9. The prime minister of India from 1966 to 1977 and again from 1980 to 1984, when she was assassinated. She was union minister of Information and Broadcasting immediately before her first term as prime minister, which was when Ghatak was appointed vice principal of FTII. The more popular version of the events is that Satyajit Ray recommended Ghatak for the position.
10. When Ghatak fell ill soon after finishing the shooting for *Titas Ekti Nodir Naam*.
11. A gold medallist in film direction and screenwriting at FTII, Abraham made four full-length films and three documentaries in a short career that ended with his death, at forty-nine, in 1987. *Agraharathil Kazhuthai* (1977,

Donkey in the Brahmins' Village) and *Amma Ariyan* (1986, Report to Mother) are his most celebrated films.

12. Towards the end of *Subarnarekha*.
13. Gramsci, an Italian Marxist philosopher, writer and politician, was a founding member of the Italian Communist Party, and a staunch critic of Benito Mussolini and Fascism. He was imprisoned in 1926 after a trial, where the prosecutor said, 'For twenty years we must stop this brain from functioning.' He died at the age of forty-six while still imprisoned, though at a hospital, in 1937.
14. A stage designer, Sen worked with some of the greatest theatre directors from the 1940s to the 1990s and was a founding member of the Delhi chapter of IPTA.
15. A film editor, he worked on every Ghatak film except the penultimate one, *Titas Ekti Nodir Naam*, which was shot and edited in Bangladesh. Joshi was also the editor of landmark Bengali films like *Baksha Badal*, *Basanta Bilap*, *Fuleshwari*, *Dadar Kirti*, *Kony* and many others.
16. In *Subarnarekha*.
17. In *Subarnarekha*.

Baba and Ritwik

MOINAK BISWAS

We had shifted to a better house in the adjoining neighbourhood by then, but my playground and playmates were in the lane we had left behind. On one end of that lane was a high wall, and across the wall was the Gobra mental hospital.

You could see the inmates from this side. They wore striped uniforms and stood holding the bars of their cells, just like prisoners. Occasionally, some of them would jump the wall and try to run away, but they were caught almost immediately and taken back to their cells. The local people were enthusiastic about helping the hospital authorities in these situations.

People with mental-health issues and drunkards inspire fear in children—and this seems to hold true across the world. So, when Baba and Ma told me one day that I would have to go to the mental hospital and drop off food for someone, I felt nervous, to put it mildly. This was 1969, and the person I was to take food for was a familiar name in our household: Ritwik Ghatak.

From Baba's writings, we know that he met Ritwik for the first time around 1951. When the Communist Party of India was banned, Baba sneaked out of Assam and came to Calcutta, where he spent about three years. During this time, Ritwik often visited Baba's set-up in the Wellesley area, and Baba would visit Ritwik's home on Harish Mukherjee Road. They also met at Bhupati Nandy's house in Park Circus. Salil Chowdhury and a few others would join these addas from time to time. Barring the brief period in between when Baba was jailed, there was no gap in these meetings.

Baba composed two Bhatiyali songs (boatmen's songs) during this period. One was '*Padma kao, kao amare*' (Tell me, O Padma), and the other was '*Amar mon kaande Padmar chorer laigya*' (My heart weeps for the banks of the Padma). Not only was Ritwik especially fond of these songs, both set against the backdrop of Partition, he also contributed to the composition of the second one. He was witness to the composition of another of Baba's songs from the time—the lengthy ballad, '*Dhakar daak*' (The call of Dhaka). Written in the wake of the language movement of 1952 in East Pakistan (now Bangladesh), the making of the song lit a fire in Ritwik. Around the same time, he started working on *Nagarik*.

While the film was being planned, Baba would often join the meetings at the residence of Bhupati Nandy, the main financier of the film. There was yet another connection between Ritwik and Baba. In the 1940s, Ritwik's wife, Surama, had been Baba's comrade in Sylhet and Shillong, where they were involved in organising cultural programmes and protests for the Party. Both their families were from the Surma river valley, and she was in fact named after the river—though Baba used to call her by her nickname, Lokkhi.

The early 1950s was a time when Baba started to grow disillusioned with the work of the Indian People's Theatre Association. His writings from this time are quite clear about his view that the political crisis had started to impact the Party's cultural activities, causing it to lose direction and purpose. Ritwik was perhaps affected by this more than the others were, and it took a toll on his political as well as personal life. In 1954, he wrote a sharp critique of the Party's cultural line, titled *On the Cultural Front*, and sent it to the Party leaders. He would have frequent discussions with Baba while putting together the document. Surama has written that Ritwik had sent the last copy of the tract to Baba. There's no doubt that these experiences brought them closer.

Within a year of writing the document, Ritwik was expelled by the Party. Ritwik and Surama married the same year. We can find glimpses of this episode of Ritwik's life in *Komal Gandhar*.

Ritwik had wanted Baba to sing in *Nagarik*. In Baba's words, 'I was quite unwell then, and sickly. That's why I didn't agree.' Baba had recommended his friend Mahananda Das for the song in question. Ritwik was very happy with Mahananda's singing and recorded the song with him. However, the version of the film available to viewers now doesn't have the song.

For *Meghe Dhaka Tara*, too, Ritwik had wanted Baba to sing a song on camera. Baba didn't agree because of his 'celluloid fear'. On that occasion, he sent Ranen Roy Chowdhury—whose style of singing was similar to Baba's—to sing in his stead. Thankfully, we can see and hear Roy Chowdhury's amazing rendition of '*Kandiya akul hoilam bhobo nodir pare*' (I'm crying my heart out by the river of life) in *Meghe Dhaka Tara*. He has written about his experience of going to meet Ritwik with Baba's letter in hand.

Baba didn't manage to turn down Ritwik for *Komal Gandhar*. He didn't have to appear on screen, but had to sing a song. Ritwik demanded that the 'komal gandhar' note (E-flat in Western music) had to be used in the song. In the film, the song can be heard in the Lalgola scene, where Montu Ghosh plays the dotara and Bijon Bhattacharya sits on the banks of the Padma, singing '*Epar Padma, opar Padma, modhye Jagnar chawr / taar-i modhye boishya achhen Shib Sadagar*' (Padma on this side, Padma on that, Shib Sadagar sits in between, on the sandbar of Jagna).

So it was 1969 when Ritwik was admitted to that high-walled mental hospital in our neighbourhood. It was decided that his food would be sent from our house; the hospital authorities had given us the necessary permissions. My parents went out to work on the weekdays, so it fell on me to take the food across to him on those days. It might sound like child abuse to today's readers, but like many young children in those days, I was regularly sent out to get groceries for the household from the bazaar that was more than a kilometre's walk away. I enjoyed it too, because a trip to the bazaar meant I could flick a quarter coin and buy myself a few jalebis.

With this wealth of experience behind me, I was found eminently suitable for the task of taking food to Ritwik. I must admit that I had a funny feeling in my stomach to start with. I must have had a prayer on my lips when I walked in through the gate the first time, the tiffin carrier

Ranen Roy Chowdhury sings '*Kandiya akul hoilam bhobo nodir pare*' in *Meghe Dhaka Tara*; © Ritwik Memorial Trust

in my hand. Later, there was a sense of pride that I had entered that scary place and come back unscathed, having finished my job.

Much later, I realised that there was great significance attached to the whole thing.

I vaguely remember walking into the facility, asking various people where to go, reaching a building and standing in front of it. Ritwik was standing on a balcony slightly higher than where I stood, smoking a beedi. I gave him the tiffin carrier and stood there with my hands in my pockets. He asked me who I was. I clearly remember saying, 'I am Hemango Biswas's son.' In Bangla, one does not use the 'am', but I did, in my nervousness. It made Ritwik break out into a guffaw. A tall, thin man, standing up on the balcony, and laughing at what I had said—laughing at the person who had made such an effort to bring him his food!

The following Sunday, Baba and Ma had gone to the hospital to meet Ritwik. Surama Ghatak had been there too. When they returned, I realised I had been the subject of much merriment owing to that grammatical slip. After this, a cousin accompanied me on a few visits—my maternal aunt's daughter was visiting us during her holidays, and it wasn't terribly difficult to persuade her to come along.

I don't think I ended up going to the hospital too many times, but I remember one particular visit quite distinctly. Ma had packed some ilish maachh for him that day. Ritwik opened the container, took one look, and returned it to me, saying, 'Take this back. And tell Boudi that I am from the banks of the Padma, a single piece of ilish doesn't cut it for me.' Ma was quite upset at hearing that. When Baba came back from work and heard the story, he said he would ask Ritwik what this was all about. But I don't think he got around to it. The two of them, especially Ma, spoke about the incident for long afterwards.

One day, after a visit to the hospital, Baba told Ma in a low voice that Ritwik had told him, 'Please explain to these people, Hemangoda, that there is no point using electric shocks on this swine.' I was a bit shocked by that. I thought that sort of thing only happened in movies, even though I hadn't seen too many at the time.

Anyway, after a while they stopped administering electric shocks because some people with influence had become involved. Ritwik's daughter Samhita has written about this. But it's also true that Ritwik was on good terms with the doctors and nurses at the hospital—one can catch a glimpse of it in the play he wrote about his experience there, called *Shei Meye* (That Girl). This is the curious thing about that play: the principal character of Shanti, an inmate, was administered electric shocks by the doctor who didn't seem to have an alternative. It's clear that the writer of the play—Ritwik, that is—was trying to talk about his own pain through Shanti. But the character of the doctor is that of a sensitive and caring person. There is no criticism of his conduct. In the play, in fact, Shanti returns home cured.

Ritwik got patients and employees of the mental hospital to act in *Shei Meye*. I have heard that the poet Binoy Majumdar, who was also admitted to the hospital at the time, had taken part in it as well. Baba has written that Ritwik had been trying to get him to arrange music programmes at the hospital. There was a government budget for cultural programmes, and Ritwik had been trying to get funding from there.

I don't know if the programme they eventually put together featured *Shei Meye*; it's possible that Ritwik produced a number of plays while he was there. The day Baba sang there, a number of patients sang songs and recited poems. One of them put on a magic show, and there was a play too, as far as I can remember. There was a proper shamiana and a stage for the show. Was I asked to attend? Or did I go on my own? I can't remember, but I do recall sitting on a sheet on the grass. Everyone sitting around me had the striped uniforms on. Some of the calmer ones among them went on stage to perform—one of them sang the Tagore song '*Mone ki dwidha rekhe gele chole*' (You left leaving me hesitant). I sat there, scared stiff. Children hadn't yet discovered trauma in those days. A child in similar circumstances today might have had to be admitted to the same hospital.

What happened during the climax of the evening became the stuff of legend in our home.

Baba's troupe was singing '*Bhedi anashana mrityu tushar tufaan*' (Through the winter's cold and famine)—his translation of the Red Army choir's 'Partisan's Song'. And as soon as they sang 'Comrade Lenin-*er ahobaan, chole mukti senadal*' (At the call of comrade Lenin, there arose the partisans), all the patients stood up and marched out of the pandal. We found out later that the dinner gong had gone off. Those who were meant to hear Lenin's call may not have heard it, but these people heard their bell. It is apt that the place was later renamed Pavlov Hospital.

I am also reminded of *Subarnarekha* as I write this essay. That film attempted to assimilate insanity. I won't get into a detailed discussion here, but if you pay attention to the way the film unfolds, there is a pattern of time passing, and people losing their minds, or going off to outer space, like the cosmonaut Gagarin.

Baba has written about his discussions with Ritwik about *Subarnarekha* during this period at the mental hospital. Baba always said that, in the tragic climax of the film, when the character of Iswar reaches Sita's room, there is no sense of despair or blemish, but, 'like Dostoyevsky, he is crying for them'. However, at that time, standing at the cusp of Naxalbari, Baba felt Ritwik's film was about one side of the river whose other side was Gopiballabhpur.

Baba had asked Ritwik, 'Would you be able to capture the reality of Gopiballabhpur?'[1]

'I will think about it,' Ritwik had replied.

Baba had lent his copy of Felix Greene's book on China[2] to Ritwik. A few years later, Ritwik had brought Baba a screenplay. It was the screenplay of *Jukti, Tokko aar Goppo*. Listening to Ritwik narrate the story, Baba felt their conversations around *Subarnarekha* had a role to play in it. Baba watched *Jukti* at Parijat theatre in Howrah about a year after Ritwik's death. I was with him that day. It was the first Ritwik film I watched.

Thinking about *Subarnarekha*, one is reminded of Federico Fellini's 1960 film, *La Dolce Vita*. Not only because Fellini's music is cited—the connection runs deeper. *La Dolce Vita* had a profound impact on Ritwik. In his extraordinary essay on the film, he writes, 'That Fellini chap says both "*krato smara*" and "*kritang smara*" [the involuntary act of remembrance as well as the deliberate act of recalling past actions]—just like the all-seeing sages of our *Kathopanishad*.' Towards the end of *Subarnarekha*, we find Iswar and Haraprasad travelling in a taxi at night. Through the window of the taxi, we see the moving lights of the city, and we hear the voices of the two drunkards in the background: 'Haven't seen the atom bomb, haven't seen the war, haven't seen the famine ...' At one point, Haraprasad whispers, '*Krato smara, kritang smara*.' *Kathopanishad* comes before this: at the beginning of the scene, we hear him saying, '*Uttishthita jagrata prapya baran nibodhata*' (Being fully awakened and unencumbered).

The gap between the two films was around two years. Ritwik must have watched *La Dolce Vita* for the first time in 1960 or 1961. Baba had once asked me, 'Have you people watched *La Dolce Vita*?' Being a young film society member, I thought I should use the opportunity to present some 'general knowledge'. But then Baba said, 'Ritwik wanted to show me the film. He came and said, "Hemangoda, come, let's go and watch a cosmic film."'

Ritwik Ghatak's letter to *Dainik Assam*

Damaging rumours were circulating about Ritwik's sanity after he was admitted to the mental asylum in 1969. A couple of Assamese publications brought out reports defending him. *Dainik Assam* carried one such report, which was sent to Baba by its editor. Baba shared it with Ritwik, who wrote a letter to *Dainik Assam.* It came out in the newspaper (translated into Assamese) in early January 1970. *Kagaj,* a Bengali little magazine, reprinted it with Biswas's help in its autumn issue of 1981. Here, I translate it from the Assamese as the original letter is lost.

To, the editor of *Dainik Assam,*

Astonishing!

I am astonished.

While various publications in Calcutta are busy spreading delicious slander, you have remembered me despite your busy schedule, and reported the bold truth.

A couple of months ago, my respected friend Hemango Biswas showed me your newspaper. I found a sharp voice in it rising above the howl of wild animals, a voice in my defence.

I was feeling profoundly helpless at the time. The fault is mine. I had failed to fathom how difficult a commitment I had made in life. Failing to handle the consequences of my calling, I headed for self-destruction. I have no qualms in admitting that I had lost all faith in people. At such a moment, your paper, and the *Cartoon* from Assam, reported the truth about me in a way that made me regain belief in humans.

But it took me time to come out of the evil circle. The process has caused me immense pain. I regained self-control with clenched teeth, which gave rise to a harshness of mind.

But I have managed to come out.

I won't thank you, since your work deserves more than that. You have brought back my faith in life. How can it be repaid?

It cannot be.

Still, you should know that even if I cannot do much practically, in my mind I hold you in high esteem of gratitude. And if ever I get the chance to bring out the Assamese people's great tradition of art and culture, I shall try to repay the debt through my humble work of art.

I have long-standing interest, artistic interest, in Assam. I have a relationship of marriage, of course, but I have had other opportunities to learn about Assam. I often wonder if I could do something. Film is the most powerful medium today. Can't I say something with its help?

I feel frustrated as I cannot think of anyone who would help me realise this dream.

Perhaps an opportunity will emerge now. And if that happens, I may have something to show to you.

But your journalism is amazing! Please accept my thousand salaams.

Yours,

Ritwik Ghatak

This translation of the second instalment of the series 'Babar Golpo' (Stories of My Father), originally published in Banglalive.com *on 30 July 2020, is included here with permission from the author. The letter published in Dainik Assam was not part of the original essay.*

Moinak Biswas is professor of Film Studies at Jadavpur University, Kolkata. Among his publications are Apu and After, Revisiting Ray's Cinema *(2005),* Chaplin *(1997, 2000) and* Ujan Gang Baiya *(1988, 2018). He edits the* Journal of the Moving Image *and* Kolkata 21. *He has written and co-directed the award-winning Bengali feature film* Sthaniya Sambaad *(2010). His video installation 'Across the Burning Track' was commissioned for the 11th Shanghai Biennale, 2016.*

Notes

1. The peasant struggle in Gopiballabhpur in the late 1960s and early 1970s was part of the larger Naxalite movement.
2. Felix Greene, *Awakened China: The Country Americans Don't Know*, Doubleday, 1961.

I wish he had lived to enjoy the glory of his global status

JOY BIMAL ROY

We have had countless guests in Godiwala Bungalow, but the memory of one stands out above the rest.

Sometime in the early 1970s, a Bengali gentleman landed up unannounced at home. He looked like he had seen better days. His entire demeanour was one of defeat, someone at the end of his tether. His clothes looked as though they hadn't been washed in a long time, and he also appeared to be a bit tipsy. It was obvious from the manner Ma greeted him with that they had known each other for a long time. She addressed him affectionately as 'Bhoba', and she was palpably distressed at seeing him in this condition.

I was dying to know who he was, but had to wait till he left to find out. Ma said he was a film-maker called Ritwik Ghatak, and he had worked with Baba many years ago in New Theatres. But that was not the only connection, because our families had known each other all the way back to their days in Dhaka, before they moved to Calcutta in search of better prospects. I digested this information but his name didn't ring any bells. And then he invited us to see a special show of his film *Ajantrik* in the Films Division auditorium.

I was so overwhelmed by the film that I wept at the end, and even at that young age sensed that Ritwik Ghatak was a tour de force and a master

There's so much happening on the set: *Komal Gandhar*;
© NFDC – National Film Archive of India

of cinema. I was not surprised to hear many years later that he was more popular in France than Satyajit Ray was.

Soon after his first visit, he came over again, accompanied by two young acolytes. He was definitely drunk this time. He slurred as he explained that he had not been able to make a film in years, but he wanted to make a fresh start. So he was planning to write a script, which, if approved, would get him a loan from NFDC. Ma was delighted by the news and promptly invited him to stay with us while he wrote the script. Bhobakaka happily accepted her offer and landed up soon after with bag and baggage, and the two acolytes in tow. Ma realised they would be staying too. She arranged for their stay in our cottage next door, so that he could work in peace, and also be out of her hair, thereby killing two birds with one stone.

Little did she realise that she had taken on one of the biggest challenges of her life. Though she knew Bhobakaka drank, she didn't know he was a complete alcoholic. Soon after, the houseboy who went to clean his room came back in disgust and reported that there was a foul stink and there were empty bottles lying around. Ma pulled up Bhobakaka, who heard her out meekly and said he would stop. But of course he didn't. Things seemed to get worse, so Ma questioned the acolytes and discovered that Bhobakaka had made no progress on the script.

She demanded to see Bhobakaka immediately. He landed up with an abject and apprehensive expression on his face. I have rarely seen Ma more angry. She said he should remember he had a family to maintain, a wife and young children. This was his one chance to redeem himself and he was throwing it all away for alcohol. She told him that he was being extremely irresponsible and she wanted him to promise her that he would not drink again until he had completed his script. She warned him that she would not allow him to leave till he had finished it. To my surprise, Bhobakaka literally fell at her feet and wept, and promised to honour her word. And he did.

And that was how the script of *Jukti, Tokko aar Goppo* was finally completed.

Bhobakaka was a changed man at the end of his stay. He looked well kempt, well fed and purposeful. He touched Ma's feet when he left, telling her that he thought of her as he did his mother. Quite a compliment! In a happy ending, NFDC approved the script, sanctioned the loan and the film got made. I wish I could end by saying 'and they lived happily ever after', but Bhobakaka's life was like a Greek tragedy, and I suspect he died an unhappy man.

How I wish he had lived to enjoy the glory of his global status, acknowledged as one of the all-time greats of Indian cinema.

This essay, from Joy Bimal Roy's self-published Ramblings of a Bandra Boy, *which tells stories from his life, and of living a life in cinema, being the son of iconic film-maker Bimal Roy and celebrated photographer Manobina Roy, has been included here with permission from the author. The excerpt has been lightly edited for house style.*

Joy Bimal Roy has been a producer and director himself, having started his career as an assistant to Shyam Benegal.

RITWIK AND I

PART ONE: THE COLLABORATORS

Bari Theke Paliye was a happy interlude in my life

PARAMBHATTARAK LAHIRI

The association between the Ghatak and Lahiri families goes back to the late 1940s. To a place called Chirimiri (also spelt Chirmiri), which is now in Chhattisgarh.

My paternal grandfather, Bibhutibhushan Lahiri, was a geologist with the Tata group. At some point, he had moved with his family to Chirimiri, which was, and continues to be, a major centre for coal mining. When he discovered large deposits of coal there, my grandfather spoke to his bosses at Tata and suggested that they should set up operations at Chirimiri. They saw no sense in doing anything in that out-of-the-way town. So my grandfather quit his job and started his own business there. He spoke to the maharaja of the area, called Korya, and his words to the king are legend in my family: 'You finance me, and I will connect you to the civilised world.' That's what happened. The business was massive, and he brought in unemployed boys and girls from our ancestral village of Shantipur (in West Bengal) to work there. They have recently put up a statue of Bibhutibhushan in the area. It became a Bengali colony, with schools and colleges and a cinema hall, also a football team and other things my grandfather built.

One of Ritwikmama's elder sisters—Dollypishi, Sampriti Devi—was living there at the time with her husband, the manager of a coal mine, and their children. Sometime in the early 1950s, Ritwikmama, after completing his tenth-standard exams, had come to visit Dollypishi. And he became very close to my mother and her sister, Tapatimashi, who treated him like a brother. They used to call him Bhoba. He used to call my mother by her name, Debi, and my mashi Didibhai (elder sister). My father, who would go on to become a movie producer and produced Ritwik's films *Ajantrik* and *Bari Theke Paliye*, was Pramod-da to him. It was a relationship that continued until Ritwik's death in 1976. To date, we are occasionally in touch with some of his relatives.

We moved to Calcutta, to Rashbehari Avenue, after the coal mines were nationalised following India's independence. My grandfather built our house, Sarbatabhadra, and we settled down in Calcutta.

Not long after this, my father decided to produce films. The family already had a film distribution business. His brother knew Tapan Sinha, who had just made *Kabuliwala*, and they discussed the possibility of making a film together. That film was *Louhokopat* (*The Iron Gate*), made in 1958, which did quite well commercially. Around this time, Baba met Satyajit Ray and asked him about doing a film together. Satyajitbabu told him quite frankly that he did have a script, but it was unlikely to do good business. My father wasn't put off; he just wanted to make good films. So they made *Parash Pathar* (*The Philosopher's Stone*) together, which was also a 1958 release.

Our house was filled with discussions around films and plays, there were rehearsals for plays … I was just a child then, but I met the greatest talents and legends of the film industry at home. Pankaj Mullick sat there and sang some of his great songs—for two-three hours! Sarbatabhadra was a melting pot for the industry.

Ritwikmama too would visit. He had already made *Nagarik* by then, though the film had not yet been released. One day, while everyone gathered was throwing ideas around, Ritwikmama said he wanted to make a film. Baba told him to go ahead. Ritwikmama said he had an idea called *Ajantrik*. Baba said fine, do what you want.

It was based on a short story of the same name by the writer Subodh Ghosh, and set in a coal-mining town. Ritwikmama was in his early thirties at the time. My father realised that the film wouldn't do well at the box office, but he liked the idea. Also, honestly, Ritwikmama was a bit like the child around the house, and he wanted to do something, so my father was being indulgent.

At this time, I would have been about ten years old, and wasn't really interested in films. I was a good student, and my mother wanted me to focus on my studies. None of the films Baba produced, apart from *Louhokopat*, made any money, but that was all right. All of them are regarded as great films. Sadly, it had to end somewhere, since we couldn't keep losing money.

With all this background, let me come to *Bari Theke Paliye* now, which is the story you want to hear.

Shibram Chakraborty was known as a great writer of comic stories. I think this was the only story he wrote that was made into a film.

I remember the time well. *Ajantrik* had flopped, and they were going to make *Bari Theke Paliye*, and were looking for the lead actor. Ritwikmama wanted a young boy who looked pure and unspoilt. He had to look curious and mischievous. Not complicated. Not urbane. The film was about looking at the world through his eyes.

I remember so many young actors coming to audition in our house those days, but none of them appealed to Ritwikmama. He just didn't find the right face. And then he turned to me.

He knew me, obviously. I should have mentioned that he was living on the top floor of Sarbatabhadra at the time. With his wife and daughters. As tenants. Though he never paid the rent. He had made a couple of films, but hadn't made a name yet. One hadn't released. The other had flopped.

A lot of people have asked me why Ritwikmama took so long to spot me if I lived in the same house as him. The answer is: Ma. If Ma scolded him, Ritwikmama turned into a mouse. Ma was a formidable woman, and she wanted to have nothing to do with films. In fact, I hadn't even been allowed to go watch the shooting of the first three films that Baba had produced. I am an only child. All of us were scared of Ma. I don't even know how Ritwikmama decided I would be Kanchan, or how Baba and he convinced Ma. I still can't believe she relented, but obviously she did. *How did she agree*, everyone always wondered. No one knows to this day. And now we can't know.

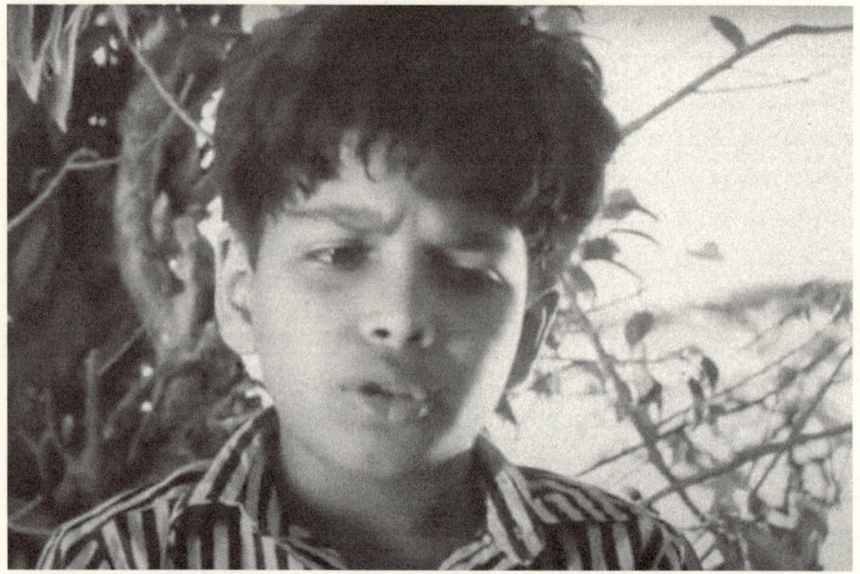

Boy wonder—Parambhattarak Lahiri's acting career began and ended with *Bari Theke Paliye*

Acting was fun, but it's not something I had ever thought of doing. On the sets of *Bari Theke Paliye*, I knew everyone: I called everyone—technicians and actors and director and producer—either kaka or mama or mashi or pishi or something. It never felt like work. It was like a game. I suppose my face was right for the role.

But now, all these years later, I remember the little details. I remember that the first scene that was shot was also the first scene of the film. I am studying, doing my homework, in the house in the village. Someone had come and complained about something I had done. My mother—played by Padma Devi—first explains to me why I should not be fooling around, and then my strict father comes and catches hold of me by my ear and throws me out of the house. Interestingly, in my own house, my father used to spoil me, while my mother was strict. After that, the shots were not always in sequence. I think scenes were shot based on where we were. So all the village scenes were shot in one go at the start, though they appear at different times in the film. It was a village near Diamond Harbour.

Everyone has always said that I was a natural in *Bari Theke Paliye*. Let me tell you, I was just being myself. Ritwikmama just asked me to tackle each scene the way I would in my real life. I was mischievous, I was curious … people talk about my smile and my eyes, but I wasn't acting, really. I was just being myself. I read a lot of books, so I had an imagination. I was quite innocent, as everyone was then. Now everything has changed, of course. And I was the right age. I didn't even know how to swim. In one scene, I almost drowned, but then managed to clamber out.

Along with Ritwikmama, Kali Banerjee and Padma Devi also made things easy for me. They were both such wonderful people. They showered me with love, and at no point did it seem like I was working. That said, I speak very quickly, gabble a bit. I did then too. My speech is not always clear. The words tend to jump over one another. I think that didn't work in the film, but everyone seemed happy with it. The restlessness of the character came through, I suppose? Although I think Ritwikmama tried various tricks to edit it while dubbing. The one thing that I found tough was running barefoot behind the fire engine … I got blisters on my feet.

Earlier, there was the turning point in the film. When the beggarwoman, who had lost her son after moving to Calcutta as a refugee and was looking for him, is beaten up on suspicion of being a kidnapper, I shout 'Don't hit her, she is my mother', and then I stand quietly. Haridas (played by Kali Banerjee) comes to me, and I ask him, 'Why is there so much misery here?' Like in Oscar Wilde's *The Happy Prince*, which Haridas refers to. He tells me the story later.

I remember, one evening, one of the people in the unit said to me, 'You have started so well, now you will soon be "Param Kumar", and become a star.' I got very angry. I didn't want to be any Kumar. I wanted to study. That's what I really wanted to do. I never acted again. In plays or movies or anything. This was the start and this was the end. Ma was the reason, partly, but I was also good academically and wanted to focus on that. You won't believe me if I tell you that I never met the young girl who played Mini after the film was over. The film was a bit of a pause in my life. I have heard that she married and moved to the US, but I have never met her.

So many people have asked me over the years why I never acted again. I find the question silly. I didn't. Isn't that enough?

Ritwikmama was like a family member. My mother and my mashi loved him. In fact, my mother was very angry when he got married. She scolded him: 'You have no money, no home, there is no certainty, how can you marry?' Remember that, at the time, he didn't drink. It was more about practical issues. He moved to Sarbatabhadra with his wife and Tuntuni, his first child, and lived on the top floor. Bulbuli, his second child, was born in that house. He never paid rent, but he was one of ours. I remember, one day, my father was playing '29', the card game, with his friends downstairs. Ritwikmama suddenly turned up. He went to my mother, bent down in front of her, put something down and rushed away from the room. He had left two hundred-rupee notes. He must have got it from somewhere.

As for me, well, I was the hero of a film, but I didn't get paid a paisa. And then I spent my whole life working with State Bank of India. In India and overseas as well. For thirty-five years. I don't even have the shirt I wore in the film. I used to have a single still from the film, but I don't know where it is now. It was just a happy interlude in my life. Nothing more.

Parambhattarak Lahiri played Kanchan, the lead character, in Bari Theke Paliye.

'I am very happy I made two films with Ritwik even though they were flops'

An Interview with PRAMOD LAHIRI

***Nagarik* didn't get a theatrical release. In such a situation, why did you take a risk with a story like *Ajantrik* and a director like Ritwik Ghatak?**

There's a long history to this. I knew Ritwik from the time he was in his teens. He used to visit Chirimiri in Madhya Pradesh, where we lived at the time. I think he was more involved with theatre then. When he was in Rajshahi, he used to bring out a magazine as well. When we met, we used to discuss cinema, and people like [Vsevolod] Pudovkin and [Sergei] Eisenstein. My family obviously had an interest in cinema. We have been in the distribution business for forty years now. So that was there, and we used to travel to Calcutta to watch the latest English films once in a way.

Ritwik was also my wife's close friend. They were like siblings. My sister-in-law and my wife didn't have a brother, so he became like a younger brother to them. We were a large family, and my son and my nephew called him 'mama'. But my wife didn't want him to be involved in the theatre or in cinema. She wanted him to do some proper work.

Anyway, then he made *Nagarik*. He used to write to me often, telling me about the difficulties he was facing while making the film. He finished the film in 1952. My wife and I went to Calcutta and watched *Nagarik*

Keshto Mukherjee as a street magician in *Bari Theke Paliye*; he had made his acting debut with Ritwik's *Nagarik*

with him. It was an outstanding film. I had also been thinking about making a film. But since I was busy with other things, I hadn't given it a serious thought yet. I started *Louhokopat* [Tapan Sinha, 1958] first, in 1957. Then I was told that Satyajit Ray's unit was sitting idle. He wanted to make *Jalsaghar* [The Music Room, 1958], but Chhabi Biswas was in Berlin, so he couldn't start. I thought that a man like Manikbabu [Ray] shouldn't be sitting idle, I must help him. So I got in touch with him through my elder brother [Prashanta Lahiri], and we started *Parash Pathar* [The Philosopher's Stone, 1958].

But I had wanted to make a film with Ritwik all along. We had a few stories in mind, including Bibhutibhushan Bandopadhyay's *Aranyak*. I really wanted to make *Aranyak*. We had a few discussions about it too. In between, *Parash Pathar* was completed, and I had given Ritwik my word about *Ajantrik*. I had told Ritwik that I wouldn't be able to handle three films—*Louhokopat*, *Parash Pathar* and *Ajantrik*—simultaneously, so he should push back his dates. Ritwik said something very remarkable in response. He said, 'I am ready to push back my dates. A director like Satyajit needs to make his film first. You should finish his film.' So I started work on *Parash Pathar*.

But there was pressure at home. They asked me why Tapan Sinha and Satyajit Ray should be prioritised over Bhoba. I had to give in. So we started *Ajantrik* as soon as we could. This is the story of how *Ajantrik* happened.

What sort of discussions did you have about the script of *Ajantrik*?

I had a weakness for the story [by the Bengali novelist Subodh Ghosh]. Ritwik and I worked together on the script, and I gave him a lot of freedom with the script, which was rewritten seven-eight times. But I let him have the final say on it. It seems astounding, but we ended up with about two lakh feet of negative exposure. Three cameras and four cars were at the location all through.

How much did you end up spending on the film?

One lakh and thirty-five thousand rupees, a pretty hefty sum for the time.

How much did you get in return?

Oh, don't talk about that. We couldn't even recover the cost of the prints and the publicity. We had made sixteen prints of the film. Within three days, they were all returned to us. I think I earned around thirty thousand rupees from Calcutta. It was a total flop.

You took *Ajantrik* abroad too. What was the reaction there?

Yes, to Cinémathèque Française first. [French film archivist and cinephile] Henri Langlois was full of praise for the film. He didn't want to return the print. He wanted to keep it there. I had to make him understand that I had brought the film to show it around the world. So he said that I should call him from whichever country I visited last, and he would get the print collected from there. He showed the film to everyone he could. While in Paris, I spoke to various embassies and invited people for a screening. Everyone loved it and praised it. I had printed a synopsis of the film in French, Italian and German, so everyone could understand it.

You didn't try to give it a commercial release there?

No one wanted to take the risk.

What about competitive festivals?

No, but it was shown at the Asian Film Festival later, in 1962. Recently [in 1975], at the festival in Delhi, I showed the film to Zelito Viana [the Brazilian film-maker]. He had won the Silver Peacock for best film [for *Os Condenados*]. A critic from the French newspaper *Le Monde* was with him. Viana praised the film a lot, and the critic asked me how I had the courage to make the film twenty years ago. He had heard of Ritwik. He said, 'I know about him, he was crazy. How did you get him to make a film like this?'

So *Ajantrik* was a flop. Why did you then decide to make *Bari Theke Paliye* with Ritwik, when the story wasn't one that was likely to be commercially successful?

I knew Ritwik, and I knew the fire he had in him, the passion for cinema. And both *Nagarik* and *Ajantrik* were outstanding films. And he had understood what mistakes he had made in them. We discussed making *Akal Basanta* [a story by the Bengali writer Samaresh Basu, which Gulzar adapted for a Hindi film called *Namkeen* in 1982]. Ritwik and I made some progress with the script. But we couldn't make the film because of a technical issue. Then we thought of making a film with *Sundarbane Arjan Sardar* [a novel based on the lives of tribal people in the Sundarbans by Bengali novelist Shibshankar Mitra]. We worked on the script, it was ready, but we couldn't make the film because of some issues. But both of them would have made good films. We were wondering what to do. Ritwik said, 'Pramod-da, let's make a children's film.' So we started working on *Bari Theke Paliye*. But this one flopped too. *Parash Pathar*, *Ajantrik* and *Bari Theke Paliye*, all of them were flops. I didn't try my hand as an independent producer after that. But I did connect Ritwik with many people in the industry.

So you didn't think of making another film with Ritwik after *Bari Theke Paliye*?

No. I didn't want to make any more films at all. But I am very happy to have produced two films with Ritwik. I made four films with three prominent directors. I had a strange connect with Ritwik. I couldn't think of working with a director after Ritwik.

This interview, first published in the Bengali magazine Chitrabikshan *in a special issue following Ritwik Ghatak's death in 1976, has been translated by the editor with permission from the publishers.*

Pramod Lahiri produced Ajantrik *and* Bari Theke Paliye *with Ritwik Ghatak as the director; his son Parambhattarak was the lead actor in the latter.*

'Ritwikda made impractical demands of his cinematographers'

An Interview with DINEN GUPTA

How did you start working with Ritwikbabu?

Ramananda Sengupta was the cinematographer for *Nagarik*. I was his assistant. That was 1952. Ritwikda seemed to be fond of me, and I got an idea of his great camera sense during the course of that movie. He used to ask me to do small things, 'we should get a long shot for this' or 'focus on that', and then discuss what would improve a shot, realistic lighting, etc., etc. And we agreed on most things. I just did what he asked me to.

Once *Nagarik* wound up, I started working as an independent cinematographer. We connected again when he started work on *Ajantrik*.

Ajantrik was my second or third film [second, based on IMDb listings] as an independent cinematographer. I worked very hard on it. Ritwikda and I used to fight and argue a lot too. He used to make impractical demands at times. 'I want a shot like this. The focus should be on this. The focus should be on that too.' When the argument reached its peak, we would be forced to call off the shoot. This happened a few times. I was adamant that it wasn't possible. He was hellbent on making it happen. Then, finally, we would arrive at a compromise.

Cinema is a director's medium. The cameraperson and other technicians have to do what the director wants.

On many occasions, Ritwikda would draw pictures of how he wanted the scene to look. But there is a big difference between a drawing and camerawork. I would have to explain it to him, and he understood eventually. But he would want me to think and innovate, and deliver what he wanted, and to that end, he knew how to rile me up and motivate me, talk about what other cinematographers had done. I took up the challenge, but some things were just not possible technically.

Then *Ajantrik* released. It was a landmark film, but not many people watched it. After that, we came to *Bari Theke Paliye*. It was based on Shibram Chakraborty's story. That also didn't do well commercially. Then *Meghe Dhaka Tara*. I was quite busy at the time, working on a few projects. Ritwikda wasn't too enthused by the story to start with. But eventually decided to do it. It got made. It released. It was very successful.

Then he made *Komal Gandhar*. I didn't like the script at all. Anyway, I didn't work on that film. [Dilip Ranjan Mukhopadhyay was the cinematographer for it.] *Meghe Dhaka Tara* was my last film with Ritwikda. I was supposed to do *Koto Ajanare* with him, but I was very busy at the time and didn't have the dates he wanted. Of course, I did the photography for Ritwikda's documentary on [the classical musician] Allauddin Khan.

You were talking about Ritwikbabu's camera sense. Did he look through the camera a lot himself, or ...

Of course he did. He did it a lot. He knew how to operate the camera; he wasn't entirely dependent on me. He would keep looking at the shot, and only when he was satisfied would he say, 'I want this.'

But I have to say that Ritwikda liked my work. When you work in a film, it has to be like an orchestra. The director and the technicians have to be in sync, and the technicians should be able to figure out what the director wants just by his gestures. I always felt that. Whichever director I worked with, I tried to understand the director and know what he wanted. I never tried to tell the director what I wanted. The director has chosen the story. He has worked on the script for six months. I am not so arrogant

Jagaddal, never short of words when Bimal does something she doesn't like—sing a tuneless song in this case

that I would listen to the script for an hour and tell the director how the shot should be taken.

Ritwikbabu used to say that he wasn't a film-maker but a creator, and his technicians must work according to his wishes. How did that play out?

Since I worked with Ritwikda, when I directed my first film [*Natun Pata*, 1969], at every stage I tried to work the way he would. I had tried to learn everything from him—how actors should function, the movement of the camera, everything.

Now, Ritwikda's approach was different from everyone else's. The way he spoke about the camera, if you look at the theories, a lot of what he said was wrong. But if you look at the total effect, he was correct. Like, he might ask for a long shot and then, wham, a close-up. Most of us work to a rhythm. Long shot, mid shot, close composite shot, close-up. Ritwikda would break this rhythm. So when I took a shot like that, I felt I was making a mistake. But when he placed the music on the shot, put everything in place, it gave you goosebumps.

I have worked with all the major directors in Calcutta—Satyajitbabu [Ray], Tapanbabu [Sinha], Rajenbabu [Tarafdar]—but Ritwikda had everything in his head, the total picture. Only in his head, not in the script, not in the shot division, nothing.

Then how did he coordinate with the technicians?

I don't know how he worked with other cinematographers, but with me, he discussed things a lot.

Let me give you an example. *Meghe Dhaka Tara* had a Tagore song: '*Je rate mor duwarguli*'. It was taken in one shot. The camera moved forwards, it moved backwards, all in one shot. It moved from Supriya Choudhury's close-up, back and forth. He told me, 'I want a design, I don't know why it isn't coming to me.' He pointed to the bamboo fence of the house, and said, 'Just burn that fence completely.' I told him, 'It's a scene with light. It will look bad if you burn the fence.' He asked me, 'What's the best you can do?' I said, 'I will put a white cloth in the back, and throw very harsh light on it. Then rays of light will come through the gaps in the straw wall of the shanty, it will feel like a glare.' He was happy. 'Try it,' he said. I tried more. I felt that if I made the wall a little out of focus, the rays of light coming through would form stars. So, Supriya was made to change her position, and it looked like the stars were shining from behind her. The effect was perfect. This sort of thing happened a few times during shots. I always had this freedom.

Tell us about some similar innovations from *Ajantrik*.

Say, in the last scene, when the scrap dealers are taking the remains of the car away in a cart, Ritwikda decided that the headlights of the car should come on. That way, it feels like there is some life left in the car, that its eyes are dazzling. It was very difficult to do this. The car was moving, and he wanted the car's headlights to dazzle for Bimal—and the audience—one last time. It took a lot of time to get that right. It needed a reflector to move with the cart and for the light to be reflected on to the headlight … and shoot it at the same time. We managed it eventually. You have seen it.

There was no back projection in *Ajantrik*. Kali Banerjee [the lead actor] didn't know how to drive properly at the time. But Ritwikda told me that

I couldn't use back projection for the shots of him driving. There was one shot of Bimal driving to the railway station. I had to be strapped to the footboard of the car. I was doing my work. And I suddenly saw that Kali Banerjee was all frazzled. He couldn't stop the car, which was going at top speed. The car was going downhill, and his foot was on the accelerator. As it hurtled down, large rocks were being scattered here and there. I could have been hit any moment. But I kept quiet and continued doing my work, since I couldn't do anything, I was tied up. Ritwikda was most appreciative. You see, I never told Ritwikda that I couldn't do something. Maybe I told him about focus, etc., but if he wanted a shot, I never said it couldn't be done.

Another shot in *Ajantrik* involved two cars moving towards each other from opposite directions. And they stop facing each other. One car was going up the hilly terrain, and our car was going downhill. We were shooting in Netarhat [now in Jharkhand], and there were no proper roads there at the time. I was sitting with my camera on a platform that had been strapped on to the bonnet of our car. I was strapped too. I should have realised that the car could skid. Obviously, it did, it skidded some distance after the brake had been pressed, and crashed into the other car. The headlights were smashed. But Ritwikda was very satisfied. He guffawed, and said, 'Very good, this is exactly what I had wanted.' He always had that sense of humour and was appreciative of good work. If you worked hard to get something right, he appreciated it. I don't know how the actors felt about it, but I enjoyed it. Every shot required a lot of work, and he praised you if you got it right. I liked that very much.

A shot in *Ajantrik* had to be taken in a Santhal hovel. They were all completely drunk. I was lifted on to the top of a car and asked to shoot 'like a documentary'. I was doing my work, and suddenly I felt sticks landing on my head and back. They didn't want us to take pictures. And Ritwikda was standing some distance away, laughing.

Sometime later, he asked, 'What happened?'

I said, 'You saw what happened.'

He said, 'See, this is what alcohol does to you.'

When Ritwikda worked, he had no relationship with the clock. In fact, he couldn't stand it if someone kept an eye on the time.

You worked in quite a few films with Ritwikbabu. Which of them gave you the most satisfaction?

Ajantrik.

Why? The camerawork in *Meghe Dhaka Tara* was more mature.

Maybe it was more mature, but I don't think the camerawork in *Meghe Dhaka Tara* was appreciated as much. But it was in *Ajantrik*. There was a lot more scope to do interesting things in *Ajantrik*. He knew how to get the best work out of a cinematographer. If you see his last film, *Jukti, Tokko aar Goppo*, the cinematographer [Baby Islam] did very good work. I think anyone who had some sense of the camera would have done outstanding work with Ritwikda. In that sense, I am grateful to him.

This interview, first published in the Bengali magazine Chitrabikshan *in a special issue following Ritwik Ghatak's death in 1976, has been translated by the editor with permission from the publishers.*

Dinen Gupta started his career as an assistant in the camera department with Kankabatir Ghat *(1955) before working as cinematographer in* Antariksha *(1957). He worked in three films with Ritwik Ghatak as the chief cinematographer—*Ajantrik, Bari Theke Paliye *and* Meghe Dhaka Tara, *apart from being an assistant on* Nagarik*—and later turned director with* Natun Pata *(1969). He made thirty-three films as a director.*

There was always an attempt to sideline Ritwikda

SUPRIYA CHOUDHURY

Not everyone gets what they deserve during their lifetime. Ritwik Ghatak was among those get-nots. He didn't get the fame or the fortune he deserved. Not that he was inferior in any way to anyone else.

It's unfortunate—sometimes the truly talented go unacknowledged. Even we are to blame.

Let me start by telling you about my first meeting with Ritwikda.

I was shooting for *Agni Sanskar* [1961] and *Shuno Baranari* [1961] at the time. *Amrapali* [1959] had just released. We had just moved from our house on CIT Road to a new house on Hindustan Road. The day after the move, Bishu (my then husband Biswanath Choudhury) and I were planning to go to Bijoli to watch Ritwik Ghatak's *Ajantrik*. The plan was to stop at Dwarik afterwards and pick up some luchi and chholar daal. Anyway, I always read at night before going to sleep and was reading a book on the night of our move too—*Chena Mukh* by Shaktipada Rajguru. I was so moved by the book that I told Bishu the following morning, 'If I could play the role of the lead character in this book, I wouldn't want anything else in my life.' We went to watch *Ajantrik* as planned that evening. Just as we were entering the theatre, the strap of my slippers broke. I liked *Ajantrik* very much, but we couldn't go to Dwarik, because of the situation with my slippers.

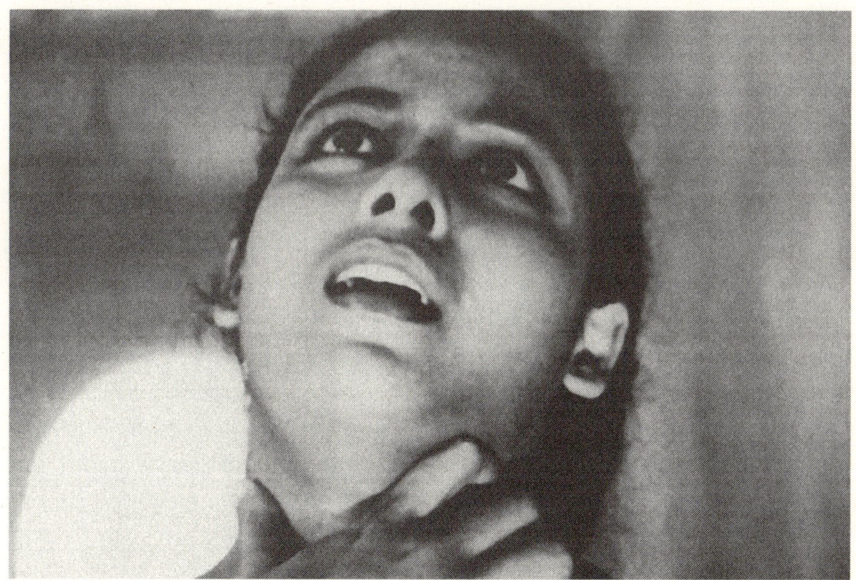

'He knew how to get the best out of an actor'

The next day, I had gone for a shoot to Studio No. 2 at New Theatres. I met Khoka [Dinen Gupta, the cinematographer and film director], and he told me, 'Go meet Ritwikda. He is looking for a heroine for his next film.' Khoka was a close friend. But I didn't have the best experience with the directors he had asked me to meet so far. So I told Khoka, 'I won't go to meet him. If he agrees, you bring him to my house.' I also told Khoka that I had watched *Ajantrik* the previous evening [Gupta was the cinematographer of the film].

Ritwikda visited me that same evening. A tall man, he spoke very politely and sincerely. He said he was planning to make a film based on Shaktipada Rajguru's *Chena Mukh*. I jumped out of my seat. I couldn't believe that my dream would come true like that. We started chatting like old friends. Ritwikda soon moved from the familiar and friendly 'tumi' to the informal 'tui'; and I also quickly moved from the formal 'apni' to 'tumi'. And *Meghe Dhaka Tara* began soon after that.

The last bit of the film was shot first. In the mountains of Shillong, where Nita, my character, is telling her brother, 'Dada, I wanted to live.' Ritwikda tried to shoot the rest of the film in a refugee colony, but people would crowd around and not let us shoot, so that idea had to be dropped.

Then, of course, the set was built on the large ground at Technicians Studio.

Without putting down any other director, I must say that I haven't seen another director work with the sort of sincerity that Ritwikda did once he settled down behind the camera. He knew how to get the best out of an actor. The other quality of his films was the naturalness in them. I think some other directors, in trying to achieve that sort of naturalness, ended up making things artificial. In *Meghe Dhaka Tara*, Gitadi's [Gita De] sudden wail at losing everything, Anil's [Anil Chatterjee] rolling on the floor laughing … I found all of that so natural. I found most other directors trying to find ways to avoid these things. The truth is that Ritwikda knew all aspects of film-making—camera, music, drama … it was all at his fingertips. I think many of his contemporaries were scared of his genius. Maybe that's why there was always an attempt to sideline him.

Ritwikda was a very simple man. And people like that are often very sentimental. Maybe that's what led to his alcoholism in later years. Another group of people were equally responsible—the ones that made sure Ritwikda wasted away.

The first time I saw Ritwikda holding a glass of beer was on the first day of shooting for *Komal Gandhar*. We had an all-night shooting schedule at New Empire theatre. I told him that I wouldn't shoot if he didn't throw the beer away. Ritwikda accepted my condition.

I couldn't give him a long sequence of dates for *Komal Gandhar*, since I had a lot of work at the time. One day, I was shooting at New Theatres, and I suddenly saw a tall figure strolling about near the gate in the drizzle. I went out and met Ritwikda. 'Come with me for an hour,' he requested. I managed to get out. I had to 'manage' so many things for Ritwikda. He had a car at the time, and he took me straight home. And I saw Lokkhiboudi [Surama Ghatak] sitting at a sewing machine. Ritwikda said, 'Remove the make-up.' I protested, but somehow I got ready. The shot was taken: me, my cheek pressed against the iron rods of the window, looking at the rain.

Many shots in the film were taken like that, Ritwikda coming and asking me to leave the shoot I was part of and go shoot his scenes. If you pay close attention, you'll see that my make-up is not the same in every shot. In some cases, I didn't even get time to remove the make-up I was using in the other films.

Ritwikda found unique ways to track me down. Once, I was in Darjeeling to meet Soma [her daughter from the first marriage]. She was studying in Loreto Convent at the time. And who do I see there but Ritwikda. If I didn't love and respect him so much, would I have tolerated all this?

As I was saying, I couldn't shoot properly for *Komal Gandhar*, since I was quite busy with other projects. But that created no problems for Ritwikda, he was a magician. Let me tell you why I say that. After he had completed the shooting of *Komal Gandhar*, he took me to see the rushes. I saw myself singing '*Aaj jyotsna raate shobai gyachhe bone*'. But how did that happen? I hadn't shot for it. I turned to Ritwikda, stunned, and asked him about it. He said, laughing, 'You were not there, so I got Punu [his assistant Punu Sen] to wear a saree and do the shot.' Imagine! It was so perfect that even I couldn't tell the difference. How could the audience tell?

This article first appeared in a special edition of the Bengali daily Aajkal *on 25 February 2001. Translated by the editor with permission from the publishers..*

One of the foremost actors of Bengali cinema, Supriya Choudhury (8 January 1933–26 January 2018) acted in two of Ritwik Ghatak's films, Meghe Dhaka Tara *and* Komal Gandhar, *in a rich filmography spanning five decades and over fifty movies.*

'*Komal Gandhar* was much ahead of its time'

An Interview with ANIL CHATTERJEE

How did you come in contact with Ritwik Ghatak?

I was in college at the time. At Indian People's Theatre Association, there was a plan to stage Shakespeare's *A Midsummer Night's Dream* in Bengali. I acted in it. I met Ritwikda during the rehearsals. We stayed in touch. I moved to cinema, as an assistant director. Ritwikda was also trying to make films. He made *Nagarik*. I had a small role in it. Unfortunately, the film didn't release.

It's fair to call *Nagarik* a collaborative film about the socio-political realities of the time. Was it mostly shot in studios or on location?

I don't think a film of that calibre about contemporary reality has been made to date in India. But it was shot primarily in the studio, because shooting outside was complicated at the time.

Did Ritwikbabu act out scenes for the actors, or did he only explain the characters and the situations?

Ritwikda was a fine actor himself, and acted in lots of IPTA plays. During the shooting of *Nagarik*, I saw him enact some scenes for the benefit of Bulbul [Satindra Bhattacharya, who played the lead role of Ramu] and

Ketaki [Dutta, who played Uma]. When I worked with him in later films, I didn't see him do this; he would only explain the scenes to the actors. But yes, at the start of his career, he did this with certain actors; he would enact the scenes for them. He changed his approach later.

The script for *Nagarik* was ready when the shooting started. That said, Ritwikda never quite completed his scripts, or what we call screenplays. He always improvised a lot. He would improvise on the sets, change things. He changed the dialogues, rewrote them. And he did this quite easily.

Now tell us something about *Ajantrik*.

I had a small role in *Ajantrik*, but I saw the whole film being made in front of me. I was working as an assistant director on other films then, and was a part of *Ajantrik* almost as an observer, like a student. Ritwikda had asked me to be with him.

What were the changes you saw in Ritwikbabu between *Nagarik* and *Ajantrik*—had he become more methodical or more disorganised?

When *Ajantrik* was being made, I remember the producers, Pramod Lahiri and Prashanta Lahiri, saying, 'What madness is this, Bhoba? How can we have a film with this battered, old car and its driver.' Since there was no screenplay yet, we didn't know what shape the film would eventually take.

***Nagarik* didn't get a release. *Ajantrik* and *Bari Theke Paliye* were flops. Then he made *Meghe Dhaka Tara*. Did you see a change in him through all this, did he seem like he wanted to compromise with the box office?**

Absolutely not. Though he would keep saying, 'These idiots are forcing me to make a commercial film.' All of you have watched the film. I don't think there was any commercial element in it. The only reason it became popular is that it touched people. There was a new experiment in it when it comes to content and form. It was about life, about refugees, that atmosphere, that period … I don't think anyone managed to capture all of it in quite the same way before or after *Meghe Dhaka Tara*. No one had heard of Supriya Choudhury at the time. No one would have

Anil Chatterjee played a key role in *Meghe Dhaka Tara*, as he did in *Komal Gandhar*

heard of Anil Chatterjee either. So there was nothing commercial about it. The distributor, Mahendra Gupta, had suggested a different ending to the film: the sister should survive, and she would return home with her brother. Ritwikda shot that ending. But he told me, 'This ending will not be used, I will shoot an alternate ending. This film must end in tragedy. The sister must die. She can't survive.' He didn't compromise.

Had his approach or style as a film-maker changed by then?

Of course, his style had evolved. People who managed to watch *Nagarik* can speak about this at length. But I think his approach had become a lot more 'real' by then. The sets for the film were made on the grounds of the studio, but it wasn't what you might call the interior of the studio. We used to shoot day scenes in the day and night scenes in the night. Ritwikda and his cinematographer Dinen Gupta had found some innovative ways to use light. Like, if we needed to reduce the harshness of the light sometimes during the day scenes, the entire set would be covered with tarpaulin. They used the light that filtered into our houses through the gaps in the fence extensively. Especially if you look at the sequence of the song, '*Je Raate Mor Duwarguli*'. They used natural and artificial light for that, keeping the time of the day in mind. When Ritwikda made *Nagarik*, there was no need to bother with all this. But when he made *Meghe Dhaka Tara*, he controlled the light all through.

Komal Gandhar, which he made next, was a much more mature film, but I suspect it was much ahead of its time.

Tell us about the next two films you made with him, because neither was completed, and not much is known about them.

You are talking about *Koto Ajanare* and *Ronger Golam*. *Koto Ajanare* might have been the first film where Ritwikda had an opportunity to work with some degree of financial freedom. When there is money to make a film, and if money is spent on the technical mounting of a film, everything can be so sparkling, the sets, etc. A lot of the film had been shot, but it couldn't be finished, unfortunately. A lot of actors and technicians had the opportunity to do a lot of good work in that film.

When *Ronger Golam* started, Ritwikda was quite unwell. The location was at the Kopai river, very close to Santiniketan. We shot for three-four days. And then some distributor came and advised him to use famous actors in the film. Anyway, the film wasn't shot after that. Ritwikda wasn't well, as I said, but the little work he did on the film he did with enormous confidence.

You have worked with so many important directors. How different was the experience of working with Ritwikbabu?

In Ritwikda's films, in some cases, we find a bit of an influence of the stage—stylised acting—in some characters. This is true of all of his films, but not necessarily all his characters. Some of his characters overact at times. That's because of what the film is trying to do. If Ritwikda used a character that was over-stylised, he always used another character alongside who was more natural. This was because of his years in the theatre, and of his own background as an actor. Some of his shot compositions were like you would see in the theatre. Like in *Komal Gandhar*. His love for the stage would come to the fore in some of his films.

This interview, first published in the Bengali magazine Chitrabikshan *in a special issue following Ritwik Ghatak's death in 1976, has been translated by the editor with permission from the publishers.*

Anil Chatterjee, a much-loved Bengali actor perhaps best known for Satyajit Ray's Mahanagar *and Tapan Sinha's* Nirjan Saikate, *acted in Ritwik Ghatak's* Nagarik, Ajantrik, Koto Ajanare *(unfinished),* Ronger Golam *(unfinished),* Meghe Dhaka Tara *and* Komal Gandhar.

Ritwikda hid the scripts, he wanted his actors to be spontaneous

MADHABI MUKHERJEE

I didn't pay heed to what Ritwikda used to say then, but I do now. He'd say, 'What are these films you act in—no one will remember them.' And I used to argue with him: 'I can't be irresponsible like you are.' He wouldn't reply, just laugh in that way so typical of him. That only made me angrier. But the man I found so irresponsible, so unconcerned about everything then, I now understand was so right. Isn't it true that an artist's main responsibility is towards their art? Ritwikda isn't around anymore. If he had been, I would have owned up to my mistake.

Sometime before *Komal Gandhar* was made, Sailenda, from Ritwikda's production team, came to my home one day. He asked me to go meet Ritwikda at his Bhowanipore home. I did, I went and met Ritwik Kumar Ghatak. He read out the screenplay of *Komal Gandhar*. It was decided that I would act in the film. Some days later, Ritwikda informed me that the producer had asked for someone else to play the leading role. He asked me to try one of the other roles, but I didn't agree to that. Maybe that was a wrong decision too.

Ritwikda's habit was to keep changing his script as he went along with the filming. During the shooting of *Subarnarekha*, I watched two female actors playing significant roles. But, in the film itself, one of those actors

Within a three-year span, Madhabi Mukherjee played the lead in Satyajit Ray's *Mahanagar* and *Charulata*, as well as in Ritwik's *Subarnarekha*

had only one shot. That's why I wonder—what if I had done that role in *Komal Gandhar*, and would Ritwikda have kept all of it in the final film?

The Ritwikda behind the camera and the Ritwikda outside the film sets were totally in conflict with each other. Seeing him drink and hurl abuses at everyone, you didn't get to see the fire that was always burning inside him. I have seen so many directors lose their cool when working with the junior actors. Ritwikda would tell them, 'Ma, it won't work if you do it like that' or 'Baba, you sit here like this, rest your back'. He was always calm and cool-headed then. He knew how to make people work.

In *Subarnarekha*, my character was supposed to lip-sync to a song. He used to keep asking me to memorise the song. The tape recorder the song used to play on was a weak machine. But that's what played during the shooting. Despite using such an anti-cinema technique and method, he managed to get the lip-sync right. I don't think anyone else could have done it. In one scene in *Subarnarekha*, the sister watches her brother appearing. At the time of shooting, we realised that the lens required to take the shot the way Ritwikda wanted was not available. He placed a lens from his spectacles in front of the camera lens to get it right. Can you imagine that?

I am eternally grateful that I got a chance to work with both Manikda [Satyajit Ray] and Ritwikda. But the two were so different from one another—if one was restrained, the other was the complete opposite. The actors in Manikda's films got the script well in advance, but Ritwikda preferred to keep the script hidden away. He wanted the actors to be spontaneous, act without preparation. The two of them had a lot of respect for each other, but when they met, they would argue about everything.

Manikda had been invited to attend the premiere of *Subarnarekha*. I think it was screened at Basusree. At the end, the two of them came face to face, cups of tea in hand. Ritwikda started, 'In which film was Madhu better—yours or mine?' Manikda replied, 'In mine.' Ritwikda didn't agree. And they started arguing. Now I understand that they were just discussing and debating each other's work. I was irrelevant. Manikda never spoke ill of anyone. And behind his back, Ritwikda would say, 'Don't watch films by anyone other than that giraffe. The rest are all buffoons.'

Although I ended up not working with Ritwikda again, our relationship didn't change. The taxi metre would start from eight annas (half a rupee) in those days. Once, Ritwikda suddenly turned up at my house in a baby taxi. He got off and told me, 'Madhu, pay him.' I saw that the fare had come to four hundred rupees! This didn't happen just once, it was fairly routine.

I went to Bangladesh not long ago. A gentleman came and introduced himself, but I couldn't place him. Then he said that he had come to my place with Ritwikda—and I remembered. Ritwikda knew that I wouldn't give him money for his alcohol, so he would try various tricks. Once he told me, 'Give me twenty rupees, otherwise I won't be able to get my ration.' I didn't flinch. So he said, 'Okay, fine, they will all remain hungry.' I thought maybe he wasn't lying, and I should give him the money, but then I remembered that Lokkhidi (Surama Ghatak) had asked me not to give him any money. I had to go out for a shoot, but I realised that I was feeling uneasy about refusing money to someone like Ritwikda. So I went to Lokkhidi on my way to the shooting location and gave her the money. I told her, 'Whether you need it or not, keep this. I can't keep my calm and work if you don't take it.'

At the same time, I have seen this same Ritwikda put his hand into the pocket of his kurta, pull out a fistful of coins, and give it to a technician who needed the money. Truly, it was so difficult to understand this man. His talent went unrecognised in his lifetime. This pained Ritwikda no end. It is my good fortune that I got a chance to work with him, spend time with him.

This article first appeared in a special edition of the Bengali daily Aajkal *on 25 February 2001. Translated by the editor with permission from the publishers.*

One of the icons of Bengali cinema, Madhabi Mukherjee was also a collaborator of Satyajit Ray's in movies including Charulata, Mahanagar *and* Kapurush, *and has acted in Mrinal Sen's* Baishe Sraban *and* Calcutta 71. *She acted in Ritwik Ghatak's* Subarnarekha.

Ritwikda's process was his own

MAHENDRA KUMAR

'Sorry, I can't take you'—I had been turned away by a number of film directors. I had come to this city [Calcutta] with a dream: to be part of the cinema world. And of course I had heard of Ritwik Ghatak, the unconventional film director who had made a film called *Ajantrik*, the story of a relationship between a man and his car. 'Try him,' said my friends, 'even as a person, he isn't like any of the rest … he might give you a foothold.'

At Technicians Studio, Ritwik Ghatak was shooting his latest film, *Bari Theke Paliye*. Being a runaway [from Kashmir] myself, the title of the film resonated with me. If he is that unconventional, I thought to myself, I could try to meet him without an introduction, or even an appointment.

That evening, as I reached Technicians, I saw many a young man and woman crowding the gate and not being allowed inside. A taxi came up to the gate and blew its horn. The young people were shooed away, and with a big salaam, the watchman opened the huge gate. No questions were asked, and the taxi went in.

If I come here in a taxi, I'll be able to get in, I thought. So I walked back to the nearest taxi stand, got inside one, and ten minutes later, the taxi honked at the gate of the studios. The gateman, with a big salaam, opened the gate, and I entered the land of my dreams.

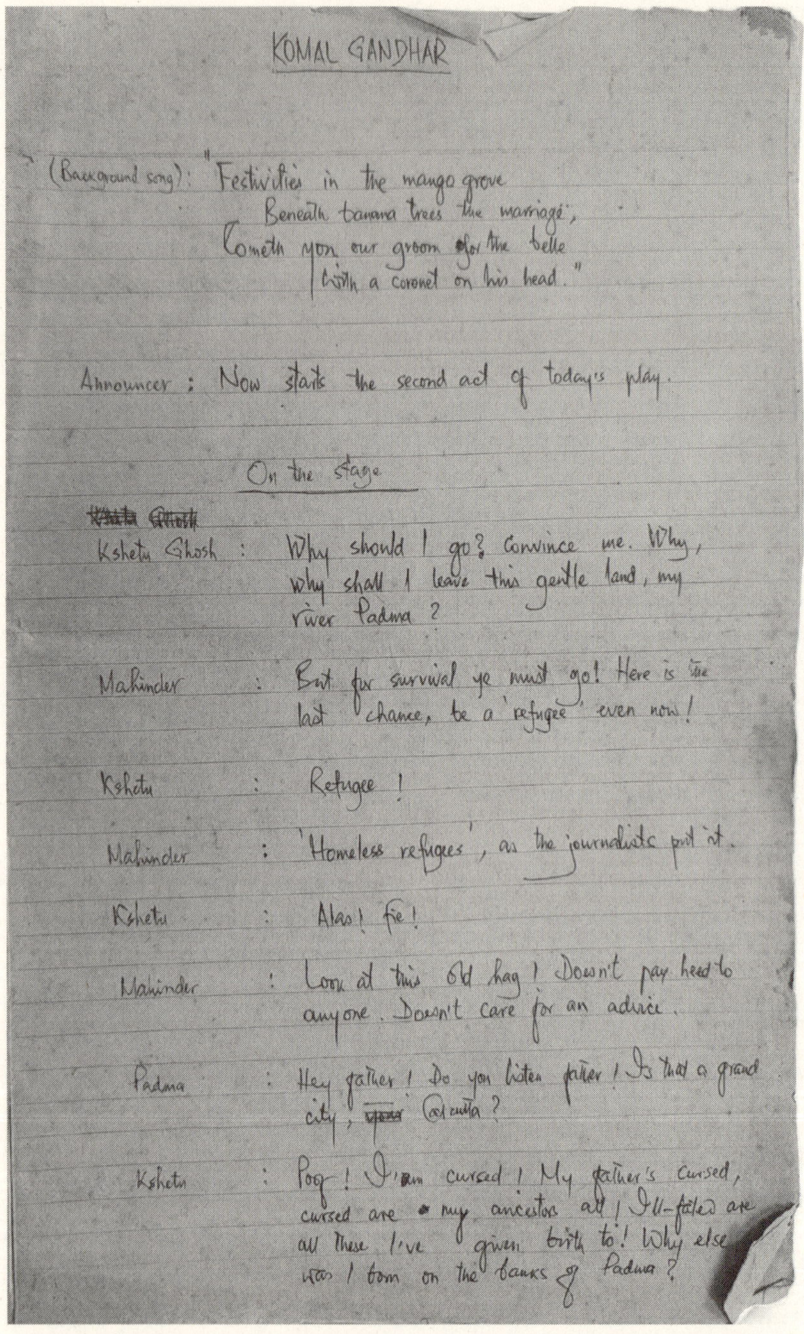

KOMAL GANDHAR

(Background song): "Festivities in the mango grove
Beneath banana trees the marriage;
Cometh yon our groom for the belle
With a coronet on his head."

Announcer : Now starts the second act of today's play.

On the stage

~~Khetu Ghosh~~
Kshetu Ghosh : Why should I go? Convince me. Why, why shall I leave this gentle land, my river Padma?

Mahinder : But for survival ye must go! Here is the last chance, be a 'refugee' even now!

Kshetu : Refugee!

Mahinder : 'Homeless refugees', as the journalists put it.

Kshetu : Alas! fie!

Mahinder : Look at this old hag! Doesn't pay heed to anyone. Doesn't care for an advice.

Padma : Hey father! Do you listen father! Is that a grand city, ~~your~~ Calcutta?

Kshetu : Pooh! I am cursed! My father's cursed, cursed are my ancestors all! Ill-fated are all those I've given birth to! Why else was I born on the banks of Padma?

They say Ritwik, once he got down to it, was one of the most meticulous film-makers around; © Ghatak family archives

The shooting had just ended. The place was bustling with people. They all seemed in a hurry to leave. I had to find the director before he, too, left the studio. I went from person to person with a beseeching 'Where can I find Ritwik Ghatak?'

In the fading light, I nearly bumped into a tall person wearing a cap, a vest and jeans.

'Could you please tell me, Sir, where I can find Mr Ritwik Ghatak?'

'You are talking to him, sonny boy. What can I do for you?'

'I want to learn cinematography. Can I join your unit?'

'Join up. There's a shoot on. Early morning tomorrow. Ask the production manager the time and the place for you to report.'

That night was as sleepless as it was beautiful. So were the lights on the desolate roads before the break of dawn the next day. I trudged towards the appointed place, arrived much before the scheduled time, sat on the footpath and waited. My harmonica and camera were, as always, with me. I made myself comfortable by the wayside. And then, softly and slowly, I played the harmonica, some made-up melodies and some known ones, unaware of the passage of time, or that I had a listener for my music.

'Hey! Ritwik Ghatak wants to see you,' said one of the assistant directors, breaking my reverie.

I went over to Ritwik Ghatak's car.

'Do you know what you were playing,' he asked.

'Yes,' I said. 'Swanee River.'

'Do you know who wrote it?'

'Stephen Foster.'

'Do you know the words?'

'Yes.'

'Can you sing,' he asked.

'A little,' I said.

'Then come on in.'

The car started and sped off for Surjipur. The rattle and drone of the engine was accompaniment enough for my untrained, enthusiastic voice. And the words '*Old Folks at Home*' were sung with all the yearning for a home that my life was missing.

'Where is your home,' he asked me. I hemmed and hawed, and my reluctance to answer brought forth a burst of laughter from him, and he told the others in the car, in Bengali, 'He has run away from home, and my film is called *The Runaway*.'

Immediately thereafter, the subject was changed, never to be brought up again by him. I felt at ease. This consideration for other people's feelings, whoever they might be, was a quality he had. For me, this aspect always overshadowed his image as a great film director.

As we began shooting for *Subarnarekha*, the unit had been inflicted with chess fever. Umanath Bhattacharya, Madhabi Mukherjee, there were others too, were all good at chess. I had also won a prize at a tournament at the YMCA. So Ritwikda asked me to teach him chess.

A new set of chess pieces and a board were bought the next day. In the evening, the whole unit was there as Ritwikda enthusiastically watched the pieces being laid out. Just that very moment, Ajoy Chakraborty walked in. He was a man of eminence and wealth. Affectionately called 'Paglada', he had also produced a few films.

'Ritwik, you play chess,' he asked with enthused surprise. 'I challenge you to a game, any stake.'

Instantly, Ritwikda retorted, 'See if you can defeat my assistant, then you can think of challenging me. Come, take my seat.'

I was up against a very good chess player. But he lost the first game, perhaps because he had underestimated me. As luck would have it, he lost the second game too. Paglada was a sporting man. He beamed at me and said, 'You are a good player.' Then, while taking his leave, he told Ritwikda, 'I will come again someday, but not to play chess with you. You must be terrific!'

Ritwikda saw him off to the gate. He returned as jubilant as a schoolboy. All of us were writhing with laughter, as if we had scored a victory over a rival team. But the real credit for the success of that glorious evening was Ritwikda's—in chess history, his was the most remarkable 'opening move' for a beginner.

Being on location for the shooting of *Subarnarekha* was a rich experience, seeing first-hand how a master craftsman creates a film; in a way, his process was his own.

The selection of the location, the time and the season were as important to him as the cast. The background sounds, or the music, would be either pre-recorded or already at the back of his mind. So were the 'pace' of the camera movements and the actors' movements. Armed with all this and other things beyond my ken, he also had a very alert mind that could deftly convert situations into part of the symphony of his films.

An example …

The death sequence of Abhiram's mother had been set up, ready for the camera to shoot, when the whistle of an incoming train was heard. We were informed that the fast express train would soon pass by that platform without stopping. The shot had to be deferred by a few minutes.

As Ritwikda paced the platform impatiently, the train whizzed past with the staccato beat of the wheels on the rails. All of a sudden, Ritwikda's attention became riveted on a little puddle of water, right at the edge of the platform. The light was pulsating in it, like the throbbing of a human heart.

The scene was shot. Then, none of us knew why, we all waited. The camera was trained on that puddle of water. The next express train came by, with its thundering staccato clatter, piercing doppler shriek and pulsating light, to help that little puddle of water get included in the history of modern cinema.

The last shooting schedule of *Jukti, Tokko aar Goppo* went very well. My only responsibility was to look after Ritwikda. While doing this, I took a lot of photographs—of him at work and at rest. These pictures say: here is the most dynamically efficient film-maker who understands his craft so thoroughly and is so intense about conveying what he wants to say.

As the shooting drew to a close, Ritwikda was a happy man. The last day of shooting had been reserved for the climactic scene, where his character gets shot in the crossfire of bullets between two warring viewpoints. *I have a rendezvous with death at some disputed barricade*—that's where he wanted to see the face of truth. We had to start very early since the day's programme was packed.

I had woken up slightly before the alarm went off. I found Ritwikda sitting up in bed and in great pain. We started getting ready. The pain was increasing. As we left the room, it seemed the pain had become unbearable. '*Teere eshe tori dub-be*?' (Will the boat sink so close to the shore?), he muttered. Then he braced himself and said, 'Tell the unit to proceed, we will follow in half an hour. I'll be inside. Don't come in unless I call you. Let the door be open—stand outside. And don't let anyone in.'

I signalled to a member of the unit and conveyed Ritwikda's message to him. And then I waited. Through the slightly open door, I could hear sounds. Of intense pain being stifled. As the sound of the motorcade carrying cast and crew members and all the equipment receded, I thought about his words, 'Don't let anyone in.' It was so important to defer our departure till he could enact the rendezvous with death. *What's your hurry?* The pain relented in ten minutes, and then sleep took over for twenty minutes to prepare him for the day.

He came out, in exactly half an hour, and had his breakfast. Then, while walking towards the car, he said, 'Today, be very careful. Stay very close to me all the time. Be very alert. I leave it to your discretion to stop the shooting at any time if you think there is a need to take rest or food or drink.'

When we reached the location, he was as vivacious as ever, and the shooting continued without anyone being aware of what he had been through, or that the climax sequence was fraught with danger.

At one point, I whispered to him to take a break and have something to eat and drink. 'Later,' he said, wanting to carry on with the shooting. I whispered again that there was a risk the shooting would have to be totally stopped. 'Okay,' he said, so casually, and we moved to a tree-shaded area.

He was quite calm now. He sipped his drink and had his food. And I had time to muse. What was this being? He could flit from the serious actor to the vivacious director, from joking with his crew to being intensely involved in the shooting and then quietly acquiescing to rest … all this while being in pain and under the threat of passing away at any instant?

I had, whenever I was sure that all was well, taken a few photographs. Till the 'shot' where the bullet hits him in the stomach.

Then, after a number of shots, a look from him signalled that the climactic shot was next.

'Only one shot,' he told the cameraman Baby Islam. 'No close rehearsals.' Baby Islam had brought a 9.5 mm lens from Bangladesh specially for that particular shot. Mechanically, Ritwikda moved and kept asking the cameraman what dimensions of the frame he was occupying. Then, right up to the camera he went and touched the mouth of the country liquor bottle to the filter of the lens and asked Baby Islam, 'How much should I bend so that my head remains within the upper limits of the frame and the mouth of the bottle also stays in the frame when it touches the filter-guarded lens?'

Soon after, 'All set! Make sure there's only one take.'

From his position, Ritwikda commanded that the camera should start, resumed the motion from the spot where he had been shot, and then, in great pain, holding on to his stomach, he tottered towards the camera.

The dividing line between great acting and real life is perhaps only theoretical, undiscernible. As the camera whirred, the pain seemed real. After the shot, was that pain acted away for the benefit of the crew?

Only after the sequence was over, when he pulled out his beedis and matches, the grin on his face said the crisis had passed.

This essay is from the Mahendra Kumar collection, courtesy the National Film Archive of India, Pune and the Centre for the Study of Social Sciences, Kolkata. It has been lightly edited for publication.

Mahendra Kumar was a part of Ritwik Ghatak's crew for many of his full-length films and documentaries from the late 1950s till Ghatak's death in 1976, mainly as a still photographer but often as an assistant cinematographer. He continued to live in Calcutta till his own death in October 2016 at the age of eighty-one. He remained close to Ghatak's family members till the end.

We had liberated Bangladesh, how could handling Ritwikda be more difficult?

HABIBUR RAHMAN KHAN

I was born in 1945. By the 1960s, I wondered, why were we partitioned? Who gained from it? I was not the only one thinking that, of course. I didn't know, yet, that across the border, in Calcutta, a man twenty years my senior was thinking the same thing. Actually, that's not saying enough. Ritwik Ghatak—Ritwikda to me—was perhaps affected by the Partition much more than me, much more than anyone I knew.

At that time, the late 1960s, we had bigger issues to deal with than Partition—my country Bangladesh had to be liberated. We did that in 1971. I played my own small part in it, as part of an underground group. And by the start of 1972, all I wanted to do was to make a film with Ritwikda. Earlier, I used to tell my friends that I would make a film with Ritwik Ghatak. They would tell me that I was being silly, Ritwik Ghatak would never set foot in Pakistan. I said, yes, Ritwik Ghatak won't come to Pakistan, but he will come to Bangladesh.

I didn't know anything about cinema. I was just a boy in my mid-twenties; my father, a businessman, had money. And I wanted to make a film with that money. Not any film. But a film directed by Ritwikda.

I didn't know Ritwikda. I had read some essays by him and had heard stories about him, which I found fascinating. The thing was that both of us, though I was about half his age, were stuck in the same place—Partition. Not the partition of India, but the partition of Bengal. Only two parts of India had been partitioned, Punjab and Bengal. Why do we call it the partition of India? It was the partition of two states of India, the two states that troubled the colonial masters the most, the two states that newly independent India's rulers were also the most worried about. It was wrong. Bengalis were one community. Religion is a separate matter; it's a personal choice. All of us in Bengal were happy together. Divisions were created by people with vested interests. Divisions that are yet to leave us. Divisions that, I fear, have only grown deeper. Between Bengalis on the two sides of the border. Between India and Bangladesh. Within India. Within Bangladesh. Everywhere.

But let me first tell you how I found him. It's the first of many memorable stories …

On Bhasha Dibosh (literally, Language Day) in 1972, some of us had organised a function in Dhaka, and had invited Satyajit Ray, Ritwikda and Sombhu Mitra. A man called Barun Bakshi, slightly older than me, had come with the group from Kolkata, and we were talking about doing a film jointly, a collaboration between the two countries. He asked me if I wanted to speak to Satyajit Ray. I said, 'No, I want Ritwik Ghatak.' Imagine my cheek!

He went back to Calcutta and called me after a month or so, asking me to go across. He had found Ritwikda in a park somewhere. He didn't have a place to live in at the time; Barun had taken Ritwikda to his own home at 8B Beniapukur Lane and, after some treatment and rest, he was better.

So, I went and spoke to Ritwikda. He said he wanted to make *Titas Ekti Nodir Naam*. I said, 'You do whatever you want, but you have to do it with me.' He agreed. He took me to a small screening room above Jyoti cinema hall. I think the censor board used to work from there. He showed me *Subarnarekha*. I fell in love with the film and with Ritwikda straightaway. The rights for the book—by Adwaita Mallabarman—was with a trust. Satyajit Ray was a director of that trust. They gave us the rights for a small sum of money, and I remember Satyajitbabu saying, 'This is the right film for Ritwik.' I hadn't read the book at the time, but I read it immediately after that conversation.

'For everyone who has grown up in Bangladesh, the rivers are the lifeblood'; © NFDC – National Film Archive of India

What I mean to say here is that it was not important for me what the film was about, or what the story was. I just wanted to make a film with Ritwik Ghatak. That's all.

Baba considered cinema haram. Being a rebel, I argued with him. I told him, 'You do business, you live on the interest from the money you have in your bank. That is haram too.' There was a lot of shouting and crying but, to cut a long story short, he agreed to finance the film. I spent eight lakh and twenty-four thousand Bangladeshi taka to make the film. I don't even know how much that was, or how much it is now.

Those days, a regular film used to be made at a cost of around one lakh taka in our country. People often ask me why it cost so much to make *Titas*. If you watch the film, you will see how huge the canvas was. It was shot in three schedules. In the summer, in the monsoon, in the winter. A lot of it was shot in the monsoons. It had to cost a lot. The actors and

Ritwikda didn't cost much, but the shooting itself was expensive. We shot the whole film on location, near Brahmanbaria (north-east of Dhaka).

One day, he told me in Bangaal, the language we spoke in, 'I have a reputation for leaving my films incomplete. You can take the horse to the water, but what can you do if the horse doesn't drink the water? I will not finish your film either.'

I told him, 'If the horse doesn't drink the water, I'll kill the horse. If the horse is of no use to me, I don't want the horse.'

He was flabbergasted. 'You will kill me?'

I said, 'I didn't say that. I was talking about the horse. But I won't let you leave the film unfinished.'

Ritwikda laughed a lot. He had grown very fond of me. I loved and respected him, but I also hated him at times. He was so impulsive.

Let me tell you two stories—these are also about money.

On the first day of shooting, we went to a location. It was a place close to Dhaka. We had around a hundred people in our unit. He took a look at everything through his viewfinder—thrice—and announced, 'Pack up!' I asked him what this was all about. He said, 'These people are poor. They will get paid for doing nothing today. And some of your money will be spent. Everyone benefits.'

Thankfully, he didn't do this pack-up business too often. Once he started working, he worked diligently. But it was all very difficult those days. There weren't proper bridges over the rivers, communication systems weren't modern, carrying all the equipment and everything was cumbersome. Still, we worked to a proper schedule.

Another day, in the evening, he said he wanted to eat Chinese food. I took him to a restaurant. He ordered seven-eight things, though he was not a big eater. He picked at his food, had a bit of this and a bit of that. And wasted almost everything. I asked him, 'What is this, Ritwikda?' He said, 'You're part of the bourgeoisie, and I spent a little bit of your money. What's the problem?'

Everyone said making a film with Ritwikda would be impossible. I thought, how difficult could it be? You can call it the brazenness of youth, but we had just liberated our country; how could making a film be more difficult, how could handling Ritwik Ghatak be more difficult?

To be honest, it wasn't. It was a joy. But it needed tact at times.

Like when it came to alcohol.

For one whole year, for the entire duration of the making of the film, he and I shared a room. Wherever we went, I stayed with him. In hotels, in guest houses, in the homes of friends. Even in Calcutta. He didn't have a home at that time, and his wife, if I remember right, was in a place called Sainthia, far away from Calcutta. When we went, we rented a flat in Karnani Mansion, on Park Street.

In Bangladesh, we don't manufacture alcohol, and I have never had alcohol. But I knew that you got Scotch whisky if you knew the right people. I organised that. Ritwikda only drank Scotch whisky for the whole duration of his stay in Bangladesh.

The agreement with him was that he would get three pegs in the afternoon and six pegs in the evening. And I would serve him. I would mix a lot of water in the bottle, so it was diluted. He wasn't used to drinking Scotch; in India, he drank country-made liquor. Sometimes, if we didn't have work, I would give him stronger drinks. I remember him saying once, 'Arre, Habib, this is giving me a high today. What have you brought?' I would say, 'I don't drink, Ritwikda, how would I know? I have just given you whatever I got.'

I felt Ritwikda suffered from a dual-personality syndrome. I don't think it had ever been diagnosed or treated. He wasn't the same two days in a row. One day, he told me, 'I have wasted a lot of your money. I will write you a script, like I have done for many others, and you make a commercial film with it. You will make a lot of money.' But I hadn't started out wanting to be successful. I just wanted to work with him. So, I declined.

On other days, he would get angry at small things, argue, fight, be unpleasant. I also wouldn't cede any ground. I would answer back and argue. It was almost like he wanted to be angry. It didn't matter if there was a reason for it or not.

One day, I took him to see some weapons. After the liberation war, whatever weapons we had were stored in a godown. I showed him.

He asked, 'Why did you show these to me? I have no use for them. I don't want to see all this.'

I told him, 'We fought with these.' I wanted him to know that I could be a bit evil at times.

In between, there was a delay because he had to go to Bombay to meet Mr Karanjia, chief of the National Film Development Corporation. This was in connection with a loan Ritwikda was getting to make *Jukti, Tokko aar Goppo*. I went with him. Mr Karanjia asked me once, 'Does Ritwik do his work properly?' I told him, 'Most of my film is done, it's progressing very well.' Everyone in India viewed Ritwikda with suspicion, because of his reputation as an eccentric person. They wondered if the money would be used properly. I wasn't lying. Work was going well at the time.

To go back to where we started …

I have told you how we met. At that point, I hadn't even seen a movie camera. Ritwikda sat down with a pen and paper and made a huge list, and called it a requisition slip. I had no idea what was happening. But I accepted it. After the liberation, nothing seemed impossible. And I had money. I sent people all around, and we got everything we needed.

The first time we went to see the river Titas, he asked me to stop the car at one point. And he walked straight into the river. He walked in, till the water came up to his knees. He bent down and started splashing the water on his face. Over and over.

After a while, standing on the shore, I asked him, 'What drama is this?'

He said, 'You won't understand.'

I said, 'I will if you make me.'

He said, 'I never thought I would be able to come to Bangladesh, to this country, to see the rivers again, to make a film here. I am trying to convince myself that I am here, at the Titas.'

And then we started shooting. I think that, apart from Ritwikda and Ustad Bahadur Khan, the music director, everyone was from Bangladesh. Although, really, they were also Bangladeshi—Bahadur Khan was born in Brahmanbaria. And we all used to have so many addas, especially in the evenings, when Ritwikda had his drinks and we sat around him.

'There are no movie artistes. They are not needed. An artiste is like a moving set property,' he said once.

I argued. 'How can that be? There are so many famous and popular actors. How can they not be relevant?'

'No. An actor can't do anything beyond what the director says. He is just a prop.'

The next day, there was a shot. The character of Basanti is in the forest, with the man with the bow-and-arrow. Ritwikda asked the actors to do various things. *Move a bit to the left, to the right, raise the chin, turn this way*. 'I am taking some close-ups,' he told them.

Then he turned to me and asked, 'Can they do anything outside of what I tell them?'

That night, he conceded, 'There are just a few actors in the world …' He didn't take names; he just went into deep thought.

The film got made, more or less on schedule. One of the scenes I remember most vividly still is where the character of Magan Sardar tells the character of Kader Mian, 'I have destroyed the lives of many people. Let me destroy you as my last act. You keep your mouth shut. I promise you, after that, I will turn over a new leaf.' It ends with Kader Mian telling Magan Sardar, 'Yes, I wish you to become a better man.'

There's also the scene that haunts me even to this day. When the young Basanti lures the letch to her house and shuts the door to the room with the other women waiting inside. They beat him up and threaten to tear off his clothes. It was such a powerful scene. At the end, they carry him out of the room and throw him in the river.

There is obviously a retaliation, and the climax. 'I don't have a mother-in-law or a sister-in-law at home. You think I am scared of any man?' And Basanti rushes, leaps and grabs the man by his clothes … like an angry goddess, her hair open, flying around, and she shakes the man like a rag doll and then pushes him away and he runs.

And who can forget the extended scene with the long boats? It was shot over many days, with so many people.

It's been fifty-three years since the film was made, and I turned eighty last year. So I don't remember everything anymore, but I do remember most of the film. It was a simple story, about simple people, told simply. Nothing complex.

So many people have done their PhDs on *Titas Ekti Nodir Naam*. It's an epic poem, like the Mahabharata. Just think of the canvas. When I was twenty-seven, when I watched the film after it was ready, I didn't understand it at all. Then I started watching it once every week. And I became obsessed with it. I think it's a film that, to like it, you must be a bit mature, older, more aware.

I later produced Goutam Ghose's *Padma Nadir Majhi*, which was written by Manik Bandopadhyay. Someone once asked Adwaita Mallabarman, what's the difference between the two stories? He had said, 'Manikbabu is a wordsmith. He is an artist. His book is a work of art. I have just written the story of my life.' Because he was from the Malo community, about whom the story was.

For everyone who has grown up in Bangladesh, the rivers are their lifeblood. Even today, when I see a river, I can feel a tug. The rivers attract us; they call out to us. Me. Ritwikda.

If Ritwikda had been alive, I would have wanted him to direct another film for me. About the death of democracy in Bangladesh, my Bangladesh, his Bangladesh.

Habibur Rahman Khan produced Ritwik Ghatak's Titas Ekti Nodir Naam, *which released in 1973. It was Rahman's first film as producer. He went on to produce a number of other films, including* Padma Nadir Majhi *(1993) and* Shankhachil *(2016) by Goutam Ghose.*

The mad professor

BISWAJIT CHATTERJEE

A whole generation of film-makers in this country is indebted to Ritwikda, who took Indian cinema to the global stage, even if he didn't get the sort of recognition some others did in his time. He was a dear friend, though he was older than me, and lived with me in Bombay for a while—those were wonderful times.

I can tell you lots of stories about Ritwikda, but not all of them might be right for this collection. What I want to talk about is his single-mindedness, his genius, his ability to win over people and his determination to do good work even when he was in poor health. And I want to talk about the respect everyone had for him.

Sometime in 1969, Ritwikda was in Bombay. I can't remember why he was there. It was after his stint with the Film and Television Institute of India in Poona. He was estranged from Suramadi, his wife, by then, though I was in touch with her off and on, and would meet her when I visited Calcutta. He was staying with Abhi Bhattacharya, the actor, who was also his relative. Now Ritwikda was a wanderer. He lived in his own world, went from place to place, didn't have any roots. And he had a problem with alcohol, as is commonly known.

One evening, I was at home when I heard a commotion outside. My assistant went outside to check and returned to tell me that a man had fallen down outside our gate and was hurt. I went out to check. It was

Ritwikda. He had hurt his head, and there was blood on his face and on his white kurta-pajama. He couldn't walk; he had to be supported as he got up. But he recognised me, and kept saying 'Bishu, Bishu' to me. I asked for him to be brought in, and called my doctor, who came quickly and cleaned the wounds and stitched him up. He had to rest. I put him up in the spare room.

Once he had rested and was feeling better, he told me, 'I want rice and daal.' So, the cook made hot rice and daal for him. And then he had the medicines the doctor prescribed and went back to sleep. In the morning, I realised that he had no memory of what had happened the night before. It was terribly sad, the way he was wasting away his life. But what could I say? I told him that I was like his younger brother, and that he could stay at my house for as long as he wanted. I used to live alone at the time, and only my staff would come by when required. It was the best I could do to keep him safe—he was not the sort to stay in one place for too long. But fortunately, he agreed.

It was a time when many talented and even established people from Calcutta—singers, actors, film-makers, film technicians—would come to Bombay, and we, who were already in the city, would help them. Pashupati Bhattacharya, Kumar Sanu's father, turned up one day. He was a musician. He arrived with a suitcase and everything, ready to stay with me. I used to call him 'Mastermoshai'. He moved in, and Ritwikda got a friend. The two of them would spend all day chatting and singing. I would go off to work. I couldn't do much to help Ritwikda with work, but I had arranged for Mastermoshai to teach Beena, Pradip Kumar's daughter, singing. (She became an actor too later.) I could chat with them when I came back from work in the evening. All of us loved music, so there was a lot of fun.

Sometime after that, things had started to get tense in Bangladesh—it was East Pakistan at the time. We used to get the news in the newspapers in the mornings and listen to Sheikh Mujibur Rahman's speeches on the radio in the evenings. I could see Ritwikda's agitation when he listened to the speeches. He would pace around the room, saying, '*Eta onyaay, eta onyaay*' (This is unjust), reacting to the actions of the Pakistani army. You could see his love for Bangladesh, which he was known for. '*Amar maar opor otyachaar, ami shojyo korte parchhina.*' (I can't tolerate my mother being tortured like this.)

Nargis came out of retirement because she couldn't say no to Ritwik

He would say that the truth of the situation needed to be told to the world. I asked him if he wanted to speak to journalists—I could invite some—but he had no interest in the media. So, I thought, I work in the movies, he was from the same profession, we could do something together, surely.

I asked him, 'Ritwikda, can't we make a film?'

'The idea, Bishu,' he said, excited. 'Let's do it.'

We discussed it, and I said, 'What if I produce it?'

'You?!'

'Yes, why not?'

'That's a fantastic idea. I'll write the script right away.'

He was mad. He was a genius, but he was like a mad professor. He immediately went into his room, shut the door and started writing the script. When I met him the next morning, he had not only written the whole script, but he also had the shot breakdowns, a list of how many actors and technicians would be required, everything.

Ajoy Biswas, who had made *Prothom Prem* (1965) with me—and later remade the film in Hindi as *Sambandh* (1969) with Deb Mukherjee in my role—was in Bombay at the time and would come to my house often. I asked Ajoy to get the unit ready, and said, 'You tackle him,' since Ritwikda was famously difficult to work with.

'You have to act in the film,' Ritwikda told me.

'What role,' I asked.

'You have to play a muktijodhdha [freedom fighter].'

'Sure, why wouldn't I do it?'

Once I agreed, he said, 'I want Nargis. I can't make the film without her.'

But Nargisji had retired officially by then. Ritwikda, however, was not to be discouraged. 'I want her.' If he wanted something, he got it. There was no question of any compromise.

I was close to Sunil Dutt and Nargisji, so I told Ritwikda that I could introduce all of them, but that I wouldn't be able to do anything more.

We went, and when Nargisji saw Ritwikda, she was overjoyed. 'Arre, Ritwikda!' She was just four years younger than Ritwikda and, later, in 1981, died at almost the same age as him—at fifty-one. Not just Nargisji. Whoever I saw with Ritwikda showed him so much respect, so much love. It was almost like they were ready to fall at his feet. It was respect for his talent and ability as a film-maker.

Ritwikda called her 'Baby'. I did a double take. I knew that everyone at RK Studios called Nargisji 'Baby'. I didn't know how Ritwikda knew that. Perhaps from the time he worked with Filmistan. So Ritwikda said, '*Hum* film *bana raha hai,* Bangladesh *ke upar. Us mein tumko karna hai.*' [I am making a film, on Bangladesh, and you must do it.]

Nargisji protested, saying that she had retired as an actor. 'What will people say? Try to understand.'

But Ritwikda wasn't the sort to understand. So he said, 'You are not acting, you are doing something for the country, think of it as something you are doing for all humanity.' He described what was happening in Bangladesh.

Eventually, Nargisji agreed. She had to be Ritwikda's 'Banglaar Ma—Mother Bengal'.

But she had a condition that Ritwikda couldn't say no to. She wouldn't shoot outside, since that would attract attention, and presspeople would turn up. The shooting had to happen in her house.

Ritwikda was undeterred. 'Yes,' he said. 'We will shoot your scenes under that tree. We will install a tulsi tree there. Everything I need with you can be done here. All you need to do is wear a red-bordered saree, but I will arrange that.'

Then he went off to Kaifi Azmi to ask him to write the lyrics for the songs. Bahadur Khan, of course, was always with Ritwikda. I remember him shouting at Bahadur Khan, '*Tum kahan se* music *seekha? Tum gobet hai!*' (Where did you learn music from? You are an idiot!) He would shout at everyone, but not with malice. *Gobet*! *Gadha!* (Idiot! Donkey!) He would sit down with the instruments and demonstrate to Bahadur Khan exactly what he wanted. He would do that with everyone. But that's also because he knew everything. He knew the A to Z of film-making. He held everyone's hand, but got others to do the work finally. No one would say anything in response. I don't think anyone feared him, everyone loved him.

I never got a chance to act with Satyajit Ray—he only made films with Soumitra Chatterjee, and a couple with Uttam Kumar—but I got a chance to act for Ritwik Ghatak. It's a matter of great pride for me as a Bengali actor. I did whatever he asked me to. 'Smile.' 'Turn around.' 'Look this way.' 'Come forward two steps.' He knew what he wanted; I did what he wanted. No questions.

Ajoy and I arranged for Ritwikda to travel to the Bangladesh border once, and we managed to get him into Bangladesh with his unit. It was a troubled time, so it was risky. But he was a very brave man, almost reckless. He went, even though it wasn't easy. They crossed the border illegally and shot in the jungles on the other side. Ritwikda came back with a smile on his face.

It was a two-reel film, like a documentary, that very few people watched at the time. But I enjoyed working with him. Ritwikda asked for whomever he wanted, and he managed to get them to be part of the film. Dilip Kumar, Manna Dey, Hemant Kumar, S.D. Burman, everyone helped with the film in some capacity or other. Dilip Kumar even sang a song for it.

The film was made in 1970-71, and after Bangladesh was liberated in 1971, I went to Dhaka to meet Sheikh Mujibur Rahman to give him a copy of the film. He greeted me warmly, held me by the shoulder. I remember I was in a dhuti-kurta. So was he, and he also always wore a black sleeveless jacket. He spoke very sweetly to me. Where we sat, there were large portraits of Rabindranath Tagore and Subhas Chandra Bose behind us on the wall. He told me how he admired the two stalwarts. More recently, when Bangladesh celebrated fifty years of liberation from Pakistan, Sheikh Hasina, the prime minister at the time, felicitated me, among others, for being a 'friend of Bangladesh'. Like I had with her father, I presented Sheikh Hasina with a copy of the film and some photographs from the shooting.

Sheikh Mujib also admired Ritwikda. I didn't know anyone who didn't. I met many people in my life, great people, fantastic people. There might be just one or two people among them whom I consider geniuses. Ritwikda was one of them.

Biswajit Chatterjee, popularly known just by his first name, is a veteran actor in Bengali and Hindi films, as well as a producer and director. He produced and acted in Ritwik Ghatak's short film Durbar Goti Padma, *released in 1971.*

His passion banished reason and logic

BHASKAR CHANDRAVARKAR

It was in the small hours of the morning, 3.30 a.m., at the end of April. An extremely hot Poona summer. Yet, the early dawn was cool. Cool, calm and joyous. A tall man—over six-feet tall—clad in white dhoti and kurta, was engrossed in beating the life out of a variety of instruments in the recording studio at the Film and Television Institute of India.

He got them to produce unusual sounds. He blew on the Indian flute to get a shrill, whistle-like sound, banged the Burmese gong and carried on thus for a fair while. This was the well-known Bengali film-maker Ritwik Kumar Ghatak. Our music recording session and his drinking had started simultaneously the previous evening. He went off to sleep by 9 p.m., having had a peg too many. Certainly more than he could hold. But was now refreshed as only Ghatak could be in the early hours after drinking that much. The recordist, the orchestra crew and I were flabbergasted by this show, unable to understand what was happening.

Only after two months did we hear and see and understand what all that noise was about.

When the short film this was all for was complete, it left all of us stunned. The weird sounds Ritwikda had created that early April day suddenly came alive as we watched *Fear*. Months later, I happened to see many—almost all—of his films. Most of them are object lessons for students who want to learn the use of music in films. If one were to set out to list films that make the best use of music, Ritwikda's *Meghe Dhaka Tara* would lead the rest, while his *Subarnarekha* would probably take second place.

A treasure house of creative and volatile ideas, his soundtracks are immensely educative. *Meghe Dhaka Tara* displays his powerful hold on sound, the other half—to a musician, the better half—of film. *Meghe Dhaka Tara* depicts the victimisation of an innocent young woman from a refugee family that has migrated to India after the Partition. Owing to family commitments and economic strain, the woman virtually sacrifices her life. The film is based on a short story, I believe. Ritwikda, in his script, introduced one brother as a singer. This gave him the opportunity to skilfully underline the film with music, which makes a simple but powerful story scale great heights. Jyotirindra Moitra, who had scored the music for the film, was conscious of Ritwikda's ideas and approach, and the sound and music of the film belong to Ritwikda as much as they do to the music director.

Generally, music in films is associated with sounds created either by musical instruments or sounds emanating from the vocal cords. But Ritwikda, in defining music, gave it much wider range and connotations.

Meghe Dhaka Tara opens with some broken phrases of Raga Hamsadhwani. You hear the sound of a train shearing through the strains of the raga. Then the birds are chirping. He heard the whine of a projector leaking in from the projection room and advised the recordist to mix it with the other sounds. And all these sounds together transport you to a complete and lucid world of music.

The world blossoms slowly as the film unreels. Towards the end, one hears the complete, fully woven Raga Hamsadhwani of which one has only heard a few broken strains in the beginning. The words '*Laagi lagan sati pati san / Param sukh ati anandan*' (Her whole being exists for him alone) move the listeners deeply. The slow unfolding of the raga from the glimpses of swaras to the drut cheez (allegro vivace) is a salient feature of this soundtrack. It is very skilfully woven in with the other sounds.

There is also the subtle use of other ragas, such as Bairagi, Asawari, Malhar and Bageshri. There were also a Rabindransangeet—'*Je raate mor duwarguli bhanglo jhore / Jani nai to tumi ele amar ghore*' (I knew not

There aren't too many books by or about Ritwik in English, but he has been widely written about in Bengali

that you came to me the night the storm broke down my doors)—and a Bhatiyali song sung by Nirmalendu Chowdhury, a sweet and penetrating Assamese folk song sung when a bride is sent to her husband's home, Pahadi songs sung by the people from the hills. All these are intermixed with masterly exactitude and intensity.

Ritwikda was of the view that the whole soundtrack, flowing alongside the visual track, must be treated as the music track. He believed in, and worked towards, the goal of fortifying this track with 'music'. We had heard about how he made the track 'thick' at a mixing and recording session in a Calcutta studio, like he did with the use of the projector noise. While mixing, he heard it from the other room. Obviously, the glass pane on the projection window was missing. A live track was also being fed into the mixer from the studio. Ritwikda heard the whine for a while and then advised the recordist to leave it as it was. 'Let the window remain open,' he said. 'The sound of the projector mixed with the others is lending the track an added and effective perspective ... I prefer it that way.' He had a knack for incorporating uninvited or the most accidental of sounds into his soundtracks to enrich them.

His sensitivity could turn mundane sounds into creative music. The effects track of *Meghe Dhaka Tara* is replete with these—the drone of frogs croaking by the river, the sounds of a train and of other vehicles, the chirping of crickets in the night, the not-so-uncommon sounds of rain, the wind and gale, the noises made by children reciting the number tables, the crackle of a boiling rice-pot cooking atop a choolha, but, above all, the one effect-sound of breathtaking intensity, and more effective, perhaps, than any music, the one that cuts through to the inside of your heart: the sound of the whiplash. (It is used when Nita, the heroine, discovers that the man she loves—and believes loves her—is actually about to marry her younger, somewhat skittish, sister.) The sound of the whip turns like a hacksaw blade inside you.

In the last scene of *Meghe Dhaka Tara*, Nita is in a sanatorium in the hills being treated for tuberculosis. Shankar, the singer-brother, comes to meet her. One hears a Pahadi song seconds before he enters the sanatorium. The gamak (vibrato) in that song is like the stab of a dagger catching you unawares. One finds the undulation in the pitch terribly inauspicious, though one may not understand the language at all. Yet, perhaps all is well as Nita is seen sitting alone reading a letter. One sees the tall hills, the green valleys, the beauty all around. This beauty and warmth unprepares you for the wet, cold slap in the next two minutes that shakes you violently to the innermost depths of your being. Nita's sobs and the ominous vibrato of the folk song suddenly discover their relationship. They become the collective sob of downtrodden and exploited womanhood. No soul in the auditorium is left untouched as Ritwikda weaves Nita's sobs into her words: '*Dada, ami bachbo, ami bachbo*' (Dada, I want to live, I want to live). His use of reverberation in this sequence is unique. I have watched this scene not less than twenty-five times and can unashamedly say it still moves me. Many of my colleagues have seen it two, three, four times too, either because they admire it or because they want to test their strength. It is impossible to hold back the tears or to push away the lump in the throat. The force, the impact and the intensity of this soundtrack remains unmatched by any film-maker in the world.

In the creative and short life he lived, Ritwikda achieved much more than a lesser person would have in a longer lifespan. After getting his master's degree in English literature, he worked in a textile mill on a daily wage of one-and-a-half rupees; he rode elephant-back in the thick jungles of Assam, directed plays as a member of the Indian People's Theatre Association, heard the masters of classical music, played the flute and made his best films before he turned forty. He was a gandabandh shagird (sworn disciple) of Ustad Allauddin Khan, among whose pupils number Ravi Shankar, Annapurna, Ali Akbar Khan and Pannalal.

Sadly, Ritwikda lacked a sense of proportion. His love for music, like his taste for alcohol, knew no bounds. His passion banished reason and logic. He did not know when to stop.

The song '*Lagi lagan*' in *Meghe Dhaka Tara*, for instance, starts when Shankar, now a famous singer, returns home. It is cut abruptly on a beat. This scene is followed by a simple dialogue sequence and, as it ends, lo! the song is back. Exactly where it had been left off—two-hundred feet of film in the past.

Very often, he does not bother to visually justify the sounds or the instruments used. Bhatiyali singers are seen plucking their one-string tukaris, but later, when Shankar sings in a street, the soundtrack teems with tabla, tanpura and swaramandala sounds as if it were a mehfil rather than a lone singer in the street. The crackle of the boiling rice pot is at times overdone. The very idea of using the sound of the whiplash bespeaks the expressive artistic calibre of the film-maker. Others may have used it once. But not Ritwikda. He uses it three times, and each time it seems to linger a little longer than it did before, than it should have.

Someone once dared to ask him, 'Dada, don't you think you create melodrama by overdoing things?' He answered, 'Son of a pig that you are [he swore often], you are bound to think so. It is the right and privilege of an artist to take the leap from the ridiculous to the sublime. That's what I have done, and I am sure I have succeeded.'

This essay was first published in Cinema Vision India, *Year 1, Edition 4, 1980, and has been reprinted with permission from Arun Khopkar. It has been lightly edited for house style.*

Bhaskar Chandavarkar was a musician and a composer of music in the cinema and the theatre, where he worked with luminaries such as Mrinal Sen, Girish Karnad and K.G. George, among others. He taught film music at Film and Television Institute of India in the 1970s.

DISCOVERING RITWIK

An electric whip

MAITREESH GHATAK

There's no one left to torment with an electric whip
This middle-class affluence and smugness
You've left, the swagger's gone, humility has arrived.[1]

– Shakti Chattopadhyay, 'For you, Ritwik'

In an elegy written right after Ritwik Ghatak died, the poet Shakti Chattopadhyay compared the impact of his films to the lash of an electric whip. Where the electric whip hits one the hardest depends on one's perspective and preoccupations. I have often thought that how viewers respond to Ritwik Ghatak's films is akin to what is called the Rorschach test in psychology, i.e., what one sees reflects one's thoughts and preferences, and not just the image on the screen. Perhaps this is true of all works of art, maybe even life. Those who are politically inclined will see in Ritwik Ghatak's films a ruthlessly clear-eyed critique of society, politics, relationships—what humans to do to each other. Those who are invested in a certain idea of 'art cinema' will appreciate sequences of sheer cinematic beauty, involving both visuals and music, but may frown upon touches of melodrama and a sense of humour that sometimes borders on the pantomime (for example, the sequence of a groom going to his wedding at the beginning of *Ajantrik* with the old car sputtering on bumpy rural roads and the groom, somewhat childlike in demeanour,

The eccentric taxi driver and his beloved old jalopy;

making exaggerated gestures and expressions ranging from discomfort to fear, and the background music taking on a comical tone).

For me, the resonance of his films extended beyond shaping a certain cultural and political sensibility or an appreciation of the power of art when I first watched them. Revisiting his films later in life made me reflect on my own academic work. As an economic theorist, I am interested in understanding the role of monetary incentives versus intrinsic motivation (for instance, commitment to people and causes) in driving human agency. To me, many of Ritwik Ghatak's films dramatise a core dilemma of individuals operating in a market economy: the inherent risk of destroying what we intrinsically value in our pursuit of success.

Monetary incentives fundamentally make you work for someone else. As the famous Bob Dylan song puts it, 'Well, it may be the Devil, or it may be the Lord / But you're gonna have to serve somebody'—usually someone with money and power. This may not draw on the vast reservoir of human motivation and creativity, leaving you feeling unfulfilled even after notching up the material markers of success. Or worse, you might take up any available economic opportunity to make ends meet, leading to the stunting of potential, both for you and your community, and create a huge gap between the life you could have lived and the one you end up living. On the other hand, pursuing your passion often runs the risk of failure, in terms of not receiving the critical appreciation you covet as well as economic hardship, and you could end up imposing this cost on your loved ones.

Interestingly, this tension between the profitable and the meaningful is central to the two personal anecdotes I have about Ritwik Ghatak, who died when I was only eight years old.

Of the few occasions when I met him—he was my grandfather Manish Ghatak's youngest brother—there is one that I remember well, from 1974. My mother introduced me to a tall, somewhat scruffy looking middle-aged man with very piercing eyes and said, 'This man is your chhotodadu (youngest granduncle) and he makes films.' This was in Berhampore, a mid-sized town about two hundred kilometres north of Calcutta, where my grandfather had built a large house with a garden. There was always a stream of visitors—family, friends, as well as stars from the Bengali literary world—because my grandfather was a novelist, poet and short-story writer who wrote under the pseudonym 'Jubanashwa' and was a leading figure in the neorealist era of Bengali literature known as the Kallol (named after a magazine) era. However, Berhampore was a sleepy town, and films (mostly Hindi) would land there some years after their original release, and I, all of five years old, had just seen *Haathi Mere Saathi (Elephant, My Friend*, M.A. Thirumugam, 1971). My parents were not into mainstream Hindi films, but because this was publicised as a 'children's film', one of my aunts had arranged to take a bunch of us cousins to a local film theatre called Surya.

Haathi Mere Saathi was a hit film starring Rajesh Khanna, about the friendship between an orphan and an elephant, who start out by performing at street corners to earn a living. The film did not make much of an impression on me, but I did enjoy watching elephants dancing or kicking a football with their trunks. So, hearing that this dadu of mine made films, I asked him if he had made *Haathi Mere Saathi*. He responded affectionately, with an impish grin, 'I wish I had, kiddo, then I would not be in such a sorry state.' While said light-heartedly, his comment clearly captures the tension between staying faithful to one's artistic vision and pursuing commercial success.

My mother also recounts a similar exchange between Ritwik Ghatak and my uncle Abu Ghatak, who was only a few years younger and more like a sibling than a nephew to him. Abu Ghatak spent some time in Bombay working as a film journalist as well as a directorial assistant and associate screenplay writer to directors such as Bimal Roy and Shakti Samanta. He is credited as an associate writer for story and screenplay for the film *Chinatown* (Samanta, 1962). At an event in the Berhampore Film Society, now named Ritwik Sadan, Ritwik Ghatak gave a talk highlighting the challenges of making innovative films and criticising mainstream commercial Hindi films. In the question-and-answer session, my uncle, a polite and well-mannered man who was also quite mischievous, slyly asked, 'But, Mr Ghatak, who wrote the screenplay for *Madhumati* (Bimal Roy, 1958)?' Of course, it was an in-joke and got the expected laughs from an audience that knew the family well, but looking back, I can see an interesting parallel with my own naïve exchange with Ritwik Ghatak in 1974.

I was reminded of these exchanges when I discovered Ritwik Ghatak's films in my early teens, a few years after his death. It felt like being hit by lightning. I first saw *Meghe Dhaka Tara* on Doordarshan in the early 1980s, during the regional films slot on a Sunday afternoon. On the surface, it is a family drama about the economic struggles of a lower-middle-class Bengali family displaced by the Partition. The protagonist, Nita, shoulders the burden of being the sole breadwinner, giving up her dream of pursuing higher studies. She is eventually diagnosed with tuberculosis and sent to a sanatorium in Shillong. The scene at the sanatorium, in which her anguished cry—of wanting to live—echoes through the hills, delivers the emotional equivalent of a gut punch. There is a double allegory at play about the literal and metaphorical wasting away of human life: those around Nita, her family members and the fiancé who ends up marrying her sister, also seem to be afflicted by a wasting syndrome, a moral atrophy caused by their callousness and selfishness. Even the most sympathetic of them, her elder brother Shankar, who understands what Nita is going through, chooses to put his own dreams of a musical career above the immediate needs of the family and Nita's well-being.

The tragic force of the sanatorium scene is foreshadowed in the subversive use of a well-known Tagore song '*Je rate mor duwarguli bhanglo jhore*' ('The night when my doors broke down in the storm') in an impromptu duet sung by Shankar and Nita in the film, with the voices provided by eminent singers Debabrata Biswas and Gita Ghatak (the latter also acted as Nita's somewhat selfish sister). In this sequence, Ritwik Ghatak manages to convert a spiritual song, which finds comfort in the presence of god in times of crisis, into something more emotionally radical and raw; the fact that there will be no god to save Nita makes the song more like a dirge for a death foretold.

Many years after my first encounter with the film, the British Film Institute organised a Ritwik Ghatak retrospective in 1996. As I happened to be visiting London then, in what turned out to be the beginning of a long association with the London School of Economics, I watched some of his classic films for a second time, and saw audience members, who had no direct connection with Bengal, the mythology around Ritwik Ghatak or the trauma of the Partition, weeping quietly as the film dragged us through the emotional equivalent of a stormy sea.

I was struck then by the similarities between *Meghe Dhaka Tara* and *Ajantrik*, perhaps my favourite Ritwik Ghatak film. To me, the popular translation of *Ajantrik*'s title, 'The Pathetic Fallacy', does not quite capture the pithiness of the Bengali title. The alternative one, 'The Mechanical Man', seems more appropriate. The literal translation of the word 'ajantrik' is 'unmechanical', and that may capture the double irony of the film: a man spends so much time with a machine that others joke he himself resembles a machine, while viewers see—through the protagonist's eyes—a machine that seems almost human and its connection to a man almost in terms of a human relationship.

The storyline of *Ajantrik* follows the eponymous short story by the distinguished writer Subodh Ghosh fairly faithfully. It focuses on a somewhat washed-out middle-aged taxi driver, Bimal, who is known as Bimal Master in the neighbourhood, and played brilliantly by Kali Banerjee. Bimal's rugged, somewhat scruffy appearance matches that of his decrepit Chevrolet car, with which he shares an emotional bond that, for the lack of a better term, is love. Some of the more amusing moments of the film suggest that the 'feeling' is reciprocated. For example, a pretty woman dressed as a bride rides the taxi with her companion, who appears to be, but eventually turns out to not be, her husband. While shy and awkward, Bimal is clearly intrigued by and somewhat attracted to her, and during their brief exchanges while the car is parked, the swivelling headlights of the car that Bimal calls Jagaddal (literally meaning a heavy immovable object, an apt name for a big, old car that often breaks down) resemble human expressions, ranging from eye-rolls and sideward glances, suggesting envy at his mate's attention being diverted.

It is the ending that reminded me of *Meghe Dhaka Tara*. Years of heavy use on rough terrains takes a toll on the machine, which breaks down, and Bimal, who is normally quite frugal, tries to overhaul the entire engine to give the car a new lease of life, but all his efforts fail. This is like Nita succumbing to tuberculosis because of hard work and chronic poverty, and Shankar making a last-ditch effort to cure her by sending her to a sanatorium, which too ends in failure. The anguish both Shankar and Bimal feel seems similar—it is grief for a loved one's passing away, tinged with a sense of guilt at not having done enough or having exploited them for selfish gains.

Indeed, the two films have a structural similarity, even though the stories and the settings are very different. Both explore the tragic consequences of human or human-like relationships getting tangled up with economic necessities. The tragedy lies not just in the fate of the protagonists, who do not survive, but also in the lives of those who loved them and have to carry the burden of loss and guilt. Whether it is Shankar in *Meghe Dhaka Tara* or Bimal in *Ajantrik*, their losses are final and devastating.

Both films end with a suggestion that life goes on despite individual tragedies, and that those who have departed leave something behind for their loved ones, whether it is a memento or images that evoke their memories from happier times. In the final scene of *Ajantrik*, a child is seen playing with the horn of the car that has been sold as scrap metal; when he toots it, Bimal rushes out as if expecting the return of his beloved car;

when he sees the child, he smiles, and his eyes fill with tears. *Meghe Dhaka Tara* ends with Shankar, in a state of grief-stricken numbness right after Nita's death, staring intently at a young woman walking down the same muddy dirt road Nita used to take to go to work. Suddenly, the strap of this young woman's chappal breaks and she looks back at him, smiling awkwardly; as she walks away, limping slightly, Shankar's stony reserve crumbles, and he breaks down crying. One could give similar examples from *Komal Gandhar* and *Subarnarekha*, illustrative of Ritwik Ghatak's way of capturing how humans are broken by life, and yet, turn around. This is not deep philosophy or spiritualism, but an almost childlike, instinctive embrace of everyday life with all its love, heartbreak, grimness and soaring beauty.

There is clearly an economic critique in Ritwik Ghatak's films, of hopes and aspirations of individuals being crushed by poverty layered with an examination of the political circumstances—Partition and displacement—and the oppression of gender norms that precipitate such hardship. But if we go beyond these structural parameters that are specific to a particular time and place, and look at these films from a more abstract point of view, certain themes emerge to make us reflect on the intertwining of human relationships (or between humans and human-like beings) with economic necessities. When it comes to a relationship with someone or something, can we always disentangle our selfish or instrumental interests (what it can do for me) from intrinsic emotions such as empathy, loyalty and love? In a given social and economic context, where choices are limited and resources are scarce, is a conflict between the two inevitable?

From one angle, Shankar is selfish, and he puts his dreams of making the best use of his talents as a classical singer above the needs of the family, and so the burden falls on Nita, eventually sucking the lifeblood out of her, literally and metaphorically. From another angle, Shankar clearly loves his sister, is the only person in the family other than her father who seems sensitive to the struggles she is going through, the only one who *ever* does anything for her; he gets her admitted to a sanatorium for treatment, and in the end, is clearly stricken by grief when she passes away.

Similarly, Bimal is a selfish man on one level—he has a reputation for being miserly, strikes a hard bargain with customers who desperately need a ride, and does not seem to mind driving Jagaddal over rough terrains even as the car creaks and splutters like an ageing beast of burden. On another level, he shows touches of genuine tenderness (like pouring water in the engine's cooling system as if giving a glass of water to a loved one who is thirsty) and bristles if anyone appears to criticise Jagaddal's run-down appearance. Moreover, when Jagaddal breaks down, he spares no expenses in trying to repair it, as if a close relative or friend were in need of medical treatment and saving them overrode everything else.

Perhaps it is utopian to imagine a society where human beings (or human-like beings, from Jagaddal to AI) do not exploit one another and nobody is driven by monetary incentives. Given Ritwik Ghatak's well-known association with leftist political and cultural organisations, we are perhaps justified in seeing a vision of socialism as a model of an ideal society in his films. We also see glimpses of tribal life as a model of a society not corrupted by the logic of the marketplace in some of his films, such as *Ajantrik*, although these remain chimerical. But even if no such ideal society is in the immediate horizon, we know that an economic system where everything can be reduced to a monetary value (like the scrap value at which Jagaddal's carcass is sold) dehumanises us and destroys everything that is precious and unique in relationships between people, between people and nature, and between people and inanimate objects (one can think of attempts to protect heritage buildings and sites in the same way).

Is there a way out of this? Ritwik Ghatak's films seem to point to individual agency, to attempts to defy the oppressive forces that reduce us to becoming an exploiter or an exploited, and to the struggle to protect all that is precious and unique to us from the destructive logic of the market. While such struggles inevitably tend to fail in Ritwik Ghatak's films, they also point to the possibility of a different kind of trajectory. Therein lies their power to inspire generations of viewers, like the tragic heroes in myths who stand up for something beyond personal survival or the attractions of power or fame (think of Karna in the Mahabharata).

But this inspiration comes at an emotional cost to the viewer. In Ritwik Ghatak's films, a childlike wonder at beauty in all its forms (music, nature, hopes and the dreams of ordinary people) is tinged with an awareness of the grim realities of life. The films are preoccupied with how people cope with losing something precious, whether it is a dream or an ancestral home or a decrepit car. That might explain the somewhat surprising posthumous popularity of his films even among viewers who are not necessarily part of a typical art-house audience or drawn to progressive politics. The Tagore song that Nita and Shankar sing in that unforgettable sequence in *Meghe Dhaka Tara* serves as a commentary on his films and his life—it breaks us, but it also lifts us.[2] That realisation is the electric whip his films torment us with.

(*Acknowledgement: I thank Manishita Dass for helpful discussions and comments, and my mother Lipi Ghatak for refreshing my memory about the anecdotes involving Ritwik Ghatak.*)

Maitreesh Ghatak is professor of Economics at the London School of Economics. His main areas of research interest are development economics, public economics and the economics of organisations. He writes regularly on economic, political, cultural and policy issues for a broader audience in various newspapers, magazines and blogs in both English and Bengali.

Notes

1. Translated from the original in Bengali ('…আর কেউ নেই যে কড়কাবে বিদ্যুচ্চাবুকে / এই মধ্যবিত্তি, সম্পদ, সন্তোষ মানুষের / তুমি গেছ, স্পর্ধা গেছে, বিনয় এসেছে') by the author.
2. For those not familiar with the original song, which is reproduced below, this is a translation by me:

   The night when my doors broke down in the storm
   I didn't know that you had come to visit me
   It all turned dark; the lamp went out
   I reached out to the sky, but who was it for?
   I lay crumpled in the darkness thinking it's a dream
   Little did I know that the storm was your flag of victory
   In the morning, I looked and saw that you are standing
   All over the emptiness of my room.

Ritwik Ghatak: Reinventing the cinema

JONATHAN ROSENBAUM

I have no way of knowing if Ghatak ever saw Jacques Tati's 1953 masterpiece *Mr Hulot's Holiday*, but when I look at his second feature, *Ajantrik*, it's hard not to be reminded of it. Tati discovered with that film—while introducing his most famous character, who went on to appear in his next three features (*Mon Oncle*, *Playtime* and *Trafic*)—that Hulot didn't even have to appear onscreen every time he was to be evoked. All Tati had to do was duplicate the sound of Hulot's car: a rattling antique and an embarrassment that very early on in the picture becomes closely associated with him, identifying him from the outset as the odd man out among vacationers at a summertime beach resort.

There's a similar association made between Bimal (Kali Banerjee), the cab-driver hero of *Ajantrik*, and his own broken-down car. The fact that this car has a name, Jagaddal, and is even included in some rundowns of the film's cast, also seems emblematic of this special symbiosis. And it's interesting that Ghatak also uses some artificial-sounding noises on the film's soundtrack that oddly evoke science fiction, as if to express his fascination, his bemusement and amusement, with Bimal talking to and more generally treating his 1920 Chevrolet as if it were both a living creature and an extension of his own personality. (In interviews, Ghatak stated that he spent many years thinking about the philosophical implications of this relation between man and machine—a relation that seems especially pertinent to the technology of cinema itself.) And offscreen as well as onscreen, the various sounds that Ghatak uses to characterise this vehicle through various stages of health and fitness are a major aspect of the film's tragicomic tone—as important as the music or the sound of Bimal weeping when Jagaddal finally and irrevocably breaks down. The sound of this wreck being pulled away in the final scene is especially harsh and poignant, yet the sound of the detached car horn still wheezing and honking when an infant squeezes it allows the hero some sense of triumph and joy in the film's final shot.

In short, we have to acknowledge that the sound of this picture is far more than a neutral accompaniment to and counterpart of the images. And more generally, when we consider the soundtracks of some of Ghatak's other features, such as *The Cloud-Capped Star*, it is tempting to imagine that Ghatak in effect created these features at least twice—once when he shot them, and then once again when he created their soundtracks.

On the British Film Institute's DVD of this film, there is a detailed introduction by the former *Guardian* film critic Derek Malcolm that puts much emphasis on its sound. Although Malcolm speaks of the film having an innovative use of 'natural sound', which I rightly or wrongly interpret as 'direct sound', I've been told by Ghatak's son Ritaban that none of his father's films employ direct sound, and that all of them, by technical necessity, are post-dubbed. But this latter fact only emphasises the degree to which Ghatak's soundtracks are composed, and what I find most striking about his highly unorthodox methods of sound composition are the ways that they essentially 'rethink' the dramaturgy of the visuals and affect the ways that we look at these visuals by drawing our attention towards certain details and away from certain others.

This principle is facilitated by the way that Ghatak seems to compose both his visual mise en scène and his aural mise en scène in discrete layers. He frequently employs deep focus cinematography, permitting a certain counterpoint between background and foreground details that on occasion reminds me of the early films of Orson Welles. (The last time I saw *The Cloud-Capped Star*, at the Ghatak retrospective held at the Jeonju International Film Festival in South Korea, I was especially struck by certain similarities to Welles's second feature, *The Magnificent*

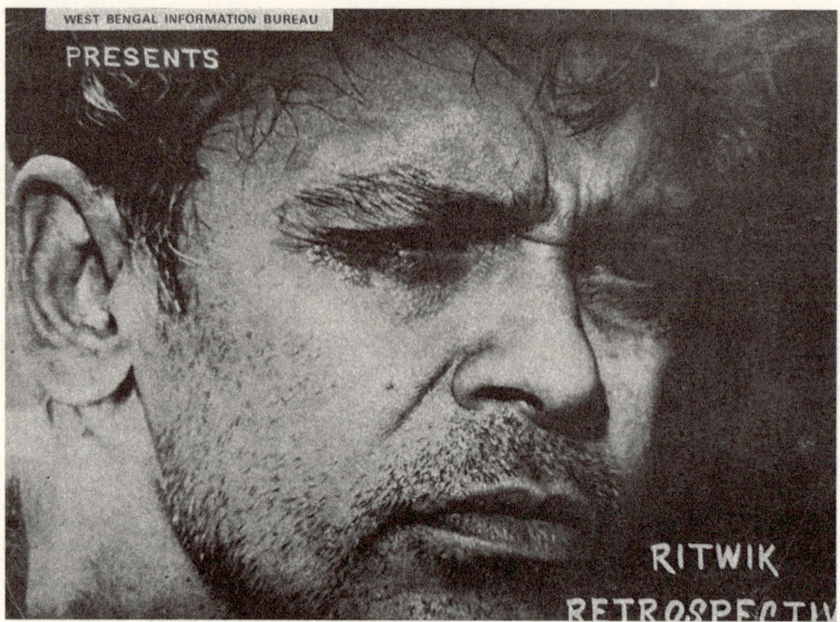

Ignored so much during his lifetime, recognition for Ritwik has come after his death

Ambersons (1942)—another tragic portrayal of the shifting fortunes of a family set against a larger backdrop of a culture in relentless decline, with a great deal of emphasis placed on the sacrifices made by some of the family members.) And Ghatak's sound is often layered between music, dialogue and sound effects that can be naturalistic (such as the sound of food cooking on a grill, which Malcolm mentions) or expressionistic (such as the recurring sound of a cracked whip, which Malcolm also mentions). Much as our visual attention can shift in certain shots from foreground to background and back again because of the construction of the layered images, our aural attention might shift at times between music, dialogue and sound effects, which might in turn affect the direction of our gaze in relation to those images.

There are two basic ways that a film-maker can relate to film history: to work within an existing tradition or to proceed more radically as if no

one else has ever made a film before. I think it would be safe to say that at least 99 per cent of the films we see in theatres are made according to the first way. The Danish narrative film-maker Carl Dreyer and the American experimental film-maker Stan Brakhage are two of the rare exceptions who might be said to have followed the second way. Even though they too worked to some extent in existing traditions, their principles of editing and camera movement and tempo and visual texture are sufficiently different to require viewers to move beyond some of their own habits as spectators in order to appreciate fully what these film-makers are doing artistically. Without making such an effort at adjustment, one's encounters with the films of Brakhage and Dreyer are likely to be somewhat brutal in their potentiality for disorientation.

Ghatak, I believe, is another rare exception who followed the second route I have described, and one who provides comparable challenges of his own. And his methods of composing soundtracks for his films as well as his ways of interrelating his sounds and images are among the things I would point to first in order to describe his uniqueness as a film-maker.

One might conclude, in other words, that he reinvented the cinema for his own purposes both conceptually, in terms of his overall working methods, and practically, by rethinking the nature of certain shots he had already filmed—specifically, by starting and/or stopping certain kinds of sounds at unexpected moments, sometimes creating highly unorthodox ruptures in mood and tone.

It might be argued that these ruptures were not necessarily intentional. At least I've found no acknowledgement of them or of many of Ghatak's other eccentric film-making practices in his lectures and essays, such as 'Experimental Cinema', 'Experimental Cinema and I' and 'Sound in Cinema', all collected in *Rows and Rows of Fences: Ritwik Ghatak on Cinema* (Seagull, Calcutta, 2000).

But by the same token, I find little, if any, acknowledgement by Carl Dreyer of his unorthodox editing practices in his own writings. And the issue of artistic intentionality remains a worrisome one in any case, because artists aren't invariably the best people to consult about their own practices, and it can be argued that what artists do is far more important (at least in most cases) than what they say they do. And the radical effect of Ghatak's ruptures in his soundtracks strike me as being far better illustrations of his manner of reinventing cinema than any of his theoretical statements.

To put it as succinctly as possible, they reinvent cinema precisely by reinventing us as spectators, on a moment-to-moment basis, keeping us far more alert than any conventional soundtrack would. And this makes them moments of creation in the purest sense.

Jonathan Rosenbaum was a film critic for the Chicago Reader *from 1987 to 2008. While living in Paris (1969–1974), he worked as an extra for Robert Bresson and as a script consultant for Jacques Tati, before working as assistant editor for* Monthly Film Bulletin *and staff writer for* Sight and Sound *in London (1974–1977). The author of a number of seminal books on cinema, he has also taught at State University of New York at Stony Brook, New York University, the School of Visual Arts (in New York), the University of California branches at Berkeley, San Diego and Santa Barbara, the University of Chicago, the University of St Andrews (in Scotland), the School of the Art Institute of Chicago, KinoKlub Split (in Croatia), and FilmFactory (in Sarajevo).*

A sort of homecoming: Rediscovering Ghatak

JAI ARJUN SINGH

'Bari?' slurs the middle-aged man with the ridiculous head-dress, sitting with a friend in a Calcutta nightclub during an evening of revelry. The one-word subtitle at the bottom of the screen reads: 'Home?' The man starts to get up, the head-dress is accidentally knocked off. He chortles like a child. We get a point-of-view shot. Everything is blurred.

His drunk friend having toppled to the floor a few seconds earlier, a nervous waiter has proposed that it may be time for them to go home. In response, our speaker says the word 'bari' almost indignantly—as if the very notion of having a home to go back to is outrageous. What home can there be? After all, as the director of this film has been quoted as saying: *everyone* is a refugee. Or a castaway.

The man with the funny head-dress (with a pointy crown? Devil's horns?) is the actor Abhi Bhattacharya, whom I knew from a few Hindi films—including in charismatic performances as Vishnu and his avatars in mythologicals (the 1965 *Mahabharata* and the 1974 *Har Har Mahadev*). In those roles an actor has to be assured and smug, an omniscient god imparting quips and wisdom with equal aplomb while a sudarshan chakra hums atop his finger. But the 'Iswar' played by Bhattacharya in Ritwik Ghatak's *Subarnarekha* is vulnerable and rootless, from the beginning of the film (set in 1948) to the current scene, set in 1962. Trying to maintain

Ritwik explains exactly what he wants—during the shooting of *Jukti, Tokko aar Goppo*; © Arun Khopkar

his personal integrity despite the circumstances, working hard to bring up his much younger sister and a Partition-orphaned boy. Yet, ending up in a place where dignity has no meaning, where life can only be understood as an absurdist comedy.

For me, this scene—near the end of a superb film which I experienced a good print of for the first time just a few weeks ago—brought an epiphany or two. But I'll come to that.

'Difficult, Demanding, Undisciplined'

From the beginning, I had plenty of reason to be wary of Ritwik Ghatak—or, more accurately, by the *idea* of Ritwik Ghatak.

Imagine. You're growing up in Delhi, of Punjabi stock but Anglophone upbringing. In your adolescence, you become obsessed with international cinema, starting with classic Hollywood; but even as you temporarily part ways with the masala Hindi films you were weaned on, the so-called 'regional' cinemas of India remain very distant, much less accessible than the Kurosawas and Godards and Fellinis. They are a nebulous-looking blob with one name standing above all others as indicative of 'foreign-language' Indian films—Satyajit Ray. Whom you saw when he was receiving an Oscar on his deathbed, the last of many felicitations by an international community who probably didn't know there were other Indian film-makers worth celebrating.

In your environment, though, even Ray is a remote figure. In the early 1990s, there are very few videocassettes of his films to be found, hardly any with good prints or comprehensible subtitles (only in the embassy libraries perhaps, a privilege of living in Delhi). A few years later, post college, Bengali friends (mainly the editor of this present book) tell you with a mildly patronising air that the subtitles in the prints you *did* see were inadequate. You only *thought* you had watched and enjoyed *Goopy Gyne Bagha Byne* on Doordarshan—but you hadn't. Anyway, even if the subs had been excellent, you couldn't have grasped all the nuances of the original language: the rhymes, the nonsense verses, the non-sequiturs and strange juxtapositions, the cultural allusions.

And here we were talking about a much-loved children's film by the best-known Indian film-maker globally—someone whose works are often described as being universally appreciable because of their humanism, the gentleness of their telling (and also, importantly, because the cosmopolitan Ray was influenced enough by major Western film movements, including classical Hollywood, to speak a cinematic language that other cultures could quickly grasp).

Despite my pretensions as an aspiring movie historian, I fully got to engage with this giant only in my mid-twenties, when a festival showed excellent prints of many of his films, well curated and contextualised with post-screening talks.

And if Ray could be intimidating, what hope then of grasping Ritwik Ghatak, always defined in opposition to fortune's favourite child?

Here was the other pole in all those intellectual discussions featuring Bengali colleagues and friends—the *enfant terrible* who seemed to go out of his way to be alienating and hard to slot. Though Ghatak had received posthumous recognition, his legacy had not been well preserved and he still seemed out of reach, both in terms of the availability of good prints and in terms of the films' subject matter or their maker's uncompromising lens. He was often described, even by those who preferred him to Ray, as 'undisciplined and very demanding'. These are not welcoming signs for an outsider trying to enter a new cinematic culture.

Shortly after those Ray screenings mentioned above, I watched Ghatak's most celebrated film, *Meghe Dhaka Tara*, at another small festival, in a blurry print with subtitles that flickered and (being in yellow) were barely visible against the lighter parts of the frame. The screening felt like a token gesture, and with little understanding of context, I was bored and annoyed. I couldn't grasp the family relationships, who was whom, the nature of their bonds, I couldn't yet see the very special, luminous yet troubled quality of Supriya Choudhury's face in the lead. Worst of all, the audio was very poor, and the powerful sound design—such as the haunting, plaintive use of Umasangeet—was lost. All I dimly gathered was that here was a story about a sad family being visited by one tragedy after another, and with a long-suffering woman (was she daughter or daughter-in-law?) at the centre.

On some visceral level, I *was* stirred by Nita's cry of 'I want to live!' (meaning both 'I want to stay alive' and 'I want to experience life in its fullness') into the void, the camera circling to show the treetops. But even that powerful moment (and the equally stark closing image, a fade to black from her brother's stricken face as the reverberating strains of the Uma song begin again) was divorced from larger meaning. The image and the sound stayed with me and came back at unexpected times: while reading about the Bengal Famine in a book, or when speaking to the film-maker Anup Singh—director of the gorgeous *Qissa*—and learning about his adoration for Ritwik Ghatak's cinema. But I retained no sense of the film as a whole entity.

Then came a viewing of *Ajantrik*, on that accursed Fourth World creation, the 'VCD'—not a better experience. And half a viewing of either *Komal Gandhar* or *Subarnarekha*, by which time I had mentally tuned out. Though the rational part of me knew I wasn't watching these films the way they needed to be watched, another part submitted to the cliché-illusion of Ghatak as dull or pretentious. Perhaps I had begun thinking that a film-maker this undisciplined didn't *deserve* better prints, that these films could only have very niche appeal to viewers who had a special masochistic love for the Partition theme. 'I can't think of a reason why a non-depressed person would want to watch Ghatak,' an acquaintance said once in a group, and I didn't know enough to disagree.

Other close encounters happened. At the FTII, Pune in 2017, there was an imposing drawing of Ritwik Ghatak on a wall, glowering exactly as you'd think he would. I had written a book on Ghatak's one-time friend and collaborator Hrishikesh Mukherjee, and in fact was at the FTII for a special tribute to Hrishida; and given what we know about the latter's trajectory, it was easy to imagine that this pictorial Ghatak was looking balefully at me. How *dare* someone who fancied himself a serious film buff waste a whole book on the man who made fluffy, 'compromised' Hindi films like *Gol Maal* and *Chupke Chupke.*

Of course, as it happens, Ghatak was involved in the writing of the first film Hrishida directed, the 1957 *Musafir*—an unusual work, with three discrete stories linked only by a common house. I had loved the film, but given how different it was in terms of narrative structure to Mukherjee's future, mainstream work (starting with the heavily Raj Kapoor-influenced *Anari* a year later), it only served to consolidate my dim ideas about Ghatak being a forbidding figure. About everything he touched becoming tarnished with the ponderous or 'arty'.

Ritwik, at the Right Moment

It was only a few weeks before writing this piece that I got a chance to discover how misleading these impressions were, and why Ghatak had such an intense following among those who knew him well. In a span of a few days, I watched four Ghatak films in reasonably good prints—two of which (*Ajantrik* and *Meghe Dhaka Tara*) I had watched before, as mentioned, in unsuitable conditions—and this time I was rapt. By each of them. From start to finish. Even though they represent such a range of storytelling (from a man who sometimes gets pigeonholed as being a Partition-melodrama specialist).

Sometimes, even if you began your cineaste journey as a teenager hungry to experience and engage with *everything*, you have to wait decades for the right moment to present itself.

The first thing I noted was that Ghatak could be funny and playful. Which made nonsense of another of those accumulated impressions—in this case derived from a very snarky, very quotable line from a Satyajit Ray essay. In a putdown of Ghatak's students Mani Kaul and Kumar Shahani, Ray wrote: 'It is strange that both Kaul and Shahani should acknowledge their debt to Ritwik Ghatak, who taught them at Poona, when the only Ghatak trait they seem to have imbibed is a lack of humour.'

Though such pronouncements mustn't be taken too seriously, and though Ray was complimentary of Ghatak in general, this remark chimed with what others had told me (and my own encounter with *Meghe Dhaka Tara* in that faded, cloud-capped print). While Ray had a lightness of touch, an instinctive knack for seeing the humour in a situation, Ghatak was easily labelled—from a distance—as grim and pedantic. (How could it be otherwise, if all you know of the man is that he was obsessed and tormented by a historical tragedy?)

But now, watching *Ajantrik*, I noticed the jerky, silent-comedy-like quality of Kali Banerjee's expressions as Bimal in the earliest scenes, when we don't know much about him and have only seen him as a scowling, possibly alcoholic loner. I noted how he squints intently at the currency notes he has been handed or the wide-eyed gestures as he angrily orders his passengers to get off and push the car. And there is of course the slapstick, the droll use of sound effects to make the car Jagaddal appear sentient: sighing after 'drinking water', expressing jealousy or pleasure. (Bimal himself sometimes seems mechanical in comparison.)

Or, returning to those sight gags in the final passages of *Subarnarekha*, the back of Iswar's head, with the horns atop it, bobbing along as Haraprasad (played by Bijon Bhattacharya) rants about apsaras and gods, ambrosia and whisky, and the use of brown sugar recommended by the holy scriptures. And the equally funny scene that follows, in a taxi, where Haraprasad continues misquoting old texts and lamenting that the sages of yore knew naught of war and riots, Partition and the Bomb. All this while we see drunk-eye-view images of buildings and street-lights passing in the night outside.

But equally, these comic moments are heightened by the pathos that moves alongside them or is just around the corner. Laughing at Bimal and his attachment to his expressive vehicle, we are implicated as the narrative continues and we come to understand him better. The sense of violation when children throw handfuls of mud at the car, and at him, is made more urgent because of the earlier lightness. Likewise, those sublime moments involving the drunk Haraprasad are a set-up, keeping us distracted while *Subarnarekha* heads for a shattering tragedy involving Iswar and his estranged sister Sita.

My journey of rediscovery—and a first sense of the magic this film-maker could create with images, sound and music—really began with one of his least canonical works, *Bari Theke Paliye*, about a boy named Kanchan running away from his village to Calcutta. In its own friendlier, more accessible way, this wonderful 'there and back again' narrative deals with the themes of alienation and belonging (or un-belonging) that run through the more serious political films. Though I wasn't thinking about that initially.

Until watching *Bari Theke Paliye*, I hadn't realised Ghatak could be such a gentle and empathetic observer of children. I loved the great transition from the happy song '*Amar ei Haridaser bulbul bhaja*'—sung by the 'old' chickpea-seller Haridas (Kali Banerjee again)—to the intense imagery of Haridas removing his beard and vigorously scrubbing his face, now looking sinister to the young boy, like a kidnapper who might put him in a big sack. (Or like the city's dark underbelly revealed below a benevolent Santa mask.) As it happens, Haridas *is* very much a good guy, but the sense of danger and mystery in that transformation remains.

Then there is the simple but effective use of bubbles to show Kanchan's dreams and fantasies, including the lovely sequence where he imagines sending luxurious goods home to his mother, delivered by a little boy with a beard. Or the song about the Howrah Bridge being constructed with thousands of beams and struts. (Imagine how it would be if millions of *people* could be united and solidified like this, sings the bard.)

Amidst all this come a couple of clearly 'serious' scenes. I was startled by the moment where Kanchan meets his new friend Mini's mother, and the melancholy, sickly woman opens up to him, treating him not as a child she has just met, but as someone who can understand her pain: the pain of a girl lost, afraid she will fade away one day in the city, forgotten and insignificant, far from the village she grew up in. This is followed by a complex scene where the family listens to a song about a mother on the radio.

'Mother' and 'nation' are often synonyms in Ghatak's work, I would soon learn. Kanchan's pang of longing for *his* mother has been echoed in a scene where Haridas mentions how he 'ran away' from home too, after India was partitioned, leaving behind his job as a teacher. This is light talk, but it creates a link between Kanchan's innocent adventure and the dislocation of Partition refugees sundered from their native places. In both cases there are new opportunities, but there is also an irresolvable sense of loss. Kanchan, at least, will get to go back home.

The Meaning of Home

Returning, for a minute, to that grotesquely funny-sad scene in the Calcutta pub in *Subarnarekha*: when the intoxicated Iswar said 'Bari?!' and the subtitle 'Home' appeared, I had an a-ha moment. 'Bari' meant home. So the title of *Bari Theke Paliye* probably translated to 'runaway from home' or something such. The official title is 'The Runaway'. Having picked up smatterings of Bangla by listening to friends, having heard the common word 'bari' often enough, I could probably have told you what it meant if specifically invited to think about it. But when I saw it as part of *Bari Theke Paliye*, it had rung no bells. Now I got it.

'Running Away from Home' would have been a clunkier title, but the idea of 'bari' is absolutely central to Ghatak's oeuvre. Much as there is to savour in the films I have watched (and more will reveal itself as I re-watch them), the theme that resounds the most for me is the idea of home. What does it mean? What can it encompass? Can it be two or three conflicting things at once?

Can home be a beloved car? (Bimal's Jagaddal, we learn, has been with him for fifteen years, since his mother died—a key piece of information, casually dropped in.) Can home be a nightclub where confidences and banter are exchanged with an equally lonesome comrade? Or a mythical El Dorado, like the one that Kanchan imagines? Or the one hinted at in other films, with the running theme of a better place just out of reach, beyond the horizon: such as the vision of blue hills with the birds and butterflies in *Subarnarekha* (when reality is a barren landscape jumbled with rocks). The adult Sita (played by Madhabi Mukherjee) remembers this deceptive fantasy so well from her childhood that she tells her little son the same story, clarifying only that she didn't go there but saw the way from a distance.

And what does home mean for a fearful child? An early, horror-movie-like scene in *Bari Theke Paliye* has Kanchan's father suddenly appearing and grabbing his ear. One senses a kinship here with children who are not yet citizens of any world apart from the one that adult hegemony keeps them in. By the end, the film might appear to offer this 'lesson': that home is your own house, the place where one returns to and feels secure; and that a stern parent might really be someone who cares for you. And yet, the fear on Kanchan's face, the tears in his eyes in the first scenes are very real too, and you realise that, at the very least, he needed to make the journey.

Nita, the protagonist of *Meghe Dhaka Tara*, wants to get away too; her family's house is a prison and a source of suffocation. 'This is a forlorn house—how does it matter whether one sleeps in the inner room or the outer room?' she asks at one point. The warmer 'home' she might aspire to is away from the family, in the hills she yearns to see.

For some outliers, being caught in no man's land—like the protagonist of Manto's *Toba Tek Singh*, lying below the barbed-wire fence—can be a homecoming too. 'You want to be suspended in space too?' Haraprasad asks Iswar, shortly after a reference to Yuri Gagarin being the first man in space. Again, this is part of a funny exchange, except that they are both in limbo, like the Trishanku of Hindu mythology.

In Ghatak's world, home can also be a space between past and present, where these seemingly irreconcilable worlds meet or converse. As in the sudden, scary appearance of a pagan god (a behrupiya dressed as Kali) in *Subarnarekha* while little Sita plays in a modern space, an abandoned airstrip (an earlier scene having shown us the remnants of a giant plane, a mechanical beast with its maw exposed to the elements). Or the car in *Ajantrik* representing modern technology but also reflecting the most primal human emotions (and becoming family for a man with a possibly tragic refugee past).

In *Bari Theke Paliye*, the wide-eyed Kanchan, newly arrived in the city, is counting floors on a skyscraper when he is almost hit by a car and saved by the wild-looking, bearded Haridas who seems like a fakir from another time. There are many such meeting points between the new and the primitive. No wonder Arun Khopkar wrote of Ghatak, 'The remarkable thing about a true romantic is that they can leap from their own time to another in a trice. [He] was *at home* in all cultural spaces, in all milieus. As though with a time machine, he could traverse eras in minutes.' [Italics mine.]

Room for the Refugee

But to watch Ghatak films can also be to see a refugee from world cinema—someone who didn't 'belong' (like Ray did) in the world of international film forums or festivals—creating a new cinematic space and idiom, a special home, for himself.

Watch the unusual framing of that *Subarnarekha* scene where Sita is playing, humming to herself. It should be the centre of our (and the camera's) attention, but at one point she moves towards the left and completely out of frame, while the camera tracks rightward towards emptiness; this is followed by the next disorienting shot (preparing us for Sita's own fright when she runs into 'Kali'). Here we see part of the airstrip ground without knowing exactly where she is or where she will re-enter the frame.

Or the song between brother and sister, Shankar and Nita, in a dark room in *Meghe Dhaka Tara*, done as a complex single take that begins with Shankar at the extreme left of the frame as he sings into the darkness; then pans left to reveal Nita sitting next to him, as she picks up the song; then moves back to encompass them both in a long shot, and then forward again to become intimate with them again.

Or the image of the just-married woman passenger laughing during Bimal's altercation with someone on the road—he sees her in the rear-view mirror, a shaky reflection of her shaking with laughter. The fragility of that shot is typical of Ghatak's avoidance of 'clean' or 'organised' framing in favour of what felt right to him emotionally and viscerally. Such decisions can lead to a director's technique being called 'raw' (as opposed to 'polished'), but when done with this sense of purpose—as part of a mise en scène involving visuals and sound in constant interplay—they feel like an exciting new approach to a medium.

Rootless, always searching, untethered, sidestepping conventional filmic grammar, not belonging to an identifiable school (even given his regard for Eisenstein and others)—these are vital aspects of Ghatak's craft. Especially when set against the more respectable Ray, who was seemingly at home in everything he did, and at home in the wider world too: an urbane, well-travelled film-maker who could mingle easily with the Renoirs and the Brandos.

Of course, Ghatak not being a 'global' citizen doesn't mean that his fans have to follow the same path. Inevitably, I brought my own pop-cultural references to what I watched of his films. The beautiful scene near the end of *Bari Theke Paliye*, where Haridas likens himself to a lake and young runaways to the swans being nurtured by it ('Runaways like you will come, I'll look after them') reminded me oddly of Holden Caulfield's fantasy of being a 'catcher in the rye' in Salinger's novel. When the woman travelling in Jagaddal jokes about the hole in the car's roof, but also observes that the sky looks so beautiful through that hole, I thought of the Leonard Cohen lyric 'There is a crack in everything / that's how the light gets in'.

And even when it comes to the 'home' (or 'lost home') motif so endemic to Ghatak, I think of John Ford's *The Searchers* (1956) with its famous images of John Wayne framed in solid or shattered doorways, neither inside nor quite outside. Or the mythical 'Green Place' that Furiosa remembers from her childhood in *Fury Road* (2015).

Whimsical, random connections? Of course. Irrelevant to what Ghatak himself was trying to do? Probably. But that's how we often make sense of the art we consume, relate it to other things we have processed at much earlier stages in our development, delight in serendipitous links between cultures and tropes. Or ruefully discover treasures that might have enriched our lives much earlier. After that first viewing of *Meghe Dhaka Tara* two decades ago, I put it in my shortlist of supposedly 'great' films that had left me completely underwhelmed (along with Fellini's *La Dolce Vita* (1960), Andrei Tarkovsky's *Ivan's Childhood* (1962), Theo Angelopoulos's *Ulysses' Gaze* (1995), and a few others). Today I would have little hesitation in placing it on a top twenty favourites list.

Even now, in 2025, it is hard to find good, sharp prints of Ghatak's films that are *also well subtitled*: in my experience, it has usually been one or the other. For those of us on the outside of Bengali culture and language (and did anyone relate to outsiders better than Ritwik Ghatak?), a few strange possibilities present themselves. You might watch a film first on an average print with the subtitles, and then immediately see it again in the better, un-subtitled print while each scene is fresh in your mind. Or, as Shamya suggested to me, watch both prints simultaneously on separate devices (which will demand rapid eyeball movement from the words on one screen to the images on the adjacent one). Or otherwise sit with a Bengali friend willing to play benshi, a vocal accompaniment to the images.

It's both amusing and sad—but also apt—that the work of a form-transgressor like Ghatak may have to be experienced this way, even at a time when he has been widely feted and brought into the fold. But as I have learnt, the most 'difficult' thing about this director is getting to watch his work in the best possible conditions. Once you have the apparatus to do this, the films themselves invite you in and are warmer, more accessible than you might have imagined. This may not be the warmth and humanism of a Ray or a Renoir … or an Ozu (though Ghatak might have empathised with Setsuko Hara—heart-stopping smile on her face—looking into the camera and assuring us that yes, yes, of course life is disappointing). But it is often something more: a man who may have been driven to despairing nihilism in real life, finding beauty and grace even while telling tragic stories about outcasts and loners and people exploited by their own families. And doing this with care and creativity, using every available tool of a medium that he claimed not to care much about. *Of course* the Ghatak on the FTII wall was frowning—but the films are alive and vibrant, and they smile.

Jai Arjun Singh is an independent writer. His books include Jaane Bhi Do Yaaro: Seriously Funny Since 1983 *and* The World of Hrishikesh Mukherjee. *Most of his columns, reviews and essays are on his blog Jabberwock (http://jaiarjun.blogspot.com/). He is currently working on a book of personal writings about the intersection of cinema and life.*

Ritwik's trees

SUMANA ROY

I always put it down to coincidence, the easiest way to explain things. Ritwik Ghatak and I were born on the same day, though half a century apart, and plant life would come to frame the way we both experience the world. I am fifty years old now, exactly the age Ritwik died at. Writing this essay with that awareness—strange as it is confusing—takes my thoughts in directions they might not have otherwise.

There's a tree in *Sahaj Path*, the first tree I ever saw. That can't be true, of course, because I would have been about three then, in my first year at school. It is in the generic nature of trees to not be remembered, but this is slightly different. It's not a blob of green that I remember as a tree; it's black, black as soot, like burnt tree trunks. The tree, though, is not burnt—it is alive, a human sits inside it, as dark as the tree and its foliage, as dark as its shade. Sounds a bit childish, I know, but no other living form had enchanted me like this. I say 'living' with caution and affection, for I would discover a living likeness of the soot-black tree soon. On a bus from Siliguri's Court More to Bagdogra, where my father's sister lived—a journey we made no more than twice a year, in spite of the short distance, for the lack of availability of transport and time—I would see it. The bus was moving slowly, its speed curtailed by the rush of workers emerging from the Chandmoni Tea Estate. There it was, outside the window to our left—it hadn't moved since the last time I'd seen it. A tree exactly like Nandalal Bose's.

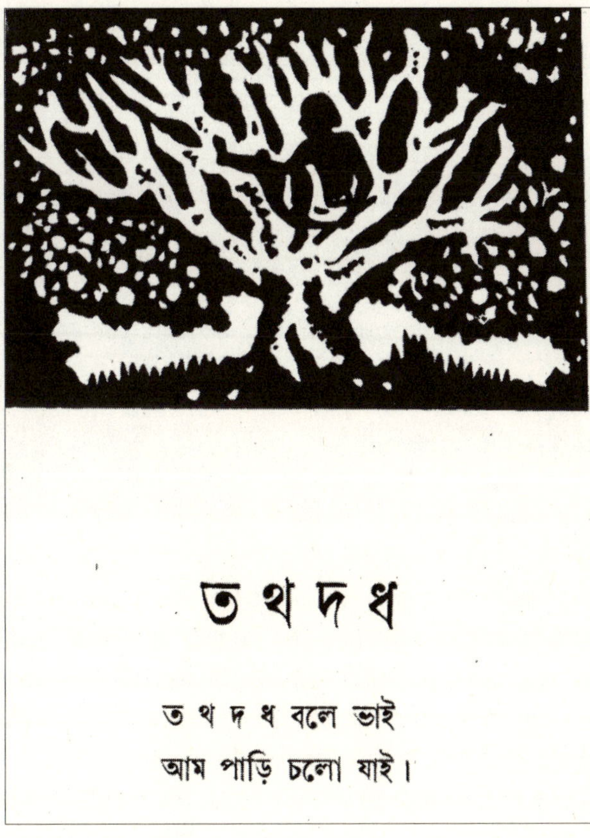

Ritwik would have seen that tree in *Sahaj Path*. It is with such a tree that *Meghe Dhaka Tara* begins, its branches spread wide, without shyness or self-consciousness, as if to expose its leaves to all the light it could get. It is to the right of the screen, Nita walks out of its shadow. I could also rephrase this: the tree releases Nita into the world after protecting it from the glare of the world, perhaps of life. It is tempting to see the tree as analogous to the protective womb, after which the human is left on its own. For the first forty seconds of the film, the camera looks at things that don't move—the trees. The camera shows no interest in looking for a human, such is its initial indifference to the centrality of the human figure in art. A woman in white emerges out of the shade and shadow of the trees, a black-and-white contrast emphasised in a black-and-white film; so similar to Nandalal's linocut.

The canvas begins to move. A train passes by. A man is singing, *aa aa aa aa*. His back is to the audience. The camera isn't interested in his face. It takes in the vegetation by the river bank. Sharp, tall grass pierces the top half of the frame, they poke the sky. From looking for punctures in the sky, we are dragged downwards to the earth, to a torn slipper on a human foot. The camera has become plant-like—it is moving like trees do, in the north–south axis; like plants, it has become indifferent to the human face.

After the restoration of attention to human affairs, to the crises of poverty, particularly new poverty (surely there must be a term equivalent to nouveau riche for those suddenly rendered poor by catastrophic circumstances), the camera seems to long for a sighting of the plant world again. Only four minutes have passed. It's enough to give us a sense of the family whose life we will be following; it's also enough to tell us that human lives will be complemented and annotated by the histories of their changing neighbours, plant life. 'Nabin Sangha' enters the frame. Humans, tall and small, chew the foreground, but it's only as much real estate as the mouth occupies on the face. Behind them is the sky, made jagged by the uneven height of trees. It is not just an assemblage of different species of trees that we see, but a more urgent history of settlement, of planting. Pollinators, mostly two-footed ones like those in the foreground, are responsible for their settlement on this land. Ritwik is giving us a history of dislocation, of people as much as of plants. The name of the neighbourhood club, common in Bengal and other spaces that came to accommodate Bengalis evicted by the forces of history, is telling—the plants are as 'nabin', new, as the humans here; they might soon be propagated to other places, near and far.

In Ritwik's films we see a new kind of horticultural unit, one that emerged so naturally that it hasn't been recorded in our architectural or ecological history. Neither garden nor forest, it is as domesticated as it is wild. In Rabindranath Tagore, for instance, we find both an admiration for the beauty of the garden and an instinctive rejection of it as a unit foreign to landscapes and geographical formations such as ours. In practice, both he and his son Rathindranath—who would adopt favourite characteristics of Japanese, Italian, French and Mughal gardens into Santiniketan's Uttarayan, the cluster of four houses that Rabindranath would design and live in—were internationalists, welcoming of travelling flora from other continents. As a concept, though, Rabindranath seemed to be suspicious of the garden, the way the unit had come to be imported from outside the Indian subcontinent, particularly Europe. The controlling impulse necessary to design and execute gardens would have challenged his ethics and aesthetics. They would have been too neat, too premeditated. 'Bon' over 'bagan' for him, the forest over the garden, though he would have been thinking of the jungle more than the forest, a space then still outside human intentionality.

Satyajit Ray, in his foreword to Ritwik's book *Cinema and I*, writes about the latter's lifelong preoccupation with the Partition, how it shaped his films, gave them their subject and energy. What hasn't been noticed is how the post-Partition Bengali family is seen through the concomitant new ordering of plant life. Land had been divided, how could the creatures of land, humans and plants, live in older units anymore? 'Unit', after all, is the root word for 'unity', and, with that gone, how were we to find plants except in fragmented and foraged units? This is what Ritwik—like John Clare, who was disoriented by the Enclosure Act of 1809, the privatisation and fencing of shared land—records in these scenes: broken sentences, broken song, broken land, its broken vegetation. Orchards, forests, gardens, fields, they are units of unbrokenness, a way of looking at the world where looking becomes equivalent to owning. The ambition of the zamindar was to own as far as his eyes could see. The philosophical idea of the plantation must owe to this, the idea of unbroken rows of the same plant as well as the ownership that comes from this manner of control and ordering. The people in Ritwik's films do not have the luxury of such a 'vision'; time limits their lives as much as space does. They live from day to day, and, in *Meghe Dhaka Tara*, from month to month, salary day to salary day. In this, they are like trees, they who live outside capitalism, outside mortgage and pension and EMIs.

In these films is the 'bagan', garden. But the architecture of Ritwik's gardens is arbitrary, its scope and ambition limited by space and poverty. What can the gardens of a homeless people look like? Indifferent to expectations of geometry and species that had given form and beauty to gardens in Japan and Italy, for instance, these borrowed spaces became an archive of their ad hoc living. Grammatical gardens are a record of ambition and purpose, the gardens in Ritwik's films are a record of foraging and found plants, found and functional art. The trees are not here to add beauty, just as human faces and bodies do not exist to draw attention to the beauty of their anatomical form. They are just there—like the sky is, or like shadows are, because they are. Our eyes meet them like they do relatives of our own species, without formality or introductions. Yes, they are relatives, for they live alongside humans in residential spaces, by the well and by a stream, bringing shade to a tin-roofed house, fruit to a half-starved family, outliving the human who brought them here.

My heart bustles in recognition when I see them, for I grew up in such a neighbourhood myself. In Siliguri's Ashrampara, my neighbours, families whose memories and eating and living habits were formed by the agricultural produce and rivers of Bangladesh before they, like seeds, were flung into spaces unfamiliar to their ancestors, created such gardens. Chilli plants by a streetside water drain, pumpkin and bottle gourd vines climbing on to tin roofs of kachcha toilets, unseasonal marigold flowers from a leftover garland used to worship a goddess, fresh coriander from seeds scattered near the well, where they grew beside ghritakumari, and there, often, a banana plant offering fruit, flower or stem, and always, always, an assembly of kochu leaves, waiting to be devoured. Roses became fences, valued more for their thorns than their flowers, to keep strangers away more than to attract; the tulsi that would, every Saturday, bring together a congregation hungry for the airy sweetness of batasha, thrown up into the air, Hari-r loot, then gathered from the earth and put urgently inside mouths; shandhya malati and nayantara, that flowered better when neglected; and greens, so many kinds of shak that it seemed the Bengali had evolved from the cow. Every morning, flower thieves, with a lanky bamboo pole in their hands, collecting flowers for their gods, never missing an opportunity to break a branch from a tree to plant in their garden—finding and foraging, planting and pollinating.

From the 'sangha' to 'sansar', the club to the room, Ritwik makes this migration through song: '*Ghorete bhromor elo gunguniye*'. The bee's come singing into the room. Where there is bee, there must be flower? What we have instead of the glamour of flowers—and I'm struggling to remember whether the camera ever pays attention to flowers at all—is bamboo. The strips of bamboo and the stripes of the saree that the women wear mirror each other all through his films until he's established, almost naturally, that the refugees of his world are like bamboo: this is their habitat, they will stick to each other to form clusters, they will be chopped off from time to time, used, repurposed, taken away from their family, but the roots will allow growth again, life and height, length and the seeking of light, until they are dismembered again. The stripes in the women's sarees run parallel to each other, like the strips of bamboo in the walls of the room do—the ends of both, saree and fence, have to be cut abruptly. Sometimes they continue on to men's bodies, to the stripes of their lungi.

Perhaps no other film-maker has documented the culture of everyday bamboo design in eastern India with such an artist's homely attention as Ritwik. These moments of distraction from the thoroughfare of human traffic are almost akin to a tendril looking for support, for something to hold. The varying rhombuses of bamboo fences give the eye this hold, this pause. The ninth minute of *Meghe Dhaka Tara* is long, the eye spans and embalms, it takes in details of the weave of the bamboo before it moves to something that Ritwik's camera turns into its relative: hair, hair on the heads of women, Nita's in a bun, Gita's left open, the craft and compulsion of human hands on bamboo visible, as it is in the bun; the freedom of the bamboo groves, alive and loose, as in Gita's open hair. Nita's name bears the etymological impress of ethics and morality, a human-brokered life; Gita's name derives from song, it is freer, as much as music is free, or freer than morality. Ritwik's eyes look for echoes, they find it—echoes of bamboos in the sarees, particularly those that Gita wears, where the shadow-and-light serve-and-volley dims and glows.

About a quarter of an hour has passed. Ritwik returns the trees of the first scene to us, we now see more of them, more of their bodies; we see more of the river, too, which pushes the trees out of the frame slightly, gently. What takes up space are the shadows of these large-bodied trees, their girth a visible birth certificate, a mark of fixity, perhaps even of constancy, who can tell, in contrast to the river whose water moves, like the people

in the film. The brother—played by Anil Chatterjee, in one of the most unforgettable characters in cinematic history—sings, his accompanists are birds, they cry, though I don't know why the English language calls their tongue 'bird cries'. Like a musician uses caesura, Ritwik uses music: for a break between stanzas. In the film's first scene, Nita emerges from the trees, not exactly like Venus from the sea in Botticelli, but the shared lineage of human and the elements, plant and person, is established right away. A little more than a quarter of an hour later, she walks from the right to the left of the screen. Her brother sits under a tree, rehearsing.

Ritwik ensures that we see him as part of the tree trunk, the bodies of humans assimilated by the camera's angle as once was possible in mythology; Nita, too, is part of this gift of the gaze: she, her brother's lone audience, melds with the aerial branches of the tree.

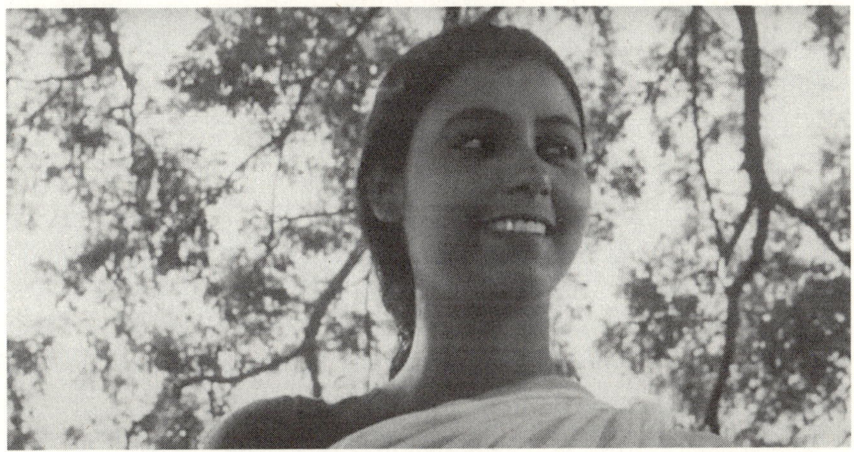

She, provider, sister, daughter, girlfriend, has to become more than one species. This is why Nita moves out of her Krishnachura- and Radhachura-like body to become bamboo soon after, the transition happening as soon as she gives some money to her brother.

It's Nita's birthday. A Jagaddhatri Pujo will take place. Ritwik has decided to abandon subtlety. Jagaddhatri, as her name indicates, is a goddess of the earth; according to the Kena Upanishad, she asks the elements, Agni and Varuna and Vayu, to move a blade of grass. Ritwik takes Nita, her father and brother to something like grass. Coconut and betelnut trees, tall, and taller than the hills in the background. They walk on the unlaid road, through marshland and paddy fields, the stalks ankle-deep in water. Other species crop up on the screen: boatman, shaluk, lotus. 'Poetry of the earth is never dead,' one of the characters says. Jagaddhatri; the plants. Ritwik doesn't leave it there—like Bibhutibhushan in *Pather Panchali*, he emphasises the beauty that can be had by those without money, like Apu's sister Durga in the novel, like Nita's singer-brother in this film. 'Dhanyo khetra', the blessed land, the land of such agricultural bounty is a phrase central to Ritwik's vision. For the Bengali audience, there would also be the cultural conditioning of '*Dhono dhanye pushpe bhora*' of D.L. Roy's song, the celebration, in spite of Partition, of the plentiful plant life that made Jibanananda's 'Rupashi Bangla'.

Children run out of a small school a few scenes later. As if to frame this freedom, Ghatak allows a branch to graze the frame from the left. To him, the plant world is a metaphor that emphasises, by contrast, the unfreedom of social life. 'How do you all stay indoors in the evening? I find it difficult to breathe,' says Gita, to which Sanat, still undecided between the two women, 'music' and 'morality', offers to take Nita out for a walk. Their house is framed by trees, their father by an umbrella, the heads of both mirroring each other, as it is possible only in a drawing book. Sanat complains about Nita being chained down by responsibilities, to which she offers a stronger metaphor for the loss of freedom: 'Besh toh, make a glass frame and put me inside it, like a wax doll.' And, almost immediately, two opposites are offered: marshland and meadow, there is

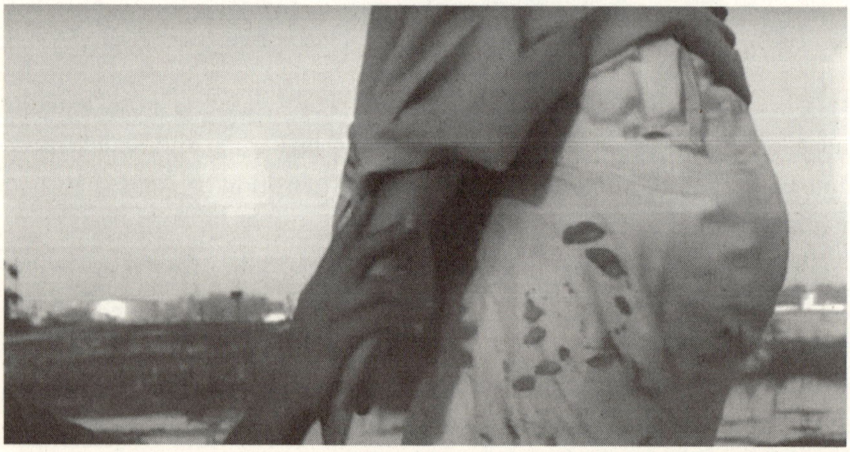

freedom in both, even if there is stickiness. For when Nita stands up to go, leaves stick to her saree. Over and over again, Ritwik turns her into a tree, a giving tree.

A job has been found, she requests her brother to drop her off at Sealdah. The landscape changes; it's thornier, wilder. The tree is different—it is no longer on the right side of the screen but the left; it has more branches than leaves, it is less spread out, some of its branches even amputated. Soon the camera is on the brother. He's singing, entering the world of plants, whose bodies are flecked by light and shade; wild grass waits nearby in every frame.

Nita, though, was doing the opposite, emerging from the trees. The camera refuses to move; it has become the tree. Nita passes by, he asks her for twenty-five paise, to shave, and the camera begins moving. The brother runs after her, his shadow slightly thinner than the older, time-fed trees. The branches offer shade, they also stand rooted while humans are rendered homeless. The camera, momentarily happy to be a tree, now begins running—it, too, is scared of becoming homeless.

Catching up with her, he realises that it is not his sister, only someone in the same generic white saree with a slim border. The unknown woman smiles. Her eyes are downcast, instead of the goddess' halo, her bust-sized image: the white saree with the border running like a train line whose other track has been eaten by time or water; the echo of that thin horizontal line in the vertical strap of her handbag, a marker of her working woman status, a new self in a new land. Not halo but branches of trees crowd the frame. She is of the trees, even if she has a face, even if she is human.

The woman smiles. The brother laughs. He begins singing.

Another tree appears. Now it's to the right of the screen. He is standing under it and singing. The camera moves with him as he walks. His shadow moves. The shadows of the branches remain still. He moves from right to left, a bit like the Urdu script at first, and then like musical notation, the arohan and abarohan, travelling to and fro, to and fro, the return to the 'sama', the home. But where is home? Do shadows return to the trees at night?

Ritwik changes the composition of the halo that announces a goddess' status. The branches of trees a little while ago, now it's smoke from the mother's cooking that frames her face, so that the halo is diffused, a blur, in spite of the branches of the trees right behind, as distant as cloud. Another woman enters—her hair is open, her saree is striped, the bamboo seems to be emerging out of her body, she goes out for a walk by the lake. It is Gita, with Sanat.

Nita is walking back home. Irregular dots of darkness fill the screen—blobs of tree heads, their fraternal twins lying as shadows on the ground, more restful. Nita's face is dark, light falls on a portion of her hips. Books clutched to her chest, she walks; her sister and boyfriend are sitting by the water, singing. Nita looks, then looks away, walks past the scene. The camera moves to the sister and her new audience. Her shoulder-length hair has been left open. For a moment they look like branches of the tree behind her—both move. The camera moves too. Gita is laughing after her flirtatious sermon to Sanat about staring at her with his mouth open. Nandalal's tree, from *Sahaj Path*, is behind her. Its many branches make her look like a many-armed Durga; the man is made to look like Mahishasur. She jumps, he follows.

We are inside stripes again: bamboo walls, fences, light and darkness. The composition is of an afterlife of the plant world—wooden windows with sticks inside them that keep animals away and divide the sky and the view. The sister in the striped saree enters through the gate; all is bamboo and wood, even the sister. Ritwik takes care to emphasise their form and texture, a continuation of their life, a life made possible by a new host and

a new environment, like the refugees of Partition have had to adapt to. Bamboo and smoke, different as they are in behaviour, move in various patterns and orientations, making the walls of the house look like a happy museum of the afterlife of trees themselves. From inside the house, various kinds of plant life emerge, among them, paisleys trapped inside diamond-shaped cages on Gita's blouse.

Things change, Sanat and Gita are married, living in a flat in the city: the bamboo patterns, Nita's saree, now in a dark colour. Instead of a house scavenged and salvaged from bodies of plants, we see a skylight in iron frames. The soft stripes of bamboo and clotheslines and sarees have given way to the stern lines of glass and steel, staircases and doorframes, ventilators and windows. Nita's bag is now a pattern of checks. The door curtain, in all likelihood a Manipuri weave not uncommon at that time, has diamond-shaped rhombuses.

As soon as the door opens, the camera moves to the solid lines of the threshold. These lines are bureaucratic, they keep apartments sturdy, they want to serve ambitions of permanence; how different they are from bamboo, in whose DNA it is to be ad hoc. Smoke cruises up here, too, but it's not the smoke of Nita's mother's kitchen; not clay oven but ashtray. Ritwik is showing us the props of culture: a Bankura clay elephant stands beside truncated shadows of window bars, tuberoses in a vase on the table, puppets on the wooden cupboard, nature is being diminished here, everywhere.

But the camera is restless for the lines in Nita's home, its stripes: clothes, clotheslines, serrated tin roofs, bamboo nailed together, diagonally falling shadows. These are informal lines and rhombuses that derive from the grace of the natural world. It is the freedom of this informality that allows shadows to enter frames before human figures, shadows picking clothes from ropes and wires, slightly ghost-like, more like trees. Ritwik relies on the light-and-shadow opera to highlight the human drama through the eaters of light, the trees.

After the light and night of '*Je raate mor duwarguli bhanglo jhore*', of '*shob je hoye gyalo kalo*', of everything turned dark, the camera moves like a plant, like the eye, searching for light. And then it moves like writing in the Devanagari script: trees and houses, conical tops, roofs, tin, concrete, all of these in a rush, so that it seems like the camera wants to escape from homes and the homeless for now, till it rests and waits, on foliage, on plants, to the ad hoc gardens that connect inside our eyes to indulge the sense of what is now called 'social forestry'.

The father, leaning against a tree for support, speaks to a doctor about Nita. One displacement happens after another—Nita, first rendered homeless by history, now moves out of the house to a bamboo room nearby, her equivalent of a temporary tent, her 'nirbandhobpuri', a town without friends; then she has to leave home for Reid Chest Hospital, another instalment of displacement. Ritwik begins making her more tree-like with greater urgency, as if that could protect her. After the audience's discovery of her tuberculosis, we meet the trees—they take over the screen, Nita's head now a blob emerging from the lower bottom of the screen. She's being displaced from the screen too, history repeating itself over and over again. In a darker saree now, she's the colour of tree trunks and branches, until she merges with the tree trunk in a scene.

Ritwik is cutting out something else simultaneously—shade and shadow. By the ninetieth minute, the shade of trees is gone. There's just bare land, the shadows of the trees far away are like birds whose shadows don't reach the earth. A train cuts the screen. She, like the trees, doesn't move. A couple of minutes later, she opens her umbrella standing under a tree, a double umbrella as it were. Every now and then, Ritwik's camera surveys the land: palms of various kinds, a leafless plumeria, after the news of Gita's pregnancy. In the foreboding of both birth and death,

Ritwik turns to plants. After the camera shows us Nita's blood-stained handkerchief, we see trees moving wildly in a storm, and her curly hair, as if they were relatives.

The vegetation around Reid Chest Hospital is different—a coniferous-looking tree stands to the left of the frame, it offers no shade, only the

fur of fog and the skin of the sky. Nita is sitting, her brother comes with news about Gita's son, their two-storeyed house, until she breaks into one of the most famous dialogues in Bangla cinema: '*Dada, aami kintu bachte cheyechhilam*', Dada, I did want to live …

The camera loses balance as it were and surveys the trees. That's how the film ends—with tree and tree and tree, almost like how it began, except for the woman who has gone missing from life, from the screen.

Fifteen seconds into *Subarnarekha*, no image has been given to us, nothing except the auditory, 'Vande Mataram'. The first visual: trees, slim, unrevealing of age, a bamboo in the middle, another an arc; the

cohabitation of various sizes, even shapes. The Indian flag goes up on the bamboo pole; another bamboo, bent, serves as trellis over a gate.

In bamboo as flag pole, Ritwik is hoping for the new Indian nation to have the tensile strength of bamboo, to be flexible, supportive and all-purpose, for all its citizens to make whatever they can of it. For the moment, though, there's chaos and uncertainty, differences more than unity—a teacher in a new school teaches English and history, another Bengali and Sanskrit, history and historiography available only to those living in English; Dhaka versus Pabna; caste divisions. A child's mother is lost. The word 'udbastu', refugee, floats around. Gandhi's assassination emerges as newsprint in a newspaper office.

Nabajibon Colony, the new settlement for those without homes, is constructed almost entirely of bamboo, as if the new ('naba') life ('jibon') must have the plant's resilience. Ritwik draws the opposition between the old and new through metaphor. Both the sarod and the ektara are musical instruments that derive from plant life, but he gives us classical music before a Baul's song. Hence bamboo—for the people, like the people; the roofs, doors, windows and walls of the houses in Nabajibon Colony, the Baul's musical instrument. In the first ten minutes of the film named after a river, we see bamboo being split and cut everywhere. Partition, people, plants. A bamboo republic.

Ghatshila's plants enter the census of our imagination: bamboo, banana, papaya, species that grow easily, often on their own, without care, like these people must. When the little girl Sita asks her brother whether Abhiram, the boy who has lost his mother, will come with them to the new place, we are given no answer, only a sign, almost Buddha-like—she plucks a flower and leaves. The mill, where her brother has found work, is beside a sal forest. After reaching Ghatshila, the first thing Sita says is, 'Dadamoni, come and see how beautiful the garden is …'. The little boy Abhi is still crying. An oleander—poisonous oleander—stands behind him. Rabindranath's song sprouts: '*Aaj dhaner khete roudrochhayay lukochuri khyala re bhai, lukochuri khyala*'. Sunlight and shade are playing hide-and-seek on the paddy fields … What grass was to Jibanananda Das, paddy is to Ritwik. It's to the paddy fields that his homeless want to return. Paddy and bamboo, related sub-families.

We see a barren landscape from time to time, stony, bare-branched trees, but in their forms is still the intimation of being alive—unlike the ruins of the aircraft from World War II, with its exposed steel rods, weeds around it, the camera making it look like a foreigner, a UFO, the runway unfriendly, trees pushed to its corners, like eyelashes in the eyes. Sita and Abhi run through a place with different kinds of plant life: the bare and low, spiky and tender leaves. Some of these are inside the ruins of the airfield's buildings; no roof or inhabitants, no windows, no doors, only frames, like the leafless trees.

Ritwik is intentional. The little girl is called Sita for a reason, the story of her name from the Ramayana is abridged for us in a dialogue—how the Sita of the epic was found in an agricultural field, her link with ploughing cultures, and, though we are not told this yet, how Sita returns to the earth after her test by fire, a premonition of what is to happen to the Sita of this film. 'Sita is the daughter of the earth …' We are shown that earth: of rocks, river, bark, stone and trees with tiny heads, and tiny human heads half-hidden among large rocks. Outside their house are lonely species: a few palms, shrubs, skinny young trees, standing without discipline or order. They are at home.

Abhi returns from the city, educated and eager to finish writing his novel based in Ghatshila, for which he has found a 'big publisher'. Both he and Sita are surprised to find each other grown up, their bodies longer,

their hearts in longing, they walk through the sal forest. The trees are tall, very tall—the camera, so long habituated to a sparser population of trees, goes a bit mad, it begins moving from left to right, taking in the trees one by one, until it is overwhelmed. This is Ritwik's interpretation

of Wordsworth's 'Ten thousand saw I at a glance'—the uncountability of this unit of plant life, its impress, its freedom and rush, its nurturing and caging.

The sense of time—and space—in the forest, where one can't tell when the first tree was planted, that this is a history very different from those that have been written about human lives, allows Abhi to begin talking about his novel. It might have been classified as autofiction today. He begins narrating the story of his life, third person to himself. Walking towards the trees, he raises his arms—they becomes branches, and he a tree for a moment.

The camera then moves to the back of his head, so that he, like the other citizens of the forest, becomes part of this republic of faceless beings, the trees.

He asks her a question, to which she says 'no'. Light and its opposite fall on her face, and the camera integrates her into the blur of trees behind. How long has she felt like this, this 'love', Abhi asks Sita, without using the word. 'A long time,' she replies. The camera goes berserk in trying to capture this sense of Time—Ritwik does a few 360 degrees, all we see are the trees of this forest, long trunks, and then the river.

Abhi and Sita return to bamboo, to home, to the vines that are growing on bamboo trellises, to the houseplants. Occasionally, we spot oleander, a

palm or two, overgrown green in the pilot's clubhouse, or a flower vase on a table when someone says 'caste is everything'. When Abhi's mother dies and he recognises her from memory, Ritwik takes us to the child Abhi, and where is he? Swinging from a tree, like only a little boy can.

Twenty seconds later, after the graceful undulations of the roots from which the little boy was hanging, and the shade of the banyan, both unquantifiable and amorphous, we see the sternness of electric poles in a railway station. Their relationship is shown through plant metaphors: trees skirt the agricultural fields as they talk, while the tanpura, made from a gourd, is strung; when the wedding is fixed against her wishes, a dry palm leaf scratches the frame; when Abhi leaves and Sita asks whom she should share her sorrow with, the camera shows treetops far away.

The wedding day arrives. The alpana of paddy stalks, grain and leaves sit on the floor, leading our eyes to Sita, whose face is painted with stylised designs from the agricultural world. And suddenly she's gone. A woman says that she was scribbling something. The camera focuses on the alpana, its details, leaf and leaf and stalk and leaf, and the plant alpana grows and glows towards light.

Years pass, trees and peace have disappeared from their lives in the cramped city. Listening to her sing, the little son asks, 'Ma, what do the dhaaner khet, the paddy fields, look like?' The song will return at the end of the film, but, before that, there are other plants. Haraprasad, having lost everything that he valued, returns to Iswar and tells him that he's a

'baajey-pora taal gaachh', a blasted palm tree. The landscape turns barren gradually.

In the end, though, the little boy Binu, orphaned, stands with Iswar, his newly found maternal uncle, under a tree. They have just got off the train, Iswar has been asked to vacate his residential quarters. Homeless once again, the camera turns to a tree. And then to song and soil, to the wave on the paddy fields—the literal and the figurative find a home: '*Dhaaner khete dheu* ...'

The film ends as it had begun—by resting on plants.

Water in instalments, river, rain, ripple, inside boat, on plant, on tree. Water and sand, mother and child, river and bank. Trees by the river, like ripples of heads. Three minutes of this survey of life by the river Titas, and our eyes rest on an old tree at last—we meet its relatives, not on land, but their reflections on water.

Soon more, not alive but their afterlife: boats, trees now travelling on water, unimaginable during their life on land; bamboo, fence, wall, house, basket, where grain is being winnowed, thatched homes. They come alive again, rounded trees and dancing papaya plants. They return to water, to

boat, its wood, but mostly its bamboo, arcs and shelter, fish caught and put in baskets, covered with a flat woven bamboo piece. To land again, where the tree's roots are, where they provide the shade necessary for dance and home, for celebration under trees. The canopy—tree branches become Ritwik's sky; two tree branches connect two corners of the screen, like a ceiling connects walls; men fight with them too, with bamboo.

Ritwik begins to make us see, again, the optical osmosis between plant and person …

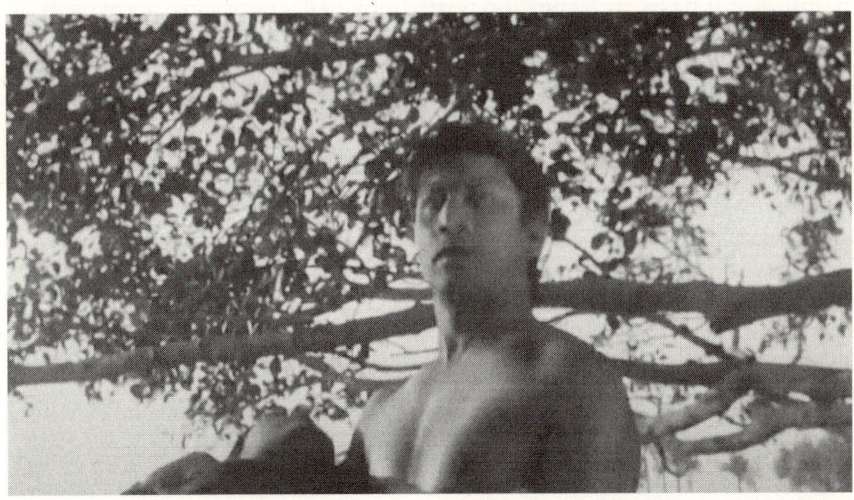

… an unconscious woman in a man's arms, horizontal, is like the tree branches in the following scene; the floral patterns on the bride's forehead, the wedding garlands, the eating and rejection of light, darkness and luminosity, how Ritwik's camera catches light falling on the flowers in

the garden and those on the wedding saree, the shola kadam flower on the topor, the groom's crown. These are echoed visually by the houses of bamboo and straw, as if they too were topor-like, and the palm tree behind the small temple. At the moment of leaving her parents', the bride weeps holding a plant—the holy basil in the tulsi mancha—and her butterfly tiara makes her plant-like.

There is no getting away from this way of seeing. Ritwik shows us the boatman's katha, its stylised botanical patterns; he warns the husband about his wife's beauty gathering attention with a proverb borrowed from—what else?—the plant world: '*Lau er opor najar lagau na kintu*', be careful that the bottle gourd doesn't catch attention. A close-up of the woman's middle-parted hair is turned into a relative of the sugarcane leaf's long midrib; shadows of leaves dance on the bodies of women so that their bodies and limbs become branches.

Ram's aged, scraggly beard is not very different from the straw hanging from the roof.

There's the stamp of the botanical everywhere: flowers on dhaak, diamond patterns of bamboo designs in kitchens, straight lines of jute sticks, bow and arrow; a galaxy of water hyacinth amidst which sit planets

of boats, boats of potatoes. Tree shadows lick the water everywhere, old trees snuggle up to their shortened noon shadows, the dheki moves up and down and up and down, avoiding the hand that feeds it grain, crushing grain. Men and women erupt in anger, the violence of the plant idiom: '*Tomarey kauwa ja, oi dhaan khete giye kauwao ta*', telling you something is like telling the paddy field …

The little boy's name is Ananta. Infinite. He runs through the paddy fields blowing a paper horn.

Nabajibon, paddy, bamboo, it is to this that Ritwik returns, this is how history is reborn.

Sumana Roy is the author of How I Became a Tree *and* Provincials: Postcards from the Peripheries, *works of non-fiction,* Plant Thinkers of Twentieth-Century Bengal, *a book of literary criticism,* Missing: A Novel, My Mother's Lover and Other Stories, *and two poetry collections,* Out of Syllabus *and* V. I. P: Very Important Plant.

A new look at Ritwik Ghatak's Bengal

RATIK ASOKAN

In February 1972, three months after the close of East Pakistan's bloody war of secession, the Indian film-maker Ritwik Ghatak travelled to Dhaka, capital of the new nation of Bangladesh, as a state guest. It was a kind of homecoming. Born in 1925 in the eastern part of Bengal province, then an undivided state in British-ruled India, Ghatak grew up in the region before he relocated west to Calcutta in the early 1940s. Since 1947, when the province was split in two during the Partition, its western half going to India and eastern half to Pakistan, he had not returned east.

As his flight crossed over the river Padma, which runs down Bangladesh, and on whose banks Ghatak had played as a child, the director was so moved that he burst into tears. 'I felt that Bengal in plenty and beauty as I knew her years back was still there untransformed,' he recalled some years later. Inspired, he returned to Bangladesh the same year to shoot a film, his first in a decade, *A River Called Titas*. But up close, he saw that the world of his childhood had all but disappeared. 'Everything has changed out of recognition—people's thought, mind and soul,' he admitted. 'They have lost culture.'

The partition of Bengal looms large over the cinema of Ritwik Ghatak. In eight grave, ravishing films, made in an intermittent career that spanned the first three decades of Indian independence, he returned time and again to the calamitous event which had deeply scarred him. Sometimes, as in his wayward masterpiece *Subarnarekha*, he reckoned with the suffering unleashed on the refugees of Partition; in other movies he approached the subject more obliquely. Always he drenched his plots in old Bengali literary and mythic allusions, as well as the region's classical and folk music, as if expressing a nostalgia for an undivided past.

Made in response to specific political crises, his movies retain all their urgency four decades on. For the issues Ghatak grappled with—displacement, cultural conflict, state violence—have never really gone away in India.

Ritwik Ghatak was born into the Bhadralok (roughly 'gentlefolk'), a small class of educated, upper-caste Bengalis who exercise an outsize influence on the region's politics and culture. His father, a magistrate, was a scholar of Sanskrit; his oldest brother, Manish, was a well-regarded poet. Like a good Bhadralok child, Ghatak grew up immersed in Bengali literature, music and art—all of which he loved and drew on in his films. ('In his heart and soul, Ritwik was a Bengali film director, a Bengali artist, much more of a Bengali than myself,' Satyajit Ray observed of his friend and sometimes rival.) Yet, for the Bhadralok itself, Ghatak had little admiration. His films expose the arrogance of their casteism.

Ghatak came of age during the 1940s, a decade of seismic change in Bengal. It was a period bookended by a famine created by the Crown in 1943, in which more than three million villagers starved to death, and the horrific riots in 1946 that foreshadowed Partition. These events dispelled any illusions he harboured about the future of India. In all his films, and particularly the Partition Trilogy, the new nation is presented as something fractured, unstable, permeated with violence and doomed from the outset. The contrast with Ray—see his glowing Apu Trilogy—could not be starker.

Ghatak's pessimism is already evident in his third film, *The Runaway*. It is the story of a child who flees his dreary village and tyrannical schoolmaster father to wander through Calcutta. The journey begins with a long, early-morning sequence—shots of the Howrah Bridge emerging against a dim sky; bustling streets seen from a low angle—that wonderfully evokes the

Ritwik played the lead—himself, really—in his last film, *Jukti, Tokko aar Goppo*; © NFDC – National Film Archive of India

dreamlike immediacy of childhood. But the plot soon darkens as its hero becomes a kind of street urchin, mingling with migrant workers, beggars, victims of famine and even thugs who try to kidnap him. 'Why is there so much pain here?' he wonders late in the film, before returning home chastened.

Ghatak's most comprehensive statement about independent India is to be found in the great Partition Trilogy, shot between 1960 and 1962. In these films, he uses the vehicle of a marginal figure, the refugee, to tackle the social ills eating at the heart of Indian society. *The Cloud-Capped Star* is a fervid, Dostoyevskian tale of a young woman who allows herself to be exploited by her conservative family. *E-Flat* is a parable about the collapse of political idealism. *Subarnarekha* directly confronts caste.

The films are loose allegories of Partition. Each is structured around a romantic separation, with Ghatak suggesting a parallel between the fierce yearning that his young leads feel for each other and a greater desire, unhoused in any single character, for a unified Bengal. In crucial moments, the metaphor is made almost explicit. For instance, early in *E-Flat* the two main characters look across the tributary of the Padma which separates India and what was then East Pakistan. 'What do you know about what one feels when one is deprived of one's homeland,' Bhrigu, the child of refugees, asks Anasuya, whose mother, we learn later, was killed in Partition-related riots. 'I know,' she replies. 'I know.'

'Film is not a form,' Ghatak liked to say. 'It has forms.' He himself had little interest in the then-predominant convention of neorealism, preferring to draw on 'lower' modes like the musical and the melodrama (in this, his work resembles Douglas Sirk's and Rainer Fassbinder's). His achievement was to turn these genres on their head, channelling their intensity into more critical and surprising directions. Meanwhile, he drew brilliantly on other Indian cultural traditions—music, theatre and mythology—to texture and burnish his plots.

Ghatak found realism woefully inadequate for depicting the brutality of Indian society. Instead, he fashioned a special kind of melodrama to convey how Hinduism deformed the lives of men and (particularly) women, constraining them in fixed social roles, circumscribing their aspirations. In all his films, he works with familiar, even clichéd, Indian types—spoiled son, vicious mother-in-law, long-suffering daughter and so forth—only to unsettle them, subjecting his characters to a series of moral and intellectual challenges.

This interrogation plays out most powerfully in *The Cloud-Capped Star*, the story of a refugee family in Calcutta. The film is focused on Nita, the oldest of four siblings, who single-handedly keeps the family solvent, while everyone else—vain sister, childish brothers, cruel mother and hapless father—shamelessly sponge off her. As the plot lurches from one crisis to the next, she grows ever more self-effacing, taking on a growing number of responsibilities: an ideal caregiving Hindu daughter. She even rejects the man she loves for fear of the marriage expenses (he then marries her younger sister). Only at the film's conclusion, when she is dying from tuberculosis in a sanatorium in the hills, does Nita realise what she's allowed to happen to her. Her final words are heart-rending.

'I want to live,' she cries to her brother. 'Tell me just once that I'll live.' The camera slowly pans around the surrounding valleys, forming a circle, as nature silently looks on.

The Cloud-Capped Star also showcases Ghatak's predilection for mythic allusions. Raiding the cultural treasure chest of Hinduism, both its high Vedic and folk strains, he litters the film with images, songs and motifs, creating an elaborate web of references, almost another level of storytelling, rather in the manner of T.S. Eliot in *The Wasteland*. In dramatic moments, he dissolves from a close-up of Nita's face to the yajna mandap (or holy pyre) in the house courtyard, suggesting that she is being ritually sacrificed for her family. Early in the film we learn that Nita was born on Jagaddhatri day; as the film scholar Ira Bhaskar has noted, she is modelled on the goddess Jagaddhatri, a universal sustainer and avatar of Durga, who 'was born out of this smoke [of] the transmutation of human desires'.

Yet, the mythic dimension of Ghatak's characters is not always clarifying (or convincing). Sita in *Subarnarekha* is an elusive, exceedingly passive figure who evokes various fantasies in the minds of men. For her brother, she is the chaste, self-sacrificing Durga; to her love interest, she is Krishna's divine, musical lover, Radha; a passing villager tells Sita she is the earth-mother Sita of the Ramayana. These are stifling expectations, yet Ghatak offers no critique of them. Likewise, he leaves Sita's passivity unquestioned, giving her few desires of her own. In the end, bereft of a larger critical purpose, the myths simply cloak her lack of inner life.

The drama of identity-formation instead unfolds in the language of Ghatak's cinematography. Forgoing a frontal address, he prefers extremely angled shots, shooting both from above and from far below, so that his figures always appear slightly off-kilter, as if larger or smaller than life. To similar effect, he uses wide-angle lenses that emphasise the depth of field, almost embossing people against a backdrop, in the style of mannerist paintings. In crucial moments he uses extreme close-ups to make the actors' heads seem to float and wobble in a space, underscoring the fractured sense of self. 'Ghatak's cinematic devices … give the figure in space this uneasy location,' the art critic Geeta Kapur has noted, 'on the join as it were, between reality and irreality'.

Before coming to cinema Ghatak worked with the Indian People's Theatre Association, a troupe affiliated with the Communist Party of India. Founded in 1943, the IPTA pioneered a form of street theatre that combined elements of folk music and drama with a revolutionary message (imagine a lively, non-doctrinaire variant of Mao's propaganda outfits). For seven years, he wrote, directed and acted in IPTA productions, rising to the rank of squad leader. In 1955, he was formally expelled by the CPI for criticising the party's increasingly dogmatic cultural agenda.

Ghatak drew on these experiences in *E-Flat*, a heavily autobiographical film set in the world of Calcutta theatre. More generally, the imprint of the IPTA is all over his aesthetic; his dialogue, for instance, has the snap and expository tone of the stage. It is also likely that IPTA gave him the confidence to use music so daringly and copiously in his films. Not only do several of Ghatak's characters sing—Nita's brother is an aspiring musician; Sita takes vocal lessons; *E-Flat* it is about a musical theatre troupe—but at the outset of each story he establishes a set of musical motifs that recur at key moments throughout, as in a tone poem, often in counterpoint to the drama. 'With our common habit of describing cinema as a visual art,' he wrote in his brilliant essay 'Sound in Cinema', 'we are tending to forget altogether the importance of the world of sound by itself.'

Part of what attracted Ghatak to IPTA, and later to cinema, was his desire to reach a mass audience. A lifelong Marxist, he wrote polemically about the state of Indian film, often attacking contemporaries, including Ray, for ignoring the country's countless social problems. Yet, at the same time, he warned against all forms of political 'sloganeering'; personality was for him fundamental to art. He spoke of both aspects of the film-making process—the task of raising social awareness and the desire to capture beauty—in combative terms: 'A million clenched fists rise to the sky militantly asserting their existence, even as the beams of a fledgling sun fall aslant on a cluster of paddy stalks, touching their edges and turning them into shimmering lines. The film reports from both frontiers, fights both fights.'

Alas, Ghatak's own military campaigns ended in failure. All his films, with the exception of *The Cloud-Capped Star*, were out-and-out box-office flops, which is unsurprising since little money was put into marketing them (the producers made the self-fulfilling assumption that such challenging art would have few takers). Worse, critics on the left denounced Ghatak for bourgeois pessimism and decadence, charges he repeatedly and vainly denied in print. Early in his career, he took to drinking heavily; by the mid-1960s, he was an inveterate alcoholic. His students at the Film and Television Institute of India, where he served as a vice principal between 1964 and 1965, remember a brilliant man who was often drunk. 'Keep a bottle of liquor in one pocket and your childhood in another,' he advised young directors.

By 1962, Ghatak's career seemed to have sputtered to a halt after only six films. But in 1972, more than a decade after his last production, he managed to pick himself up to shoot *A River Called Titas*, a stunning historical epic, based on a novel by a lower-caste writer, Adwaita Mallabarman, with funding from a Bangladeshi production house. (Ghatak admitted to an interviewer that he was drunk during most of the process, though he clarified that his 'drinking did not interfere with the shooting'). Two years later, he made his last movie, *Reason, Debate and a Tale*, an abrasive, Godard-esque essay-film, in which he plays a washed-out, alcoholic intellectual, a caustically refracted version of himself. In its painfully direct reckoning with social privilege, political failure and personal shortcoming, there is nothing like it in Indian cinema—or, for that matter, Indian literature. In 1976, a year before the film was officially released, Ghatak, fifty, died of chronic alcoholism.

Ghatak's posthumous reputation has grown steadily in India; today he is a cult figure in art-house circles here. What accounts for the change in fortunes? In the first place, history has proved his political instincts right. Ghatak's fears about the conservative elements within Hinduism; his premonition, in *Titas*, of environmental disaster; his fixations on homelessness and the metaphor of the refugee: all of this has come to feel awfully resonant in the past few decades. Last August, the BJP government implemented a 'Citizen's Registry' in the northeastern state of Assam, turning some two million people, most of them poor Muslims, stateless overnight, making them refugees in their own country. The plan now is to compile similar registers in the other states. (Last December, responding to massive civil protests against the registries, the BJP's youth wing shared a montage of clips from the Ghatak's Partition Trilogy on social media, in a shameless and confused attempt to demonise Muslims.)

Over time, Ghatak's formal innovations have also come into focus. In his brief career, he opened up film to the possibilities of music, the epic, the essay and also visual abstraction, blazing a trail that many others have since followed. If an indigenous tradition of Indian cinema can be said to exist, it begins with him. (Ray, for all his varied moods, hardly looked beyond the conventions of European realism.) Finally, Ghatak had a direct influence on Indian cinema at the FTII, where he mentored a group of students who went on to become notable directors in their own right, including Mani Kaul, Kumar Shahani and John Abraham.

If these film-makers did not match their guru's achievements, that is perhaps because they belonged to a more cynical generation, lacking the deep and tortured political idealism, as well as the moral clarity, that allowed Ghatak to respond to the cruelties of Indian social life in the ways that he did. Now the BJP, in its deluded quest to create a Hindu Rashtra, has once and for all exposed the fractures beneath the veneer of India's democracy. Perhaps that will push film-makers to a new social reckoning. Until then, Ghatak's films are a reminder of how badly the country is doing, and what it might have been. 'This stuff you write, only sadness, struggles and tears. I don't like it,' someone tells Abhiram, a young lower-caste writer, in *Subarnarekha*. Abhiram smiles, then replies, 'But this is what I see all around.'

In 2024, 'Poetry and Partition: The Films of Ritwik Ghatak', a landmark series at Lincoln Center, brought together seven films, five of them excellent new restorations, allowing viewers to revisit this neglected, path-breaking artist.

This piece was published in The New York Review *on 25 January 2020. It has been edited lightly for house style.*

Ratik Asokan is a writer based in New York City.

A means to an end: Ritwik Ghatak's life in the theatre

AMBORISH ROYCHOUDHURY

Little Bhoba's life of rebellion began in right earnest with forgery. Mymensingh Mission School was ill-equipped to contain his restive soul. Presented with the slightest opportunity, he would slink away. In the mid-1930s, his brother Manish Ghatak brought him to Calcutta and enrolled him at a prominent school, where Bhoba continued to play truant. Frustrated, their sister devised a way: she would sign his exercise book every day as he left home, and the school principal had to countersign it when he was done with school.[1] The boy, inevitably, discovered the benefits of forgery. But his short stint at the Calcutta school also introduced him to an art that held him in good stead later on.

Circa 1936, visitors to Calcutta's Maddox Square Park watched an eleven-year-old deftly playing Chanakya in amateur productions of Dwijendra Lal Ray's classic play *Chandragupta*. This was a beginning of sorts. As World War II broke out, the boy Bhoba, Ritwik Ghatak, had to return to Rajshahi, but he continued to act in plays, mostly Tagore's works, like *Achalayatan* and *Daak Ghar.* Ritwik would occasionally also take up the mantle of director. These engagements were still little more than childhood indulgences.

As a young adult, Ritwik's creative impulses found an outlet: literature. He began trying his hand at short stories and novels. At this time, his worldview wasn't yet fully formed—and then came a monumental tragedy that would torment Ghatak for the rest of his life.

1943 saw the outbreak of the Great Bengal Famine that killed over three million people. Rotting corpses littered the streets, and emaciated humans with bones jutting out of their bodies would roam about, crying 'Phyaan dao!', begging for the starchy water left over while cooking rice. Rice was so scarce that even the middle class could barely afford it. It was common to stumble upon dead bodies on your way to work or school. Ritwik was deeply disturbed. His experience of the famine is why, in 1944, he experienced the first intellectual jolt that would begin to shape his psyche.

It is difficult to pinpoint when or where, but sometime in late 1944, Ritwik saw Bijon Bhattacharya's seminal play *Nabanna.* Ritwik was nineteen at this time, and Bhattacharya was thirty-eight. They would go on to collaborate gloriously, but that was still a few years away. *Nabanna* was the first major production of the newly formed Indian People's Theatre Association. The play depicted the horrors of the Bengal Famine and its impact on the peasantry and working class. The stark, realistic portrayal of *Nabanna* was a far cry from the ornate and gaudy dramas that had become a staple in Bengali theatre. In the words of eminent theatre historian and commentator Samik Bandyopadhyay, it 'captured the real' in all its 'nakedness'.[2] Ritwik testified later in an interview: 'It changed all my thoughts. It was so novel and unexpected at the time.'[3]

Nabanna also had a profound impact on a fifteen-year-old budding theatre enthusiast called Utpal Dutt. He later said about his experience: 'The crowd scene was startling. It was huge. Eighty people on the stage or more, without any set design to speak of. Just a sackcloth hanging behind them … we see the 1942 movement, and the police opens fire, dispersing the crowd. Everyone running around on stage, and then fighting back … it was spectacular.'[4]

To Ritwik, the play represented a visceral protest against colonialism. Until early 1942, life in Bengal had been tranquil for him. In Ritwik's words, 'a placid, undisturbed life'. In quick succession, the region saw a series of distressing events—the Japanese attack, the Quit India movement, the famine. It was a period of great turmoil, and as Bengal reeled, Ritwik sought answers in Marxist politics, as politically conscious youth did

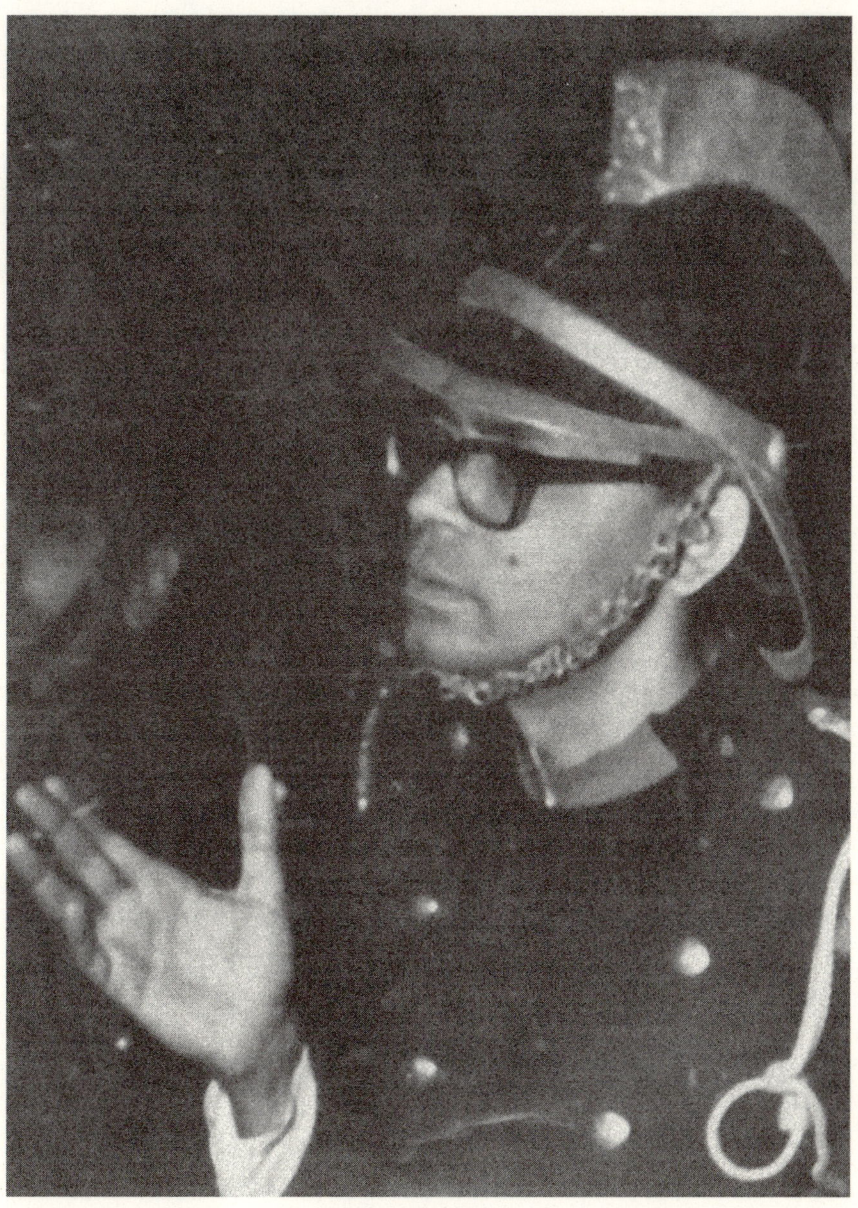

Not in a costume for a play, this is Ritwik at an exercise of the civil defence guards during the 1965 India–Pakistan War, while at FTII; © NFDC – National Film Archive of India

those days. And then came *Nabanna.* It reinforced his emerging belief in Marxism and nudged him towards a membership of the IPTA. He realised that theatre could be a potent weapon for social change.

At this time, Ritwik was already associated with the Progressive Writers' Association. He had believed that literature was his true calling because it helped him say the things he wanted to. And yet, it already seemed grossly inefficient. Readership was limited, restricting the number of people he could potentially reach out to. This is when *Nabanna* opened up a wholly new avenue for him. The kind of response it was getting made Ritwik acutely aware of the power and the reach of the theatre. 'I found that this was a much more potent medium than literature and also most immediate. I became very much associated with IPTA.'[5] IPTA's core philosophy, as Ritwik saw it, was to serve the people, standing by them in moments of crisis and telling their stories.

By most accounts, Ritwik began working with IPTA in 1948. He had by then already played Jinnah in a production by Kranti Shilpi Sangha. As Ritwik's engagement with the theatre was deepening, he was confronted with the event that would leave the deepest scar on him and profoundly mark his work: the Partition. It was a cataclysm Ritwik never recovered from. During his stint at the IPTA, he acted in several plays, with one of the first being a new production of *Nabanna*, directed by Sombhu Mitra and staged in 1948. Another was Tagore's *Bisarjan*, also directed by Mitra around the same time. In 1949, Ritwik appeared as a farmer in Biru Mukhopadhyay's play *Dheu.* Legend has it that, with his make-up on, Ritwik went to Utpal Dutt and asked for money. So convincing was his act that Dutt chased him away.[6] Bijon Bhattacharya and Ritwik were discovering that they were kindred souls, despite the two decades that separated them. Ritwik acted in Bhattacharya's play *Kalanka* and in a production of Dinabandhu Mitra's classic *Nil Darpan* that Bhattacharya directed.

In February 1949, B.T. Ranadive, a hardliner in the Communist Party of India, sidelined the then general secretary P.C. Joshi, one of the driving forces behind the IPTA. Ranadive advocated an armed struggle to topple the Congress-led Nehru government at the Centre. As a consequence, the party was banned in West Bengal and some other places. This had a direct impact on the IPTA, which was part of the Communist Party's cultural wing. Its activities were suspended for a while, and when the ban was lifted in the early 1950s, IPTA was no longer as influential as it was in its heyday. Ritwik was asked to run the Central Calcutta branch of IPTA, where he was soon joined by Dutt. By this time, Dutt had built quite the reputation for his theatre work, having established his own group called the Little Theatre Group. Dutt and Ritwik acted in a host of plays together, starting with yet another staging of Tagore's *Bisarjan* on 21 March 1951.[7] In April, both acted in a Bengali adaptation of Nikolai Gogol's *Inspector General*, called *Officer*. The original translation was by Pramathanath Bishi, but the team didn't like it very much. Ritwik himself adapted it afresh, and this was the version that was staged. Dutt directed both *Bisarjan* and *Officer*. Then they collaborated on Panu Pal's play *Bhanga Bandar.* On 23 April 1952, Niren Roy's translation of Shakespeare's *Macbeth* was presented in Bengali, in which Ritwik acted under Dutt's direction. Dutt starred in the eponymous role.

Around 1951-52, Ritwik started working on original plays. The first play that he set about writing was *Dalil,* but found himself increasingly preoccupied with news about thirty-one people who died by suicide within the span of a month. Putting *Dalil* aside, Ritwik compiled a reportage on the incidents called *Suicide Wave in Bengal.* This research had a profound impact on him as well, and he wrote and directed a play about the suicides called *Jwala* (1952). 'Each one is a true character,' he later said, '*Jwala* is really a documentary.'[8]

Much like those real-life cases, Ritwik's characters end their lives in the face of destitution, unemployment and injustice. The play was a depiction of the troubling fissures that had arisen in the sociopolitical fabric of Bengal. This was followed by *Dalil* (1952) and *Sanko* (1953–54). *Dalil* foreshadowed Ritwik's cinema in its preoccupation with the Partition. His resolute voice and political conviction had reached certain maturity by now. *Sanko* was about communal violence in the aftermath of the Partition, and the deep distrust that existed between Hindus and Muslims in the region.

Besides these original plays, Ritwik had translated two of Brecht's plays, *The Caucasian Chalk Circle* and *Life of Galileo.* In the light of IPTA's waning influence since the ban, Ritwik was commissioned by the group's Provincial Draft Preparatory Committee to prepare a document reinforcing its cultural and political ideologies, hoping to reinvigorate and renew the theatre movement. The document he prepared was titled

Mulnitir Khoshra/On the Cultural Front. In it, Ritwik outlined the duties and responsibilities of IPTA members on behalf of the party. He reiterated the need for a cultural front in the face of the growing influence of fascism the world over. A crucial aspect Ritwik highlighted in the document was the need to revive folk art forms and integrate them with IPTA's own narrative platforms in order to resonate with the rural masses.

By 1955, Ritwik had moved away from IPTA, concentrating on his film work. Just as he had once embraced theatre as a better platform to reach a wider and more diverse audience, he now realised that cinema was an even more powerful mode for reaching the people. But he didn't abandon writing plays altogether. After what was to be his final film, *Jukti, Tokko aar Goppo*, he had plans to film a story titled *Shey Bishnupriya*. He had even submitted the screenplay to the National Film Development Corporation. The film didn't materialise, however, and Ritwik turned it into a play called *Jwolonto* (1975), in which a woman's life is utterly destroyed by the activities of antisocial elements.

Ritwik wrote his last play while lying on a bed in a psychiatric institution. Seven years before his untimely demise, he had been institutionalised to recover from a bout of mental illness. For inclusion in this new play, he translated the eighth canto of Kalidasa's *Kumarasambhava*. The story of a young woman in a mental institution, the play was called *Shei Meye*. Ritwik got some of his fellow inmates together and staged it in the compound of that establishment. It was to be the last work of theatre that Ritwik Ghatak was a part of.

Amborish Roychoudhury is a National Award–winning writer, biographer and film historian. He has authored three books and written for Outlook, Firstpost, The Quint *and other publications. His latest book is on Raj Khosla, the veteran Hindi film-maker.*

Notes

1. Aritra Som, 'Niche Adiganta Padma…', *Prohor*, https://www.prohor.in/ritwik-ghatak-the-revolutionary-film-maker-of-bengal.

2. 'In Conversation with Samik Bandyopadhyay', *Sahapedia*, https://www.sahapedia.org/conversation-samik-bandyopadhyay.
3. Interview, *Chitrabikshan* (Bengali), Kolkata, 1973.
4. Translated from Arup Mukhopadhyay, *Utpal Dutta: Jiban O Srishti*, National Book Trust, 2011.
5. Ritwik Ghatak, 'Cinema and I', in Banerjee, S. (ed.), *Rows and Rows of Fences: Ritwik Ghatak on Cinema*, Seagull Books, 2001.
6. 'Ritwik-ke tariye diyechhilen Utpal Dutta', Anandabazar.com, https://www.anandabazar.com/patrika/various-stories-of-ghatak-s-works-in-theater-1.408022.
7. Arup Mukhopadhyay, *Utpal Dutt: Jibon o Srishti*, National Book Trust, Delhi, 2011.
8. Debjani Halder, *Ritwik Ghatak: Indian People's Theatre Association Birth, Growth and Decline*, https://www.academia.edu/34496969/Ritwik_Ghatak_Indian_Peoples_Theatre_Association_Birth_Growth_and_Decline.

Ritwik's *Sanko* is still relevant

TARIT CHOWDHURY

On 6 December 1992, the fight for space between the prehistoric and the historic in Ayodhya caused deep fissures to appear in the image of India as a secular nation: kar sevaks of the Ram Mandir desecrated the Babri Masjid. Communal riots left the nation bloodied in the days that followed. Standing there, in that time in history, scarred, I wondered which play to stage, which play *should be* staged. Out of the treasury of history, I pulled out Ritwik Ghatak's *Sanko* (*The Bridge*), a play that transcended time. I heard myself say, 'This, this is the play I was looking for, this play is the most appropriate right now.'

Before we staged *Sanko* in 1993, the play had been produced only a handful of times. The riots of 1946 and 1950, and the fragmented independence of the country in 1947—this five-year period in the history of Bengal, shameful and one of moral uprising at the same time, was the subject of Ritwik's play, his third. In 1955, Group Theatre staged *Sanko*. Then, in 1958, Biswarupa Theatre did. Ritwik directed it himself. Although we have heard that a wing of the Gananatya Sangha wanted to stage the play, I am not certain that it was staged anywhere after 1958.

Almost thirty-five years after that, on 17 March 1993, we staged *Sanko* as part of Roopdaksha group. By the end of December 1997, the production completed fifty nights.

At the time I was thinking of this essay on *Sanko*, newspapers and television channels were muddying the waters with their inane, immoral

The script of *Jwala*—Ritwik's award-winning play—was released as a slim book

shouting and screeching. Not just you and I, the whole world must have been spending sleepless nights wondering if America and Osama bin Laden and the Taliban were taking us towards World War III. Where did Osama bin Laden come from all of a sudden, and why did he feel such enmity towards America? How did things come to such a pass? The questions were inevitable.

Ritwik wrote *Sanko* in the context of the events of 1950–54. The communal riots of 1946, then the independence of our fragmented country in 1947, more riots in our Bengal and in East Pakistan in 1950:

Sanko took in all of this, and went into the next few years to record new chapters in the history of humankind, while being self-reflective too.

To describe the play as one about communal harmony is to oversimplify it and insult Ritwik's layered and deep creation. Why does Sagar betray Mohsin and help the rioters kill him? And then, why does the same Sagar, now remorseful and in search of peace, run across to Mohsin's family across the border? And why, indeed, does Sagar hold Mohsin's sister Jaba's hand and walk towards a future guided by history? If you do look for these answers, you will realise that the resistance in *Sanko* begins as one against imperialism and colonialism, and that one of the many poisonous claws of imperialism and colonialism is … communalism.

The British had stumbled upon a wonderful idea to govern India undisturbed: divide and rule. *Pit the Hindus and the Muslims against each other, and they will fight and kill, and we can rule in peace.* In much the same way, the American imperialists had created Osama bin Laden to destroy the socialist Soviet Union in the 1980s. Soviet Union collapsed in the early 1990s, and Osama bin Laden soon became a sworn enemy of the United States. He said that communism and America were both his enemies.[1]

In *Sanko*, the Chowdhurys invest in Dasarath and Co. to shield them from attacks by Muslims. But Dasarath himself catches hold of Chowdhury's daughter Rama in the gully and, grabbing her hand, threatens her with a knife. This reminds us of something very recent. The extremists handcrafted by the American imperialists stole American aircraft and crashed into the great symbols of American financial power and defence and intelligence, the World Trade Center and Pentagon respectively, on 11 September 2001. But why did this happen?

It's within the seemingly impregnable framework of imperialism that the virus that will destroy it one day is hidden. Over time, the virus gains enough strength to destroy the foundations of this grand imperialist edifice. So many years ago, Ritwik wrote about this inevitable truth in *Sanko*, about the destruction of the imperialists' pimp, Chowdhury. But while the imperialist forces still run amok, it's the innocent among us who lose their lives. 'That night, all night, thousands of women and children, wrapped in torn sheets in a vast maidan, below the gulmohar and krishnachoora trees, on the footpath next to the railing of the park, slept clutching the boxes that held everything they had and their torn burkhas. They didn't sleep; they shivered. Their eyes looked like they were without light. Sagar, their lips had turned blue in the cold. Why does this happen, Sagar?'

Parallels to what Ritwik said about those shelterless people can be found along the refugees from Afghanistan after 9/11, and among American citizens too.

History tells us that all imperialist powers must collapse one day. But for the humiliated, downtrodden people, the day of freedom won't come strolling. The unshackled masses must be prepared to welcome that day, greet it. That period of waiting, of preparing, is most cruel and tough. The freedom-seekers are scarred as they go through the ups and downs of that road to self-discovery. As Sagar and Jaba were scarred. The Sagar of the 1946 riots and the Sagar that stood in front of Jaba now were very different individuals. Sagar had once turned Mohsin over to the rioters. He had needed four years of preparation to make his confession to Jaba. That fight was as much with himself as it was with the many germs of the rotten society of his time. It was a multi-pronged battle. The day Sagar handed Mohsin over to the rioters, it had become clear that the symptoms of imperialism attack our unconscious self too, they build nests there. The way out of this is the battle for introspection that freedom-seekers wage. But Jaba's battle was even tougher. In her brother's killer, she had created her freedom fighter, her man for eternity, her partner for life. But where does Jaba find the strength to wage this war? The answer to this is also in Jaba's dialogue: 'The strength of love. The strength of love for the living.'

Jaba had to leave home for her battle. Sagar wanted to be her partner. But when Jaba chose Sagar, her father, mother and even her brother-in-law Kshitishbabu were uncomfortable about it. This led to a debate. When talking about his father, Mohsin had said that his father was a researcher of history. That he had been researching the Bengali community and Bengali language. So he is open-minded about history, but is he ready for the fight for freedom? To push against the boundaries of middle-classness? In the end, the fight Ritwik is concerned with is not about a specific piece of land, or of a specific time, or a specific objective. The fight is for a symbol—freedom of the people. It's a fight at many levels. Economic, social, cultural. After overcoming her initial hesitation, Jaba's mother comes forward and accepts Sagar as her daughter's chosen one.

At that moment, she turns into the universal mother. Her identity is that of an internationalist, of humanism. A mother who says, 'The cows are of different colours, but the colour of their milk is the same / After roaming the world, I find all the sons are of the same womb.'

Or the mother that says after finding the courage to send her children to the fight for freedom, 'Let them go, let them then come back without worrying. Let everyone prosper. Let peace come leaping out of the sky like clouds.'

As we bring the curtain down on *Sanko*, still searching for the warmth of such mothers, we wait in fear of World War III …

This piece was first published in Natyaroop. *It has been translated and edited by the editor for this anthology with permission from the copyright holders, Ritwik Memorial Trust.*

Tarit Chowdhury was an eminent theatre artist and director.

Notes

1. 'I did not fight against the communist threat while forgetting the peril from the West. [...] I discovered that it was not enough to fight in Afghanistan, but that we had to fight on all fronts against communist or Western oppression. The urgent thing was communism but the next target was America. [...] This is an open war up to the end, until victory.' (Ahmed S. Hashim, 'The World according to Usama Bin Laden', *Naval War College Review*, Vol. 54, No. 4 , Article 3, pp. 20–21.)

READING RITWIK, WRITING RITWIK

Assembly line:
A poet's reflections

JAYANT KAIKINI

Amidst the river Padma
An island half-lit, half-shrouded
People who look like drawings made from fresh woundlines
Walk across the river, melting into it.
Artists and poets think,
It is a reflection of the colours of the sunset or the sunrise.

They say there used to be an unseen train plying
between night and day,
between rehearsal and final show,
between half passion and full hunger,
between 'Komal' and 'Shudhh',
between lanterns and shadows on the wall.
They say there was an unseen rail
but why have the tracks
suddenly stopped at the shore
as if the umbilical cord is cut
with a pair of scissors?
As if there is nothing in front of it
and the same river flows
across that
like a stranger.

Beyond is the same old town
everything in it right there,
I see it but I cannot reach it.
Just yesterday, we had been to the house across these banks
to our daughter's home
today, they say it is a different country.
Kids from there would come in
Burmanda's boat to their school on this shore.
This school is a different country for them now.
Who has been left behind? Where?
Which child's toy has rolled under which cot?
Who has forgotten things and where?
As if a father has gone mad
searching for his young daughter lost in a fair.
All have gone mad on either
side of the river.

That is why, Ritwikda,
rivers haunt you.
In the veins of your work, the river is spreading,
overflowing its banks, expanding its shores.
Every intense, tumultuous individual
hesitates to come into the surreal light.
or any spotlight.
They refuse to play any role in it.
The sand dunes on the banks of the Padma
fly like blank, square sheets of paper
that have abandoned poets.
They become sails
of fishermen's boats in a stormy Titas.
This river breeze chokes everything and everyone.

Who said
you cannot wound flowing water?
Here the river itself was the weapon
to break a big home.

Ritwik explains a scene to Bijon Bhattacharya (L) and Abhi Bhattacharya (C) during the shooting of *Subarnarekha*; © NFDC – National Film Archive of India

Was the boat tethered with a thin, sacred thread at the bank? Look how it breaks free, rowed by a little boy's hands, and sets forth towards other worlds. Ultimately to the city, to Calcutta. What kind of a city is this? Drawn in steel and iron, filled with cement. Are those cars or turtles? Are these buses or tigers? Has everyone fled here from their villages, poor homes, cruel fathers, and come to this big city? Like me? When did they come? In search of what? Uprooted people seeking places to hide their faces. Haridas, with the fake beard, says he had come in search of his mother. Rather unusual. Children, like me, often run away from home. But why did Haridas's mother run away? Abandoning her son? Who was lost? Son or mother?

The day the mother passed away, look how the ramshackle Chevrolet car 'Jagaddal' became a soulmate, a friend, almost a mother to the taxi driver. (Not a coincidence that the same actor, Kali Banerjee, plays Haridas and the taxi driver Bimal.) How did the beloved Jagaddal feel the taxi driver's fleeting thoughts and speak to him? How did those rusty, lidless eye-like headlights show the way and then roll over in dismay? How did the radiator cough for attention and then gulp down water, sounding like a parched old woman? The taxi driver becomes mechanical, while the ageing car becomes more and more humane, unmechanical. Culminating in the taxi driver's garage, the makeshift operating theatre. The driver becomes the surgeon with his gloves on, conducts a surgery on the car … Abdomen ripped open, its inner organs exposed, webs of pipes and veins jumbled, leaking grease and pain. The moment Jagaddal's heart starts beating again, time stands still.

(*I'd bet the railway crossing pan shot of* Ajantrik *is a precursor to the single shot of Sonny Corleone in the toll-gate scene in* The Godfather.)

The Hooghly river flows, as strong as the iron that the Howrah Bridge is made of. But not strong enough to destroy that man gazing at the lady for vadhu pariksha, bridal examination. Not strong enough to stop those men who are taking the women away from the refugee camps. Not strong enough to douse the fire of intolerance. The pages of a calendar, with beautiful landscapes painted on them, flutter in the wind. Open the window, and lo, you see a garage right in front of it. A car's open bonnet stares back like a crocodile. Close the window, you're back in the suffocating heat. Under the light post is a violinist who plays only when he is paid. He is also hungry. He remembers those who have listened to his music from a distance without paying.

There lies a pond of turmoil. On the banks sit hapless, homeless refugees, without jobs, consoled only by the trees around them as if with plumes and feathers. Their reflection settles ever so silently on the water in front of them, only to be trembled and dispersed by a passing train every now and then—a train that moves on the bridge of unsaid words. The star that is hidden in the clouds walks down three flights of stairs, avoiding the elevator in broad daylight to search for a job …

Father–daughter, mother–daughter, little sister–big brother, big sister–little brother, such a vast speechless web this is, all within a ten-square-foot refugee household. Wherever they sit, they bring with them their childhood songs. When she asks her elder brother, 'Do you still remember that song we would sing in our childhood,' he says, 'Oh yes, of course—I didn't forget.' And so he sings a Rabindrasangeet for her. Along with the song, the light that filters in through the household's woven thatch wall turn into stars for you, Ritwikda. Affection is the only hope for you. *Je raate mor duwarguli* … In that one song, the entire cosmos enters that tiny place. There is the young woman, washed ashore on the banks of the Titas, with her bridal make-up and the sandalwood-paste dots on her eyebrows still breathing. Perhaps you saw those very same stars in those dots above her eyebrows …

An old, abandoned war-time airfield with the remains of an old, crashed warplane. The children of fishermen run and play in and out of the ruins. Is this a dried-up river? Is it a runway? Is it a river of cement? Sita asks her father-like elder brother, 'Why is everyone asking me if I am grown up?' No, you're not, he says, and pats her to sleep.

The journey from villages of clear water to smoky cities, every woman a flowing river, with her several tributaries. She will create her own banks, breaking, flooding those masculine rocky riverbanks, she is antaraganga, with a lamp in her heart. Silent, alone, but never lonely.

She is grass, sprouting like vertical brush strokes, in a barren horizontal landscape.

Her fight is for a right to dignity amidst total ruin, devastation. Be it in submerged fishing villages, the big city or the refugee camps.

'She's a flirt, avoid her'—who said that?

'Girls are becoming experts at pickpocketing and dominating now.'

Dear Ritwikda, by playing the protagonist in *Jukti, Tokko aar Goppo*, your voice unveiled itself with gravitas, becoming more present. Your angst, your helplessness, your compassion for the marginalised and the politically wronged, your hope for a better tomorrow, all amplified in that voice. Amidst the rebel refugees, you particularly like the name of that teenage girl, Bangabala, whom you shelter in your small refugee group. You wander amidst the tribal folk with your group. The tribal mask-maker sees Bangabala as the devi. Your wife had taken your son away to lead a better life. Now you have come very near to the village where they live. Now you want to see your son, just once. She won't let you into her house. You have just one wish—that you may see your son's face once, in the morning rays of the sun, before you go away.

Ritwikda, all your images flow together as if along an assembly line—like the ones that are in the factories. A conveyor belt. Where all the different, disparate parts are continuously assembled and pieced together. Like a hurtling river, an assembly line. Like gathering hundreds of shards of the shattered souls of lives that were destroyed by the river itself, an assembly line. To this, the background score, the coughing, the schoolchildren reciting their mathematics tables, the chorus of a play, the hungry boatsman's song, the starter sounds in the garage, the melody of khayaals and '*Akash bhora shurjyo tara*' … The sound of warplanes flying dangerously low, '*dekho bhor bhayi*', the steam engine's siren, the fire engine's bell, all resound in your voice.

'Think, think, train yourself to think, it will help society …'

'Think, think, train yourself to think, it will help society …'

This essay has been translated from the Kannada by Srajana Kaikini.

Jayant Kaikini, a renowned writer in Kannada literature, is a poet, a writer of short stories, a playwright, a film lyricist and scriptwriter.

Abandoned lives, afterlives

BRINDA BOSE

আমার সেদিন হারিয়ে গেল কোথায় কখন
কেমন করে হারিয়ে গেল জানে না মন।
আজকে এখন ভাবতে বসে,
অবাক লাগে হিসেব করে,
ছন্দ-ছাড়া ছড়িয়ে ফেলা আমার জীবন।
এমন কথা ছিল না কো,
করার কিছু ছিল তো গো,
স্বপ্ন ভরা তীব্র হৃদয় ছিল তখন।
আজ নদীর পারে এসে,
চুরাই তো মন বসে বসে,
সব দেখারই শেষে এসে দাঁড়াই এখন।

—ঋত্বিক ঘটক

Lost my yesterdays, when and where
and how they were lost, the mind knows not.
Now when I sit down to ponder,
It feels strange to calculate and wonder,
This rhythmless, scattered life of mine.
This was not how it was meant to be,
Surely there was something to be done,
A dream-filled burning heart there was then.
Today as I reach the river's bank,
As I sit, sit and collect my mind,
At the end of all seeing have I come to stand.

—Ritwik Ghatak, found poem, untitled (my translation)[1]

Ritwik did not start his creative life with making cinema, but with writing poetry, plays and short stories. He was, however, dissatisfied with most of his written expressions (especially poetry). He did go on to find his métier in cinema, his films constituting an aesthetic revolution, but he left so much undone there too. He passed away in only his fifty-first year, leaving behind unrealised projects, unfinished films, scripts and notes. Ritwik has been described as the *enfant terrible* of the avant-garde for his fearless experimental work on screen, but I would like to pick up on some other elements of his life's work which may make him avant-garde in spirit and letter. Amongst them is his propensity to attempt and abandon creative mediums, leaving a trail of finished and unfinished material that has surfaced—sometimes as found objects—to construct a persona for him that lies outside of the cinema he is best known for.

Another is his intimacy with a sense of failure, incommensurate with his achievements in a brief life. Yet other elements, perhaps entwined with this sense: an uncontrolled consumption of liquor, a vulnerability to volatile loves, hates, friendships, artistic hopes and dreams, a feeling that something vital had slipped out of his grasp because he had been unable to harness his ideas to the art he had envisioned. And yet—like the best of the avant-garde—Ritwik spawned afterlives like almost no other in Indian art cinema. He has inspired tributes and implorations in word and art through the decades, his singular craft and even more singular mind hailed. There are poems and essays addressed to him. A slew of film-makers who were his students, each iconic in their own right, have formed a Ritwik lineage, though he actually taught at the Film and Television Institute of India, Pune for only a brief stint. Material related to him continues to be discovered in unlikely archives. Yet, one cannot help but rue all that was left undone. No celebration of Ritwik is entirely divorced from regret, his or everyone else's; recognitions of incompleteness and then even an impoverishment, and annihilation, of the aesthetic, splintered by moments of blazing incandescence.

Ritwik was a thinker and a creature of words—as were many others in his wake, notably his students at the FTII, Mani Kaul, Kumar Shahani, John Abraham, all towering film-makers—and he thought acutely about poverty, boredom and death, along with carousing life and art. He succinctly captured the precarious, isolated, surging power of the creator:

> The director should feel isolated from his medium of expression …
> At the end the man should emerge as a hero with all his fallacy.
> When he is absolutely alone and on the verge of suicide, he is offered an alternative.
> He has to leave all art work and go away into some lonesome spot to earn his living. He accepts.
> He goes to the spot. Nature is beautiful around him and he falls in love with it.
> It seems that a happy ending is in view. But that is not to be.
> He tears up the landscape with his own hands, literally.
> And then there is the atomic explosion turning the seawater into a huge mushroom.[2]

It is with this embedded sense of love, urgency, isolation, precarity and self-destruction that Ritwik feverishly pursued his creative work. In *Masocriticism*, starting his discussion of 'The Afterlife of the Avant-Garde', Paul Mann puts on record an inability to be certain of his own conclusions: 'I cannot offer you things I have conceived through hard labor, things I have established and know to be true. All I have to offer you are suspicions, fears, urges, superstitions, habits, the faintest of glimmers …'[3] If such a fragmented, disjointed sense of knowing and creating has been seen as characteristic of modernisms at large, it is even more pertinent to the avant-garde, an outlier modernism that has not just been proclaimed dead many a time but also, perhaps, powerless to be born. In fact, it is upon assuming such a death that Mann in *Masocriticism* is poking and prodding at remains and remainders.

My attempt here is to explore some of the remainders of Ritwik's relatively small but creatively enormous body of work—not the cinema he is best known for, but the bits and pieces he produced because he fell, if briefly, in love with those forms before abandoning them. I try to track their, and his, afterlives. I suggest that this is a significant legacy of the avant-garde Ritwik, these offerings in fragments that do not add up to a completed jigsaw puzzle, but provide 'the faintest of glimmers' to lead us at best to a felt, faulty yet incisive perception of his body of work. Ritwik was dogged by a sense of not reaching where he passionately wanted to with his art, succinctly captured in the poem '*Aamaar shedin haariye gelo*' (Lost my yesterdays). It is one of only two poems that have been located

The library at Nandan in Kolkata is named after Ritwik; @ Shamya Dasgupta

yet (though apparently there may have been, once and somewhere, a small published collection of his poetry). In this poem, he rues 'this rhythmless, scattered life of mine. / … Surely there was something to be done / A dream filled burning heart there was then / … At the end of all seeing have

I come to stand.' This is not a feeling that came to him at the end of his life, but assailed him from the very beginning of his creative work.

As we know now, it did not stifle him, instead leaving him restless, searching, suspicious, dissatisfied. Rani Ray, in her introduction to her translated collection of Ritwik's short stories, writes of his exposure in childhood to a variety of cultural influences. 'His earliest attempts to give shape to these various streams of impressions and ideas were in the field of poetry. But he soon realised that he was not made for it. He recalled those days in a humorous vein in his later life: 'As usual with Bengali boys—and I believe it's the same with the French—whenever the creative urge comes up within them for the first time, it breaks out into poetry. So, my artistic activities also began with a few badly written poems. Then I realised that it was not my cup of tea. I knew that I would never be able to enter even the fringes of a hundred-thousand mile stretch around "poesy"!'[4] Ritwik's own admission of 'a few' poems seems to indicate that there might once have been a published collection; the two poems that have yet surfaced tell us that his attempts at 'poesy' were not as fruitless as he had rather harshly judged them to be. In any case, until there is another surprise discovery, we must make do with the two poems that are extant, as proof of a literary 'glimmer' that came and went without much ado. There is, of course, so much that is soaring, lyrical, poetic about his films—in the real, in the mythic, in the tragic, in the humane—that we may well argue that his penchant for poesy bent from the literary towards the visual as he abandoned the forms that seemed to short-change his imagination.

As Ray notes, Ritwik's twin inspirations as he grew up—for his artistic turn and for his political thought—came from close family. His brother Manish Ghatak, twenty-three years his elder, was a writer of fiction and a pioneering member of the well-known Bengali literary group Kallol, writing under the pen name of Jubanashwa. Kallol was constituted of a politically charged set of young men, committed to writing realist accounts of the subaltern classes of Bengali society. Ritwik was undoubtedly influenced by their zeal and his eldest brother's early fame. Sudheesh Ghatak, another brother of his, had trained in camerawork for documentaries in the UK, and in the 1930s had worked with New Theatres in India, making feature films. Ritwik imbibed these aesthetic and political leanings from his brothers. In the 1940s, even as storms were gathering for multiple political upheavals in India and the world, Ritwik was growing into adulthood and awareness, and he began to shape his complex perceptions into short stories.

Ray quotes from an interview with Ritwik in 1973: 'I began to write stories from then onwards. But the urge to write stories was not like those earlier vapid and hollow attempts at composing poetry. Even at that early age, it was the desire as a political being to protest vehemently against the wickedness, the villainy, the oppression that I saw around me, which drove me to write short stories.'[5] In the short story and, soon after, the theatre script, Ritwik found a transient literary calling. He first wrote short stories prolifically over three or four years from the year of Independence and Partition, 1947, and returned to them in the 1960s, after a spate of ferocious film-making that did not bring him instant fame or money. By his own count, he wrote over a hundred short stories that were often published in some of the leading literary magazines of Bengal. Despite the fact that it was cinema by which Ritwik later became justly famous, critical assessments have deemed his short story writing as commendable and powerful in its own right.

For a short while, he also started and ran a literary magazine called *Abhidhara*, which had a proclaimed Marxist outlook and carried some of his own short stories. It may be superfluous to say that this trajectory of frantic, frenetic, creative experimentation—dabbling in poetry, becoming politically committed to particular ideologies, immersing in an aesthetic form (the short story) with enormous zeal for a stretch of time and then moving on, founding a vernacular literary magazine which was dissolved for lack of funds, scrambling to find other mediums (theatre, then cinema) to work in, giving in to despair, giving up, alcohol, loneliness, ill-health—have been characteristic of the avant-garde, marked by restlessness, self-doubt, vaulting creative ambition, vicious self-criticism, failures of the spirit, the mind and the body. It has, even and perhaps especially at soaring heights, been signified by death or a series of imminent deaths.

Why is radical artistic practice doomed to be short-lived, to mutate, even to die without realising what may have been its full potential? By Paul Mann's reading, not only is death inevitable for the avant-garde because it is bound to capitulate to capitalism, but it is also doomed by the very condition of existing, of becoming known, exposed:

> 'In general, it seems the avant-garde died because it was unable to sustain its alterity, its difference, its otherness ... The avant-garde died because all major forms of anti-art or aesthetic resistance end up in the very museums and cultural institutions that they began by calling into question ... [but let us] gather them into another diagnosis: the avant-garde died of exposure.
>
> It died by revealing itself to its enemies ... It buried itself alive in the very manifestoes, events, collages, poems, and assemblages in which it proposed to live a disruptive and utopian existence.'[6]

If this is so, then the avant-garde cannot resist or overturn this death; it is inevitably written into the very reason of its coming into being. One must hasten to clarify that 'death' here does not necessarily—or even frequently—mean oblivion. It is not that Ritwik's art, in any of its many forms, was doomed to a forgetting beyond a brief life: it means that the form itself was abandoned, because it could not be sustained or perpetuated, it could not reproduce itself endlessly; it would become then like a magic trick whose formula one was now privy to. It may be revelatory, therefore, to return to the abandoned forms, the remainders, the fragments of visionary insight, to seek fresh understandings of mind and craft. How, for example, did dream and delusion meet and merge in Ritwik's romantic vision?

I take, to begin with, a story of Ritwik's that will not seem, in its location or concern, typical of the artist's expected milieus, to think a little about its implications. The short story is titled 'Ecstasy' the English word is put down in Bengali script as a title, creating a linguistic dissonance before the story begins. It was written in 1949, two years after the creation of two nations by a geopolitical partition that affected the very being of the man—and, as we know now, about a year before he gave up his explorations into this genre of creative expression for a long time. The male protagonist of the story, speaking in the first person, is weary of a warring existence on every front and has escaped to an idyllic setting. The story begins with a two-word sentence:

> পালিয়ে এসেছি।[7]
> *I have escaped here.*

This is the escape of a weary spirit taking a flight of imaginative fancy. The surroundings are verdant, beauteous. The mind, instantly at peace, savouring an idyll, almost inevitably calls forth its muse, an amalgamation of imagination and reality, changing shape to match the circumstances in which it will appear. But now, in the distance is an apparition like no other he has ever encountered. He sees a tribal girl collecting water from the rapids under a twilit sky. He is mesmerised. A description of his vision of her is fulsome, ecstatic. Her black hair, tied back in a bun at her nape from a middle parting, glistens with oil; her skin is healthy, dark; her eyes are large, petal-shaped.

> ক্ষনেকের জন্যে তাকে নিচু হয়ে জল নিতে দেখলাম যখন, সে এক অনবদ্যরূপে আমার সামনে প্রতিভাত হলো। সে যেন এই বনপ্রদেশে পৃথিবীর আদি নারীর প্রতীকরূপে ভেসে উঠলো। [8]
>
> *As I watch her bending low to collect water, she assumes a shape of perfection in my eyes. It seems that in this wilderness the earth's first feminine form has been washed ashore.*

Certainly, the story captures in the lushness of its description an essence of 'ecstasy'. Why is the title an English word? Is there no equivalent in Bangla for a milieu and a sensibility that is embedded in Bengal? There are, and yet Ritwik chose to throw his Bengali readers into his story with a sort of dislocation, a jolt, a curiosity. The story then proceeds to describe an infatuated rapture, the infatuated, in his ecstasy of desire, fantasising that he will give up everything he knows to follow the wild beauty to her tribal village community, and live, sing, dance and love to their unknown, beckoning tunes. The world may begin to disintegrate outside of his ecstatic existence; he will neither know, nor care:

> তখন হয়তো কান্নায় পৃথিবী ভেঙে পড়বে। ঘুমের ঘোরেও সে ছটফট করবে, তৃতীয় মহাযুদ্ধ হয়তো রক্ত-তান্ডবে কাঁপিয়ে তুলবে দশ দিক। আমি তার কিছুই জানতে পারব না। ... নাঃ, কালই যাব আমি মেয়েটির খোঁপায় পরিয়ে দিতে পলাশগুচ্ছ। ওখানেই থাকব।
> ... যে-স্বাদ পেয়েছি, যে-রস ক্ষরিত হচ্ছে এই বনে-প্রান্তরে, তার মধ্যে লীন হয়ে আমি পাগল হয়ে যাব। [9]

Perhaps then the world would dissolve into tears. Even in sleep she would toss and turn, perhaps the third world war would shake up everything on ten fronts. But I will not know any of it ... Nah, indeed, I must go tomorrow, to adorn her hair with a bunch of palash flowers. And I will stay on there.
... that-taste that I have received, that-nectar that flows through this forest-wilderness, in them I will disappear and become a lunatic.

His fantasy is complete, framed by dark trees adorned with the blazing red flowers of the flame of the forest tree; it is as palpable as it can be. And then deep in the throes of its ecstasy, Ritwik shakes up his own dreamscape, almost like the world shattered by war and dissolving in tears:

তবু মেয়েটিকে বিয়ে করে চিরকাল সুখে থাকতে পারব তো![10]

Still, after marrying the girl, will I be able to live in happiness forever!

'Ecstasy' is blown away in a swirl of sober thought, as it perhaps must. The swift change in mood is like a whiplash; ecstasy, after all, can harbour no doubt, nor any wish for permanence. It can only be distilled into a moment that passes.

In three short stories written during a brief phase of coming back to the form after a break of almost two decades, Ritwik searches for absolution in the mythic when he returns—as always in his work in all mediums—to the feminine form: beauty and death, alcohol and divine rapture, violence and rebirth. In 'প্রেম'/'Love' (1968), 'ঝংকার'/'Chime' and 'মার'/'Attack' (1969), there is no longer space and time for musings on passionate desire blossoming in the wilderness or even the sobriety of transience. The stories have shrunk even further in length, have sharpened in precision and despair. In 'Love', a pair of radiant lovers meet on the banks of the raging river Padma—the river always central to Ritwik's imagination—in a lowering storm. A betelnut tree and a cinnamon tree are swaying and creaking, berserk in the rising wind. Beside them, below them, a boy and girl stand facing each other, seemingly resolute in the face of the rage of the skies, the river, the trees, the wind. He looks at her face. She smiles and kisses him, and tells him that it is only for him that she is here, despite the storm. It is a moment of perfection for him; he crushes her to his chest.

> এটা এ মুহূর্ত। এটা তো পরের মুহূর্তে আর থাকবে না।
> … ও তাকে বুকের মধ্যে জাপটে ধরল, তারপর মেয়েটির নিজের সুগন্ধি চুলগুলো দিয়ে মেয়েটিরই গলা পেঁচিয়ে ধরল এবং মেয়েটাকে মেরে ফেলল, ভাবল এই মুহূর্তটা অক্ষয় হোক।[11]
>
> *This is this moment. This will no longer last in the next moment.*
> *… He crushed her to his chest, then taking the girl's own fragrant hair coiled it around her neck and killed the girl, thought let this moment be imperishable.*

Death conquers ageing, conquers changing events, conquers the tarnishing of memory and freezes the moment of perfection.

In 'Chime', a man of broken dreams, loves and lives has retreated to the forests to meditate on how to find again the musical instrument of his prayers, a Saraswati veena. Looking to love people, wounded many a time, abandoned by society, he has taken to drink even as he attempts over and over again to carve the veena out of a battered old instrument. Frustrated, he flings it away, and a loud jangle is heard. He sits with his hands covering his face, from time to time taking a sip from a bowl of alcohol. Suddenly birds begin to sing. Hearing a soulful song, he raises his head to see an exquisite woman in front of him, dressed in white, riding a swan. Bemused, he asks her who she is. She laughs and instructs him to pick up the veena, now miraculously whole, and hand it to her.

> তিনি দিলেন।
> মহিলা সেটিকে নিজের হাতে নিয়ে এক অপরূপ লীলায়িত ছন্দে গ্রহণ করে একটি ঝংকার তুললেন। একটি ঝংকার।
> অপরূপ সব শুভ্র।
> জগৎ এইখানেই শেষ।[12]
>
> *He did.*
> *The woman took it in her hands, and embarking upon a sublime lilting tune strummed a chime. A single chime.*
> *The world ended here and now.*

In 'Attack', Ritwik forages among the deep seas of Indian mythology to retell the love story of Arjun, the brave and able warrior, and Subhadra, his beauteous, courageous and accomplished beloved. How they fought off the arrows that rained upon their chariot and rose to the skies above to celebrate a celestial wedding amidst those who honoured them. How the lovers teamed up perfectly—Subhadra expertly steering the horse-drawn chariot, Arjun wielding his bow and arrows with deathly precision—to defeat their enemies in a counter-attack. Ritwik chides the Bengal of his times for forgetting to mine the riches of the land's ancient mythology for the ultimate wisdom on life and how to live it. The lessons that he believes have been forgotten by his fellow men are the power of passionate love and the art of attack, exemplified by the story of Arjun–Subhadra whose son Abhimanyu was its emblem.

> সোজা মার। মার না দিলে ব্যাপার জমবে না।
> ... আজকের বাংলাদেশের চারপাশে যা দেখা যায় সেরকম সুভদ্রা কোথায় হবে, সেরকম অর্জুনদেব কোথায় হবে। কিন্তু নিশ্চই এরা বাংলাদেশে আছে। তারা হবে আমাদের উত্তরপুরুষ।
> অভিমন্যুর মতো মায়ের গর্ভ থেকে তারা চক্রব্যূহ ভেদমন্ত্রের কৌশল শিখেছে। এবার এরা মেরে ফাটিয়ে দিক। এদের ফাটানোর একটা ব্যাপার এসে গেছে। সামনের রক্তিম শিমুল গাছটা মোটামুটিভাবে সেই কথাই বলছে।[13]

> *Straight attack. Nothing will ever happen until there is an attack.*
> *... Going by what one sees all around Bengal, where will Subhadra come from, where will Arjundeb come from. And yet they must be in Bengal. They will be our progeny.*
> *Like Abhimanyu, they have learnt in their mother's womb the art from Vedmantra Chakravyuha. Now they should simply attack and blast. Something of the art of blasting has come to them. In front, the incarnadine shimul tree is saying something like that.*

Ritwik's philosophical investment in human passions, in divinity, in mythology and in revolution came from his deep and abiding love for people. In the second poem by Ritwik that is available to us so far, he proclaims this love, with sincerity, simplicity and humility.

মানুষ
তোমাকে ভালোবাসি।
এইভাবে
পৃথিবীর ইতিহাস বারবার
বদলে গেছে,
তবুও মানুষ সবসময়ে বেঁচেছে।
আমরা পাগলের মতন জীবন
চালিয়ে গেছি
কিন্তু, এটাই জীবন?
আমাদের দিয়ে পৃথিবী তে কিছুই হয় না,
কিছু নয়।
মাগো তোমার হচ্ছে শেষ কথা।
তোমাদের ওপরে এই পৃথিবী রয়েছে
বেঁচে
এই কথা বলার অধিকার আমাদের নেই।
কারণ আমরা তোমাদের পরিত্যক্ত সন্তান।
মাগো, তোমরা, তোমাদের পায়ে ধরি।
আমাদের ফেলো না।
আমরা এখনো বেঁচে আছি, মা আমাদের মনে রেখো
মা, আমাদের মনে রেখো।

People
I love you.
In this way the history of the world over and over
has changed,
Yet, people have always survived.
We have like lunatics our lives
pursued
But, is this living?
Nothing at all that we do sustains the world,
Nothing.
Mother of ours, yours is the last word.
It is on you that the world
rests
We have no right to such utterances.
For we are your abandoned children.
Mother of ours, we fall at your feet.

Do not forsake us.
We are still living, Mother, do remember us
Mother, remember us.[14]

Coda

Ritwik is remembered not simply for his genre-altering work in cinema but also for the devotion he inspired, and for generations of film-makers after him whose aesthetic practices he shaped—or they themselves shaped, often in conscious, sometimes unconscious, tribute to him. It may be expected that a film-maker of Ritwik's stature would have students whose own films would remain in dialogue with their teacher's work; in this, we know that the names of Kumar Shahani and John Abraham (along with Mani Kaul) are often spoken of with Ritwik Ghatak's. What remains more unusual are the words that they composed after the untimely passing of the master: Kumar Shahani's essay, titled 'ঋত্বিক, তুমি ফিরে আসবে' / 'Ritwik, You Will Return' and fittingly translated into Bangla, was published first in a newsletter on the occasion of a film festival in Dhaka in 1995, and since then collected elsewhere. An enthralling, lyrical enactment of a monologue with himself—a self now bereft of Ritwik—unfolds through stories of all that transpired and much that did not, but was felt along the veins through which the blood-ties swam. Towards the end, Shahani writes:

> ঋত্বিক, তুমি ফিরে আসবে ধানের ক্ষেতে, হয়তো বক-সারসের মাঝে, দিনান্তের মেঘে, হয়তো কোন রমণীর সঙ্গী রাজহাঁস হয়ে, হয়তো উত্তরার রক্তিম পায়ে বাঁধা ঘুঙুরের ঘন্টি হয়ে।
>
> *Ritwik, you will return to the wheat fields, perhaps among the cranes-storks, the twilight clouds, perhaps as some woman's companion swan, perhaps as the bells on the anklets tied around Uttara's rosy feet.*

Surely there can be no better way to picture his return.

John Abraham, maverick artist in the great tradition of Ritwik—who died at the age of fifty in 1987, about ten years after his master, and who wrote short stories as well—left a poem that is both a tragic lament for, and a cerebral invocation to, the (im)possibility that was Ritwik.

RITWIK DAA! RITWIK DAA!
Ritwik Ghatak,
in partition, not physically of willingness—the country departed
Out of his outer consciousness—cosmic consciousness
none of his mistakes,
Reactions—natural reactions—reflections
Ritwik Ghatak,
refugee, unborn, unwanted, unbearable
penetrative towards the Victorian hangover
of the Tagorian corruption of thinking
Life was more important to him
than the words in praise of god,
the god of Victorian Tagorian thinking.
Hence, he was rejected from the Bengalian thinking
Ritwik Ghatak—the name doesn't suit
the hierarchic thinking of the Raynian Zamidarian thinking
Perhaps, the long echo of the forgotten factors
that becomes reminiscence of
the 'death of the salesman' or otherwise
the long columns and no more Chhabi Biswas,
Cardiac arrest is common.
The death of Ghatak is uncommon.
Nay, Ritwik Ghatak
I remember,
a tall man
his hands moving around my shoulders,
catching me with the feeling of nearness,
rather than imperialism—
the man who stands before me questioning my manliness
loosening his hands to shake my hands in appreciation of manliness
recognizing each other—
abiding in each other
kicking on my ass and telling me
'Get up, awake shoot'
I remember, not with sentiments
with awakening proud, Ritwik Ghatak
Ritwik Daa,

let me call you Ritwik Daa,
I know that you are no more.
But I am, alive for you
Believe me.
When the seventh seal is opened
I will use my camera as my gun
and I am sure the echo of the sound
will reverberate in your bones,
and feed back to me for my inspiration.
Thank you Ritwik Daa,
I am thanking you
not with impotency and insipidity
Ritwik Daa,
I remember you,
when the words fails to criticize you,
Ritwik Daa,
eternally you are
in my brain
in my spirit and
in my Holy Ghost
Amen.

Ritwik embraced dissipation and life's vivacities with equal—if equally self-destructive, self-enhancing—fervour; he valued life as much as he did not give a damn. He pulled fantasies and fears and dreams and sorrows close, held them tight in his art till he choked the life out of them. And him. What remains, complete and incomplete, gems, rubble and remainders, abandoned and collected, is enough for numberless afterlives. As Abraham assures his 'Ritwik Daa' in a macabre visual evocation,

When the seventh seal is opened
I will use my camera as my gun
and I am sure the echo of the sound
will reverberate in your bones,
and feed back to me for my inspiration.

One is taken back to the lovers in Ritwik's stories who left, or died, or killed their beloveds to freezeframe an instant of perfection. The echo of that abandonment, or death, reverberates. The rest, lives.

Brinda Bose is professor at the Centre for English Studies, Jawaharlal Nehru University. She writes on modernist literature, art and cinema, gender/sexualities and humanities in the university, and translates Bengali poetry. She is currently editing a two-volume collection on avant-garde aesthetics in India.

Notes

1. All translations in this essay, from Ritwik Ghatak's Bangla, are mine. This poem, in Ritwik's handwriting with his signature, was reportedly found in a scrap shop by S.M.M. Ausaja among Pandit Ravi Shankar's papers. From the *Facebook* page 'The Ritwik Ghatak Experience', https://www.facebook.com/photo/?fbid=2416668768432081&set=a.290662387699407, accessed 17 May 2025.
2. Ritwik Ghatak, 'A Scenario', *Rows and Rows of Fences: Ritwik Ghatak on Cinema*, Seagull Books, 2000, p. 103. (Published originally in *Drishya*, no.18, July 1974).
3. Paul Mann, *Masocriticism*, SUNY Press, 1999, p. 1.
4. Ritwik Ghatak, (translated by Rani Ray), *Ritwik Ghatak: Stories*, Niyogi Books, 2018, p. 11.
5. Ritwik Ghatak, Interview, Reprinted in *Chitrabikshan*, January–April, 1976, p. 65.
6. Mann, *Masocriticism*, pp. 3–4.
7. Ritwik Ghatak, *Ritwik Ghataker Golpo*, (Bengali), Dey's Publishing, 2022 reprint, p. 47.
8. Ibid., p. 48.
9. Ibid., pp. 48–49.
10. Ibid., p. 49.
11. Ibid., p. 120.
12. Ibid., p. 122.
13. Ibid., p. 125.
14. Ritwik Ghatak, 'Manush' (lit. People), poem, *Prothomoto* (little magazine, editor Samar Chanda), Year 5, Issue 7, Sept–Oct 1987.

A testament of youth

MANISHITA DASS

I first saw *Komal Gandhar* with a childhood friend at Nandan, the state-run art theatre complex in pre-liberalisation, pre-internet Calcutta, in the late 1980s, either in our last year in high school or first year in college. All we knew about the film was that it focused on the travails of a leftist theatre group and had been read as an allegorical commentary on the Partition and the bifurcation of Bengali culture. Having seen *Meghe Dhaka Tara* earlier, we braced ourselves for a sombre story and an emotionally wrenching, if cinematically brilliant, experience. Instead, *Komal Gandhar* had unexpected touches of humour, intermittent moments of levity and an unmistakable note of hope providing a counterpoint to the sense of loss that pulsed through the film. Despite our initial hesitation ('Are we really supposed to smile? Is this meant to be funny? Isn't this a film about the tragedy of the Partition?'), we soon found ourselves softly chuckling over the youthful irreverence and exuberance of the members of the theatre group, the comical expressions and breezy colloquialisms they adopted at times, and their often-playful interactions with each other. Our chuckles did not go down too well with some of the earnest cineastes who frequented Nandan, armed with the mandatory jholas, scruffy beards, and unsmiling seriousness; they cast pained glances at us, despondently muttering under their breath about the frivolity of youth, even though most of them were only a few years older than us.

Komal Gandhar focuses on the emotional bonds and frictions forged in the crucible of cultural activism; © NFDC – National Film Archive of India

What the disapproving dadas (whom we had christened 'the bearded brigade') missed, perhaps, is that *Komal Gandhar* is not only a film about the tragic aftermath of the Partition, or a story of 'two individuals, Bhrigu and Anasuya, and of the chasm of the past that separates them',[1] and of their yearning for a lost homeland. Nor is it only an elegy for the much-mythologised left cultural movement that emerged in the 1940s under the banners of the Indian People's Theatre Association, the cultural wing of the undivided Communist Party of India, and had a transformative impact on the young Ritwik Ghatak. The film is also a testament to youth, a paean to committed theatre, and a fond remembrance of how youthful idealism, resilience and *joie de vivre* found an outlet in making plays for the people—and created a luminous space of hope, delight and camaraderie, even in the shadow of the Partition. *Komal Gandhar* does not offer a faithful chronicle of the IPTA movement or an inquiry into its intellectual underpinnings. Instead, it translates experimental impulses from leftist theatre into film form and conveys something of the exhilarating experience of being young, idealistic and part of a creative community committed to using art and performance to fight for a better tomorrow.

The IPTA movement, a broad-based progressive coalition, was not the result of a party directive. It emerged out of the activities of several local, left-leaning cultural groups (e.g., the Youth Cultural Institute in Calcutta) that used performance to mobilise political opinion and to raise money for the victims of the Bengal Famine of 1943. Consolidating itself in the context of the CPI-led peasant and workers' movements in Bengal, Kerala and Andhra Pradesh (Telangana), the movement was sustained—up to a point—by close interactions between the IPTA activists (not all of whom were members of the CPI) and their rural and urban working-class audiences. Squads of cultural activists, mostly in their late teens and twenties, would go out to perform in villages, towns and mill areas, using agitprop theatre, songs of resistance, dance, skits, puppetry, pantomime and posters, and drawing on regionally specific, popular traditions of dramatic performance.

Ghatak was more of an engaged spectator and fellow traveller during the movement's initial phase. He credits *Nabanna* (*The Harvest*), the groundbreaking IPTA play about the famine written and staged by Bijon Bhattacharya in 1944, with changing 'the course of his life' and thinking,[2] and leading him to join the IPTA by 1947. He played a prominent role as an actor, playwright and director within the IPTA during its second phase, in the early 1950s; *Komal Gandhar* opens with the enactment of scenes from a play about refugees, titled *Dalil* (*Document*), that he wrote and staged to great acclaim at the IPTA National Conference in Bombay in 1953. However, ideological conflicts and his growing discomfort with hardening party orthodoxies soon led to his departure from the IPTA in 1954.

While the IPTA movement started disintegrating in the 1950s, its initial phase in the 1940s was characterised by a heady mix of cultural ferment, radical idealism and political fervour. Ashok Mitra (1928–2018), a leftist Bengali economist and essayist who, like Ghatak, came to study in Calcutta (one of the epicentres of the movement) in the early 1940s, remembers this period as a time poised between crisis and utopia. It was darkened by the collective trauma of war, famine and deprivation, but suffused with a sense of possibility and a sense of solidarity with 'the people'—not just of Bengal or India but people involved in struggles for decolonisation and social justice across the world: 'Calcutta, circa 1943-44 [...] it was the season of famine and epidemic, but the city was pulsing with a commitment to establishing life in the face of apocalypse. Mass mobilization was in full swing; Hitler was retreating in Europe; despite many challenges, the message of the Tebhaga movement was being spread through the villages of Bengal; the tram-workers of Calcutta, the jute mill workers of Barrackpore, the iron-foundry workers of Howrah were all learning the magic formula of proletarian solidarity [...] Thousands of young men and women were joining the movement, spreading across the countryside, following the instructions of the party to base themselves in working-class neighbourhoods [...] Think of how powerful the movement was then, riding on a tidal wave of emotions [...] how we were swept away by the waves of the left cultural movement, propelled by the Progressive Writers Association and the Indian People's Theatre Association, with the conviction that we were moving closer to our dream ...'[3]

Participants in the IPTA movement, as well as fellow travellers such as Mitra and Mrinal Sen, repeatedly recall this short-lived phase of the IPTA in Bengal and elsewhere as being successful in 'reaching the grassroots' and 'in bringing about an identification' between the activist performers and the audience.[4] Even when looking back more critically at this period, Hemango Biswas, a prominent musician, composer and IPTA stalwart, acknowledged that, despite its many 'weaknesses, contradictions, and conflicts', the IPTA nonetheless provided a mobile platform that enabled Indian artists and intellectuals to come close to 'the toiling masses' and to identify with the latter's 'causes'.[5] Biswas argued that the IPTA thus temporarily succeeded in truly becoming a 'mass medium' in the 1940s, through a fusion of the political and the cultural fronts: IPTA songs, for instance, became powerful weapons of mass mobilisation, and were amplified and popularised through 'waves of the political movement'.[6] Salil Chowdhury, the renowned composer who was Biswas's comrade in the 1940s cultural movement, also described the IPTA as an unprecedentedly broad-based and organic formation, shaped by the involvement of not just middle-class intellectuals and students but also peasants and workers. He saw the IPTA's formal experimentation as being driven by the urgency of political communication: of creating art that 'could directly communicate with the people' and speak eloquently to their experiences.[7] In other words, this was a time when, however briefly, the left cultural movement became an authentic 'mass' movement, or could have been imagined as one.

We see a fleeting glimpse of this in *Komal Gandhar* when a poor Dalit woman comes up to Bhrigu, the intense young director of the group named Niriksha, after a performance in a rural area, and tells him about her son, who had been a casualty of war and famine, like the characters in the play. She gives a visibly moved Bhrigu a medal belonging to her dead son, urging his troupe to keep performing across the country to keep alive the stories of her son and the millions of others who had lost their lives. For the most part, however, the mass audience courted by the IPTA movement or Bhrigu and his comrades remains a shadowy presence in the film, and the theatre group's links with a mass political movement are left implied. Similarly, the political turbulence coursing through the streets of post-Independence Calcutta stays largely off-screen, occasionally erupting into the soundscape through the tumult of protest marches, the chanting of slogans and the rat-a-tat of police firing in the distance. Though the film is often described as a document of the IPTA movement, it does not seem particularly interested in exploring the political backdrop and the cultural history of the movement or the ideological rifts within it, almost taking the audience's contextual knowledge as a given. In that sense, it is perhaps more of an insider film than Ghatak's other films, some of its resonances being accessible only to those with a certain kind of contextual knowledge about, and orientation towards, the left.

As the film's epigraph indicates, *Komal Gandhar* chooses to focus on the emotional bonds and frictions forged in the crucible of cultural activism: 'Theatre-crazy young men and women come together from various places, form a theatre group, and then a family within that group, knit together by affection, love, envy and jealousy. Thus, they don't have a family life in the conventional sense of the term. This film tries to depict a chapter in the history of such a family.'

The Bengali left emerges in this film not so much as a political formation as a cultural community and an extended family of choice. Having grown up within a close-knit, quasi-familial network that emerged out of the leftist movement of the 1940s–50s (in which my father was an active participant), I find *Komal Gandhar* compelling as an unconventional 'family drama' that moves kinship away from biology to affinity, from what one is to what one does or desires or aligns with. My fascination with the film, shared by many others of my generational cohort, no doubt has something to do with the access it offers us to a time and space that we never knew but that partly shaped our ways of being in the world (besides having a significant impact on the Indian cultural landscape). *Komal Gandhar* allows us to imagine springtime in a troubled land, when our parents (or grandparents), their friends, the director and the left movement itself were young and hopeful, even in the wake of calamity and in the face of daunting challenges, and not yet weighed down by the burden of history or the freight of disillusionment.

When Ghatak made the film, he was in his mid-thirties and had already been forced to leave the IPTA. The cultural movement had long since lost its unity and creative momentum. *Komal Gandhar*, however, is imbued with the youthful energies and optimism of the IPTA movement in its initial phase, though the film alludes (through the tensions between Niriksha and their rival group, Dakshinapath) to the internal strife that contributed to the IPTA's decline. The machinations and middle-class smugness of Dakshinapath only throw into relief the fresh-faced idealism of the young theatre workers affiliated with Niriksha and their dedication to the cause: Bhrigu (Abanish Bandopadhyay), with his angst, intensity and combination of gruffness and vulnerability; Anasuya (Supriya Choudhury), with her warmth, sensitivity and emotional expressiveness; Jaya (Chitra Sen), with her girlish effervescence and dancing feet; Rishi (Anil Chatterjee), with his bright eyes, bohemian air and gift for set design and lighting; the quiet Kunal (Dwiju Bhawal), who collaborates with Gagan (Bijon Bhattacharya), an older theatre enthusiast, to write a play about the Bengali political landscape that Bhrigu praises as 'the first attempt at epic theatre' after *Nabanna*; and even the somewhat sardonic Shibnath (Satindra Bhattacharya), whose love for the collective life of the theatre ultimately trumps his narrow personal interests and leads him to return to the group he had left in a huff.

Komal Gandhar repeatedly evokes an alluring vision of an artistic collective through its use of much-loved IPTA songs from the 1940s and the 1950s, sung for the film by IPTA stalwarts such as Debabrata Biswas, Preeti Bandopadhyay and Jyotirindra Moitra. These include fragments from *Nabajiboner Gaan* (*The Song of New Life*), a musical drama written and composed during the famine by Moitra (also the music director of the film) and widely performed by IPTA activists for mass audiences; '*Eso Mukto Koro Andhakarer Ei Dwar*' (Come Open the Doors of Darkness), a song that was apparently extemporised by Moitra for a meeting at the University Institute Hall in the 1940s and went on to become an anthem for leftist youth; '*Abaak Prithibi, Abaak Korley Tumi*' (You Confound Me, World) and '*Bidroho Aaj, Bidroho Charidike*' (Rebellions Everywhere), poems by the young communist poet Sukanta Bhattacharya, set to music by Salil Chowdhury. In the film, we see the members of Niriksha often singing and dancing to these moving songs of heartbreak, protest and hope in their rehearsal room, with Jaya usually leading the performance. These scenes convey something of the affective force and utopian spirit of IPTA's choral performances from the 1940s and early 1950s (often invoked in reminiscences of IPTA's agitprop practice), and their power to bind people together into an emotional and kinaesthetic community.

In crafting these scenes, Ghatak was drawing not just on his memories of working within the IPTA in the early 1950s but also on his nostalgic recollections of its heyday in the 1940s. Like his use of IPTA songs and singers, his decision to cast well-known IPTA activists from that phase in major as well as minor roles has as much—and sometimes more—to do with their iconic significance as with the demands of the narrative. Bijon Bhattacharya (as Gagan), Montu Ghosh (as Bansi), Gyanesh Mukhopadhyay (as the political worker Debu Ghosh) and the legendary singer Debabrata Biswas (in a cameo as an unnamed 'friend' of the group who appears near the end of the film, ostensibly to participate in its comeback show) bring with them traces of an embodied history of the IPTA into the film. *Komal Gandhar* thus becomes—at least for viewers like me—an affective archive of the IPTA movement: a constellation of after-images and echoes, political sentiments and unrealised possibilities, painful as well as cherished memories and feelings from different yet overlapping times, places and spaces.

Unfortunately, the contemporary reception of *Komal Gandhar* revealed more of the sectarian tendencies within the left that the film satirises than of the communitarian spirit that it celebrates. According to the singer-activist Preeti Bandopadhyay, Ghatak was 'heartbroken' by the harsh public criticisms of the film by some of his erstwhile comrades; they dismissed his work as melodramatic, overlooked the innovativeness of his film language, and veered towards ad hominem attacks.[8] To this day, rumours circulate in Calcutta about a concerted attempt by the CPI (as well as the Congress) to sabotage screenings by planting people in the audience with instructions to sob loudly at funny moments and to guffaw during serious scenes. Whether the CPI played a role or not, first-person accounts by members of the film's cast and crew confirm that the first screenings of *Komal Gandhar* in Calcutta (at Radha and Purna) were disrupted by viewers booing, swearing and throwing shoes or stones at the screen, vandalising the theatres and loudly making derisive comments; for instance, Abanish Bandopadhyay reports jeers about Bhrigu lacking a comb with which to tame the unruly locks flopping over his eyes. Abanish and Satindra recall lying low for a few days, for fear of facing the ire of the public on the streets.[9] Though a public plea by luminaries such as Bishnu Dey and Uday Shankar (who had seen and liked the film) persuaded distributors and theatre owners from immediately cancelling all screenings, it ran for barely three weeks and was a resounding flop, unlike Ghatak's previous film, *Meghe Dhaka Tara*.

The film's dismal reception dealt a huge financial blow to Ghatak, who had invested his own savings in the film. According to some of his associates, it also marked the beginning of his gradual descent into frustration and alcoholism. However, Ghatak himself reacted with a characteristic show of insouciance by repeatedly asserting, 'My audience has flopped, not my film.'[10] Chitra Sen recalls him reassuring her after a disastrous first show at Purna, 'Mark my words, viewers will be praising my film thirty years later.'[11] True to his ironic predictions, the critical reputation of the film and Ghatak's work has soared in India and abroad in the decades since its release and especially since his untimely death in 1976. Ghatak would no doubt have chuckled over the hushed reverence expected of viewers at the house-full show at Nandan where I first saw *Komal Gandhar*.

That first encounter with the film definitely played a role in sparking my interest in the cultural history and memory of the IPTA movement, which would later become a major focus of my academic research and writing. Over the years, the film has also become inextricably tangled in my mind with Ghatak's last testament to what he described as his 'troubled times': the explicitly autobiographical *Jukti, Tokko aar Goppo*, in which he casts himself as a 'frustrated, alcoholic intellectual' trying to articulate his politics of dissent and artistic credo against the volatile political backdrop of contemporary West Bengal. Every time I see Ghatak's face in this film, ravaged by illness, alcoholism and his anguish over 'a world on fire', I am reminded of the youthful energies of *Komal Gandhar*. And of the haunting echo of the future in Bhrigu's recollection of what his father, a man broken by the Partition, had said on his deathbed: 'I had begun my life with such a limpid rhythm—should it have ended like this?' ('*Jeeban-ta shuru korechhilam ki nirmal chhondey—ei bhabey shesh hoye jawa ta ki uchit?*')

Manishita Dass is a reader in Film & Global Media at Royal Holloway, University of London. Her publications include Outside the Lettered City: Cinema, Modernity, and the Public Sphere in Late Colonial India *(OUP, 2016) and* The Cloud-Capped Star *(BFI Film Classics Series, Bloomsbury, 2020). She is writing a book about the cinematic afterlives of the IPTA movement.*

Notes

1 Ashish Rajadhyaksha, *Ritwik Ghatak: A Return to the Epic*, Screen Unit, 1982, p. 83.
2. Interview, *Chitrabeekshan*, August–September 1973, Reprinted in Shibaditya Dasgupta & Sandipan Bhattacharya (eds.), *Sakkhat Ritwik*, Deepayan, Kolkata, 2000, p. 59. All translations from Bengali sources in this essay are mine, unless otherwise noted.
3. Ashok Mitra, 'Ekti Premer Galpo' (A Love Story), in *Kobita Thekey Michhiley* (*From Poetry to Protest Marches*), Ananda Publishers, Kolkata, 2005.
4. Anuradha Roy, *Cultural Communism in Bengal, 1936-1952*, Primus Books, Delhi, 2014, p. 250.
5. Hemango Biswas, 'Gana Natyo Andolaney Amar Gaan' (My Songs in the People's Theatre Movement) in Arjun Goswami (ed.), *Uttal Shaat-Sottor: Rajneeti, Samaj o Sanskriti* (*The Turbulent 1960s-1970s: Politics, Society, and Culture*), Chayanika, Kolkata, 2006, p. 94.
6. Ibid., p. 91.

7. Salil Chowdhury, 'Nijer Katha' (My Story, interview by Kalpana Biswas, originally published in *Kalpurush*: Summer/Monsoon 1980), in Goswami, ed. *Uttal Shaat-Sottor*, pp. 100–102.
8. Quoted in Surama Ghatak, *Padma Thekey Titas/From Padma to Titas*, Anustup Prakashan, Kolkata, 2010, 2nd ed., pp. 61–62.
9. See *Chitrabhash*, February 2013 (Ritwik Ghatak and *Komal Gandhar* Special Issue).
10. Niharkanti Nag, 'Sei Komal Gandharer Katha' (About *Komal Gandhar*), *Chitrabhash*, February 2013, p. 140.
11. Chitra Sen, 'Ritwik Ghatak, Komal Gandhar ebong Ami' (Ritwik Ghatak, *Komal Gandhar* and I), *Chitrabhash*, February 2013, p. 129.

Ritwik Ghatak and relational virtue

ANANDA CHAKRAVARTI

Introduction

In an age where computer algorithms increasingly fragment our attention, Ritwik Ghatak compels us to confront an enduring question: what does it mean to live well with others? His cinema returns us to relational consciousness, revealing the persistent human capacity for care and ethical action even amidst disintegrating social conditions.

As with Rabindranath Tagore's *Raktakarabi* (*Red Oleanders*), Ghatak presents virtue as a form of resistance, something that goes against the grain of social decay. His protagonists are often misaligned with the societies they inhabit because they refuse to abandon human relational values—kindness, connection, love, decency. His cinema stirs us not because it rewards moral clarity, but because it exposes the cost of its abandonment. Born of twentieth-century dislocation, Ghatak's vision speaks directly to our own challenges shaped by factors such as accelerating geopolitical shifts and erosion of communal ties in urban, digital life.

His films do not merely preserve cultural memory; they reanimate moral imagination. His work transcends nostalgia, instead presenting ethical frameworks for the unfinished world.

Ghatak was a film-maker deeply attuned to the philosophical crises of his time. The trauma of the Bengal partition formed the emotional and symbolic ground of much of his work. Yet, for Ghatak, the Partition

The memorable and extended boat race scene in *Titas Ekti Nodir Naam*, which took many days to shoot

was not only a historical event. It became a metaphor for existential displacement, for the rupture between ethical traditions and lived reality.

Seen in this light, Ghatak is not merely an activist film-maker but a cinematic philosopher. Far from preaching, his films provoke thought. They explore human flourishing through relationship, sacrifice and care in a world that no longer honours these values.

Ghatak saw himself in deep continuity with Tagore—not only as a creative influence but as a philosophical precursor. In an interview, Ghatak expressed the connection: 'I cannot speak without Tagore … That man has culled all my feelings long before my birth. He has understood what I am and put it all in words. I read him and I find that all has been said, and I have nothing new to say.'[1] Yet, Ghatak translated Tagore's philosophy of spiritual humanism into cinematic language, using film to both reflect the world as well as infuse it with moral possibility.

In his cinema, the family becomes a moral field of action, a kshetra in which care, duty and sacrifice unfold. Like Tagore, Ghatak believed that flourishing is relational, not individual. His characters live out ethical values not as abstract ideals, but as responses to the real and fractured conditions of their time.

Ghatak's work speaks beyond its immediate context. It is my view that his work resonates unmistakably with the spirit of world philosophy, defined by ethicist Michael Slote as the development of perspectives '[making] use of two or more autochthonous traditions … to argue for ideas and perspectives that cannot be found within any single one of those traditions'.[2]

Crisis of Modernity and the Family

Modernity has not only changed how we live, but how we understand ourselves. Technology, capital and political fragmentation have destabilised meaning. Many experience freedom not as liberation, but as detachment. This disorientation is starkly felt in the aftermath of the 1947 Bengal partition, which tore apart kinship networks and left behind a legacy of mass psychological estrangement.

For Ghatak, the Partition was more than an event. It became a symbol of humanity's rootlessness in the present age. His films treat Partition as both metaphor and lived reality. In *Meghe Dhaka Tara* and *Subarnarekha*, the personal dislocations of his characters mirror a broader spiritual desolation. Yet, unlike Sartrean despair or classical fatalism rooted in Greek tragedy, Ghatak's cinema resists nihilism. This resistance is not an intellectual stance but a natural expression of his Indic civilisational rootedness—just as it was for Tagore. His characters may suffer, but their suffering is embedded in a worldview that never fully severs the thread of meaning, duty or becoming.

So this is not tragedy in the Western sense. As in the *Nāṭyaśāstra*, Ghatak's cinema offers grief as a path to reflection, rather than an endpoint of devastation. Even amid apparent collapse, the presence of ananda endures, sometimes hidden, but never extinguished. Like a cloud-capped star.

Against prevailing theories that frame the family as oppressive or obsolete, Ghatak reclaims it as morally significant. Despite being fractured, his families remain sites where *care* can take form. The family stands as a last bastion of relational virtue, where lifting and holding one another up still matters.

Tagore and the Assertion of Virtue

Ghatak's portrayal of virtue asserted in a world unravelling finds a powerful antecedent in Tagore's *Raktakarabi*. In that play, Nandini defies a faceless, extractive industrial empire through presence, clarity and love. Her resistance rests on an unshakable affirmation of human dignity, even in a society built on control and material accumulation. She does not escape the world—she insists on entering it truthfully. What Sitansu S. Chakravarti calls 'the inner urge that sustains our very existence' continues to press forward, even when the world turns away.[3]

Ghatak channels this same ethical energy through characters like *Meghe Dhaka Tara*'s Nita, who endures, gives and ultimately breaks—yet never stops caring. Her posture is one of quiet defiance, rather than resignation. She enacts virtue by embodying it: through her relationships, her presence and her unwavering capacity for care. Her suffering is not a sign of weakness; it is the medium through which moral intention is revealed. The world may not know how to receive her, yet that does not diminish what she gives.

This same outward-reaching, unwavering intentionality grounds the choices of Ghatak's heroines. Their truth does not await recognition. It asserts itself through the steady work of holding, protecting and continuing. Their virtue is a remembering: of what matters, and of the moral structure a disoriented world has forgotten how to see.

Virtue, Sentiment and the Moral Texture of Ghatak's Cinema

Beyond merely depicting suffering, Ghatak's cinema offers a moral vision drawn from the emotional and cultural fabric of a world fading quickly into oblivion. The care his characters express—steady, persistent, often unreciprocated—is not symbolic. It is deeply rooted in the culture Ghatak inhabited, loved and mourned. Even as Partition, industrialisation and modern detachment tore that world apart, Ghatak's films become a means of keeping its lifeblood in motion. Even in tragedy, care does not wither. It endures with steadfast clarity.

Rather than acting according to doctrine, his heroines are guided by an intuitive sense of dignity, responsibility and love. As Michael Slote writes, in the sentimentalist tradition, empathy is the foundation of moral life, rather than simply an accessory to it.[4] Similarly, in Ghatak's cinema, the orientation of familial love is not a theoretical position. His characters embody virtue, assert it and protect it with all they have. Ghatak reclaims the family as the place where virtue survives because relation endures—moving beyond notions of ideal, duty or obligation.

There is a clear connection here to traditional Indian ethical thinking. As Sitansu S. Chakravarti shows, the concept of truth is not singular but layered: 'satya' refers to factual truth, while 'ṛta' refers to truth as value, leading to existential becoming.[5] The sentiment at the heart of Ghatak's cinema—his emotional world, his aesthetic choices, his rasa—is ethical. It attunes his characters, and his viewers, to ṛta: truth not just as what is, but what ought to be. Ghatak's heroines live this truth; they do not merely state it. Their virtue is a reaching out, a remembering of moral order in a world that has forgotten how to see it.

Flourishing in the Face of Collapse

Human flourishing, as Rosalind Hursthouse reminds us, is not reducible to happiness or success. It is about living rightly, developing character and exercising judgement with moral clarity in concrete situations.[6] In Ghatak's cinema, the world is often already broken. His characters rarely find peace. Yet they persist. They show care in the everyday sense—looking after others, shouldering burdens, refusing to turn away. Their dignity isn't symbolic; it's practised.

It is often noted that Ghatak's films, while rarely redemptive in any conventional sense, retain a trace of hope. He urges his audience to see flourishing as orientation—an aspirational posture of character—rather than as an attainment. In *Sadhana*, Tagore writes of the soul's realisation as attunement to the infinite through relation.[7] Ghatak, too, seeks this attunement. His cinema does not simply depict suffering; it enlarges the capacity to meet it. The viewer is not a passive observer, but a participant in Ghatak's ethical imagination. They are drawn in, asked to feel with those who endure, and through that shared recognition, begin to become more fully human.

This orientation towards virtue as relational and context-sensitive also finds deep roots in Indian traditions, where flourishing is inseparable from duty (dharma) and moral order (ṛta).[8]

A Synthesis of World Philosophy

Drawing together Slote's ethics of care, Hursthouse's vision of flourishing, Tagore's spiritual humanism and Chakravarti's framework of dharma, ṛta, and satya, we can see Ghatak as offering a cinematic expression of world philosophy. In his storytelling, virtue is not presented as heroic. Rather, it is inherently relational. It emerges between people, in loss, in sacrifice, in the refusal to abandon love.

This vision resonates with, but also expands upon, Martin Heidegger's warning in *The Question Concerning Technology*: that modern humanity increasingly views the world as something to use rather than to dwell within. Heidegger argues that technology is not simply a tool, but a way of revealing, a mode that renders the world into Bestand, or 'standing-reserve': a stockpile of resources to be used, optimised or discarded.[9] As Heidegger diagnoses estrangement, Ghatak enacts a moral response. His cinema restores presence through the tangible power of human relation. In *Ajantrik*, for example, a battered old car is treated not simply as a tool, but as a living companion, imbued with personality and pathos.

Offering an alternative to prevailing Western philosophical stances, Ghatak's characters present compelling propositions. Their virtue is profoundly rooted in care, connection and memory. Their stance is not one of nostalgia; instead, it is immersed in ananda—the innate, existential joy that flows outward through relationships, even in times of suffering.

While European existentialists respond to modernity by asserting individual freedom in the face of absurdity, Ghatak offers another path. His films do not celebrate rebellion as an end in itself, but rather the possibility of becoming through relation. Nita's and Sita's sacrifices stem from profound moral clarity, as opposed to resignation. His work is neither declaration nor detached observation—it serves as an invitation to the viewer to be drawn in to the realm of care.

In Ghatak's moral imagination, virtue is a form of remembrance, of what matters, of who we are, of the truths (satya) and cosmic order (ṛta) that still flicker beneath social breakdown, and of dharma: the orientation towards right action, even when the world no longer provides clear direction. As Chakravarti writes, these are not fixed doctrines, but a lived framework for ethical becoming.[10]

Case Study 1: *Meghe Dhaka Tara*

Meghe Dhaka Tara offers one of Indian cinema's most unflinching portraits of moral endurance. Nita, the protagonist, bears the emotional and economic weight of a family displaced by the Partition. She does so without complaint. Her iconic line to her brother Shankar, 'Dada, I want to live', is striking because it emerges from someone who has lived entirely for others and only now, at the edge of her life, dares to assert her will. It represents clarity rather than defiance: the recognition that her life was never marginal, but central, the vessel within which the lives of others were held.

This moment does not negate her care; it reveals its cost. Ghatak does not reduce her to a symbol. He allows us to see the full texture of her humanity: duty, longing, resentment and love. Nita is not punished for weakness. She is punished for being good in a world that no longer knows how to receive goodness.

In the final scene, Shankar sees the slippers of a woman on the road tearing, a visual echo of an earlier moment involving Nita. The repetition is deliberate: a masterstroke of cinematic memory. In that instant, Nita is everywhere. Shankar's reaction—head in hands, overcome—is more than grief. It is recognition. And through that recognition, a transformation begins: first his own, and more importantly, one already underway in the viewer. This is what Ghatak meant when he called cinema a weapon. His films lay bare the ethical contradiction of a world that breaks those who care most.

Through Nita, Ghatak dramatises virtue not as heroic abstraction, but as moral clarity enacted in a society that has lost its way. His cinema becomes the space where satya and ṛta intersect—where truth is not merely spoken, but lived through those the world has forgotten how to honour. In this, Ghatak sketches a uniquely Indian existentialism: not grounded in despair, but in the fragile possibility of becoming through relation.

The image of the woman with the torn slipper becomes a stand-in for Nita, and for all those whose care has gone unseen. In that moment, we are reminded: we are all Nita. The individual expands into the archetypal. Recognition becomes revelation.

Case Study 2: *Subarnarekha*

If *Meghe Dhaka Tara* is a portrait of sacrificial endurance, *Subarnarekha* is a meditation on moral blindness: the failure of those who mean well, rather than the cruelty of villains. The film centres on Iswar, a man trying to raise his sister Sita in the wake of the Partition. Seeking stability through respectability, Iswar becomes ensnared by inherited anxieties—about status, propriety and control—that ultimately blind him to Sita's reality. His choices, made in the name of duty, lead to estrangement and collapse instead of protection.

When Sita flees an arranged marriage to be with a man socially excluded by Iswar's standards, the brother's inability to recognise her agency becomes final. Through a slow erosion of trust, she is pushed to the margins of society. Iswar, devastated by the consequences of his own rigidity, fails a suicide attempt and escapes to the city, emotionally hollow and morally adrift.

There, in one of the film's most enigmatic sequences, he drinks with his old friend Haraprasad. The two had once shared a vision of the world, but now sit together in a haze of resignation. Haraprasad, a learned Sanskrit scholar, speaks in riddles—part prophecy, part parody of what has been lost. As the night unravels, he begins to recite from the Upanishads: the *Bṛhadāraṇyaka Upaniṣad*, where Maitreyi asks Yājñavalkya, 'What should I do with that by which I do not become immortal?'; then the Īśā *Upaniṣad*, calling forth *tena tyaktena bhunjīthāḥ*, 'enjoy through renunciation'. He invokes from the *Kaṭhopaniṣad* the story of Nachiketa, the boy who turned away from the pleasures offered by Yama, the Lord of Death, to pursue knowledge of the eternal. But Haraprasad turns it on its head: 'Nachiketa was a fool. I too am a fool.' Haraprasad aligns himself with Nachiketa not as a seeker of truth, but as someone who has failed to heed its call. In calling them both fools, he confronts his own estrangement from the very wisdom he once upheld.

The absurdity is not in the texts; rather it is in the distance between their truth and the world that surrounds them. Many interpret Haraprasad's drunken monologue as comic relief; it is in fact a philosophical reckoning. He becomes the film's cosmic conscience, voicing a metaphysical awareness that flickers even in collapse. The tradition he channels does not arrive with certainty. It trembles between obscurity and challenge. It asks whether, in a world that has forgotten how to hear, the echo of value can still be felt.

And yet, in the film's final gesture, a different kind of continuity begins. Iswar, having lost everything—his sister, his ideals, his moral bearings—takes Sita's orphaned child by the hand and walks towards a new home. The act is uncertain and unresolved. But it affirms that ṛta—the moral thread binding the world together—can endure, its strength found in relation, not through doctrine.

Reflection

I write this on the occasion of Ritwik Ghatak's birth centenary. As his grand-nephew, born the year after his passing, I never knew him. But I grew up with his presence. I offer these reflections as a fresh perspective on Ghatak's enduring philosophical vision.

Ghatak's characters are more than just victims of a disintegrating world. They are responses to it. In a time increasingly shaped by technological enframing, reductionist thinking and civilisational drift, figures like Nita and Sita embody a different truth: that care, sacrifice and relationship still matter. Though their virtue is not rewarded—it is barely even recognised—it is not erased. It lingers: transmitted in a child's hand, in a torn slipper, in a voice reciting ancient parables to no one in particular.

For Ghatak, the tension between straying and staying—losing one's way yet remaining connected to something deeper—unfolds at every level: individual, familial, societal and civilisational. We may drift, splinter, forget. But the moral bearings drawn from tradition are not lost; they remain latent, awaiting recovery. Ghatak's work insists that even when satya—truth as fact—breaks down, ṛta—truth as moral order—can still be revealed. While not always visible, it can be shown. That is the charge of the artist, the philosopher, the film-maker: to awaken what remains *in potentia* beneath the surface.

Ghatak's films belong to the future as much as to the past. This is a humble contribution to what I hope will be the beginning of the next hundred years of reflection on Ghatak's work—across disciplines, traditions and borders.

Ananda Chakravarti completed his undergraduate studies in political science and mass communication at York University, Toronto. He has over twenty

years of international management experience, currently specialising in business development with a Big Four accounting firm. Chakravarti was an editor of the book, Traditional Indian Virtue Ethics for Today: An East-West Dialogue *(Palgrave Macmillan, 2024). He is secretary, International Society of World Philosophy (ISWP), located at Massey College, University of Toronto.*

Notes

1. Dasgupta and Bhattacharya, p. 110.
2. Chakravarti et al., 2024, p. vii.
3. Chakravarti, 2004.
4. Slote, p. 16.
5. Chakravarti et al., 2024, p. 297.
6. Hursthouse, p. 28.
7. Tagore, p. 27.
8. Chakravarti et al., p. 297.
9. Heidegger, p. 17.
10. Chakravarti et al., p. 2.

Bibliography

1. Sitansu S. Chakravarti, Amita Chatterjee, Ananda Chakravarti and Lisa Widdison (eds), *Traditional Indian Virtue Ethics for Today: An East-West Dialogue*, Palgrave Macmillan, 2024.
2. Sitansu S. Chakravarti, *Tagore's Rakta-Karabi or Red Oleanders*, Toronto Bengali Drama Group, 2004.
3. Ritwik Ghatak, 'Cinema and I', in Banerjee, S. (ed.), *Rows and Rows of Fences: Ritwik Ghatak on Cinema*, Seagull Books, 2001.
4. Ritwik Ghatak, 'I Am Only Recording the Great Changes' (interview, 1976), in Sibaditya Dasgupta and Sandipan Bhattacharya (eds), *Ritwik Ghatak: Face to Face*, Cine Central, 2003.
5. Martin Heidegger (tr. William Lovitt), *The Question Concerning Technology and Other Essays*, Harper & Row, 1977.
6. Rosalind Hursthouse, *On Virtue Ethics*, Oxford University Press, 1999.
7. Michael Slote, *The Ethics of Care and Empathy*, Routledge, 2007.
8. Rabindranath Tagore, *Sadhana: The Realisation of Life*, Macmillan, 1913.

Ritwik Ghatak's *Calcutta* and *Nagarik* on his birth centenary

ERIN O'DONNELL

The city, or nagar, specifically Calcutta/Kolkata, is a continual preoccupation for Ritwik Ghatak. From his first film, *Nagarik*, through to his final film, *Jukti, Tokko aar Goppo*, Calcutta is utilised not only as location and character, but also as problematic repository and symbol of the dire social, economic and cultural effects engendered by the 1947 partition of India, particularly at the often-neglected site of Bengal (as opposed to Punjab).

In Ghatak's films, the metropolis of Calcutta, which is frequently constructed in terms of exile, estrangement, separation and rootlessness (but also punctuated with distinct moments of promise and possibility) is in a tense visual and aural (sounds, music and dialogue) dialectic with the omnipresent real and imagined spectre of the countryside (a relationship that is often articulated and invoked in Indian cinema, here specifically Bengal). In the mise en scène of his films, the elaboration of this relationship is repeatedly observed in terms of staging and framing components that include the use of real locations (with the recurrent incorporation of documentary footage); claustrophobic interiors (Calcutta's cramped inner city spaces) often contrasted with immense exteriors (pastoral West Bengal landscapes); transitional border areas (refugee camps, bustees and train station platforms); and closed framing

Upon seeing Ramu, the violinist stops playing with a curt, discordant twang

forms (through the implementation of high, low and irregular camera angles, and the blocking of actors in relation to each other and within the films' settings) that promote and emphasise a sense (as in sensorial) of urban dystopia, which are juxtaposed with open framing forms (through the use of wide-angle lenses and panoramic shots) that suggest and stress a sense of rural utopia. Significantly, within Ghatak's assemblage of the space of post-1947 Calcutta, his cinematic characters not only contend with the ramifications of compulsory physical displacement, but also the consequences of an evolving (often downwards) social mobility.

Let's focus briefly on Ghatak's first film, *Nagarik*, to better understand the trajectory of the director's artistic, political and often painful personal relationship with the city of Calcutta (as it was called in his lifetime) or Kolkata (as it was officially renamed in 2001). Ghatak conceived of the story, wrote the screenplay and directed the movie. It follows the post-Partition journey of an uprooted, lower-middle-class Bengali family that has been forced to move from their ancestral home, or bari, in northern Calcutta to a temporary dwelling, or basha, in the city to find work. The film was not distributed upon its completion in 1952 (and only over twenty years later, in 1977, got a limited release) due to problems with censorship—ostensibly due to the leftist politics of the work—and lack of funds. Ghatak and his partners had incurred substantial loan debt to make *Nagarik*, and the director exhausted money he had inherited upon his father's death to finish the film.

Prafulla Chakrabarti says about the political atmosphere of West Bengal and Calcutta in 1952–53: 'The problem of providing food, shelter and employment for more than 2 million refugees was nowhere near solution. The administrative machinery was cracking under the strain. And upon everything fell the ominous shadow of the refugees parading the streets, demonstrating, holding mammoth rallies and never allowing Calcutta to forget them for a moment. All these lowered the flashpoint and the stage was set for a trial of strength between the Government and the parties of the Left. Arrayed against the repressive machinery of the State stood the disaffected population, the refugees, the workers, the so-called canaille of a metropolitan city and the petty bourgeoisie ... Suddenly Calcutta erupted in July 1953. The enhancement of second-class tram fare by the Calcutta Tramways Company was *one of the little things which were happening constantly and immediately becoming something quite different*.'[1] (Italics mine.)

How then do we think about what Ghatak has to visually and aurally say about the Calcutta of the 1940s–50s as embodied, quite literally, in *Nagarik*? Additionally, how do we contemplate the further transformation of Calcutta (in political and cinematic frames and spaces) during the remainder of Ghatak's lifetime through the 1970s and up until today? In short, does the filmic construction of the city in Ghatak's first film have any relevance for contemplating contemporary twenty-first century cinematic paradigms of Kolkata, and by extension, other Indian and global metropolises?

Keeping these questions and Chakrabarti's words above in mind, this piece employs Henri Lefebvre's (and others') notions about the production of space and modernity, specifically the production of 'modern' capitalist urban space (in all of its different modalities: interior/exterior, real/imagined, corporeal/cerebral, etc.).[2] There is a critical essay in the Lefebvre collection *Writings on Cities*, titled 'The Specificity of the City', that can enhance our understanding of Ghatak's cinematic project in/on the city in this film and open up the space that *Nagarik* inhabits—from its creation in 1952 to its delayed release in 1977 to our present moment: 'The city is a *mediation* among mediations ... A text in a context so vast and ungraspable as such except by reflection. And thus the city is an *oeuvre*, closer to a work of art than to a simple material product. If there is production of the city, and social relations in the city, it is a production and reproduction of human beings by human beings, rather than a production of objects. The city has a history; it is the work of a history, that is, of clearly defined people and groups who accomplish this *oeuvre*, in historical conditions.'[3]

Lefebvrian notions of the potential of the city to be 'mediatory', 'textual', 'a work-in-process', 'humanistic' and 'historical' are found in Ghatak's *Nagarik*.

We should pause to inquire at this moment: how does one define 'the city'? In terms of the city proper—the ostensible heart, the originary core—the so-called 'inner city' and/or incorporative of the suburbs? In terms of culture, ethnicity/ties, language(s), cuisine(s) and/or the arts that constitute and emanate from a city? Critically, the city can be defined in terms of time and space. Specifically, clock time and factory space (and the inhabited spaces of dense populations who migrate to the city for work). And equally as critically, cinema can also be defined largely in terms of a certain constructedness of time and space. Significantly, the experience of the manipulated time and space in/of cinema resonates with, and is refracted through, the experience of the constructed time and space in/of the city.

Furthermore, how do we define the 'city', in this instance, of 'Calcutta'? It is important to underscore that the city of *Nagarik*, 1940s–50s Calcutta, is a dense urban nodal point of modern Indian and Bengali history. From the supposed founding of the modern city in 1690 (challenged by a Calcutta High Court ruling in 2003) by Job Charnock,[4] an administrator for the British East India Company, to the metropolis as a hub of political agitation—against the first partition of Bengal (bangabhanga) in 1905 through the second partition of Bengal (deshbhaag) in 1947 that resulted in an independent India and Pakistan and the migration of millions of primarily Hindu East Bengali refugees to the city. Furthermore, Calcutta has served as an urban platform for the growth and evolution of the Indian People's Theatre Association and as a bastion of cultural and political leftism in a myriad of productive and destructive forms.

Now for a somewhat cursory examination of Ghatak's Calcutta in his *Nagarik*, with a particular emphasis on its beginning and ending. The spine of the film is the home-seeking journey of a family that moves to a bleak, claustrophobic dwelling in the city just after Partition to find work and to attempt to create a new home. The core family consists of Ramu, the eldest son, Sita, the daughter, a younger son, a mother and a father. Ramu is played by Satindra Bhattacharya, an IPTA actor who is in Ghatak's *Komal Gandhar*, *Subarnarekha* and *Jukti, Tokko aar Goppo*, and the noted Bengali actors Probha Devi and Kali Banerjee masterfully play the mother and father respectively. Banerjee, a fellow IPTA member, is also exceptional in Ghatak's *Ajantrik* and *Bari Theke Paliye*. The extended family includes Ramu's girlfriend, Uma, who lives nearby with her younger sister and mother, and a boarder named Sagar whom Ramu's family takes in for extra money. The opening framing sequence of *Nagarik* provides the impetus for the journey, the struggle for survival of this uprooted family, which represents the similar struggle of thousands and thousands of Bengalis.

As historian Partha Chatterjee notes: 'The most dramatic change that took place in Calcutta in the years after Independence was in its demographic and territorial space. This change had far less to do with any economic processes of urbanisation than with the consequences of a political event: the partition of the province into East Pakistan and West Bengal. The flow of refugees from the eastern parts of Bengal into and around Calcutta occurred in several spurts from 1947–1971. As a result, what was previously a rural hinterland was transformed within two decades into an urban sprawl integrally linked to the core of the city.'[5]

With this quote, Chatterjee serves to locate the historical setting for the narrative of *Nagarik*, which was made in the immediate post-Partition era. The first shots of the film are of the opening credits—in handwritten Bengali and projected upon a background consisting of pages of a Bengali newspaper, glued to a wall for public perusal. With the newspaper backdrop, Ghatak is representing a critical component of the family's journey deeper into the cityspace—its entrance into the urban modernity of Calcutta. The Bengali newspaper signifies, as Chatterjee has proposed, Bengalis/Indians as 'producers' rather than 'consumers' of their 'own modernity';[6] it establishes a space from the very start of the film to investigate, to make aware, to communicate *in a/the language of/for/by a citizen, the citizenry*. At the end of the credits is a dedication to all who contributed to the making of the film—a communal, group effort, with many of the cast and crew being former or current IPTA members.

After the credits, a panoramic montage of documentary, location footage of Calcutta (similar to the panoramic montage of Bengali landscapes at the conclusion of *Komal Gandhar*) begins, with Ghatak providing the Bengali voice-over narration heard on the soundtrack: 'I know him, I have seen him', referring to the nagarik, the citizen—immediately invoking an idealised identity of belonging—to a city, to a community, to a nation, perhaps.

The omniscient narration adds a psychological and potentially political layer to the family's geographical, social, cultural and economic journey into the space of the city. Ghatak's authorial narration functions as a form of self-inscription (his first, and in his first film, in the first sequence). While the 'voice' of the extra-diegetic voice-over is evanescent and expansive in form, the image track is rooted in the local, the specific, the particular environs of Calcutta. The panoramic sequence opens with a tracking pan of an overhead tree canopy,[7] with a pan down to a very long shot of a tiny, solitary individual walking down a country road. The sequence unfolds with a series of dissolves and pans of the Hooghly river, with its riverbanks and boats and fishing nets, on the outskirts of Calcutta; next we see a dissolve to a pan of the Howrah Bridge leading into the city, with another pan from the point of view of a car going over the bridge and under its heavy iron gridwork. As we enter Calcutta's urbanscape, the narrator declares: 'Here stands the metropolis [mahanagar], where the river silently winds its way beneath iron girders.' A dissolve to a long shot pan from the opposite side of the Howrah Bridge fuses into a series of pans of Calcutta and its city life, overflowing with buildings and people, while the narrator intones: 'While alongside [the river] flows human tears and laughter; where the difficult work of one more day has ended, and the sun sets over hundreds of lakhs of worn-out souls.'

The narration resumes with 'beneath the wire-crossed sky', as a series of pans of tram wires and tram cars is seen, and concludes, 'I saw him, in the middle of the teeming crowds, a lone citizen', as a dissolve into a high crane shot reveals from a bird's-eye view, Ramu, the nagarik, waiting for a tram to pass. The crane shot is held, as we see a barefoot old woman in a plain white sari—a widow—join Ramu, and we hear her ask him to help her cross the road. He takes her hand, and they gingerly cross the street congested with trams, buses, cars, rickshaws, pushcarts and people. In this moment, the contemporary citizen is being defined for us: a bridge from the past to the present. Here, fleetingly, Ramu exhibits optimal qualities—such as awareness and engagement, reflection and action—of a citizen of the city. The character of Ramu in *Nagarik* represents the/a romantic, utopian political self of Ghatak, at the beginning of his cinematic career, before his conflicts with the Communist Party of India came to a climax, and he experienced the sustained strains and difficulties of making avant-garde films in Calcutta.

In this compact opening, we are presented with symbols of 'progress' and modernity: bridges, government buildings, tram cars, traffic congestion. These visual markers serve as the meta-context for and counterpoint to the narrative that transpires in the interior of the neighbourhood (para) and basha as the sequence moves forward. This initial framing sequence nears completion with a cut to Ramu walking down a winding alleyway, where he hears the melancholy tune of a violinist playing in the narrow dusty lane. Throughout *Nagarik*, this wistful melody is a sonic motif associated with Ramu and is heard on the soundtrack when he frequently expresses a nostalgic longing for a return to the family's boro bari ('big house'). Here, at the end of the opening sequence, is a marked shift in the visual composition and spatial feel of the film. The establishing documentary footage of the streets of Calcutta gives way to theatrically staged studio sets. A closed framing form—tight close-ups, multiple characters blocked into the frame, irregular camera angles, dramatic lighting to emphasise the darkness of the inner spaces—replaces the open framing form of the exterior shots of the city and its surroundings. The overwhelming sense conveyed is the suffocation of the characters in these constructed interior locations. Upon seeing Ramu, the violinist stops playing with a curt, discordant twang. Ramu asks him to please continue with the beautiful tune; the violinist silently holds out his hand for money, and Ramu moves on, unable to pay.

The sequence culminates with Ramu entering the dark, claustrophobic interior of his family's new basha, where sarees and sheets are hanging everywhere, producing a maze-like appearance, as if cartographic elements of chaotic Calcutta have been replicated in the space. In these small, confining quarters he encounters his mother and Sita, who is unhappily being paraded in front of a prospective bridegroom's family. Her body is discussed in objectified fragments; as she serves food to the guests, she is instructed to loosen her hair, to turn around, to walk, and to lift the bottom of her sari to display her feet and ankles. (The commodification of women is a common theme in Ghatak's work.) While Sita undergoes this humiliation, Ramu and his mother reflect on returning to their old home, as they stand in front of a wall calendar of a village scene that throughout the film serves as an obsessive, fetishistic, symbolic visual reminder of their ideal of both the past and future. Again, in *Writings on Cities*, Lefebvre's short but relevant essay, 'Town and Country', illuminates the dynamic present in this ongoing calendar motif in *Nagarik*. Here, he continues to discuss 'mediation' in the context of the negotiation(s)/relationship(s) between the urban and the rural: 'Urban life includes original mediations between town, country and nature. As the village, whose relationship with the city, in history and in actuality, is far from being well known. As are parks, gardens, channeled waters. These mediations cannot be understood as such by city dwellers without symbolisms and *representations* (ideological and imaginary) of nature and the countryside.'[8]

The sequence finally concludes with Sita's father lamenting that he could not provide her with an advanced education—'a certificate, degree means independence'—and Ramu and his father disagreeing over the likelihood of finding employment in the city. The father states with regret: 'Our Bengal was a formative Bengal; nowadays it is a Bengal of disintegration. Like an old structure, Bengal is falling to pieces.' To which Ramu replies: 'Shouldn't I try? I know I will succeed. My aspirations are not high, just a life with a little bit of happiness.'

In *Nagarik*, the city is a site of potential revolution and political awakening (the French socialist anthem '*L'Internationale*' is a musical motif on the film's soundtrack), a climate familiar to Calcutta. From his first through his last film, Ghatak perceived his cinema as a consciously constructed, committed political and artistic exercise that strove to build a dialogue with and between the past and the present. Ghatak's sense of the social spatial construction of his modern moment rotated around an exilic sentiment and a journeying impulse in *Nagarik* (and in most of his films), which incorporates utopic and dystopic elements to present an uneasy, shifting notion of the future. In 'Evaluating Utopias', Ashis Nandy postulates a possibly productive 'creative tension' in 'the gap between reality and hope' in utopic envisioning that is relevant here: 'It is a creative tension with which some persons and cultures prefer to live. The gap between reality and hope which such a vision creates becomes a source of cultural criticism and a standing condemnation of the oppression of everyday life to which we otherwise tend to get reconciled.'[9]

As the narrative of *Nagarik* progresses, the family's home-seeking journey is primarily conducted within the confines of their suffocatingly small dwelling. The stultification of their journey is symbolised by the boundedness of their urban surroundings. The family's stymied search is expressed through their words and reminiscences, which signal a tension-filled journey of nostalgic stasis. Only Ramu is shown wandering the bustling streets of Calcutta, in locations all over the city. At this point in the story, the film's architecture is composed of cramped interior staircases, courtyards and rooms in the homes of the family and their neighbours, and the inhabitants' placement and movement within these spaces, which are repeatedly shot with a compressed depth of field and lit with hard key and side lighting so that the increasing oppression of the urbanscape on the characters is palpable. In these stifling quarters, Ramu repeatedly references and is framed with the wall calendar that has a picture of a tidy rustic house on a plot of land surrounded by trees; this is the bari of his idealised future, where he wants to live with Uma. Ramu's attachment to the bucolic calendar image illustrates his naive 'imaging' of Bengali identity. The reality of his soul-crushing, dead-end search for work in the city undercuts his vision of a future that incorporates the prospect of property ownership—an index of a successful citizen of the new nation. The family's physical and psychic space is filled with images of Sita's tired, glum, hopeless face; the mother's pining reflections about their old house; and the father's pessimistic monologues about the deterioration of Bengal and the degradation of city life. Sita is not 'married off' and slaves away with her mother in taking care of the family. Ramu's optimism quickly dulls as he is unable to find work, and the family discovers that Sagar, the boarder they have taken in, is penniless and unemployed. Uma and her family fall into increasingly dire straits, with her younger sister resorting to prostitution. And finally, towards the end of the film, Ramu's father dies.

Nagarik concludes with the family uprooted once again; they are forced to move to a bustee in the city because they can't pay their rent. Before leaving, Ramu goes to retrieve his beloved calendar. As he exits with the calendar in hand, he hears a young couple talking in the alleyway; they enter their new dingy lodging, with the husband telling his wife to be patient for he will soon find a good job. Ramu has uttered these same words to his family throughout the film. He stands, transfixed, framed in the doorway with the calendar as '*L'Internationale*' comes up again on the soundtrack. A series of increasingly rapid cuts between close-ups of Ramu and the picture of the idyllic home on the calendar occurs, until suddenly he tears—with an exaggerated ripping sound on the soundtrack—the calendar in half and tosses it to the ground. The confluence of '*L'Internationale*' with the discarding of the image of Ramu's dream home symbolises his acknowledgement of the reality of the living conditions and job prospects that lie before him, and a larger comprehension of the stagnancy of the Bengali middle class and its aspirations due to political and economic forces that inhibit its social mobility. As Ghatak related in a 1967 interview when asked about *Nagarik*: 'This was the first attempt to capture the crisis in the life of middle-class [modhyobittwo] Bengalis in the post-World War II period, realistically, in art ... A young boy dreamed he would flourish in life ... He felt around the corner a lucky good turn was waiting. However, he gradually realised that no good turn was waiting for him. It is not possible in our social structure. We, the middle class, will always remain at this economic stage, we will never rise above it. The story ends with this realisation.'[10]

For the last time, Ramu walks down the narrow lane adjoining his former shabby dwelling, where he encounters the violinist who demanded money at the beginning of the film, now offering to perform for free. The violinist plays and, for the first time, resolves the tune of Ramu's theme, as the newly conscious nagarik trudges onward, with only his dhuti and sandal-covered feet visible. The roar of a lorry engine and the twang of a broken string cause the violinist to abruptly stop playing, as '*L'Internationale*' rises on the soundtrack for the final time. Framed from behind in a long shot, Ramu strides towards the end of the rain-soaked alleyway, as the voice-over narrator, Ghatak himself, concludes: 'Around here, this was Ramu's story. The life of a nagarik, in another time and place—what course will it take? Thereafter Ramu ... but that is another story.' Despite Ghatak's pessimism expressed in the interview above, in the end, *Nagarik* creates a space to conceive of the emancipatory possibility, utopian potentiality of the city, as is pointedly constructed in the film, and ultimately embodied in the moment when the character of Ramu assists the old woman across the street. This underscores that in the city, even perhaps in the Kolkata of 2025, a life-affirming crucial political space of minute, daily, unremarkable exchanges can be found, which must always be vigilantly cultivated, and are, above all, in fact, quite remarkable.

A longer version of this talk was originally given at the CinemaSpace Conference, Chao Center for Asian Studies, Rice University in November 2011. The piece has been edited for this publication.

Erin O'Donnell is associate professor of History at East Stroudsburg University, Pennsylvania and co-editor of The Epistemic Archeology of Ashish Avikunthak: Cinema and Religiosity of Everyday Life *(forthcoming, Bloomsbury Publishing, 2026) and author of* Ritwik Ghatak's Cinematic Sensibility *(forthcoming, Bloomsbury Publishing, 2027).*

Notes

1. Prafulla Chakrabarti, *The Marginal Men: The Refugees and the Left Political Syndrome in West Bengal*, Naya Udyog, Calcutta, 1999, pp. 330–31.
2. See Lefebvre's seminal *The Production of Space* (tr. Donald Nicholson-Smith), Blackwell Publishers, Oxford, 1991, specifically Chapter 2, "Social Space". Also see, *The Emancipatory City? Paradoxes and Possibilities* (ed. Loretta Lees), Sage Publications Ltd, London, 2004, and David Harvey, 'The Right to the City', *New Left Review*, 53 September–October 2008, pp. 23–40, https://newleftreview.org/issues/ii53/articles/david-harvey-the-right-to-the-city.
3. Henri Lefebvre, *Writings on Cities* (tr. and ed. Eleonore Kofman and Elizabeth Lebas), Blackwell Publishers, Oxford, 1996, p. 101.

4. Prabodh Biswas, 'Job Charnock', in *Calcutta: The Living City, Vol. I: The Past* (ed. Sukanta Chaudhuri), Oxford University Press, Oxford, 1990, pp. 6–7.
5. Partha Chatterjee, 'Political Culture in Calcutta', in *Calcutta: The Living City, Vol. II: The Present and Future* (ed. Sukanta Chaudhuri), Oxford University Press, Oxford, 1990, p. 29.
6. Partha Chatterjee, 'Our Modernity', SEPHIS/CODESRIA, Rotterdam/Dakar, 1997; originally given as the Srijnan Memorial Lecture (Calcutta, 1994).
7. This is momentarily suggestive of Akira Kurosawa's *Rashomon*, 1950, which Ghatak had the opportunity to view at the 1952 International Film Festival in Calcutta.
8. Lefebvre, *Writings on Cities*, pp. 119–20.
9. Ashis Nandy, 'Evaluating Utopias', *Traditions, Tyranny and Utopias: Essays in the Politics of Awareness*, Oxford University Press, Delhi, 1987, p. 3.
10. *Ritwik Ghatak: Face to Face: Conversations with the Master, 1962–1977* (tr. Chilka Ghosh, ed. Sandipan Bhattacharya and Sibaditya Dasgupta), CineCentral, Kolkata, 2003, p. 23; in Bengali: Ritwik Ghatak, *Calaccitra manush, ebong aro kichu* (Cinema, Man and a Little More), Dey's Publishing, Kolkata, 2007, p. 238.

Bibliography

Prabodh Biswas, 'Job Charnock', *Calcutta: The Living City, Vol. I: The Past* (ed. Sukanta Chaudhuri), Oxford University Press, Oxford, 1990.

Prafulla Chakrabarti, *The Marginal Men: The Refugees and the Left Political Syndrome in West Bengal*, Naya Udyog, Calcutta, 1999.

Partha Chatterjee, 'Our Modernity', SEPHIS/CODESRIA, Rotterdam/Dakar, 1997; originally given as the Srijnan Memorial Lecture, Calcutta, 1994.

_____'Political Culture in Calcutta', *Calcutta: The Living City, Vol. II: The Present and Future* (ed. Sukanta Chaudhuri), Oxford University Press, Oxford, 1990.

The Emancipatory City?: Paradoxes and Possibilities (ed. Loretta Lees), Sage Publications Ltd, London, 2004.

Ritwik Ghatak, *Chalachchitra, Manush, Ebong Aro Kichu*, Dey's Publishing, Kolkata, 2007.

_____dir. *Nagarik*, Film Guild, Calcutta, 1953.

Ritwik Ghatak: Face to Face: Conversations with the Master, 1962-1977 (tr. Chilka Ghosh, ed. Sandipan Bhattacharya and Sibaditya Dasgupta), CineCentral, Kolkata, 2003.

David Harvey, 'The Right to the City', *New Left Review* 53 (Sept./Oct. 2008), pp. 23–40. https://newleftreview.org/issues/ii53/articles/david-harvey-the-right-to-the-city.

Henri Lefebvre, *The Production of Space* (tr. Donald Nicholson-Smith), Blackwell Publishers, Oxford, 1991.

_____*Writings on Cities* (tr. and ed. Eleonore Kofman and Elizabeth Lebas), Blackwell Publishers, Oxford, 1996.

Ashis Nandy, 'Evaluating Utopias', *Traditions, Tyranny and Utopias: Essays in the Politics of Awareness*, Oxford University Press, Delhi, 1987.

Her mother's son: Kinship and history in Ritwik Ghatak

MOINAK BISWAS

The Citizen's Journey and the Eternal Return

Commenting on Satyajit Ray's *Apur Sansar* (*The World of Apu*, 1959), Ritwik Ghatak wrote that the film's ending 'suffers from a major misconception'.[1] Ray's film ends with Apu walking away to the horizon, towards the camera, with his son, Kajol, on his shoulders; they are set on the path to the future. However, the novel[2] ends with Apu returning to his ancestral village with his son. As the young boy stands before the ruins of their abandoned home, the place itself and its lost inhabitants—dead family members, local gods, characters from the local lore and from the Mahabharata—begin to speak to him. They announce the return of Apu in the incarnation of the boy. The return to the bosom of the ancestral village at the end of Bibhutibhushan's novel is poignant in its very refusal to follow the archetypal novelistic journey from the country to the city. It is a return of the village itself as a lost consciousness. Ray does away with this episode, and seems to offer an affirmative image of the trajectory of the citizen.[3] Ghatak's comment, made towards the end of his career, reveals more about his own art than anything else. It tells us about his approach to questions of selfhood and narrative. Ghatak expressed deep admiration for the first two films of the trilogy, *Pather Panchali* (*Song of the Little Road*, 1955) and *Aparajito* (*The Unvanquished*, 1956), but even with *Pather Panchali*, Apu's movement away from the village at the end bothered him, he found it lacking in depth, that 'the wanderer's generous melody' was absent in that ending.

The mythical power of return would fascinate Ghatak; he was not satisfied with a form that enacted the historical flow, seeking instead to turn history itself into an object of investigation. To this end, his one important task seemed to be to give expression to the sense of violation brought on by the historical transportation of his people into the scene of the contemporary nation. He could not do this by positing a wholesome tradition and past over and against modernity, a road taken by much of popular cinema since the 1970s. He would remain strangely solitary in his choices. Ray was to write of Ghatak, 'One doesn't notice any influence of other schools of film-making on his work. For him, Hollywood might not have existed at all. The occasional echo of classical Soviet school is there, but this does not prevent him from being in a class by himself.'[4] It was as much a matter of choice as of training. His cinema was 'intellectual'[5] in the sense that there was a conscious attempt to make cinema itself a tool in the search for what, rephrasing Bertolt Brecht's words, one can call a 'fighting conception of the modern'. Ghatak's solitude should be a challenge to the critic, not least because it cautions us against using his example as one of questioning modern modes from the side of tradition, as is sometimes done.[6] Let us remember that his use of popular forms of narrative and performance did not win him any popular audience in his time.

The City of Oblivion

At the end of their night-long revelry in *Subarnarekha*, the two renegades, Iswar and Haraprasad, take a taxi ride down the streets of Calcutta. Earlier, in the pub, verses from the *Upanishad* were chanted against the theme music of *La Dolce Vita* (Federico Fellini, 1960). The great spiritual delirium of the city continues to bring cultural quotes into the spectacular collage as the two drunken friends are swallowed up by the night. On the haze of streetlights passing across the screen, we hear their voices:

'Haven't seen the atom bomb.'

Shooting in progress at what became the abandoned airstrip in *Subarnarekha*; © NFDC – National Film Archive of India

'Haven't. Haven't they?'

'Never. Haven't seen the War, haven't seen the Famine, haven't seen the riots, haven't seen the Partition … Useless—that old hymn to the glory of the sun …'

Iswar will turn up at his sister's quarter as her first customer soon after this. She will slash her own throat with a kitchen knife. Ghatak names his project with fearsome accent here: remembering not to forget.

He recorded his debt to the socialist political-cultural project of the 1940s.[7] The forties was the decade of the Bengal Famine, the partition of India, Hindu–Muslim riots, Independence. And it was also the decade of the Quit India movement, the naval mutiny, peasant rebellions, thousands of strikes, barricades on the street raised by workers, students and ordinary citizens, a decade of cultural resurgence led by the IPTA.[8] He would perceive the tragedy of the decade not so much as a failure of revolution, but as oblivion for a people. He talked about the lost Bengal in a language close to the author of *Pather Panchali*, in terms of childhood, plenitude and home.[9] But the excavation of memory in his films is not so much a matter of a return to roots as it is sometimes thought to be. It is meant to bring back the moment of rupture to consciousness, a moment that the traumatised do not know how to remember. It is possible to address the question of selfhood and form in his work in connection with the project of remembrance he undertakes, keeping in mind the essential challenge that his films pose: they sound the recall, but they refuse to accept a chronology that demands submission to its logic of violence. In Ghatak's work, to come to terms with history did not mean accepting it essentially as progress, or accepting the present as the only possible outcome of its processes, which is perhaps why the outward journey from the country to the city, figured as destiny, celebrated as movement towards an envisaged future, would make him uncomfortable. His work, in film or in writing, on the other hand, does not leave any scope to lapse back into a history versus myth argument. It proposes a much more difficult course: to lay bare the irrational substratum of the present, to make history face the other at its heart, and therefore also break open the secret alliance of realism and melodrama.

As he prised open that interlock—the combination without which realism or melodrama hardly ever functions—Ghatak had to alienate himself from the trend in more than one way. Let us remember that, around the middle of the 1950s, both realism (or art film) and melodrama (or popular film) arrived at their classic formulations in Indian cinema. The new melodrama responded to the modernising impulse of the new nation more consistently. It celebrated the urban adventure, sought to figure the journey to citizenship by capturing the seduction of the city space. The new romance it formulated was in many ways a romance with modernity. There was a visible attempt to conceive a domain of the romantic couple in its autonomy from the family domain—a desire that often ended up giving rise to unstable tropes of space. In displacing historical tragedy into upheavals in kinship relations, Ghatak was following a well-worn logic of melodrama, but let us remember how in its bourgeois articulation, the contemporary melodrama was seeking a compromise between the shelter of the old family and community on the one hand, and the dream of individualism and industrial progress on the other. Close at hand was the example of Bengali melodrama that came to be known after its most successful star, Uttam Kumar. It developed a powerful form out of this compromise, and still remains the most potent articulation of the fantasy of the journey to the city for the Bengali middle class—of the individual's emergence into the historical open without having to abjure the protection of the past. Ghatak's melodramatic turn was truly scandalous; he followed the logic of the form to its end, so that by stepping into the enclosure of primal bonds, the kernel of resistance to the individual's 'development', one could produce the most acute observations of historical processes.

The challenges of history are recognised in two ways. In the first, he tries to figure history as a horizon into which the narrative must open, and from which it draws its final coherence. The best example is probably *Komal Gandhar*, a film that does not hold together unless one uses historical memory to reorder it. Of the other process, *Subarnarekha* tells us most clearly—remembrance as not simply representation of the past, but an excavation of what has passed under the cover of historical reality. The first process has been studied in some detail already.[10] I would like to make a few points here on the second aspect of his melodramatic turn.

Ghatak took one rupture in the history he witnessed as central—the partition of Bengal. As he went on extending that event into a metaphor for everything that was alienating and destructive in the experience of his community, and talked about pervasive degeneration of his country, sometimes solely in terms of it, he faced puzzlement and even incomprehension from his contemporaries. Wasn't he being obsessed with a single event? Wasn't he living in the past, cutting himself off from the contemporary? The full irony of the situation is probably now coming to light: the Partition—a joint treachery committed by the colonial power and the nationalist leadership—cost millions of lives (mainly in Punjab and Bengal, but also in other provinces as the communal riots spread) and left millions homeless,[11] but had hardly any thematic impact on film or literature. People forgot to talk about it. In the face of the silence, the history model of narration itself had to be played with; it had to be crossed with elements borrowed from traditional community-centred forms—epic, chronicle play, allegory, musical theatre. But in the face of historical denial, Ghatak would also resort to a drama where a few hapless characters would say just that 'we deny it'. These are people who howl against the rocks saying they want to live, who place negation against negation by closing the circle before violent interdictions of change. A particular kinship relation takes on an acute dimension in this drama. It works to defeat the melodrama of couple formation even as it destroys the logic of the other, pre-bourgeois melodrama: the feudal family romance.

The First Films

With the exception of *Ajantrik*, the films from the 1950s and 1960s show a compulsive engagement with the brother–sister relationship. The absence of the couple, however, connects *Ajantrik* also to the same preoccupation. Here, the two-term pre-social bond is between the hero, Bimal, and his jalopy, Jagaddal.[12] Bimal is an eccentric, a loner; the only conversation he can have is with the car and the young garage boy, Sultan. His fellow taxi drivers make fun of him: 'Is the car a woman,' they ask. Perhaps it is, but what kind of woman? In a rare moment of eloquence, Bimal tells Sultan that, in these days of hardship, the old car gets him his day's meal; it came into his life, he says, the year his mother passed away. Let us recall the sequences with the runaway bride. The moment she appears, Bimal is seized by a strange and almost comic disturbance, which is matched by the reactions of the car (it gets murderously jealous, even tries to run over the woman). After the woman, cheated and abandoned by the man she had eloped with, leaves in the train, this play of identification—the humanisation of the car, the humanism of the story—disintegrates before our eyes. Bimal tries to catch her at the next station by taking a shortcut through the hills. The car breaks down on the way, gets reduced to the 'thing', as it were, it refuses to be human anymore. Nature stands grandly aloof, watching. The very look of the camera breaks free of diegetic sources and begins to flow in from nowhere.[13]

As the hero steps into the domain of social sexuality, as the possibility of romantic couple formation is suggested, it is the realist order of the narrative that falls into crisis. Why should transition from the pre-social to social create a crisis for the realist logic? The answer might tell us about Ghatak's distance from not only familiar forms but also from the agreed-upon equations between forms and feelings. When we move into the other kinship bond that forecloses couple formation, the brother–sister bond rather than the bond with the mother, the whole question becomes much more complex, generates formidable challenges. The conflict between maternality and conjugality is simpler—after all, Indian melodrama has been negotiating a resolution of that conflict for decades—but none of us was prepared for those brothers and sisters of Ghatak to appear as exemplars of the pure couple.

Towards the end of *Nagarik*, the unemployed hero Ramu receives a promise from his beloved Uma that she will join him in the slum his family is moving into. As she makes the promise, we see a close-up of the starving Uma: her face awash with soft light, strong backlight throwing a rim of silver dust on her hair. It reminds us of the close-up of Nita in *Meghe Dhaka Tara* at the end of the duet she sings with her brother. Uma's expression of solidarity inspires Ramu to urge their tenant, Sagar, to accept his sister Sita as his partner, to be a fellow traveller in their impending journey into the night. But the Ramu–Uma relationship is dealt with briefly, almost with reluctance, in *Nagarik*. The real emotional bonding exists between Ramu and Sita, his sister. Wasting away at home as the unmarriageable daughter, Sita can laugh and become playful only in the company of her elder brother, and Ramu finds in her the friend who knows him more than anyone else, believes in him despite his repeated failure to get a job. The parents appear at times to have become calloused by the daily privations, but tenderness is preserved in the domain of interaction between the two siblings. Theatrical use of the body at climactic points, which evolves into significant sculptural and dance-like postures in the three films of the 1960s, appears in its cruder form in the film. But significantly, these gestures appear with the same intensity in the scenes between Ramu and his sister as in those between Ramu and Uma. They come at points of emotional saturation between Ramu and Sita, when the pain of one seems to pierce the other. Names are almost never without allegorical import in Ghatak's films; they are called Ram and Sita after the divine couple from the Ramayana.

The tale of a village boy's adventure in *Bari Theke Paliye* places the mother as the princess, she is the woman for whom the boy seeks the treasure in the city. However, the sister—one who is younger in age (the elder sister often figures as an extension of the mother in Indian families)—appears as part of a proto-romance in the story. The runaway Kanchan meets the little Mini in the city, is very attracted to her and dreams of taking her home to his mother. Mini's ailing mother treats Kanchan as a son, he finds a second home in Mini's house. The two children look like early incarnations of lovers, foreshadowing the young Abhiram and Sita in *Subarnarekha*. That film will also show that, in a way, it is consistent with the 'obsession' with the mother archetype in Ghatak's films that the brother and sister should form the primary basis of love.

Against the Mandate of Separation: The Three Films of the 1960s

The overvaluation of this kinship bond in the films has gone unnoticed, but it is insistent. Nita in *Meghe Dhaka Tara* fails in her relationship with Sanat, but then the relationship is something in which she hardly participates with any enthusiasm, and it does not seem to occupy her much once Sanat's betrayal is confirmed. On the other hand, she and her elder brother Shankar create an island of happiness and belonging in the turbulent waters of the refugee home. It is the secret sharing of a language that their relationship thrives on. They exchange poems and songs of Rabindranath Tagore, indulge in childish play, together they devise means to tackle the daily humiliation of the artist and the dreamer. Sanat's marriage to Nita's sister brings on a climax. Shankar will decide to leave the house after this, Nita will begin to wither away. Before the wedding, she asks Shankar to teach her a Rabindrasangeet.[14] As they sing in duet (*The night the storm broke open my doors*), Nita's body goes through an ecstatic choreography. We know it is not merely the lover's desertion that has caused this anguish, this mourning. The ecstasy joins the two figures of Shankar and Nita into a series of iconic compositions, bringing out into the open the iconic potential in the use of bodies that the film has built up. The song is thrown like a cry against the walls made of bamboo mats, moonlight trickles in as if in answer. In the climax, the musical notes give way to sounds of lashing. Let us recall the mythical allusions in the story. Nita was born of the day the goddess Jagaddhatri (Durga) is worshipped, the wailing, choric voice in the soundtrack impersonates Durga's mother Menaka, calling her back to her bosom, to her parental home in the hills. She will set out on that journey, as if abandoning the shelter on earth where no one recognised her. Shankar is another name for Shiva, Durga's husband.

Komal Gandhar is the only film in Ghatak's oeuvre where romantic love is central. The extended metaphor is that of marriage, the love triangle serves as an allegorical core elaborated into relationships between individuals, groups and places of dwelling. Ghatak captures his own autobiography as a radical theatre activist and playwright, weaves the story of his own marriage into the plot, talks about the Partition of 1947 directly for the first time, as something witnessed by his protagonists. This audacity was greeted with silence and slander. The film was booed out of the theatres, Ghatak's old colleagues turned against it. More than the obsession with Partition, at this point it was the articulation of personal experiences that alienated his audience. But that is the task that the film sets itself. A traditional marriage song sung by women works as the leitmotif; marriage and love become depersonalised through ritual enactment. In the tussle between the two rival theatre groups, Anasuya, the heroine, works as a mediator; but her crossing over to Bhrigu's group is also an anthropological act of exchange between two sides, here put into effect by woman herself. The love story, thus refracted, connects with the theme of the reunification of divided Bengal. Conjugality calls for separation from the original family and community; it is quite possible to think that *Komal Gandhar* uses the motif of marriage, paradoxically, to suggest an overcoming of the imperative of separation. Not simply the joining of two hearts, here the theme of marriage suggests the healing of the sore of separation. To mourn the separation, a new political drama is envisaged: Bhrigu (and Ghatak himself) goes back to Kalidasa's *Abhijnana Shakuntalam* to fashion the epic form he is searching for. The scenes from the play that we see centre around the heroine Shakuntala's departure for her husband's kingdom.

At the end of the film, Anasuya and Bhrigu stand close to the railway tracks, joining hands in the gesture reminiscent of the wedding ritual. The motif of the railway track is introduced in a scene early in the film, through an inspired sequence of orchestrated spaces, action and songs. During an outing, Bhrigu and Anasuya stand at the very end of the tracks in that scene; they look beyond the river Padma and reminisce about their lost homes on the other side. From what they say, they seem to share the same family, the same home and childhood. On the second outing, in the Kurseong hills, Anasuya tells Jaya, her younger teammate, about her activist mother who was killed in the communal riots. Her mother had a rare fire in her eyes, she says, and she can see that light in Bhrigu's eyes. Later, on their third excursion in Bolpur, she will hand over her most precious possession, her mother's diary, to Bhrigu, and tell him, 'You are my mother's son, I knew it the moment I saw you.'

Subarnarekha, of course, underlines the theme in some ways. Kumar Shahani has written that the film exposes a general pathology, the self-destructive, incestuous drive of a class, which is mirrored here in the relationship between Iswar and Sita.[15] What is more interesting to note in the Iswar–Sita relationship, however, is not incestuous drive, but a substance within the kinship bond that is 'more than itself', which defies social naming, pre-exists known sexual elaborations, including incest. Iswar has no woman in his life. As he tries to build a new home in the refugee colony, he has to play the father's role to the little Sita, his sister. He leaves the colony ('deserts it', as Haraprasad says) to take up a job in the desolate Chatimpur, primarily thinking of her future. Abhiram, the orphan boy he has adopted, comes along. Sita will be his sole companion in Chatimpur after Abhiram is sent off to a boarding school. It is predictable that, in the grown-up Sita, Iswar would find the reflection of their dead mother. 'How do you look so like the mother you have never seen,' he asks her. His love is not unmixed with jealousy. His distance from the adult Abhiram and his insane anger at the realisation of the latter's romantic involvement with Sita, or his madness after her elopement with him, are all explained by narrative motivation, but the pattern of reactions has another logic—of a secret accumulation of affects. Iswar will go to the city on the invitation of Haraprasad to drown himself in the 'grotesque fun' that Calcutta is, will end up at Sita's quarter as her first client, she will be destroyed once they are reunited thus. The use of coincidence disturbed his viewers, but Ghatak did not think it was much of a coincidence. So far as he was concerned, 'whichever woman he visited would have been his sister'.[16]

As the director keeps playing with his favourite low-angle shots, the impending destruction comes to be signalled through the image. Iswar draws Sita close to him, asks her how she could exactly be like the mother she has never seen. Sita leans forward, caresses his forehead and whispers in his ear that she *is* his mother. We see the two of them in an extreme low-angle shot that takes in part of the fan whirling on the ceiling. The strain on the limits of the frame begins to point to the breaching of the borders of named relations. Later, after Sita's desertion, the frame will be repeated: Iswar would try to hang himself from the hook where the fan was hanging in the earlier scene.

Sita marries the low-born Abhiram. His mother, we are briefly told, is called Kaushalya after the hero's mother in the Ramayana. The untouchable refugee Ram and Sita grow up like siblings. When they run into the abandoned airstrip, their playful figures momentarily but strongly recall Apu and Durga running into the fields in *Pather Panchali*. They do not seem to have any other playmates except for each other in this remote and profoundly quiet country. As soon as the grown-up Abhiram comes back from the town, the film offers us their love as a simple fact, as if nothing else could have been the case. If the film strives to reveal the self-destructive drives of a threatened community, then it does so in keeping with the general value that Ghatak places on such bonding in his films, its nurturing potential is also underlined. Sita, Abhiram and Iswar spend extended days of childhood at an idyllic remove from the turbulent city. Sita loses her brother when the man–woman relationship is invoked in the space of the city, which embodies the historical present.

Tales and History

Ghatak's own essays are among the best commentaries available on the films, but he shares the silence of his commentators on this particular theme. He did feel the need to invoke psychoanalytic categories to explain some of his persistent motifs, but it was Jungian theory that engaged his attention. He needed conceptual tools that would compensate for the lack of attention to questions of subjectivity and tradition in contemporary Marxist thinking, and Jung helped him think of these questions in relation to the collective experience. Given the intellectual atmosphere he belonged to, Freud would have meant too much of a retreat into the individual. One would, however, like to know how Ghatak, with his keen anthropological interests, would have responded to the critical possibilities of rethinking the family complexes beyond individual destinies or universalist claims, as insights into the social formation of subjects, as allegories of passage into the realm of social exchange.

These brothers and sisters form a two-term relation that seems to resist the Oedipal passage, and thereby also the normative historical development of the individual. The objection to the universalist claims of the Oedipus complex has often come from anthropologists; the question, however, is not to find some variant of the Oedipus structure in Indian society or in the films in question, but to see if the Oedipus metaphor can help one understand the dynamics of resistance involved here. In a memorable essay, the poet and critic A.K. Ramanujan showed how the Oedipus tale is part of the folklore repertoire in India, but is almost always told from the point of view of the mother. Desire is directed from her side towards the son, and most often mothers narrate the story to the daughter.[17] Poetic articulations of the tales show how the gap between laws of desire and laws of the family evolve into creative consciousness in the culture. In one such tale, the woman discovers she has married her son after she gives birth to a son by him; before she hangs herself by its swaddling clothes, she puts the baby to sleep singing a lullaby.

> Sleep
> O son
> O grandson
> O brother to my husband
> Sleep, O sleep
> Sleep well.

One could imagine Sita remembering such a song before her death.

The Indian tales Ramanujan lists are surprisingly close to the Greek myth, but the very fact that most of them are mothers' stories, told by the woman, disturbs the whole Freudian theme of growth through the resolution of the Oedipal complex. The tale becomes pre-Oedipal once ordered from this perspective, in the sense that it tells of resistance to the insertion of the third term into the two-term bond that brings on the moment of the complex.[18] How to find stories that would resonate with narratives already embedded in social life? One could try to make sense of the tragic overvaluation of blood ties with such artistic problems in mind. As a storyteller, Ghatak invests the relationship with his own value and meaning, which gains resonance through the existing anthropological possibilities of ordering that relation.

As someone deeply interested in myths, Ghatak might have remembered the story of Oedipus's daughter, Antigone. This story provides the best-known example of the brother–sister relation posing resistance to the mandate of becoming a citizen. Hegel offered a famous formulation of the conflict between the two laws that arises as Antigone takes the decision of breaking the law of the city to give her brother a burial. About the relationship itself, he wrote that it is one free of transience or inequality. The sister is intuitively close to the highest form of ethical life because, as a daughter, the woman must accept resignedly the passing away of her parents; as mother and wife, she is contingent—someone else could have taken her place—and is bound by desire; in the unequal relation to her husband, moreover, she cannot 'recognise' herself in another; but in the brother, 'her recognition of herself is pure', 'the loss of the brother is therefore irreparable to the sister'.[19] These are Antigone's words from Sophocles.[20]

It has been pointed out that Antigone not only opposes the law of the family to the law of the city, but by the overvaluation of one bonding over others, she ends up violating the very economy of family relations.[21]

The allegory of the law and the state is relevant to our discussion to the extent that it illuminates the content of a resistance to the imperative of growth, to the official narrative of development in Ghatak's cinema. His contemporary Indian cinema was trying to negotiate the making of the modern Indian citizen. Ghatak's response to this obsession was to speak of the mourning that must underlie the celebration. Like Antigone, the logic of love in his films designates a space outside both family and state by positing an excess in the economy, by predating the necessary social partition of the two-term bond. The project of historical remembrance thus takes recourse in his cinema to a 'denial' of the historical separation. For a historian, this would be a dangerous thing to do, close as it is to the reactionary attitudes all too familiar to us. But, for the artist, here was a chance to extend the popular mode to the limit of genuine articulation. The melodramatic tendency of displacing the social into the domain of kinship and family is pushed beyond the limit of the triangular allegories of subject formation. The brother and sister in their love withdraw from the Symbolic, from the domain where names are fixed and destinies are already narrated. This withdrawal is meant as protest against chronicles of becoming foretold, against the genocidal victories of history.

Withdrawal from the Symbolic, from the realm of social meanings, produces silence and primal cries, inexplicable pain. How else can one explain the body in ecstasy or the voice travelling through the hills beyond the limits of the familiar world in *Meghe Dhaka Tara*? Women like Nita seem to refuse to go through the passage that would put them in contact with the outside, the adult world, because it has come as a violation of the landscape as home. The fascination with 'return' ends up in the symbolic form of a child's game here. The withdrawal can become a retrograde stand, but it is also a necessary gesture of radical negation. One of the most memorable instances of a romantic relationship, subsumed into the brother and sister bonding, is found in the protagonists of Emily Brontë's *Wuthering Heights*, Catherine and Heathcliff. Juliet Mitchell likened the retreat from the symbolic or the social order in that novel (Catherine finally says to Nelly, 'Heathcliff is me') to the discourse of the hysteric. That discourse is essential for the woman's voice to function, because there is no going back, the only way to speak is from within the regime of discourses created by capitalist patriarchy. Mitchell found an essential trait of the bourgeois novel itself in this discourse; it can produce the Mills & Boon romance, but it can also produce the truth of a *Wuthering Heights*.[22]

Ghatak never made the political films a sworn Marxist like him would be expected to make. His politics becomes emotionally so rich because, alongside the bold picturing of everyday struggles, he repeatedly captures the necessary but tragic denial by individuals to tread into the full light of the day. Nita, Anasuya or Sita are fully engaged individuals in relation to labour, daily hardships and challenges of survival. But they also seem to be unspeakably tender, almost luminous beings. The choric grocer in *Meghe Dhaka Tara* says of Nita, 'This tender girl … how can she bear such hardship?' Partly unprepared to deal with the cruelty of the world, they cling to the one who is part of their own selves. The fullness of being is gathered into this fold, the implacable sense of pain in Ghatak's cinema seems to stem from this hidden enclosure.

Such passion is not simply endorsed or negated (in fact, Nita, Sita and Iswar stand accused to some extent in the films), but is presented as material for the tragic form that neither melodrama nor realism of the day was adequate to. The formal deviations from realism that caused such misgivings about Ghatak's cinema function not in opposition to the modern mode, which the film-maker embraced, but as a critique from inside it, pointing to the cost at which such modes are assimilated into our lives.

First published in Rouge, *Issue 3, 2004. This piece has been lightly edited.*

Moinak Biswas is professor of Film Studies at Jadavpur University, Kolkata. Among his publications are Apu and After, Revisiting Ray's Cinema *(2005),* Chaplin *(1997, 2000) and* Ujan Gang Baiya *(1988, 2018). He edits the* Journal of the Moving Image *and* Kolkata 21. *He has written and co-directed the award-winning Bengali feature film* Sthaniya Sambaad *(2010) His video installation* Across the Burning Track *was commissioned for the 11th Shanghai Biennale, 2016. He has recently made the documentary,* PC: Calcutta New York Kolkata *(2025).*

Notes

1 Ritwik Ghatak, 'Ekamatra Satyajit Ray', *Chitrabhash* 18:1–2, 1984, p. 108.

2. Bibhutibhushan Bandyopadhyay, *Aparajito*, 1931.

3. A close look at the Apu trilogy as a whole, however, would reveal that Ray follows the novelist's cue more closely than Ghatak's comment would suggest. He introduces naturalist dispersal into the realist narrative and works with an incomplete separation between the individual and the natural horizon.

4. 'Foreword' to Ritwik Ghatak's *Cinema and I*, 1987, reprinted in Ritwik Ghatak, *Rows and Rows of Fences*, Seagull, Calcutta, 2000, p. ix.

5. Marie Seton was one of the first critics to use this term in her essay 'New Wave in Bengali Films' (1960), cited in Rajat Ray, 'Paschatya Samalochoker Dristite Ritwik Ghataker Chhabi,' in *Ritwik O Tnar Chhabi, Vol. 2*, Rajat Ray (ed.), Annapurna Pustak Mandir, Calcutta, 1983, pp. 112–16.

6. An example of this would be Amiya Kumar Bagchi's 'Ritwik Ghatak', *Frontier*, 7 July 1984, where he tried to read Ghatak's work in conjunction with the 'conservative' tradition of nineteenth-century Bengal, a tradition

that, in the work of the poet Iswarchandra Gupta or dramatist Dinabandhu Mitra, was more critical of the colonial rule than its liberal counterpart. The general leftist reaction to the 'traditional' aspect of Ghatak's cinema was negative, contributing to his isolation from the most likely of his patrons in the radical period of the late 1960s and early 1970s. For typical examples of such reaction, see the essays by Iraban Basu Roy and Prabrit Das Mahapatra in *Ritwik Ghatak O Tnar Chhabi, Vol 2.* The Assamese Marxist critic, Hiren Gohain, raised similar objections to Bagchi's essay cited above in *Frontier*.

7. See, for example 'Interview with Ghatak' in *Ghatak: Arguments/Stories*, ed. Ashish Rajadhyakasha and Amrit Gangar, Screen Unit, Bombay, 1987, pp. 88–89.
8. The Indian People's Theatre Association. Launched in 1943, it led a highly creative movement of politically engaged art and literature, bringing into its fold the foremost artists of the time. Ghatak and Mrinal Sen are among the direct products of the movement.
9. See his lyrical reminiscences in 'Chhabi Kora', *Chitrabikshan*, 18:1–2, 1984, p. 35.
10. The critical reappraisal of Ghatak in the 1980s stressed his experiments with narrative. The first important treatment was by Ashish Rajadhyaksha, *Ritiwk Ghatak, A Return to the Epic*, Screen Unit, Bombay, 1982 (see especially, 'Chapter Three'). Some important essays are collected in *Ghatak: Arguments/ Stories*.
11. By the end of 1947, 16 million people had lost their homes, the number of refugees in West Bengal by 1951 was 3.5 million. A conservative official estimate put the number killed in riots by 1948 at 1 million, but the actual figure is thought to be much higher.
12. 'Jagaddal' means the immoveable.
13. Which is to say that it functions like what Lacan called the gaze, a look that belongs to no one.
14. Song composed by Rabindranath Tagore.
15. 'We are made to face our self-destructive incestuous longings which are otherwise so delicately camouflaged by both our sophisticated and vulgar filmmakers', 'Violence and Responsibility' in *Ghatak: Arguments/Stories*, p 62. See also Ashish Rajadhyaksha, *Ritwik Ghatak, A Return to the Epic*, pp. 104–10.
16. In by far the best commentary available on the film, Ghatak tries to explain the 'melodramatic lapse' into coincidences in the film by drawing attention to the role played by coincidence in his 'epic' form. The central event, the

brother turning up as the sister's client, being a coincidence, everything else could be. But what kind of coincidence is it? Ghatak wrote, '(W)homever the brother might have visited would have been his sister after all.' Ghatak, tr. Moinak Biswas, 'On Subarnarekha' *Cinema Journal*, Vol. 54, No 3, Spring 2015, pp. 18–20.

17. A.K. Ramanujan, 'The Indian Oedipus' in *Oedipus, A Folklore Casebook*, ed. Lowell Edmunds and Alan Dundes, University of Wisconsin Press, Madison, 1995, pp. 238–61.
18. Sophocles's play shows how, from Jocasta's perspective, the tale is pre- or non-Oedipal, she knows there is hardly any man who has not desired his mother.
19. G.W.F. Hegel (tr. A.V. Miller, Analysis and Foreword by J.N. Findlay), *Phenomenology of Spirit*, '457', Motilal Banarasidas Publishers Pvt. Ltd, Delhi, 1998, pp. 274–75.
20. 'I would not have done the forbidden thing
    For any husband or for any son.
    For why? I could have had another husband
    And by him other sons, if one were lost;
    But, father and mother lost, where would I get
    Another brother?'

    Sophocles (tr. E.F. Watling), *Antigone, The Theban Plays*, Penguin Books, Harmondsworth, 1947, p. 150.
21. Jacques Derrida has suggested this in his *Glas* (tr. John P. Leavey, Jr,. and Richard Rand), University of Nebraska Press, Lincoln, 1986.
22. Juliet Mitchell, *Women: The Longest Revolution, Essays on Feminism, Literature and Psychoanalysis*, Virago, London, 1984, pp. 287–94.

Arguments that contradict a story: The cinema of Ritwik Ghatak

DEVDUTT TRIVEDI

Three Sanskrit words apply to the world of Ritwik Ghatak: mata, matr and maya. In his work, mata is the mother figure as measure, or matra, framing of reality that creates the falsely simulated, subjective hypnosis of maya. Such a state, according to Vedanta, is not real; the only reality or Brahman is *consciousness*. Most people define maya as the objective state of illusion, but the subjective 'telos', or purpose, of maya is an altered psychic state, so to say, possessed by the materialism (prakriti) that Others, the purusha or consciousness. This philosophical background between the subjective and objective approaches to maya creates a relationship between documentary and fiction in cinema. And one of the most expressionist, melodramatic practitioners of this form of subjective documentary via fiction: Ritwik Ghatak.

The photograph is phantasmagorical, beneath which lies a materiality. On celluloid, through Ghatak's camera, the moving photograph produces fragmentations of isolated headspace. These move in oblique ways within the frame as they are mediated by cuts that change their position. For example, the documented movement of an actor in a depth-of-field shot is different from cutting between shots with different headspaces in the same frame, thus indicating the movement between shots through cuts, or contrarily as a succession.

Ghatak's cuts deterritorialise the existence of headspace. Deterritorialisation is the process by which the signifier, namely the shot, is made nomadic. This headspace is a figuration that produces 'Grounding',[1] or the en-framing also known as 'Gestalt'. In Ghatak's cinema, consciousness arises through the Gestalt. Unconsciousness is a collective, whereas consciousness, as with Ghatak's cinema, is individual. However, the collective is a misnomer since unconsciousness is what cinema hopes to negate, namely the collective unconscious. Ghatak moves from the collective to the individual through individuation, only to expose individuality itself as the performative persona, which he then 'negates'.

In *Ajantrik*, taxi driver Bimal's fascination for his car Jagaddal as *matter-mother* is the same as the audience's fascination with cine-*ma*, 'ma' meaning mother. The moving image as the mata or Mother archetype; which becomes a spiritualism-materialism: on the one hand celluloid-matter that becomes a spiritual-projection on the screen. It must be noted that, in cinema, the Divine as *thing in itself* becomes confused with the *totality of matter*, the *noumenal*-God becomes matter-*hyle* relating back to the Mother as matter. In *Ajantrik*, Bimal's relationship with matter creates jagged sequences with Kajal, the woman he loves, viewing the car moving on the road as a montage—a development of the combination of Eisensteinian montage cells and Pudovkinian montage narrative, as used in *Menilmontant* by Dimitri Kirsanoff.

Kirsanoff improvises the cut between the camera movement, and the static camera on the tripod, as it records the close-up of the actor to create a static *decoupage* where *image and sound, supported by camera movements, create an integral flux of cinematographic chunks.*

This development was used very specifically—with deliberate tracking shots and music for distantiation and repetition of the same shot—by Alain Resnais in *Last Year at Marienbad*, which Ghatak felt was 'a secret code for neo-Fascism'.[2] Resnais subverts Schopenhauer's *absence of willing* to then deliberately *re-will* the same shot, meaning the track-in shot to the lover, which turns up twice on the edit to show a superconscious power of Will. An absence of intentionality is replaced with the doubling of intentionality, for example the same shot placed twice on the timelines, so that there is no intentionality. In this way, Resnais inverts the balance of no intentionality to signal the cinematograph as Nietzschean *Will to*

Ritwik often used extra wide-angle lens, keeping large parts of the frame empty, like here in *Subarnarekha*; © NFDC – National Film Archive of India

Power, or the Self and Other as Double: *the same shot twice*. The Will to Power is in tune with the faciality of Hitler, the symbol of fascism, that is reinforced as the passion of the Negative Christ in the films of Leni Riefenstahl.

According to legend, at the Film and Television Institute of India, Ritwik Ghatak and his prized pupil Kumar Shahani would keep watching the Lumiere brothers' *Arrival of a Train at a Station at Ciotat*[3] and hysterically laugh at what they found to be the essence of cinema: non-living matter staring at other non-living matter, or the machine looking at the machine, with the people as incidental. The Lumiere brothers' conception of cinema as documentation was followed by Georges Melies's false magic tricks; these streams eventually informed D.W. Griffith's parallel montage of actions, with the close-up of the object, usually the face, being used to make, or underline, a statement.

It was in the dialectic work of Sergei Eisenstein that the materialist view of cinema was fully developed. He used montage, or the stylised, mannerist juxtapositions of images, to mediate the shot as the cell and the entire film as a human body, with *montage as the human organ*, for example, like the heart, or the liver, or the lungs. Most notable was 'intellectual montage', where an action occurring at the climax of a film is contrasted by a set of documented moving images, the sum of them becoming a metaphor for the actions in the climax. Eisenstein pronounced this method 'intellectual montage'.

Film-makers—starting from Jean Cocteau, Jean Renoir and eventually Robert Bresson—attempted to reverse Eisenstein, so that the shot comprises entire chunks as singular and not a unity of parts, and this singularity of choreography would go into making scenes. This particular mode of stylisation, through foreground and mid-ground and counter-reflections in mirrors and such objects created a multiplicity, as in Orson Welles's *Citizen Kane*. Luis Buñuel's cinema included the unconscious irrational to enter the causal succession of events in the film, with the entry of the irrational allowing the film to reach its illogical endpoint through rationalist succession.

In contrast to Buñuel, Federico Fellini rejected his own neorealistic beginnings as a scriptwriter for Roberto Rossellini to reject cinéma vérité—a style of documentary film-making that combines improvisation with the use of the camera to highlight subjects hidden behind the obvious reality—for a phantasmagorical combination of history and fantasy that creates an *innately false* Real, and that the English dictionary calls *Felliniesque*. Fellini believed that cinema is an extension of the circus and required no literacy to be understood, there is no language or speech to be read or heard. On the other hand, his coding is more sophisticated than Hollywood in the way he creates an excess in the sexualised female as archetype, as opposed to the Mother archetype, of the collective unconscious that is visual proof of the Mother-as-Other. Ghatak is interested in this confusion between the spiritual Mother and sensuous feminine energy, which he contrasts in his film *Meghe Dhaka Tara*.

Ghatak's materiality is formalistic in so far as the conventional camera movements—such as pan, track and trolley—distance the viewer from the action before it. P. Adams Sitney, in his famous study of Ingmar Bergman's *Persona*, titled 'Kinematography and the Analytical Text',[4] refers to Bergman's deconstructivist Freudianism as beginning from and ending with the perspective of the patient. Similarly, Ghatak's subjectivity is those displaced from East Pakistan, and uncertainty about the hegemonic new name for the place they came from: Bangladesh.

In a conversation, Kumar Shahani[5] mentioned that, according to Ghatak's dictum, music was the origin of cinema, with cinema being, according to both Ghatak and Shahani, the only art form that, like music, used a higher pitch of inflection in image and sound to touch the higher realms of consciousness, while at the same time being rooted in the collective unconscious. Like the films of John Abraham later, Ghatak's films define the particular individuated quirks of characters, like Nita's slippers in *Meghe Dhaka Tara*. This is not to say that they are individualistic as they move away from a liberal capitalistic discourse to an understanding of a Whole, which is the collective-as-community.

Although Ghatak represents the archetype through character, situation and action, the expression on the actor's face documented by the camera is *an engagement in the phenomenological praxis of cinema*. According to this praxis, the subject is not a symbolised denotation of the shot as neurosis or psychosis, but a transfer in psychic states that the camera records to document the transformation of psychic states. This approach was furthered by Mani Kaul in *Uski Roti* through his study of Karl Jaspers's seminal text 'General Psychopathology',[6] which negates the Freudian symbol to create an evidence of a transformation, namely of phenomenon. Abbas Kiarostami follows Mani Kaul, except he transforms the psychic state into the symbolic nature of the Real in film through the unmediated construct commonly called documentary.

The performances in select sequences of Ghatak's trilogy and *Titas Ekti Nodir Naam* are most easily deciphered in the neurodivergent performance of Asrani in the short film *Fear*. Ghatak uses psyche and the collective irrational unconscious to pose a big question to the logical positivism of science, underlined in his sarcastic documentary *Scientists of Tomorrow*. The mythic archetypes in his feature films enter the rational causal events to allow the irrational to form a symbolised displacement from the rational of minimalism, and thereby to allow melodrama to stylise the image and fool the audiences into melodrama, which in Ghatak's case is not an affective device but a *distancing* one.

The illusion Ghatak gives is of having an intellectual grid at the centre and a contradiction of irrationalism at the periphery. The periphery is made the centre with the themes of violence, sex and death that create an expressionist melodrama where the static consciousness is at the flux of the non-self (anatman) of Gautama Buddha. Mani Kaul borrows this approach to device the Islamic 'gaze', or visual philosophy (nazar), towards the object, having cinematographer Piyush Shah not look through the viewfinder to prevent the moving shot from being appropriated through the periphery as 'wither sacral or profane'.[7] In Kaul's words, the object is sacralised through covering the profane as the blind spot, something apparent in the reverse shots in Abbas Kiarostami's films that indicate the totality of the covered or absent image.

On occasion, Ghatak does things for the sake of doing them, a maverick approach to cinematography, while creating an exhilaration of suggestive affect that is deliberately repressed in other sequences of the film, a form of suggestion through repression and over-expressionism. Kumar Shahani links to the aesthetics of suggestion or vyanjana, where the suggested mood is *repressed* until it figuratively 'bursts' and overflows. *This is not to say that the maverick sequence has no thematic layering that is already present in the scenario.* For example, he places the camera at unusual angles as in the famous sequence where Shankar steals Nita's love letter, and Ghatak places a top angle shot to remind the viewer that a shot is a whole in itself, and has a form irrespective of the storytelling—an unorthodox approach to a crucial scene in the film.

The social-religious aspect of Ghatak's cinema has to do with the resurrection of Christ as *return-to-Divine after death*. Ghatak ensures this is confused with Shiva-as-phallus to initiate the sex-death: a nod towards Freud. The socialisation of goddess worships as Bharat Mata is confused with the liberal capitalist ideology with the rotating-panning camera wedding sequences that can be confused with the Hindutva ideology. I mean to say that *the figuration of Ghatak's dialectical view of religion is such that it creates a residue more in tune with the ideology of the conservative right wing than his liberal left or communist.*

Ghatak avoids the metaphysical fetish since he views the Samkhyite dualism of Purusha and Prakriti as a dialectic, which like in Russian montage, uses opposition to move to a raised notion of consciousness, and in this way *it is not a right-wing stance*. Although he speaks of patriarchy and feminine oppression, his individuated male protagonists break from

Ghatak's grid of opposing forces, to *free up an Ubermensch*, and find their Othering in the characters named (Abhi)Ram and Sita, precisely creating the affirmative dialectic of Ram Rajya within a leftist motif.

The collective unconscious is represented in the sequences in *Ajantrik* where Bimal encounters tribals as the space that is the converse of the modernistic civilisation of the car Jagaddal: a primordial desire that is not repressed or ruptured through organisation into a striation and is a smooth formation whose possibility is low, and therefore is equivalent to a random output that is not easily rationalisable. This randomisation celebrates *counter-modernity as the authentic voice of India*. In this sense, Ghatak's approach resembles Gandhi's, although they are at either spectrum of the Dionysian and Apollonian respectively—a Gandhi that is righteous in the Apollonian sense, but has a Dionysian dance around him.

Ghatak's autobiographical metafilm *Jukti, Tokko aar Goppo* takes the idea of the theorematic in film, like in the polemical ideological films of Jean-Luc Godard and, especially, Jean-Pierre Gorin, to create an *opening out of the content* in which the character played by Ghatak, Neelkantha, faces the ultimate reality, or death, to engage contemporary political ideology in West Bengal. Once again, the confusion of narrative cinema with a cinema of consciousness which becomes a higher dimension of reality; Vittorio de Sica's neorealism gives way to the self-reflexive Brechtian shot of Ghatak pouring alcohol on the camera, hence engaging with the surface of the image and *not* its depth.

The greatest conception of Ghatak, as with Eisenstein, is the notion of the shot as representing modern civilisation through cinema; and the natural organic anti-civilisational filming that in particular Ghatak wants to return to. He does so through fragmented frames with extra wide-angled lens, keeping the mid-ground empty to show the extremes of the frame, or the whiplash soundtrack over the suffocated face of Nita, or finally, through the circular pan in which nature is distanced from itself with the problematic notion of the collective unconscious discussed above. Ghatak is wrong, since the unconscious as collective does not exist, not just in modernity, but in any order apart from feudalism, which Ghatak mounts a critique on while using the same conditions of possibility as feudalism. In this sense, Ghatak is interested in a new mannerism of the ever-same and not the ever-new that is non-mimetic of itself.

Ghatak's cinema uses the *particular*, assuming that the *universal* is a priori. It is precisely the particular through the constantly changing flux that *re-defines* the universal. Defining this universal will reveal the relationship to the particular, especially, without having to define the particular. The archetype is opposed by narrative: archetype and narrative destroy one another so that the larger form of the epic dissolves their antagonism. However, for the rest, Ghatak's cinema will continually serve as an instrument to negate Satyajit Ray's naturalism.

Devdutt Trivedi is a Film Studies lecturer and author, whose first book was CINE Interiors: The Films of Mani Kaul.

Notes

1. Martin Heidegger refers to Ground as the clearing where the sway of Dasein can evolve from Angst into the authentic Self of Being-there (Dasein).
2. *Ritwik Ghatak: Face to Face: Conversations with the Master, 1962–1977* (eds Sandīpana Bhaṭṭācārya, Siba Dasagupta, Śībāditya Dāśagupta; tr. Chilka Ghosh), Cine Central, 2003, p. 89.
3. Popular myth at FTII spread and confirmed by Kumar Shahani, that the first film is not about human beings, but a machine filming a train, another machine.
4. P. Adams Sitney, 'Kinematography and the Analytic Text: A Reading of "Persona"', *October Magazine*, Autumn 1986, pp. 112–30.
5. Conversation with Kumar Shahani at his residence at Sagar Tarang, Breach Candy, Mumbai, May 2006.
6. Karl Jaspers uses the approach of phenomenology to move from a phenomenon A to a phenomenon B and using the phenomenological apparatus to record the difference.
7. Mani Kaul, 'Approach to *Naukar Ki Kameez*', Cinemaya Dossier, https://www.scribd.com/doc/240547615/Mani-Kaul-Dossier-Cinemaya-1996 (accessed 29 July 2025).

The violence of symbols: Durga/Uma in *Meghe Dhaka Tara*

PAULOMI CHAKRABORTY

Meghe Dhaka Tara allows us to read how turning women into symbols of motherhood promotes their relentless and ruthless exploitation. The film shows how such a process violently claims women through sacrificial victimhood. Nita in *Meghe Dhaka Tara*, a refugee woman from East Bengal, provokes a critique of this process of symbol-making[1] that is part of the everyday world[2] of caste-Hindu Bengalis. Rather than explaining it as a violence of the Partition alone, the film offers a larger critique of the bhadralok class; the critique of gender violence is enmeshed with the critique of the Partition as a violent event. To Ghatak, the Partition was an unmitigated catastrophe that, among other traumatic outcomes, erased Bengal's complex history and divided its culture. The film is essentially a self-critical one: the bhadralok class so relentlessly under scrutiny is the class to which Ghatak himself belonged.[3]

Meghe Dhaka Tara critiques a tradition of gendered symbol-making from *within*. This is particularly emplotted in the film through the sacrificial role that Nita (played by Supriya Choudhury) takes on through her role as surrogate mother of her family. Sanat (played by Niranjan Ray), her former lover and now brother-in-law, tells Nita towards the end of the film that she need not continue her 'acting' (word in English) of sacrifice alone. In the British Film Institute subtitling,[4] Nita replies that 'it is not an act, it is [perhaps] penance'. Perhaps a more appropriate translation of what she says is atonement ('prayaschittwo' in the original Bengali). To the startled question from Sanat, 'Penance? What [wrongdoing have you committed],' Nita says, 'I have never protested against [any] injustice. That [indeed] is my sin.' In view of this statement, it would appear that her death at the end of the film is almost a reparation for her unquestioning fulfilment of the 'unjust' demands made of her. It is clear that the film attaches no heroism or martyrdom to the abject and gendered—'maternal'—self-sacrifice of Nita. It does not morally sanction the kind of gendered violence to which she allows herself to be subjected to.

Through the character of Nita, *Meghe Dhaka Tara* evokes perhaps the most privileged trope in Ghatak's repertoire, that of the Great Mother. This supposedly universal archetype acquires a thorough and particular form, implication and affect in his films. *Meghe Dhaka Tara* associates Nita specifically and explicitly with Durga.[5] But this is not to hail woman-power through the mother-goddess. Rather, the film emphasises the exploitative, sacrificial aspect of motherhood. Through a central allusion to the Durga myth, *Meghe Dhaka Tara* evokes not just a mother figure but a mother–daughter dichotomy. This duality is inherent in the Durga myth itself: the mother who is also a daughter. Part of the Durga lore is that, in her human avatar[6] as Uma, she is the daughter of King Dakshya and his wife Menaka, and she is the consort of Shiva. Uma is renamed Sati in her married life. Sati dies in the righteousness of a devoted wife.[7] After her death, Uma/Sati is reborn as Parvati, 'daughter of a mountain', daughter to the mountain king Himavan, a personification of the Himalayas. Shiva again marries Parvati. In a typical example of the domestication of mythic-lore, Durga stays with her husband Shiva in their heavenly abode, and visits her father's house on earth only for four days a year. Every year, Bengali Hindus worship Durga in autumn, invoking the 'mother'. Yet, because she is also imagined as a daughter of the earth, as Uma and Parvati, she is also 'our daughter'. Durga's lore in Bengali Hindu households, thus, signifies a mother–daughter duality.

It is significant that the actual character of the mother in the film (played by Gita Dey) is not a nurturing, or sacrificing, mother figure. Indeed, her aggressive desire to live and sustain her family fractures the normative ideas of Bengali motherhood within which mothers are

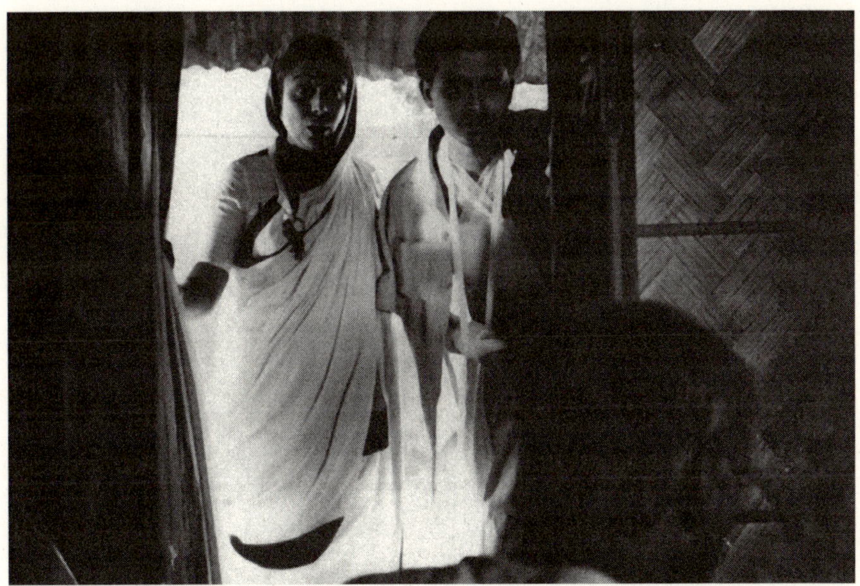

The actual character of the mother in *Meghe Dhaka Tara* (played by Gita Dey) is not a nurturing, or sacrificing, mother figure; © NFDC – National Film Archive of India

always kind, compassionate, gentle, giving, self-effacing and so on. Some commentators have read the character of the mother as a version of the goddess Kali, the fearsome goddess of destruction, and an 'other' of the nourishing Jagaddhatri/Annapurna.[8] In so constructing the mother, *Meghe Dhaka Tara* works with the good mother–bad mother dichotomy inscribed by the dominant imaginary, but imports the radical energy of the destructive mother in such a way that it fractures the discourse of love and of sacrifice that the patriarchal nationalism of the late-nineteenth century promulgated around the figure of the mother-goddess.[9] Further, by precipitating the role and the performance of motherhood on the daughter, the film inserts a third term alongside the good–bad dichotomy to form a new dichotomy, that of the mother and the daughter, thereby making explicit that normative motherhood is a constructed motherhood.

Meghe Dhaka Tara traces the 'rise' of the daughter Nita, an ordinary refugee woman, into an iconic, larger-than-life motherhood. This 'rise', as constructed in the film, is far from natural. Nita is 'framed' into motherhood through multiple registers, such as plot details, visual economy, the 'melodic' component of the melodrama and so on. At the level of plot, the film shows how sacrificial motherhood is thrust upon Nita by every member of the family. Nita is imagined through her association with Durga and Uma, as both the archetypal mother and the archetypal daughter. Nita is, we are told, born on the calendar day of Jagaddhatri Pujo. The literal meaning of Jagaddhatri—as the incarnation of Durga is named—is 'mother of the world'. Yet, Nita's girlhood is emphasised in her nickname Khuki, a word for a young girl. Her elder brother, Shankar (played by Anil Chatterjee), jocosely teases her:

> Mother, your girl is such a khuki
> She wants to catch the moon
> She can't make out anything
> She's such a khuki, mother

The rhyme, which displays a touching moment of sibling love, equally establishes her within the mother–daughter dichotomy, emphasising that she is the daughter of the house.

Visually, the film tracks the elevation of Nita into a symbol in the very opening shot of the film. *Meghe Dhaka Tara* opens with the frame of a giant tree. Nita, the protagonist, visually tiny, emerges from the corner of the frame and walks towards the camera, growing bigger as she moves closer. It is as though Nita has walked out of this giant tree. The tree is next to a lake, and she is soon framed next to the water. Both the tree and the lake clearly signify the natural plenitude, sustenance and life-giving qualities that we associate with cultural notions of motherhood. The camera establishes the insignificant ordinary refugee woman, Nita, as a tiny dot, and also that she starts to grow and become a larger-than-life force. As Ashish Rajadhyaksha writes, unlike in the standard practice in commercial melodrama, 'Where the birth of the hero or the separation of the twins is accompanied by a raging storm to indicate the cataclysmic nature of the event', the visual association with nature 'instead heighten[s] the ordinariness of Nita'.[10] Nita crosses her brother Shankar, who is practising his singing. The particular khayal he sings, '*Jai maata vilumbh taj de ma gaan guna de*' in Raga Hamsadhvani, is also suggestively an invocation of the mother goddess. Soon after, he chases her and asks for some money. The opening sequence foreshadows the process of Nita's gradual growth into this symbol of the giving mother.

Initially in the film, the shots of Nita are high-angle, the camera looking down at her, emphasising her ordinariness. However, as the film progresses, and as Nita gets more and more trapped in her role of surrogate motherhood, the shots become predominantly low-angle, the camera looking up, with Nita becoming an iconic, towering, larger-than-life, goddess-like figure. With the association already established verbally, the film starts to trace the visual connection between Nita and Durga. For example, in a famous shot that Raymond Bellour has called the most beautiful shot of the film, right after she finds out about her lover's betrayal, Nita is seen descending a set of stairs. Bellour writes in his *Rouge* piece, it 'is a very flattened shot, strongly marked by a powerful low angle'.[11] The camera captures Nita from knee up as she descends a set of stairs; these signature low-angle shots liken Nita to the towering idol of Durga as she looks to her devotees down below. The camera moves in focus, step by step, in the rhythm she descends. Eventually there is a full-face focus on Nita from chin up. In this, especially noteworthy is the framing of the actor's eyes; we see the large, exaggerated iconic eyes of Durga. Writing about a later scene, again, Rajadhyaksha has noted how the camera constructs as 'the main feature of [the icon of] Durga, her captivating, mesmeric eyes' by framing 'the whites of Supriya Choudhury's eyes in extreme close-up'.[12] When the face is framed, writes Bellour, it is by 'the camera moving only the little it takes to allow her face to be framed in an intolerable static image, in a moment of pure affection: the immobile face, the eyes always raised, one hand convulsively clasping the throat'. In the earlier shot, we can read similar camerawork noting the beginning of the process of idolisation—the symbol-making.

Although the process was anticipated earlier, compressed into the very beginning of the film, this moment of betrayal captures a very concrete move towards an elevation into symbolic motherhood. This is through a process of consecration through which the body of the woman is invested with iconic and symbolic meaning. In the close-up, when Nita clutches her throat, as if she were choking, her lips are parted, but no sound escapes her lips. She is utterly silenced. The sound that accompanies the shot is a non-diegetic sound montage, which accentuates the violence. The sound begins at the start of the shot, as Bellour describes it, 'punctuating the descent, step by step [...] very punchy shrill notes, punctuated by lacerations, like a whipping sound hissing through the air and striking a body. This continues almost to the end of the shot.' Within plot economy, too, there is no mistaking the violence of this moment: the process of consecration starts when Nita discovers her betrayal by her lover and her sister. As Nita grows into the role of motherhood, it begins to ironically strip her body of sexuality and proceeds to deprive that body of any chance of actual motherhood. This ironic juxtaposition of a constructed role of motherhood and a 'natural' one does not, I think, suggest only the violence of the former. It also makes visible, through an evocation of motherhood in its dichotomy with daughterhood, the constructedness also of the 'natural' role and its violence.

This becomes clearer with the choric lament that accompanies the scene of the marriage of Gita (played by Gita Ghatak) and Sanat that soon follows. On the one hand, in this marriage scene, there is an emphasis on the violence that Nita will never get married. Her role of supportive, surrogate motherhood to the rest of her family necessarily demands that she sacrifice her chance of marriage and motherhood, and embrace a life of enforced celibacy. Soon after Nita finds out about Sanat's betrayal, her mother broaches the topic of the marriage of her younger daughter Gita and Sanat. When the father, Taranbabu (Bijon Bhattacharya), violently protests against the idea, the mother brusquely reminds him that, had Nita married and left them, the family would have nothing to eat. On the morning of the wedding day, the mother asks Nita for her gold bangles so that she can give them to Gita. There is a blatant suggestion that Nita will never get married, and therefore she will never need those bangles. The bangles here symbolise not only any marital hopes that Nita may have harboured, but also her femininity. The symbol of motherhood that is bestowed on Nita here can indeed not be called symbolic anymore: it intervenes into the material life of the female body.

This form of non-reproductive motherhood throws into relief the exploitative labour that goes into constructing it in the first place. The 'barrenness' of Nita's life is emphasised both in the juxtaposition with the celebration of her sister's marriage and also with the celebration of Durga's image as a sign of fecundity. In a scene that soon follows, when Nita is already dying of tuberculosis, Shankar, now an established classical singer, returns home to the refugee colony for a visit. On his way back, he sings a classical song addressed to Durga, '*Laagi lagan pati sakhi sang, parama sukha ati*': On this auspicious day, you are happy with your lord and friends. The rest of the song is as follows:

Your perfumed body, your forehead
Marked with sandal paste
Doe-eyed, with sweeping lashes
May your wisdom be for your people
And [may you] be happy with your lord and friends.

The song underscores Nita's trapped existence. This is violence of one kind.

The scene also evokes the patriarchal violence of institutional marriage itself. This other kind of violence is registered when we hear fragments of a traditional folk song exposing the violence of the patriarchal marriage arrangement in which a daughter is 'given away'. It is a lament that Uma's mother Menaka sings, '*Ai go Uma, kole ai*': Come, my daughter Uma, come to my lap. The song dramatises Uma's departure from her parental home after her wedding. Let us remember that, in the myth, Uma, in her later life as Sati, will also soon be dead. The wailing lament is a wedding song, usually sung by women at the moment of the departure of a young girl after her wedding. She is to be relocated from the home of her childhood to the unknown, often unfriendly and hostile, house of her in-laws to lead a regimented, precarious life as a wife.

We do not hear the full song until a later scene that follows shortly, but the song is one that evokes Durga's daughterhood as Uma. The words of this non-diegetic choric lament sung by many female voices are as follows:

Come, my daughter Uma,
Let me garland you with flowers
You are the soul of my sad self, [you] mother deliverer
Let me bid you farewell, my daughter
You leave my home desolate [for your husband's place].
How can I endure your departure?

Other than the context of the wedding, the song also evokes the sadness on the eve of Durga's 'departure' every year after the four-day-long worship and festivities of the Durga Pujo. At the end of that period, the idol of the goddess is desecrated and sacrificed in a ritual immersion.

The mother is bid farewell to as a daughter as she departs for her marital home. The imagination that anthropomorphises the goddess also echoes the heartbreaking but banal displacement that daughters of Bengali households suffer. The annual welcome of the mother-goddess Durga is couched in the narrative of a married daughter visiting her parental home from her husband's house—the lived experience of many married daughters of Bengal, who get their annual visit to their parental home during the Durga Pujo.

The use of the song also evokes the violence of the archaic practice of Gouridaan (Gouri is another name for Durga) among caste-Hindu Bengalis, which involved the giving away of an eight-year-old girl in a marriage, often to a stranger. In an interview where he spoke of his use of old folk songs in his films—Umagiti and Gourigiti, the genre of songs of which the Uma lament is one—Ghatak rhetorically asked, 'In our society, how much space do we give to women? They are the most exploited class/ section [sreni].'[13] Rajadhyaksha cites Ghatak writing of Gouridaan in another instance: 'This created along with fear, a deep nostalgia. [...] Our folk-lores are full of this ... this is why Durga is a daughter to us; that is why autumn is a season of nostalgia for us.'[14]

Bhaskar Sarkar interprets the allusion to Gouridaan as one that 'underscores the pathos of Nita's impending separation from her family'.[15] We can agree that the central association is with Nita: the choric lament will resurface again several times in the context of Nita's impending death. However, in this moment, in a sequence which has to do with a wedding, the lament provides an associative sense of loss and violence that exceeds just Nita's death and includes the violence of the paternal giving-away of daughters that marks the gendered everyday life. It must remind us that, within patrilocal marital arrangements in Bengal, as elsewhere in South Asia and in most places in the rest of the world, women are the 'original "displaced persons".'[16] If we consider the violence of Nita never getting married as an anomaly, as a sign of a world turned ruthlessly exploitative, an out-of-the-ordinary event caused by the upheaval of the Partition, then the wedding lament connects this violence to the gendered violence of the ordinary everyday world that is not attributable to a catastrophic event alone.

Nita's association with Durga is followed through to the end, to Nita's death. The violence of the Duga myth, in its demand of sacrificial motherhood, displays the process of consecration, through which a goddess is made out of an effigy, and deconsecration, by which the effigy is not only emptied of holy signification but also sacrificed. Ira Bhaskar writes, 'A prevalent story about the genesis of Durga is the concept of Havyagni (oblation to the sacrificial fire). In the ritual of the Havan (the act of consigning mortal offerings to the sacrificial flames) is symbolised the surrender of human desires and aspirations, which are carried to the heaven in the smoke of the flames. It is believed that Durga was born out of this smoke as a transmutation of human desires, taking the form of "Jagaddhatri", the universal sustainer.'[17]

While Bhaskar writes of the sacrifice of human desires—'oblation', 'surrender of human desires'—in the creation of Durga, I am interested in interpreting the story in a manner that would attend to the oblation/ sacrifice *of the goddess herself* through the process by which she becomes the 'universal sustainer'. The goddess certainly emerges as the symbolic depository of the value of sacrifice in this myth. In addition, when we think of the process by which a goddess is made out of a lifeless clay idol for a period of the worship and the idol is sacrificed at the end, we notice the ritual sacrifice of the effigy that was the goddess for a while. Therefore, I am tempted to deliberately misread the story of Durga's genesis here, although only to a small degree, and suggest that the goddess (a daughter?) is sacrificed here in order to make her 'jagaddhatri', the mother of the universe.

The association of Nita with the Durga myth brings out the sacrificial aspect of *both* the goddess and Nita's life. This duality of the Durga myth—the mother as the daughter—captures the duality of Nita, who is at once a daughter and a (surrogate) mother; and in either role, she needs to be given away. The mythic allusion is brought to its most affective climax in a scene towards the very end of the film. By now the family is well established. Shankar is a famous singer. Gita is pregnant. Younger brother Montu (Dwiju Bhawal) has recovered from the accident he had at the factory and has earned a solid financial compensation. The mother has begun to harbour hopes that her refugee hut will soon be replaced by a two-storey concrete house. When Shankar comes back to visit, he finds out—as does the rest of the family through his discovery—about Nita's tuberculosis, which is at the very last stage. The sequence following this revelation starts with thunder and a torrential downpour, and with a joyous instrumental Malhar, the monsoon raga, playing. Nita, sleeping, wakes up to look at the rain and smiles. At that moment, in the middle of the night, the helpless, agonised, near-mad father comes to her, asking her to leave the house. He tells her, 'Go away. I've packed your things. You go away. They dream of two-storey houses! You have been "successful" [word in English in original]. You have put them on their feet, dear. [It matters little today if you are no longer there.] They pity you today. You weren't made for carrying the burden, but you had to. You are a burden yourself now. There's poison in your breath. This room is for the newborn. Go away, dear!'

In one of the shots in this sequence, the top half of her face fills the frame, her large eyes at the bottom of the screen. This shot is the reverse of the Durga-like high-angle shots we have seen earlier, marking the beginning of the process of deconsecration. At the end of her father's bid for her to leave, the 'Come to me, Uma' lament returns. The camera now stays focused on Nita, inter-cutting only once to frame the tearful, downcast face of the father. We then see Nita pick up the bundle of clothes her father brings for her, and the framed childhood picture of her and her brother, and step out into the rain. In violation of the dramatic requirement of the plot or character development, at this moment, Nita smiles. We see her full face, her open lustrous hair and her Durga-like eyes. Rajadhyaksha comments on the 'tremendous full bloodedness of this image of Nita smiling'.[18] At one level, the irony of the Uma lament is of course that, unlike in the case of Durga, Nita's father does not 'give her away' in marriage but sends her away to her death. However, in my reading, the original Uma myth, which the lament dramatises, is also equally violent, as all giving away of daughters are, even if that violence is not explicitly acknowledged in the everyday world. Ghatak's use of the Uma myth tears open its cover and exposes the violence of the original myth.

The shot ends with a close-up of Nita's rain-drenched face. One cannot call this a high-angle shot; it is rather a low-angle shot turned upside down. The visual reminder and the allusion are to the effigy of the goddess floating in the water after its ritual immersion. Then there is a quick jump to the mountains. The camera pans now, not in a smooth sweep, but in a visual reverberation, from right to left. This pan, framing the rock faces of the Himalayas in the Shillong hills, is a dizzying shot. Commenting on motion in cinema in an essay on film grammar, Ghatak writes in a 1969 essay, 'The shutter blade of the camera moves clockwise, i.e. from left to right. Hence a pan or a track from right to left, particularly done in haste, causes a distortion.'[19] Ghatak's comments here are probably the best way to explain the particularly disorienting feel to this shot.

The camera's sudden jump to the mountains visually echoes the plunge of the goddess in the custom of idol immersion in which, every year, after praying to Durga for four days, the devotees drown the idol in the holy river Ganga, or really, in the nearest significant water body they can find, caring little for environmental pollution. The idol now needs to be symbolically emptied of significance, and the ritualistic drowning of the effigy allows the goddess to return home to the Himalayas, where Durga is believed to stay with her husband for the rest of the year. In the jump from the rain to the mountains, Ghatak captures the sacrificial aspect of the idol immersion. In the film, the idol is not a painted wood-and-straw effigy, however, but a living woman. Now that Nita has given every bit she could give, she is no longer the goddess, and her body needs to be discarded.

Compared to the evocation of nature in the opening shot of the film, the giant tree and water, nature now has changed to an indifferent, 'passive' violent, bare, disorienting, cruel rock face.[20] If the earlier evocation of these symbols of nurture highlighted both the ordinariness of Nita and how she came to acquire the attributes of symbolic qualities, now the bare rock face signifies how she is no longer the repository of the symbolic values of motherhood, but a castaway effigy, emptied of symbolic significance. In terms of the plot, by now Shankar has arranged for his sister to move to a sanatorium in the Shillong hills, where she is. When he visits Nita, he seems to be carrying a hen caged in a wicker basket, presumably bought from the local market. He gives this to a nurse in the sanatorium as a gift for his sister. The symbolic signification of the cage is obvious here, but so is that of the bird inside it, which will soon be presumably killed and eaten.

Shortly after this, we see Nita for the last time, leading to another panoramic shot in the penultimate shot-sequence of the film. This shot is the key to the reading I am offering here. At the beginning of this shot, Nita is dwarfed, a mere dot on the landscape in the right-hand corner. The camera again zooms back and starts panning the landscape, but this time gently, from left to right to come to Nita. If these camera movements dwarf Nita, I argue that this is to emphasise that she is no longer the symbolic mother, the goddess, or a symbol for a force larger than life. At the end of this shot, in the middle of an innocuous, homely conversation when Shankar starts to report the happenings at home in Calcutta and how Gita's toddler 'is full of life', we hear Nita cry out: 'But I wanted to live, Brother.' She tries to control herself, but she cannot, and in desperation, she breaks into a long-drawn cry, that is part scream, part howl: 'But I really, really wanted to live … Brother, I really love to live … Brother, I will live … Brother, I will live … You just say once that I will live …' (my translation). She repeats 'I will live' several times and the cry starts to reverberate. Here, two more pan shots, one from right to left, and the other from left to right, are interspersed by a shot of the brother and the sister. The cry reverberates against the mountains and continues for a long time, but the mountains remain indifferent and unyielding.

This sequence, for which Ghatak was criticised in his own time as indulging in the worst possible kind of soppy melodrama, is key to his critique of the power of making symbols of women and the sacrificial victimhood of the individual women it claims. The individual in her, who is about to die, for whom it is too late to live, cries helplessly against the force of the symbol that has already claimed her life. This is a moment when the individual and the symbol completely separate from each other and stand face to face.[21] Indeed, the process of symbol-making is under critique by being acutely and particularly palpable in this film. There is a complete suppression, a forceful erasure of the body that is present, corporeal and labouring *for* the symbol. The stronger the symbol grows, the greater is the effacement of the body on which the symbol locates itself. Through the sensuous representative economy of cinema, the film makes perceivable exactly what is under erasure in the regime of the symbol. For instance, in the scene where the dying Nita is driven out of her home in the rain by her senile father, in a symbolic sacrifice of the mother/daughter, the camera emphasises and draws attention to what Rajadhyaksha has called the 'tremendous full bloodedness' of the present female body that is being sent to death. Indeed, the visibility of this body reminds the viewer of what is to be lost, what is to be violated, what is to be sacrificed. If *Meghe Dhaka Tara* is an allegory, a term which literally means 'speaking otherwise', where we tell one story symbolically through another, the story of the refugee woman Nita is also the story of Durga/archetypal motherhood; it shows that this symbolic motherhood consumes the body of the woman who represents it.

Ravi Vasudevan argues that, in melodramatic film language, 'personalised experience [...] relentlessly articulates itself in public expressive ways'.[22] Citing the end of Raj Kapoor's film *Awara* (1951), he writes, 'This is marked at the climax, when the drama of victimisation is given its full articulation in a speech made by the wronged protagonist that rings through the court, and declares itself part of an ensemble of victimhood.'[23] In *Awara*, the court is a site of public authority: as an arbitrator of justice and a site of secular authority of the modern State. In the language of excess in Ghatak's hands and in the post-Partition world bereft of the possibility of life for Nita, the 'wronged protagonist's speech' becomes an inchoate howl. Unlike the court in *Awara*, within the narrative world of *Meghe Dhaka Tara*, there is no higher authority in whose presence Nita can get a hearing of her story of victimhood. The indifferent mountains against which her cry reverberates in this sequence are marked by the absence of 'religious authority, the sacredness of kings, or by secular power'[24] that may otherwise mark a narrative world of melodrama. Nita's cry meets only emptiness.

The only public authority here is in the imagined spectatorship of the film text, its audience. Vasudevan points out that melodrama in Indian popular film addresses the audience in crucial ways as public rather than individuated.'[25] Ghatak did adopt this form of address if only to fracture the melodramatic form in very curious ways.[26] The public authority that lies in the audience, with whom Nita's cry may find address, is outside the narrative world and unavailable to Nita. The suspended address for its audience to hear, at the same time, also makes the film political.

Revisiting the film in the current political climate—where a certain kind of shrill ethno-religious, majoritarian nationalism raises its ugly head yet again—we might wish to think about its powerful mobilisation of women as symbols. We can recognise with Ghatak the violence that is implicated in gendered symbol-making, which we see in apparently innocent formulations every day, everywhere in our collective lives.

This essay is a revised version of a discussion that appears in the monograph The Refugee Woman: Partition of Bengal, Gender, and the Political. *Reproduced with permission of © Oxford University Press India, 2018.*

Paulomi Chakraborty is associate professor of English at the Department of Humanities and Social Sciences, IIT Bombay. She is the author of The Refugee Woman.

Notes

1. In the book, I have called this metaphor-making and developed a sustained argument about metaphors, in contrast to metonyms. Here, for the brevity of the piece, I use the broader term, symbol.
2. I take this formulation from the sociologist Dorothy Smith's book *The Everyday World as a Problematic: A Feminist Sociology* (University of Toronto Press, 1987), which combines time and space and also the personal with the political.
3. Emphasising this class critique, other commentators—most importantly Ashish Rajadhyaksha in his *Ritwik Ghatak: A Return to the Epic* (1982)—have also argued that Ghatak's critique is rooted in his irascibility with the class character of the bhadralok in the history that leads to the Partition. My reading is in that vein, but focuses on gender.
4. Unless specified otherwise, the quotes of dialogues are the subtitles from the British Film Institute DVD. In a few cases, while quoting the BFI subtitles, I have inserted my translations in square brackets.
5. The association itself is fairly obvious. Ghatak himself has spoken about it in his interviews on a few occasions. An early essay to make the connection elaborately is Ira Bhaskar's 'Myth and Ritual: Ghatak's *Meghe Dhaka Tara*', *Journal of Arts and Ideas*, No. 3 (April–June 1983). Rajadhyaksha's discussion of *Meghe Dhaka Tara* in his book *Ritwik Ghatak: A Return to the Epic* (Screen Unit, 1982, pp. 50–79) also traces the connection between Nita and Durga. Rajadhyaksha also reads a 'sacrifice' of the individual (ibid., p. 54) and suggests that Ghatak 'seeks not only an allegorical portrayal, he attempts to also open it out' (ibid., p. 59). From this point, however, Rajadhyaksha's argument is somewhat different. He continues, 'This [Ghatak] does by exposing the ritualism of the myth, by playing it out to its end but, in

doing so, suddenly raising it to the tragic' (ibid., p. 59). He takes his argument towards a reading that charts 'the material base that is hidden within the ritual that brings the past to us' (ibid., p. 77) and assesses the consequence of 'assimilation of archetypal images into dominant consciousness' (ibid., p. 60).

6. The word 'avatar' is derived from the verb 'to descend' (avataran). It is commonly translated as 'incarnation', but the root of incarnation is in the Latin word 'carnis', flesh. Spivak reminds us of this: 'the Sanskrit word for 'incarnation' (*avatar*)—has nothing to do with "putting on flesh". It means rather "a come-down [being]"' ('Moving Devi', *Cultural Critique*, No. 47, 2001, p. 123).
7. The ritual practice of *sati*, very likely links itself to versions of this legend. I have found a useful glossing of the Uma–Sati myth in Gayatri Spivak's essay 'Moving Devi', especially her citation (pp. 130–31) from Sukumari Bhattacharji's version for children.
8. Both Bhaskar and Rajadhyaksha do so.
9. Readers will find a robust discussion of the range and nature of this discourse in the first chapter of Tanika Sarkar's, *Hindu Wife, Hindu Nation: Community, Religion and Cultural Nationalism*, Permanent Black, 2001.
10. Rajadhyaksha, *Ritwik Ghatak*, p. 62.
11. Raymond Bellour, 'The Film We Accompany', *Rouge*, http://www.rouge.com.au/3/film.html.
12. Rajadhyaksha, *Ritwik Ghatak*, p. 62.
13. My translation from Bengali, from Shibaditya Dasgupta and Sandipan Bhattacharya (eds), *Sakhyat Ritwik: Ritwik Ghataker Athero ti Sakhyatkar O Ritwik Samparke Ekush Joner Lekha/Katha*, Deepayan, 2000, p. 156.
14. Rajadhyaksha, *Ritwik Ghatak*, p. 75.
15. Bhaskar Sarkar, *Mourning the Nation: Indian Cinema in the Wake of Partition*, Duke University Press, 2009, p. 221.
16. Jasodhara Bagchi and Subhoranjan Dasgupta (eds), *The Trauma and the Triumph: Gender and Partition in Eastern India*, Stree, 2003, pp. 3–4.
17. Ira Bhaskar, 'Myth and Ritual: Ghatak's *Meghe Dhaka Tara*', *Journal of Arts and Ideas*, 3, April–June 1983, p. 47.
18. Rajadhyaksha, *Ritwik Ghatak*, p. 65.
19. Ritwik Kumar Ghatak, 'Two Aspects of Cinema', tr. Samik Bandyopadhyay, *Rows and Rows of Fences: Ritwik Ghatak on Cinema*, Seagull Books, 2000, p. 67.
20. Rajadhyaksha, *Ritwik Ghatak*, p. 74.

    Reading within his Marxist criticism of the film, Rajadhyaksha finds this separation of nature from the individual as 'the emphatic denial of the romantic false-consciousness,' which he links to 'indictment of the romantic sensibility itself' and, in turn, to 'romanticism strongly etched into the middle-class' (*Ritwik Ghatak*, p. 75).

21. Rajadhyaksha also argues congruently, 'This is the only point of expression of the conflict between the archetype and the individual, but the violence with which the release comes shows the nature of the bondage' (*Ritwik Ghatak*, p. 74). However, in this reading I have developed a different idea of what constitutes this 'bondage' than Rajadhyaksha, who suggests it is the 'suffering of a whole people like her, and bound down to the rituals that have come down from her predecessors and designed to keep future generations of humanity in bondage' (ibid.).
22. Ravi Vasudevan, *The Melodramatic Public: Film Form and Spectatorship in Indian Cinema*, Permanent Black, 2010, p. 55.
23. Ibid.
24. Ibid., p. 42.
25. Ibid., p. 43.
26. Moinak Biswas argues in his PhD dissertation that, in *Meghe Dhaka Tara*, 'the melodramatic content was subverted from inside,' while in *Komol Gandhar* and *Subarnarekha*, Ghatak went a step further and 'made [melodrama] part of a field of interrogation' ('Historical Realism: Modes of Modernity in Indian Cinema, 1940–1960', Monash University, 2002, p. 190). See Moinak Biswas's essay 'Her Mother's Son: Kinship and History in Ritwik Ghatak' for a suggestive reading of Ghatak's manipulation and subversion of melodrama as a form.

Bibliography

Jasodhara Bagchi and Subhoranjan Dasgupta (eds), *The Trauma and the Triumph: Gender and Partition in Eastern India*, Stree, Kolkata, 2003.

Raymond Bellour, 'The Film We Accompany' (1992) (tr. Fergus Daly from French), *Rouge*, 3, 2004, http://www.rouge.com.au/3/film.html.

Ira Bhaskar, 'Myth and Ritual: Ghatak's *Meghe Dhaka Tara*', *Journal of Arts and Ideas*, 3, April–June, 1983, pp. 43–50.

Moinak Biswas, 'Her Mother's Son: Kinship and History in Ritwik Ghatak' (2004), *Rouge*, 3, 8 May 2009, *http://www.rouge.com.au/3/ghatak.html*.

——. 'Historical Realism: Modes of Modernity in Indian Cinema, 1940–1960.' Unpub. PhD Diss., Monash University, 2002.

Shibaditya Dasgupta and Sandipan Bhattacharya (eds.), *Sakhyat Ritwik: Ritwik Ghataker Athero ti Sakhyatkar O Ritwik Samparke Ekush Jone Lekha/Katha* (Bengali), Deepayan, Kolkata, 2000.

Ritwik Kumar Ghatak, 'Two Aspects of Cinema' (tr. Samik Bandyopadhyay), in *Rows and Rows of Fences: Ritwik Ghatak on Cinema*, Seagull Books, Calcutta, 2000.

Meghe Dhaka Tara: Cloud Capped Star, directed by Ritwik Kumar Ghatak, Chitrkalpa, 1960, DVD, British Film Institute, 2002.

Ashish Rajadhyaksha, *Ritwik Ghatak: A Return to the Epic*, Screen Unit, Bombay, 1982.

Bhaskar Sarkar, *Mourning the Nation: Indian Cinema in the Wake of Partition*, Duke University Press, Durham, 2009.

Tanika Sarkar, *Hindu Wife, Hindu Nation: Community, Religion and Cultural Nationalism*, Permanent Black, Delhi, 2001.

Dorothy Smith, *The Everyday World as Problematic: A Feminist Sociology*, University of Toronto Press, Toronto, 1987.

Gayatri Chakravorty Spivak, 'Moving Devi', *Cultural Critique*, 47 (Winter 2001), pp. 120–63.

Ravi Vasudevan, *The Melodramatic Public: Film Form and Spectatorship in Indian Cinema*, Permanent Black, Ranikhet, 2010.

Ghatak and Malayalam cinema: Reasons, arguments and stories

C.S. VENKITESWARAN

'Even when an eminent artist like Satyajit Ray is turning into an expensive display item of the establishment, Ghatak continues his lonely struggle ...'

– K. Satchidanandan, poet and writer

'Ritwik Ghatak was someone who kept away from the glorifications and temptations of both the conventional cinema before Satyajit Ray and of "art cinema" after him. Ghatak was an artist who planted his art in the burning soil of life. Instead of being adored by praises on stilts he preferred to be buried in a pagan's grave.'

– O.K. Johnny, film critic and editor of an anthology on Ritwik Ghatak in Malayalam

Ritwik Ghatak's films came to Kerala mainly through film society screenings and film festivals. In the Malayalam writings on film from that period, Ghatak had a special place. His films stood apart among the ones that circulated in those circuits. For the Malayalee audience of the time, his work exuded a raw and rare kind of energy, dramatic and intense. For the cineastes, Ghatak's films offered a visual/cultural experience that was different from the much-celebrated neorealist classics as well as the 'art cinema' that came from Europe. They also felt that his films had something essentially 'Bengali' to them. The Malayalee audience could readily connect with the socio-cultural and political ambience in Ghatak's films, as Bengali literature was very close to their hearts. Many notable works of celebrated Bengali writers—right from Rabindranath Tagore, Bankim Chandra Chatterjee and Sarat Chandra Chattopadhyay to Bimal Mitra, Tarasankar Bandyopadhyay, Shankar, Bonophul and Manik Bandopadhyay—had already been translated into Malayalam and had a wide readership.

Ghatak was also seen as part of the famous Bengali trio of film-makers. So it would be difficult to gauge or understand the extent and nature of the influence that Ghatak and his films had on Malayalam cinema without taking into consideration the other two—Satyajit Ray and Mrinal Sen—and how each one's body of work vibed with the Malayalee film audience. Of the trio, the films of Ray were the most easily available and, so, widely seen in Kerala. Some of his iconic films had been released in mainstream theatres, while his lesser known films circulated via the film society network. Unlike other states, where the film society movement was largely restricted to the cities, in Kerala it was a 'rurban' phenomenon. Film societies functioned not only in urban centres and city campuses but also in small towns and even in villages. From the late 1960s and through the next two decades, when the film society movement was at its peak, 'art films' from all over the world and from different Indian languages were widely screened across the state.

It was through the film society movement that films of the Indian new wave were seen and celebrated: a number of brochures, leaflets and booklets on film classics, the masters and the movements were produced by cinephiles and critics across the state. The period also saw the emergence of a new generation of film critics, who, through their writings in alternative or 'little' magazines and popular publications, expounded upon the political and aesthetic aspects of 'art cinema'.

Figuring prominently in all these critical writings and discourses were Ray, Ghatak and Sen. The Bengali trio and their films were admired, analysed and critiqued. But there was always the issue of selective availability, especially in the celluloid era. While the important films of Ray and Sen circulated well through the National Film Archives network, only

Go out, shoot at real locations, Ritwik always said;
© NFDC – National Film Archive of India

a few Ghatak films—like *Subarnarekha*, *Meghe Dhaka Tara* and *Komal Gandha*r—were readily available. Most of his other films—*Nagarik*, *Ajantrik*, *Titas Ekti Nodir Naam* and *Jukti, Tokko aar Goppo*—were difficult to access and rarely seen; these films became easily available only during the digital era when DVDs became popular.

Like elsewhere in the country, cinephiles and critics fought pitched battles for the three, pitting one against the other. They seemed to belong to three different schools of thought on cinema, society and politics. While Ray was considered a liberal, sophisticated humanist, Sen was seen as a champion of the downtrodden, whose films were animated by the spirit of the rebellious youth movements of the time.

Ghatak stood in between. He was a film-maker who was difficult to categorise and pigeonhole. The confluences and conflicts between tradition and modernity, the aesthetic responses and strategies that Ghatak experimented with in his narratives, the storytelling modes he relied on, and the montage and mise en scène styles he adopted were different.

He was not the typical 'art film-maker' who was overtly concerned with 'form'; nor did his 'content' stick to the set patterns of the period. It was difficult to find explicit European or Hollywood influences in his films: the characterisation and acting styles did not conform either, neither did the visual compositions and sound design.

For Ghatak, in Ray's words, 'Hollywood might not have existed at all'. Ghatak's films were neither as universal as Ray's nor as politically belligerent as Sen's. And unlike the other two, for Ghatak, Bengal was the centre of the world, and the Partition, *the* event that ruptured his world and life.

As the critic Samik Bandopadhyay observes, these were themes that persisted from Ghatak's theatre days, transforming into new cinematic shapes and idioms. 'In his films, the more earthy immediacy and reality of partition and the migration that followed, in *Dalil* and *Sanko* (Ghatak's plays), gave way to a more mythical evocation of that slice of history, now engrafted in a state of mind that had turned it all into a continuing sense of homelessness, restlessness and nostalgia for the lost home, sometimes even a quest for it, as at the close of *Subarnarekha*; the rugged realism breaking into great moments of poetry in speech and an almost dancing body ... transmuted into a cinematic expressionism far away from theatre,' Bandopadhyay writes in his foreword to *Five Plays by Ritwik Ghatak*.

Another line of comparison could be the way in which the three auteurs engaged with the idea of India in their films. Their respective bodies of work draw from each individual's own notions about the nation, people and civilisation that, in many ways, were entangled with that of borders, identities and traditions/cultures. Compared to the other two, Ghatak posed, explored and explicated these concerns/questions as a quintessential Bengali: the ideal of 'Sonar Bangla', the trauma of Partition, and the rivers and landscapes of undivided Bengal were very much a part of his aesthetics and dramatics.

In Ray, these questions are posed and expressed differently. If one considers his three trilogies—the Apu trilogy of the 1950s: *Pather Panchali* (1955), *Aparajito* (1956) and *Apur Sansar* (1959); the Calcutta trilogy made in the 1970s: *Pratidwandi* (1970), *Seemabaddha* (1971) and *Jana Aranya* (1975); and the trilogy in the last part of his career: *Ganashatru* (1989), *Shakha Proshakha* (1990) and *Agantuk* (1991)—it is possible to trace the tendencies and ruptures in Ray's social imagination and political vision. The Apu trilogy was made a decade after historic events like the Bengal Famine, India's independence and the Partition. The Calcutta trilogy coincides with war, both within (repression of rebellious youth in Calcutta) and without (Bangladesh), and the growing resentment regarding rising unemployment and large-scale political corruption. The last trilogy was made at another critical juncture in the nation's history—just prior to the announcement of the economic policies that endorsed globalisation and privatisation, and the rising tide of communal politics leading to the demolition of the Babri Masjid.

These three trilogies, almost two decades apart from each other, also mark the beginning, middle and end of his oeuvre. From three periods in his life and in the history of the nation, these trilogies reflect Ray's intense and introspective engagements with the idea of India, shifting from youthful innocence and hope in the post-Independence decades, through despairing confrontations and compromises with the establishment and mores in the 1970s, to a deep despair about degeneration at all levels by the late 1980s.

In his last trilogy, social and political issues are posed at the deepest level as a civilisational or human crisis. According to many Ray scholars, his films map the history of modern India from the perspective of an enlightened liberal.

In Sen, the preoccupations were different. One can see in him a film-maker experimenting with different themes, narrative formats and styles all through his long career. His early films *Akash Kusum* (1965) to *Bhuvan Shome* (1969) differ radically from his Calcutta films that deal with the turbulent events that shook the city: *Interview* (1971), *Chorus* (1974), *Calcutta 71* (1972) and *Padatik* (1973). They were followed by another set of films—*Mrigaya* (1976), *Oka Oori Katha* (1977) and *Parashuram* (1978)—that dug into the histories of oppression from other perspectives. The films that came after these were excavations into middle-class mindsets and worldviews: *Ekdin Pratidin* (1979), *Akaler Sandhaney* (1980) and *Ek Din Achanak* (1989). Sen relentlessly tried to wrap his art and mind around questions of oppression and unfreedom—of class, caste, gender—in all its hues and shades.

It would be interesting to compare the images and representations of the city of Calcutta that appear in the films of these three film-makers. They would present three divergent Calcuttas, seen, felt and expressed from different viewpoints: that of the refugees, the slum dwellers, the youth protesting on the streets, or that of the imperial city of colonial masters, the great city of Tagore, the city of middlemen and aspiring middle class. Another comparison could be the figure of tribals/adivasis in their films: take, for example, Ray's *Aranyer Din Ratri,* Sen's *Mrigaya* and Ghatak's *Ajantrik.*

Whether it be the presence of the modern city or the culture/life of Adivasis, each film-maker follows his preoccupations and worldviews. If the Tagorean renaissance ideas predominate in Ray, it is the influences of Marxist ideology, and Brechtian and Godardian aesthetics that animate Sen. In Ghatak, themes boil down to the elemental question of belonging, or the longing to belong, that is posed in the vast horizon of Indian civilisation. Ashish Rajadhyaksha and Amrit Gangar in their compilation *Ritwik Ghatak: Arguments/Stories* make the following observation: 'This distinction is important in the cinema: it is objectively demonstrable that the differences between e.g. Satyajit Ray and Ritwik Ghatak may substantially be traced to the choices they made vis-à-vis the Bengal School of Art that preceded them. While Ray has repeatedly reaffirmed his allegiance to Nandalal [Bose]: witness the lessons in organicity he learned in how a tree should be drawn (*Our Films, Their Films*), Ghatak was close both to Benode Behari [Mukherjee] and his friend Ramkinkar [Baij].'

So, if Ray imagined a universal, rational, secular, modern human being, for Sen, the narratives centred on the idea of class: his films were about the divisions and conflicts between and within classes. In the case of Ghatak, his vision of humanity goes beyond class and secular rationality. It was more deeply civilisational in nature, with deep roots in the soil of Bengal, drawing from its plural traditions, diverse cultures and entangled histories. This is how Ghatak puts it: 'There is an epic tradition which dominates the Indian mentality. It has seeped into the Indian subconscious. It is no surprise, therefore, that Indians are attracted to mythologies. I am a part of that tradition. I cannot think of myself without the epic tradition. I am all for it. It is in our civilisation since time immemorial. In my films, I rely mainly on the folk form. The Great Mother image in its duality exists in every aspect of our being.'

So it is not a universal humanity or class being that Ghatak was primarily concerned with, but rather with 'people' in the most political sense of the term, as a philosopher like Alain Badiou would propose:

> It is in the retrospective effect of the nonexistence of a state that the 'people' can be part of the naming of a political process and thus become a political category. As soon as the state in question is formed, regulated, and enrolled in the 'international community', the people it claims as its authority ceases to be a political subject. It becomes a passive mass that the state configures, universally, no matter what the form of the state.
>
> – *What is a People?*, 2016

In the film critics' and film society circles of those times, the Ray–Ghatak binary was an established one, with cineastes taking sides and arguing for one against the other. The 'difference' in their styles and approach was misconceived as 'opposition'. But, when one looks back more closely, it was also an argument that did not account for the many cultural and intellectual affinities and common influences that all three of them shared.

Another reason why Ghatak stood apart could be that the formal aesthetic of Ray and political radicalism of Sen were, in many ways amenable to following, imitation or emulation. The questions that Ray and Sen posed in their films, the formal strategies they experimented with and the political responses they triggered followed certain recognisable patterns. They were also much more receptive to inspirations and local adaptations, since there was something universal about them. This was not the case with Ghatak.

Ghatak's epic vision and melodramatic narrative mode were difficult to emulate, as they were animated by a certain existential and aesthetic angst that was very deeply rooted and entangled with the region's political and cultural past. Unless a film-maker was so close to their roots, so deeply wounded by history, so eager to dig deep into tradition and history in order to plumb adequate energies and excavate appropriate aesthetic forms, it was impossible to be a 'Ghatakian'.

Maybe that is one reason Ghatak remains an enigma to the Malayalees, the one who continues to haunt their imagination, posing uneasy questions about their aesthetic modularities and cultural certainties. The trauma that haunted Ghatak's life and oeuvre—the partition of Bengal—was a historical event that was, and still is, not very close to Malayalee life, probably due to geographical distance, and didn't have much of an impact on Kerala's sociopolitical fabric and, therefore, cultural discourses.

Moreover, the Malayalam 'art' cinema of those days was more preoccupied with what could roughly be categorised as two streams of influence: one, the socialist-realist aesthetic drawn from the Kerala People's Art Club, or KPAC, tradition (inspired by the Indian People's Theatre Association); and two, the tradition of existential angst and loneliness drawn from European cinema and literature. Ghatak's films did not fall into either of these categories.

Rajadhyaksha's comment in *Ritwik Kumar Ghatak: A Monograph* by Haimanti Banerjee is very relevant in the case of Malayalam art cinema aesthetics as well as discourses around it: 'As we move to *Ajantrik*, the tale of Bimal and his wayward car, we come to traditions that have remained almost entirely unrepresented in modern Indian art with its realist preoccupations.'

Beyond aesthetics, it was Ghatak's persona that seems to have had a greater influence or presence in Malayalam film discourses, especially with regard to the idea of the 'true artist'.

Among the trio, it was Ghatak who offered Malayalees the iconic image of a bohemian artist, one who is creatively and otherwise inebriated, anarchic in his art practice, always bursting with energy and has a zest for life.

Many considered John Abraham his true disciple or successor. Ghatak himself, in *Cinema and I*, mentions Abraham by name as one of his favourite students, in whom—along with Mani Kaul and Kumar Shahani and a few others—he saw the future of Indian cinema. But the influences were not so manifestly visible in Abraham's films or aesthetic vision as it was in his much-talked-about (and later, much-imitated) lifestyle of being a drunken nomad and anarchist.

But looked at closely, one can see flashes of Ghatak in Abraham's films. In *Agraharathil Kazhuthai* (Donkey in a Brahmin Village, 1977), one can see Abraham tapping into the creative sources of primal Dravidian culture, such as in his invocation of the fire god through Subramania Bharati's poem or the folk tradition of the street oracles proclaiming the arrival of good times. In *Cheriyachante Kroorakrithyangal* (The Cruel Deeds of Cheriyachan, 1979), one can see Abraham's deep fascination for his homeland in scenes where the camera meanders through the landscapes of Alleppey, its vast paddy fields and water bodies, delving into the region's history of agrarian violence as well as resistance. In the restless journey in *Amma Ariyan* (Report to Mother, 1986) through the ruins and vestiges of radical movement in Kerala, there are echoes of *Jukti, Tokko aar Goppo*.

In his article, 'John Abraham, A Donkey and the Bottle', Amborish Roychoudhury quotes Jacob Levich: 'Satyajit Ray is the suitable boy of Indian film, presentable, career-oriented, and reliably tasteful. Ghatak, by contrast, is an undesirable guest: he lacks respect, has "views", makes a mess, disdains decorum.' Roychoudhury adds: 'Pick up those colourful words used for Ghatak, and use them on John Abraham. Every word fits with equal resonance.'

In these dark, monocultural times, it is important to take stock of our cinema history through the Ghatak lens—a vision deeply concerned with the immediate and the present, even as it sought nourishment from the founts of multiple traditions, and strove for a world of freedom and creativity.

C.S. Venkiteswaran is a film critic, translator and curator based in Kerala. He writes in Malayalam and English in national and international journals and publications. He has won state and national awards for film criticism and for his documentary film , Pakarnnattam: Ammannur, The Actor. *He has curated film programmes for MIFF, IFFK, IDSFFK and the Kochi Muziris Biennale.*

The documentarian Ritwik Ghatak: People's artist, people's cinema

SANGHITA SEN

> *'I believe in committed cinema [...] committed to that contemporary reality, to the daily acts of heroism in that reality. No important work can be created without this commitment, I think [...] Because this commitment presupposes a desire for change of that reality.'*
>
> – Ritwik Ghatak[1]

In a sequence in Ritwik Ghatak's final film *Jukti, Tokko aar Goppo*, a group of Bengali intellectuals led by an eminent author (played by Utpal Dutt) is seen drinking in a park. As the conversation flows, one among them (played by Satindra Bhattacharya) insists on avoiding any critical engagement with the ongoing Bangladesh liberation war and the Naxal movement, and instead advises the author to capitalise on the crisis by writing a novel or a play. The sequence portrays the impact on the visual arts of a pervasive moral crisis; a painter from the group contrasts the docility of contemporary Bengali artists to the radical role of Spanish artists during the Civil War, citing Picasso's *Guernica* (1937) as an example. However, the painter's critical tone is countered by another member, who points to the futility of engagement with the contemporary sociopolitical crisis. In response, Bhattacharya's character brings up the dismal situation of Bengali cinema. He casually comments, 'Isn't Bengali cinema becoming increasingly inadequate and restricted?' To this, the artist mockingly raises a toast, 'Hail our decadent and rotting Bengali culture!'

While this was Ghatak's rejection of the hollow words and indifference of people with social privilege, one can also see his view of the artist as an organic intellectual. The above exchange is also a sharp critique of a segment of contemporary intellectuals and artists who spectacularise people's suffering in cultural representations without any empathic engagement or sense of solidarity, evidence of their complicity with the powers that be and lack of commitment. This polemic tone predominates almost all of Ghatak's films, including his shorts and documentaries.

In this essay, I will briefly discuss the documentaries Ghatak made and contextualise his film-making practice as part of the leftist cultural movements against the milieu of ongoing political, cultural and moral crisis in post-Partition Bengal and South Asia. Historical contextualisation is integral to understanding Ghatak's position as the people's artist rather than an auteur. The sociopolitical situation and communist movements of the 1940s and 1950s created a possibility and space for culture to be used for political purposes. This period was vital in shaping Ghatak's own practices and style of melodrama, combining elements from Bengali, pan-Indian, European and Russian cultural traditions.[2] Thus, it is important to keep this cultural history in mind in the discussion of Ghatak's films for their deep interconnections.

A political and cultural activist, he was devotedly engaged with the Indian People's Theatre Association, the Communist Party of India and trade union activism (among cine-technicians) since the late 1940s, and as actor, director, scriptwriter and producer since 1950. He started his creative journey with short stories. Subsequently, he wrote plays, became a theatre actor and director, film-maker, film theorist and educator. He used all these media of creative expressions to document the contemporary history of South Asia and offer his critique of the situation. In short: Ghatak acted as a documentarian. In an interview with Sunit Sengupta in 1967, he avowed: 'I believe in involvement as an artist. I believe there is no point in making films unless one is intricately connected with lives of people around them.'[3] An investigation of Ghatak's complete oeuvre can help us understand the processes of his radical creative practice and its intellectual foundation. Since a full discussion of these assortments will require a bigger canvas, I'm going to discuss here an aspect which often remains overlooked—i.e. Ghatak as a documentarian.

People's Artist, People's Cinema

In 1971, Puran Chand Joshi, the CPI general secretary between 1935 and 1947, called Ghatak 'the only people's artist in India'.[4] Ghatak fondly identified himself with this description. The IPTA was a beacon of the communist cultural movement that highlighted class struggle and proletarian internationalism. Continuing the IPTA tradition, he aimed to build people's cinema to transform audiences from passive spectatorship to active participation by making them stakeholders in cultural practice. He preferred cinema to theatre for its medial potential to reach a much larger number of people than theatre is able to.[5] In a country like India—with its overwhelming rate of illiteracy—cinema, theatre and other forms of oral/aural forms are the perfect media for public engagement and mobilisation. Ghatak was keenly aware of this. In a conversation with Bhupati Nandy, an eminent IPTA activist and one of the producers of his first film, *Nagarik*, Ghatak commented, 'Film is merely a medium of an artist's artistic expressions [...] albeit a powerful medium', with an ability to reach millions of people at one go unlike any other medium.[6] In another interview, he spoke of cinema's capacity to create prompt reactions amongst audiences, thus communicating his messages with a sense of immediacy.[7] So he chose cinema to agitate, educate and, most importantly, organise the people. To this end, he politicised melodrama and adopted the Brechtian *Verfremdungseffekt* (alienation effect) to enable active engagement of the audience with what is depicted on screen, drawing their attention to reality: 'involvement is necessary for the artist and alienation for the audiences'.[8]

Ghatak politicised every medium of his creative expression, including cinema, for emancipatory purposes and social criticism.[9] He acknowledged, 'I have wanted to use the cinema as a weapon, as a medium to express my views.'[10] He hoped to achieve some interrelated outcomes: to create a people's cinema as an integral part of the leftist cultural front in India, and to situate an opposition both to the elite pursuit of 'good' cinema and the mainstream cinema of entertainment.[11] This opposition was prompted by his objection to the commodification of cultural practice, driven by what film historian Ashish Rajadhyaksha describes as the ideology that methodically obfuscates issues of social relevance and constructs images only for their aesthetic value.[12] Ghatak resisted this spectacularisation and aestheticisation. Instead, he undertook an investigation of structural inequalities and the struggles of the dispossessed in his cinema by weaponising both the cinematic medium and melodrama, the genre he utilised the most.

The sociopolitical context of post-Partition India was severely fraught, with the largest mass displacements in human history and a severe refugee crisis as the consequence. The country faced devastating impoverishment that two centuries of colonial rule had brought upon it. Its hard-won independence was marred by fratricidal violence and the inestimable misery wrought by Partition—an unhealed, open wound in South Asia ever since. Realism appeared inadequate to capture this heightened misery and pain of the people. Melodrama proved to be an apt form, not just for its potential but also for the familiarity that his target audiences had with the form for centuries. Ghatak created a distinct idiom of melodrama, in which he combined elements from traditional, indigenous and mass cultural practices as well as from popular cinema. It is important to note that he did not choose cultural materials for mere aesthetic quality, but to create facets of familiarity among his audiences, so that the content and its underlying messages could be relayed effectively.

It is important to problematise Ghatak's reception exclusively as an auteur, and to affirm his position as a people's artist by illustrating his shared ideological, theoretical, aesthetic and thematic premises with oppositional cinema from across the world. Considering Ghatak solely as an auteur defeats the political objectives behind the idea of people's cinema, despite his distinct cinematic style. Furthermore, paying heed to the processes of his film-making aids a better understanding of how film-making practice and film culture in the subcontinent changed through his influence. Ghatak, along with his collaborators, forged a new way of film-making in a conscious effort to revolutionise cinema as a mass cultural form by liberating it from commodification.

Several of his films were made with active collaboration from his IPTA colleagues, people of the trade unions, the artists' guild and the general public. While engaging with Ghatak's collective film-making methods, it is also useful to remember the signature style that has led to him being labelled as an auteur. The simultaneous presence of collective practice and signature style in his work creates a challenge for neat classification of his film practice. But this is not unique to Ghatak. This challenge exists when engaging with other noted political film-makers who worked collectively and were yet singled out as the main agent behind a film project. The European model of auteurism does not adequately accommodate the range of ideological, contextual, emotional or processual elements that prompted his creative practice. The non-Western context of cultural practice—preference for collective co-creation informed by his Marxist politics, politicising the medium and attempting to forge a people's cinema—are in direct contradiction with the principles of auteurist practice. To Ghatak, film-making was not solely about art or entertainment—which is central to auteurist cinema—but about emancipation and political mobilisation that characterise Third Cinema and oppositional cinema.

In his 1956 letter to Sasadhar Mukherjee, Ghatak pointed out the problem of using cinema to create 'intoxication': 'Intoxication is easier to dish out without art. All great art is intoxication, but all intoxication is not art.'[13] This observation echoes the Adornoian caution about the culture industry's deceptive impact on the masses through the use of cinema as an ideological apparatus to perpetuate a false consciousness of reality. We can locate plenty of examples of this synergy by closely looking at the intimate bond between oppressive regimes and the culture industry that works as their mouthpiece. Examples include Leni Riefenstahl from Hitler's Germany of the 1930s and Vivek Agnihotri from Modi's India of our time, although Agnihotri has no comparable skills as a film-maker to Riefenstahl. Ghatak was keenly aware of this nefarious interconnectedness. Through his film-making practice and cultural activism, he made a rigorous effort to free cinema from the control of the culture industry. Unlike auteurist cinema, he aimed to create unpleasure and disruption.[14] He intended cinema to reveal the reality of the disenfranchised, which is seldom beautiful or pleasing or 'intoxicating'. Such a disruptive depiction of reality was to instigate the audiences to question internalised practices and prejudices. This counter-establishment disposition was at the heart of his signature style of radical cinema and film-making processes.

In his 1965 interview, Ghatak asserted: 'Cinema needs to be first and foremost committed to truth, then committed to beauty [...] here I'm not talking of aesthetic transcendentality but of consciousness.'[15] It will not be out of place to mention here that this interview took place during a very challenging time in Ghatak's creative career, with both *Komal Gandhar* and *Subarnarekha* sabotaged.[16] The fate of a documentary on Ustad Allauddin Khan he made in 1963 was similar. He made this film in collaboration with Harisadhan Dasgupta, but after the completion of the film, he was summarily dismissed, and the film was later released without giving him credit.[17] However, even during that difficult phase, Ghatak's thoughts on cinema and the artists' duty towards history and society were very lucidly political. This clarity also establishes his position as an organic intellectual committed to using his creative practices to shape collective consciousness.

Documentarian Ritwik

Ghatak has been one of the most notable chroniclers of the Partition.[18] However, this wasn't the only issue he engaged with. In his films, documentaries, plays, scripts, short stories and non-fiction writing, Ghatak touched upon a number of contemporary issues in South Asia and around the world. The broader concerns that tied the multiple issues together were inequality, discrimination, injustice and the suffering of the dispossessed. In a failing system that oppressed the weakest, the radical need for complete social change became an imperative. In 1967, referring to the shattered dreams of the protagonist of his first feature, *Nagarik*, he invoked the idea of consciousness as instrumental in recognising the reality of the dispossessed that leads to a felt necessity for change: 'You have to grasp life with both hands and change it. There is no escape—that is how history works [...] The time is changing, Sita. Don't cry. We won't cry anymore, we'll wait. Something new will emerge.'[19] *Nagarik* ends with this note of deep optimism and radical resolve as the evicted protagonist declares that he would continue to fight to bring about a better day. The soundtrack fills with '*L'Internationale*', affirming his trust in collective action. This immediately positions the film's characters alongside struggling people across the world.

Ghatak's films are strewn with evidence of structural oppression and injustice. When Neelkantha, the protagonist of *Jukti, Tokko aar Goppo*, is hit by a stray bullet and dies, Beethoven's fifth symphony plays on the soundtrack. The first four notes of the symphony convert to 'dot-dot-dot-dash' indicating the letter 'V' in Morse Code for the Victory of the Allied forces against the fascists in World War II. It is no coincidence that Ghatak used this piece of music in a film that critiqued the fascisisation of the government and its use of brutal power against political opponents, affirming hope about the sure defeat of the fascists via collective action. Right from using '*L'Internationale*' in his first film to utilising the Hindi rendition of '*La Marseilles*' in *Amar Lenin*, to the use of the fifth symphony in his last film, Ghatak skilfully weaves local contexts into the larger international context to advocate for radical collective action to transform an unjust system. It is clear that political consciousness was foremost in the philosophy of Ghatak's practice. Cinema's political function in society and relation to topicality were far more important to him than artistic quality.

There is a clear tonal continuance of this philosophy in his fiction films to his documentaries and shorts, which is why I assert that Ghatak was a documentarian. Covering a range of contemporary issues, Ghatak completed seven documentaries, abandoned one, completed one but didn't get the credit for when it was released, left one incomplete and could never make the film on Vietnam that he had planned. Besides cinema, Ghatak is also a pioneer of documentary theatre. In 1951, following thirty-one cases of suicide, Ghatak prepared a report for P.C. Joshi, titled 'Suicide Wave in Bengal'.[20] Based on this report, he wrote *Jwala* (*Agony*, 1951). He directed and acted in this play. He also directed this later as a radio play. In an interview with Prabir Sen, Ghatak pointed out, 'I selected six characters [from this report]—each one is a true character. *Agony is a documentary*.'[21] (emphasis mine) His award-winning play *Dalil* (*Charter*, 1952) is another example of documentary theatre that centres on Partition and the refugee crisis in Bengal. In 1955, he was commissioned by the government of Bihar to make *Adivasiyon Ka Jeevan Srot*/*The Flow of Life of Tribal Peoples* (35mm, B/W, two reels, 14:03 minutes) and *Bihar Ke Darshaniya Sthan*/ *The Places to Visit in Bihar* (35mm, B/W, two reels, 16 minutes). Both films were made during the first five-year plan (1951–56) and were screened throughout the country, distributed by the Films Division of India.[22]

Time spent in the company of tribal people while filming these documentaries proved extremely productive for Ghatak. In a letter to his partner and biographer Surama Ghatak, dated 22 February 1955, Ghatak wrote: 'The last few days were so hectic at Ranchi but I can't tell you how satisfying this work has been. I have been spending the whole day with Oraon and Munda people, feeling the taste of the soil, experiencing the extraordinary music and the enthralling rhythm of their dance the whole day. I'm completely blown over by witnessing their love for life despite an extremely oppressed existence. That I'm able to absorb some grains of this reality fills me with affirmation. My wish is to come back again to make a bigger film with more of this reality … We hardly work with them, but they are the heart of this country, landless peasants, semi-proletarians of the rural area.'[23]

Ghatak did go back to this area to make *Ajantrik* and yet another documentary. In 1957, he started preliminary work on *Oraon*, an experimental documentary on the tribal people in Ranchi and the Oraon tribe in Rani Khatanga village in Bihar (now Jharkhand). Although he filmed portions of it, he couldn't complete it.[24] Possibly the project was abandoned because he had to start filming *Ajantrik*, his second feature, but the first to release theatrically. Some documentary footage from *Oraon* was used in *Ajantrik*. The location of the rest of the footage is unknown.[25]

Adivasiyon Ka Jeevan Srot

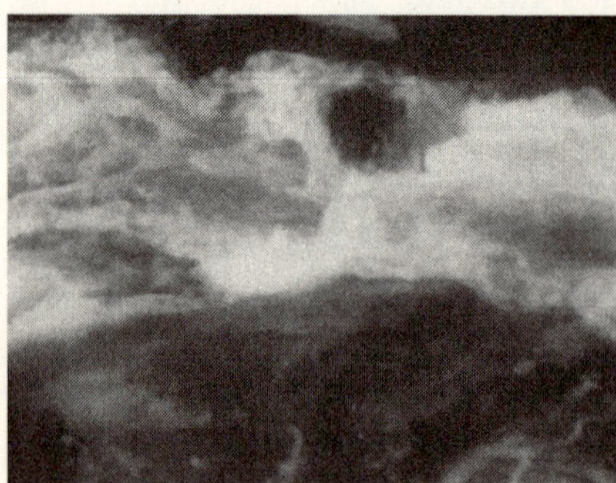

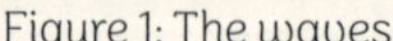

Figure 1: The waves

Figure 2: Waterfall

Adivasiyon Ka Jeevan Srot opens with visuals of the gushing waters of a river flowing through boulders and rocks and the dance performances of Bihar's tribal people, with the following voice-over narration (figures 1–2): 'Who knows in which indefinite time these waves first burst forth! Happily gurgling away, dancing rhythmically, it moved forward—to be lost in the infinite despite its limitation, to merge itself with the ocean despite being but a drop in comparison. Isn't human life also like that? It also flows like the river from a mortal life to immortality.'

We see glimpses of the daily lives of different tribes in the Chotanagpur plateau area (figures 3–6). As opposed to presenting them as objects of urban curiosity, he de-exoticised tribal people and humanised them.

In a short span, the film covers the community's jobs, social customs and marriage, economic system, election of the chief, governance, grievance redressal and conflict resolution systems, festivals, recreation and culture. With reference to how one of the tribes elect their chief with the help of a blindfolded young boy, the voice-over narration notes:

Figure 3: Newly-wed couple

Figure 4: Drum and dance performance

Figure 5: Girls playing in school

Figure 6: Man at work

'Justice is blind. This is why this tribe chooses its chief by literally staging blindness. This is how real justice could be served. Society can be happy only if one can get real justice.' Emphasising the crucial importance of collaboration ('Collaboration is the foundation of the lives of tribals') and collective cultural practices in the tribal communities, the documentary ends with a dance performance (figures 7–8) and the following narration: 'They have specific music and dance performances for each season of the year. These performances fill their being with happiness and stimulate hope. These give them energy, inspire them to carry on collectively within the community and with the outside world. This is how the tribal life continues to flow forward.'

Figure 7: A dance for every season

Figure 8: Culture of collaboration

Ghatak's commitment to social justice and inclusivity is very clear in both documentaries made in 1955. Although the second documentary is titled *Bihar Ke Darshaniya Sthan,* it depicts the cultural links of Bihar to two religious minority communities in India, the Buddhists and the Jains. The film also refers to the Maurya Empire (320–185 BCE), when Buddhism and Jainism developed in India and Bihar was a seat of international knowledge exchange and learning where students from across the world came. An intellectual with deep interest in and knowledge of ancient Indian culture, literature and history, Ghatak, it may not be a stretch to think, presented a historical and cultural continuum in South Asia from ancient times to the present in these documentaries.

As Films Division's newsreels and documentaries were mandatorily screened in every theatre in India before the screening of any film, this opportunity fulfilled Ghatak's much-desired cultural goal of using cinema to reach a wider audience, which his unreleased first film *Nagarik* had not. The smaller scale of documentary production may have also given him greater independence to work as a film-maker. This is probably why, in times of severe challenges in the industry, Ghatak always went back to making documentaries.

For example, during his stint in Filmistan Studios, Bombay, where he felt acutely restricted as an artist, he wrote to Surama on 30 June 1955: 'I don't like the way things work here. Actually, I have no work here other than doing ten-to-five in the office and writing bogus stuff. I'm not sure I'll succeed here … To do something meaningful, express one's capacity, or moving towards genuine fame seems out of reach. Everything is for a monthly income … I don't want to pay the price I have to pay here to succeed. *It will be ideal if I can earn enough to sustain us in Calcutta by writing or doing something else or making documentaries and be able to make a film every couple of years.*' (emphasis mine)

The year 1970 seems to have been very productive for Ghatak's documentary projects. He made as many as three, namely *Yeh Kyun*, *Amar Lenin* and *Puruliar Chhau Nritya*. The docudrama *Yeh Kyun* was Ghatak's response to the intercommunal riot in Bhiwandi, Jalgaon and Mahad in 1970, machinated by the Indian ethnonationalist far right Hindutva camp affiliated to the Rashtriya Swayamsevak Sangh. The film ends with a warning (figure 9). This riot took place in May 1970, killed over 250 people. A commission headed by Justice D.P. Madon was set up to investigate the incident. The commission reported strong anti-Muslim bias among the police.[26] The film offers a powerful critique of intercommunal violence and police bias in Ghatak's inimitable Brechtian style of direct camera address that he would perfect in his swansong, *Jukti, Tokko aar Goppo*. In one of the sequences, he breaks the fourth wall, and the audience sees a gun aimed at them (figure 10). Equally, he communicates a powerful message about people's resistance against such violence and the need for the peaceful coexistence of diverse communities (figures 11–12).

Amar Lenin is another significant political documentary, portraying the lives of marginalised rural farmers who are at the helm of a mass movement demanding social justice in contemporary India. The film starts with a lone unnamed protagonist (played by Arun Kumar) in rural Bengal from 'a shattered village of a fractured Bengal'. Ghatak made this

Yeh Kyun

Figure 9: Final slide

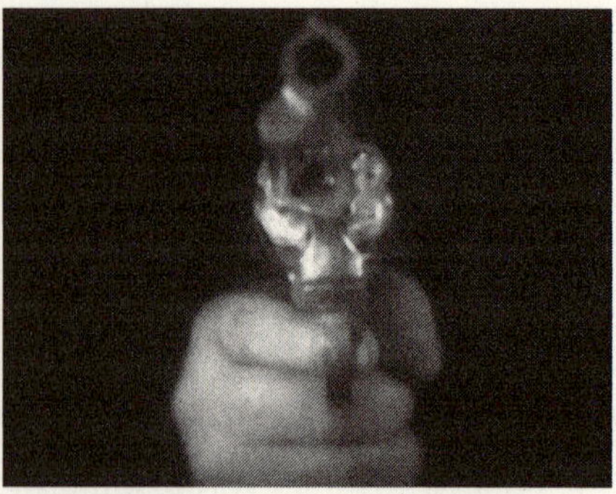

Figure 10: The gun aimed at you

Figure 11: People united

Figure 12: Peace rally

film for the United Front government of West Bengal, with Sushil Karan and Gouri Sankar Dey as co-producers.[27] This film commemorates the birth centenary celebration of Lenin, contextualising it in the premise of the revolutionary uprisings of Indian peasant and international Marxist movements. A sequence in the film shows hundreds of poor landless labourers, including tribal agricultural workers, leading an armed procession to a huge expanse of agricultural land. On reaching the field, they begin ploughing the land. The voice-over narrates, 'Empowered by the teachings of Lenin, he, along with thousands of his landless brothers, is marching to claim what is rightfully theirs' (figures 13–16).

Banned in India for its political content, *Amar Lenin* was refused a censor certificate in 1970. This created a stir in Bengal's civil society, and a number of protest letters were submitted to the competent authorities. The signatories included Satyajit Ray, Mrịnal Sen, Chidananda Dasgupta, Bijon Bhattacharya, Barin Saha and Utpal Dutt, among others.[28] A

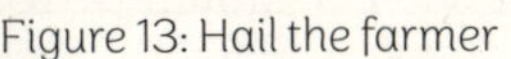

Figure 13: Hail the farmer

Figure 14: Power to the people

Figure 15: The victory of the people's war

Figure 16: Land to the tiller

separate protest letter was submitted with signatures from six cine societies in Calcutta.[29] Ghatak met the prime minister to solve the issue when the Soviet Union and the Polish People's Republic approached him to screen the film there, and censor clearance was an issue.[30] Surama Ghatak reported that the film finally travelled to Moscow with Gouri Sankar Dey, where it received some awards.[31]

The narration of this documentary shows the journey of the fictional protagonist to the metropolis and back. The similarities that *Amar Lenin* shares with *Nagarik* and *Jukti, Tokko aar Goppo* are via themes and some rhetorical connections. For example, both *Amar Lenin* and *Nagarik* begin by introducing the protagonist through a male voice-over with similar phrasing: 'I saw him …' Though the act of seeing remains the same, the context differs. In *Nagarik*, the protagonist is one among millions in an indifferent city; in *Amar Lenin*, the protagonist lives on 'the far end of the earth in a broken village of this broken Bengal'. This pronouncement of rupture in Bengal could be read along with Ramu's (*Nagarik*'s lead protagonist) father's (played by Kali Banerjee) reflections comparing the utopic undivided Bengal to the Bengal after Partition: 'Our Bengal was that of formation, and today's Bengal is that of fragmentation.'

Ghatak reiterates this idea of a fragmented Bengal in the political and moral crises in *Jukti, Tokko aar Goppo*: 'Everything is burning, the universe is burning, I'm burning.' Ghatak used documentary footage from both *Amar Lenin* and *Puruliar Chhau Nritya* in *Jukti, Tokko aar Goppo*; the footage from the first film shows people's collective resistance against the feudal landlord, while the second depicts Chhau performance as a collective creative practice. He interweaves documentary and fiction by placing fictional characters from the film's narrative alongside the documentary footage of the performance.

Considering film-making as cultural activism with emancipatory goals, Ghatak attempted to create a movement for people's cinema in India, which preceded but was very much in tandem with the global Third Cinema movement. Though his motivations were clear at the time he made *Nagarik* in 1952-53, the political connotations of his film-making practice reached its apex in the long 1960s. The geopolitical unrest of the period coincided with *Yeh Kyun*, *Amar Lenin*, *Puruliar Chhau Nritya*, *Durbar Goti Padma* and *Jukti, Tokko aar Goppo*, along with the planning of his unrealised project on Vietnam. His long engagement with the IPTA not only exposed him to the day-to-day struggles of the people, but also helped him understand their cultural taste and collective practice. Therefore, he chose the form of melodrama for its acceptance among the Indian masses, and politicised it by disrupting its traditional form and treatment.

Ghatak's primary commitment was to the people; aesthetic concerns were secondary, with film forms being determined by the content. Subsequently, he formulated his own idea of people's cinema that geared the process of decolonisation of cultural practices. The insights he acquired as a result of his IPTA connections influenced his idea of people's cinema and active as well as participatory spectatorship. His spirit of active collaboration, with an emphasis on content over aesthetics, and an idea of committed cinema for political purposes, contextualises Ghatak's film practice within the Third Cinema tradition.

In the scheme of his epic melodrama, he extensively used traditional cultural materials, which are intricately connected with the lives of Indians. However, he secularised these forms by displacing them from their immediate religious contexts, which kept it parochially tied to a prevalently bourgeois value system and conservative nationalist sensibility. Through displacement of myths and epics in his films, Ghatak augmented the process of opening up as well as subverting the traditional cultural forms. The importance of such displacement and secularisation of myth and epics appears even more pertinent, especially in today's context, when the multicultural tenor of India is under serious threat due to far-right ethnonationalists and racial supremacists utilising myth and epics to reinforce the dominator's view as the dominant view. The insights of documentarian Ghatak into the history of South Asia could show light to those who are looking for some.

Dr Sanghita Sen is assistant professor in visual communication and digital cultures at Northumbria University, UK.

Notes

1. Ritwik Ghatak, 'Film and I', first published in *Montage* 2, No. 3 (1963), reprinted in *Cinema and I*, Dhyanbindu and Ritwik Memorial Trust, Kolkata, 2015, p. 29.
   All translations mine, unless stated otherwise
2. Erin O'Donnell, '"Woman" and "Homeland" in Ritwik Ghatak's films: Constructing post-Independence Bengali cultural identity', *Jump Cut: A Review of Contemporary Media*, 47 (2004), n.p. https://www.ejumpcut.org/archive/jc47.2005/ghatak/text.html accessed on 12.06.2019.
3. Sunit Sengupta (interview with Ritwik Ghatak), 'Shilpi hishebe ami involvement-e biswas kori / As an artist, I believe in involvement', *Movie Montage*, 1967, reprinted in *Sakkhat Ritwik* (eds Dasgupta and Bhattacharya), 2000, p. 21.
4. Ghatak's letter to Surama Ghatak dated 27 June 1971, in Surama Ghatak, *Ritwik*, Anushtup, Kolkata, 2009, p. 135. Joshi helped establishing mass organs such as the Progressive Writers' Association (PWA), All India Students'

Federation (AISF) and All India Kisan Sabha (AIKS—All India Association for Agricultural Workers) in 1936 and the IPTA in 1943. Ghatak's close association with Joshi started through the IPTA.

5. Ritwik Ghatak (interview), 'Cinemar Preme Moshai ami porini / I haven't fallen in love with cinema', *Chitrabikshan*, August–September 1973, reprinted in *Sakkhat Ritwik* (eds. Dasgupta and Bhattacharya), 2000, pp. 57–71. Surama Ghatak, *Ritwik: Padma theke Titas / Ritwik: From Padma to Titas*, Anushtup, Kolkata, 2010, p. 37.
6. Surama Ghatak, *Ritwik: Padma theke Titas / Ritwik: From Padma to Titas*, Anushtup, Kolkata, 2010, p. 36.
7. Ghatak, 'Shilpi hishebe …', 1967 (2000), p. 24.
8. Ibid., p. 22.
9. Ghatak, 'Cinemar preme …', 1973 (2000), p. 60.
10. 'Cinema as weapon: Ritwik Ghatak's unknown masterworks', programme note, New York Film Festival, 1996. Archival material obtained from University of California, Berkeley Art Museum and Pacific Film Archive.
11. Ritwik Ghatak, *On the Cultural Front: A thesis submitted to the CPI in 1954*, Ritwik Memorial Trust, Kolkata, 2006, p. 18.
12. Ashish Rajadhyaksha, *Ritwik Ghatak: A Return to the Epic*, Screen Unit, Bombay, 1982, p. 9.
13. Ghatak's letter to Mukherjee dated 10 April 1956, in Surama Ghatak, *Ritwik*, 2009, p. 71.
14. Peter Wollen, in his seminal article on counter-cinema, identifies 'unpleasure' as its vital attribute along with six other characteristics including narrative intransitivity, estrangement, foregrounding, multiple diegeses, aperture and reality. Wollen refers to 'unpleasure' as a means of provoking the audiences to create a sense of disaffection to subsequently transform them into active spectators. For details see 'Godard and Counter Cinema: Vent d'est,' in *Film Theory and Criticism: Introductory Readings*, ed. Leo Braudy and Marshall Cohen, Oxford University Press, New York, 2009, pp. 418–26. Also see Ewa Mazierska, 'Retelling Polish History through the 'Soft Avant-Garde' Films of the 1960s', *Framework: The Journal of Cinema and Media*, 53, No. 1 (Spring 2012), pp. 22–39.
15. Ritwik Ghatak (interview), *Chalacchita*, 1965, reprinted in *Sakkhat Ritwik*, 2000, p. 17.
16. *Komal Gandhar/E-Flat* (1962) is about the factionalism and weakening of the IPTA, which angered some people in the Communist Party. Consequently, the film's screenings were sabotaged, and it was subsequently

withdrawn from theatres. Its failure at the box office caused Ghatak, as the co-producer, considerable financial loss. His next film *Subarnarekha*/*The Golden Line* (1963, released in 1965) didn't have any better luck. Despite a promising opening in full houses, the distributor withdrew it from theatres without consulting Ghatak. Rajshree Pictures bought the rights of the film for Rs 65,000 only and took charge of the distribution only to evade taxes on the huge revenue that they earned from another blockbuster Hindi film in 1964, keeping Ghatak completely in dark about it. Partha Chatterjee, 'Memories and Vagaries—Ritwik Ghatak', *Stage Buzz*, 12 December 2018, http://stagebuzz.org/2018/12/12/memories-and-vagaries-ritwik-ghatak-by-partha-chatterjee/, accessed on 22 May 2025.

17. In 1971, Ghatak made *Durbar Gati Padma*/The Turbulent Padma (1971, Trio Films), a docu-drama on the Bangladesh Liberation War. There were two unfinished documentary projects. The one on Indian Prime Minister Indira Gandhi he was making in 1972 was abandoned. The other was a character study of noted sculptor and painter Ramkinkar Baij that he was working on in 1975; it remained incomplete due to Ghatak's failing health and subsequent untimely death in February 1976. Ritaban Ghatak, his son, completed the film with available footage.
18. A figure, comparable to Ghatak with reference to chronicling the Partition and the pain both felt as a result of this fracture, is that of Saadat Hasan Manto, an anticolonial author, playwright, short story writer, translator, editor, a member of Indian Progressive Writer's Association (IPWA), and a dialogue writer and scriptwriter in the Bombay film industry. As Ghatak was uprooted from what he called his desh (homeland) that fell in East Pakistan and moved to West Bengal in India, Manto had to move out of his desh that fell in India to Lahore in Pakistan after the Partition. Both expressed their strong critique of the Partition through their respective creative medium.
19. Ritwik Ghatak, *Nagarik*/*The Citizen* (1953/1977).
20. Ritwik Ghatak (interviewed by Prabir Sen) 'I messed up often, but I never harmed anyone', Jalim Singh's Journal/*Journal of Jalim Singh*, September 1976-April 1977, reprinted in *Sakkhat Ritwik* (eds Dasgupta and Bhattacharya), 2000, p. 117.
21. Ibid., p. 117.
22. Inspired by the Soviet model, Five Year Plans (1951–2017) in India had been a centralised national development programme to promote equitable economic growth, alleviate poverty and advance critical sectors such as agriculture, industry, infrastructure and education.

23. Surama Ghatak, *Ritwik,* 2009, pp. 35–36.
24. Ibid., p. 219.
25. Cf. Sanghita Sen, 'Ghatak in the Shadows: Films that Struggled', *Shadow Cinema: The Historical and Production Context of Unmade Films* (eds. Kieran Foster and James Fenwick), Bloomsbury, London, 2020, pp. 109–26.
26. Report of the Working Group of National Integration Council to Study Reports of the Commissions of Inquiry on Communal Riots, Ministry of Home Affairs, Government of India, 2007, pp. 28–30.
27. Surama Ghatak, *Ritwik: Padma theke Titas*, 1995 (2010), p. 84.
28. Ibid., pp. 82–83.
29. Ibid., p. 83.
30. Ibid., p. 84.
31. Ibid., p. 84.

References

Chatterjee, Partha. 'Memories and Vagaries—Ritwik Ghatak' in *Stage Buzz*, 12 December 2018, http://stagebuzz.org/2018/12/12/memories-and-vagaries-ritwik-ghatak-by-partha-chatterjee/; accessed on 22 May 2025.

Ghatak, Ritwik. *On the Cultural Front: A thesis submitted by Ritwik Ghatak to the Communist Party of India*, Ritwik Memorial Trust, Kolkata, 2006 (1954).

—— *Cinema and I*, Dhyanbindu & Ritwik Memorial Trust, Kolkata, 2015 (1987).

—— 'Sorbagre Satyanishtha Hote Hoy, Tar Pore Saoundaryanishtha / First to be committed to Truth, and then commitment to beauty', Interview first published in *Chalacchitra*, 1965, reprinted in *Sakkhat Ritwik/Ritwik, Face to Face* (eds Shibaditya Dasgupta and Sandipan Bhattacharya), Dipayan, Kolkata, 2000, pp. 17–19.

—— 'Shilpi hishebe ami involvement-e biswas kori / As an Artist, I Believe in Involvement', Interview with Sunit Sengupta first published in *Movie Montage*, 1967, reprinted in *Sakkhat Ritwik/Ritwik, Face to Face* (eds Shibaditya Dasgupta and Sandipan Bhattacharya), Dipayan, Kolkata, 2000, pp. 20–25.

—— 'Cinemar Preme Moshai ami porini / I haven't fallen in love with cinema', Interview in *Chitrabikshan*, August–September 1973, reprinted in *Sakkhat Ritwik/Ritwik, Face to Face* (eds Shibaditya Dasgupta and Sandipan Bhattacharya), Dipayan, Kolkata, 2000, pp. 57–71.

—— 'I messed up often, but I never harmed anyone', Interviewed with Prabir Sen first published in *Jalim Singh's Journal*, September 1976-April 1977, reprinted in *Sakkhat Ritwik/Ritwik, Face to Face* (eds Dasgupta and Bhattacharya), Dipayan, Kolkata, 2000, pp. 97–127.

Ghatak, Surama, *Ritwik*, Anustup, Kolkata, Third Revised Edition, 2009.

—— *Ritwik: Padma theke Titas*/Ritwik: From Padma to Titas, Anustup, Kolkata, Second Revised Edition, 2010 (1995).

Mazierska, Ewa and Kristensen, Lars, 'Introduction', *Third Cinema, World Cinema and Marxism* (eds Ewa Mazierska and Lars Kristensen), Bloomsbury, London, 2020.

O'Donnell, Erin, '"Woman" and "Homeland" in Ritwik Ghatak's films: Constructing post-Independence Bengali cultural identity', *Jump Cut: A Review of Contemporary Media*, 47, 2004. https://www.ejumpcut.org/archive/jc47.2005/ghatak/text.html, accessed on 12 May 2025.

Rajadhyaksha, Ashish, *Ritwik Ghatak: A Return to the Epic*, Screen Unit, Bombay, 1982.

Report of the Working Group of National Integration Council to Study Reports of the Commissions of Inquiry on Communal Riots, Ministry of Home Affairs, Government of India, 2007, pp. 28–30.

Sen, Sanghita, 'Ghatak in the Shadows: Films that Struggled', *Shadow Cinema: The Historical and Production Context of Unmade Films* (eds Kieran Foster and James Fenwick), Bloomsbury, London, 2020, pp. 109–26.

University of California archive, 'Cinema as weapon: Ritwik Ghatak's unknown masterworks' in programme note, New York Film Festival, 1996. Archival material obtained from Berkeley Art Museum and Pacific Film Archive, University of California.

Wollen, Peter, 'Godard and Counter Cinema: Vent d'est', *Film Theory and Criticism: Introductory Readings* (eds Leo Braudy and Marshall Cohen), Oxford University Press, New York, Seventh Edition, 2009, pp. 418–26.

The alternative presence of Ritwik Ghatak in Indian cinema

SANJAY MUKHOPADHYAY

Long after his death in 1976, Ritwik Kumar Ghatak continues to be a mystery, a kind of enigma, in the rich tapestry of Indian cinema. Over eight feature films, and a handful of short films and documentaries, he had become a cult figure even in his lifetime. This is because all his films bear the mark of an artist trying to elevate individual situations within the larger framework of Indian history.

I am not referring only to the awareness which T.S. Eliot discussed in his seminal essay on poetic theory, 'Tradition and the Individual Talent'.[1] Also, I am inclined to locate Ghatak within the national framework of cinema. Before Ghatak—and after too—there has been a kind of commercial cinema in India that is loosely attached to Hollywood sensibilities; we have a kind of art cinema directly attached to European traditions, inclusive of French surrealism, German expressionism and Soviet montage. But nobody thought of or dared to inject, through Indian philosophical attitudes, something beyond the immediate in cinema, and venture into a kind of unknown territory full of existential interrogation.

A contemporary of Satyajit Ray's, Ghatak had a totally different agenda for the language of cinema. While Ray and other followers of art cinema believed in the representation of authentic details and a close liaison between life and image, Ghatak explored the symbolic and the metaphoric in his images, both aurally and visually. The question of the aural was, to him, of utmost importance. Before him, nobody had considered sound as a primary element in cinema construction.

Although Ghatak was committed to depicting the tragedy of the partition of Bengal, a regional holocaust, he chose not to do so through classic realistic text—an effort that was misinterpreted as anarchic and incoherent in his time. It is a measure of Ghatak's genius that he turned an essentially local experience into an expression that had universal validity. By treating cinema, above all, as an exercise in celebration, Ghatak negated any established genre distinction between the 'artistic' and the 'popular'. He was not loyal to continuity; he saw history as interactive. Naturally, therefore, he thought that unless history was punctuated with myth and legend, it would not resonate with the audience, facilitating a sensitive understanding of the human condition.

His experiences suggested a multicultural and intertextual order for history and folklore, which were then interrogated under the intense supervision of philosophical questioning. The idea of a national culture encouraged him to synthesise, almost absurdly, Nietzschean anarchic possibilities and the collective unconscious under the general umbrella of Marxian thought.

To achieve this, he would need to become a vertical invader.[2] And Ghatak was up to the task.

He liberated Indian cinema from the tyranny of visuals and lead storylines. It is through his work that, in my opinion, cinema truly became a vehicle of thought in our country. He introduced a number of issues—on the face of it, beyond the cinematic—when dealing with a particular subject. You may call it a discursive practice essential to understanding culture and modernity, but one thing is certain: in the Western world, there is Ingmar Bergman, and in the non-Western world, there is Ritwik Ghatak. Neither can be defined through their art alone. They were basically philosophers and seem to, I believe, enact a philosophical performance of truth-seeking.

Take *Ajantrik*, for instance. As Ray quite rightly pointed out, Ghatak's brilliant sense of editing, his compositions, his storytelling all demand comment and appreciation. But the intriguing question is on how tribal life is woven into that narrative. Why? One cannot be certain, but conflict

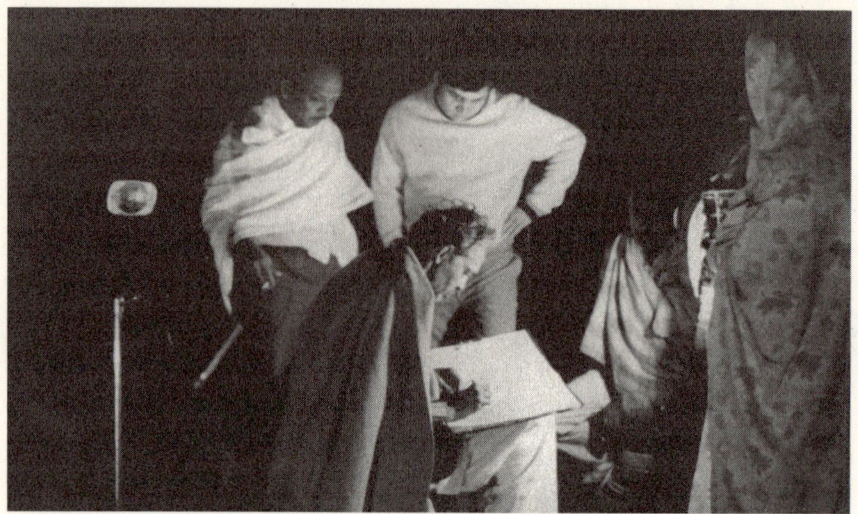

Visibly unwell, Ritwik finalises his plans for the following day of the shoot during the making of *Jukti, Tokko aar Goppo*; © NFDC – National Film Archive of India

and struggle seem to be at the heart of his thought process. Long before the study of subaltern history became mainstream, Ghatak thought of the deep structure of Indian culture, from which arose the possibility of a so-called primitive culture intermingling with the contemporary. The life of the Oraon people and the story of the vehicle come together and clash, and you can easily understand the debate.

What does *Ajantrik* mean? To Ray, it was anthropomorphism. To Jerzy Toeplitz, the celebrated principal of the Polish State Film School in Lodz, it was the madness in the character of the driver Bimal, which was a manifestation of the transformational crisis of civilisation from a feudal one to a bourgeois one. I think it was a kind of dialectical revelation—how machines are placed in the context of the emergence of modernity in post-Independence India. It's a significant question. Because our best thinkers, from Gandhi to Tagore, were largely opposed to machines. They considered machines as basically anti-humanistic. In the plays *Muktadhara*, written in 1922, and *Raktakarabi*, written in 1924, Tagore fought vividly with the mechanised order of life.

Ghatak wanted to locate machines and modernity in the culture of 1915 (when the film is set). He proved that a machine could act as a beloved. It is an achievement unheard of and unseen in our cinema. Before Ghatak, Indian cinema was not treated as an intellectual tool. Bimal is a born poet, who, in all his absurdities and anarchy, finds a place in the larger trajectory of Indian history, which includes the tribals and the local babus.

It is interesting to note that the first of Ghatak's films—*Ajantrik*—to be released was shot outside Bengal, despite his reputation as a Bengali through and through. The dialogue track included the tribal Kurukh,[3] and besides Bengalis, the Oraons played a prominent part, as did a Muslim boy from the Chotanagpur Plateau, where the film was set. This is India—and its ethos is not against mechanical impositions in certain areas. Artistically and organically, these can become part of nature and our everyday lives.

The camerawork in *Ajantrik* is unparalleled. Ghatak captured the car not in close-up but in mid- and long shots, with a bit of foreground and a bit of background. It encapsulates my thesis here: the whole landscape defines the car as a newcomer.

To Ghatak, in direct contrast to Western sensibilities, nature was not part of a mise en scène, but a part of human existence.

In this, he took his cue from Tagore, who, while discussing Kalidasa, said, 'In our oriental sensibilities, we consider nature as not a part of the narrative, but as an integral part of character formation.' He compared Shakuntala in Kalidasa's *Abhijnana Shakuntalam* to Miranda in Shakespeare's *The Tempest*, where nature plays a supporting role as a prop for her loneliness and solitude. Ghatak asserted time and again that, in India, the landscape has a role to play. If we go from frame to frame, we'll see how, in his camerawork and in his compositions, he designs the frame and sound altogether in a different mode to what was prevalent in Indian cinema at the time. As a result, like the Japanese film-maker Kenji Mizoguchi, he could go deeper into the very roots of Indian civilisation. Seen in this light, Ghatak was a discoverer as well as an inventor.

We could compare and contrast Ghatak's films with Western modernism, such as the inclusion of the Oraon ballad with that of Picasso's *Les Demoiselles d'Avignon*, which included the African mask-like faces. Or we could go back to Paul Gauguin and his Tahiti canvases. It may be argued that this association of the ancient with the modern is a kind of artistic manoeuvring to locate the true essence of the contemporary.

But in the case of Ghatak, you see that he is not a modernist in the conventional sense of the term. He goes beyond modernism. He is, like Mizoguchi in Japan, soaked in the inner soul of India. And that is why, in his films, landscapes take on unfamiliar shapes.

In *Meghe Dhaka Tara*, his most commercially successful film, take a look at the first sequence. He is introducing Nita's character. His first shot is completely non-essential. You can see 75 to 80 per cent of the space occupied by a huge tree. Nita is not a part of the narrative. It's only in the second shot that we observe her. Similarly, in the penultimate sequence, when she is screaming 'Dada, I wanted to live', Ghatak moves away from her and pans violently over the landscape, tilts the camera upwards. He wanted to establish Nita as a part of the landscape. As if the whole of nature is screaming. It is his ideal of organic linkage with the mother earth. And that is why the Partition disturbed him so much. In his reading, like in Tagore's, Bengal cannot be partitioned culturally. Indivisibility is the keyword to understanding Bengali sensibilities.

In the shot where the elder brother Shankar sees Nita at the sanatorium, the entire frame is filled with nature. Nita occupies very little space. That was Ghatak's basic argument, one that courses through everything from *Komal Gandhar* to *Subarnarekha* to *Jukti, Tokko aar Goppo*. His movies are a unique coming together of history and culture.

In the sound pattern of *Meghe Dhaka Tara*, it's astonishing to note how noise can take centre stage. Instead of removing at the editing table every incidental sound, every kind of disturbance, Ghatak included them in the sound design, mingling the incidental noise and the effect noise. It is sheer brilliance. From the sound of rice boiling to that of a falling leaf, plus folk music and Tagore songs, everything became a part of the mise en scène. It is not a narrative only of human beings, but a grand narrative that encompasses a sense of the totality, the Brahma in Indian philosophy.

In *Subarnarekha*, for instance, Ghatak redesigned, or refashioned, the epic Ramayana. And while doing so, he cast Kaushalya, the mother of the dynasty, as a subaltern bagdi bou, the wife of a fisherman, and Ram, the king in the epic, as a bagdi boy. In the platform sequence, he deliberately avoided showing the death of the bagdi bou, and a cacophony of sounds speak for themselves. Ghatak was like an invader.

In *Jukti, Tokko aar Goppo*, he used Hindu mythology to a different effect. What does Durga, the mother, represent in his eyes? It is not the elitist, Brahminical form of Durga. Look at the sound design in *Titas Ekti Nodir Naam*, where he did not show the proximity of human bodies in a lovemaking scene, but just layers of sound to indicate the intimacy. This method was extended to *Jukti, Tokko aar Goppo*, where he tried to couple a violent historical argument with the deepest moments of human intimacy.

When he used Hindu mythological references, Ghatak was accused of offending Hindu sensibilities. But think of the scene in *La Dolce Vita*, where the character of Steiner delivers the final speech where the Bible is used very deliberately and effectively. When Ghatak used 'Hey Ram' in the first sequence of *Subarnarekha* in a historically placed reference to the assassination of Gandhi, and then 'Hey Ram' in the end to a mythically placed reference to the agnipariksha of Sita, we see how he overcomes the limitations of time and creates a kind of hallucinatory moment of absolute truth.

That's why it's demeaning to limit Ghatak to being a teller of Partition stories alone. His characters are always displaced—from *Nagarik* to *Ajantrik*, everyone is out of place, in an alien land. Ghatak's relevance has only increased internationally as people across the world lose their homes and travel to far-off places to find a space for themselves. His films describe the true agony and the failures of his times as protest, as Luis Buñuel did in *Nazarin*. And in *Jukti, Tokko aar Goppo*, when he inserts, to our utter astonishment, the fifth symphony (or the fate symphony) of Beethoven, we understand that victory is Ghatak's fate; he will be victorious in the end.

In *Subarnarekha*, the Great Mother appears as a bohurupee/polymorph in the abandoned airstrip, and momentarily, we are frightened. What is this? Portents of a disaster of some sort? No. He wants to console us. He wants to say that it's just a moment of untruth. Whenever Ghatak named his characters, he largely drew on the Hindu tradition, since he considered history as part of today's story. This is unmatched in our culture.

Ghatak was interested in more than innovative adventure. His use of wide-angle lens and telephoto lens, his extreme close-ups, his location of the principal protagonists at the extreme ends of the frames, leaving wide open spaces, forces us to compare him with the great Japanese film-maker

Yasujirô Ozu, who also discovered the nuances of empty space. It was the spatial whisperings of nature that Ghatak most paid tribute to: Nita's placement in the penultimate sequence in *Meghe Dhaka Tara*, and in *Komal Gandhar*, Anasuya's placement in the river valley or the khowai. This, too, is unique—as much storytelling as it is historical commentary. Compare this proclivity with Diego Velázquez's *Las Meninas* (The Ladies in Waiting). Michel Foucault argued that, though Velázquez was a master of classical painting, in this work, he subtly investigated how structures of knowledge and representation work, giving us a new grammar for newer ways of thinking. This is also what Ghatak does when he uses extreme close-ups of Sita in the brothel scene in *Subarnarekha* or when he uses sound images to describe the political scenario in West Bengal in *Jukti, Tokko aar Goppo*. He actually made a drastic metamorphosis of the cinematic mode of realistic representation there.

By questioning established structures with the unusual frames he composed, Ghatak introduced reflexivity in cinema. And he was, it is plain to see, the first self-consciously destructive film-maker when it came to prevalent modes of representation.

There's another important piece of painting, Rembrandt's *Nightwatch*, that I think of in the context of Ghatak's cinema. People often wonder why Rembrandt, the greatest of portrait painters in medieval Europe, left the path of faithful representation and inserted apparently undesirable elegance to the frame, and why he played so passionately with gloomy, low lights. The same question may arise when we look at the '*Je raate mor duwarguli*' song sequence in *Meghe Dhaka Tara*, where Ghatak deliberately did away with normal lighting arrangements, creating extreme darkness, and along with it unimaginably extreme illumination, to prove that heaven can indeed descend on earth.

These kinds of unheard-of and unique manipulations of photographic images and aural moments are Ghatak's unique contribution to Indian cinema. He was an innovator. Ray began the practice of a believable, realistic mode of representation in cinema with *Pather Panchali*, but Indian cinema reached adulthood and a self-consciously contemporary avatar only with the release of *Ajantrik*. With the arrival of Ray, we became aware of the possibilities of cinematic reality. With Ghatak, we came to know the true limitations of the cinematic medium. He forced us to learn how art also has a right to criticise itself.

Time will tell what Ghatak contributed to the development of international cinema, but we can conclude with some honesty that he was truly in consonance with Leninist thoughts—national in content but international in form. Rarely has there been an artist like him, capable of functioning in a space of such apocalyptic ambiguity, incapable of denying reality and yet eternally questioning that reality was a fixed thing.

Sanjay Mukhopadhyay is a film historian and author.

Notes

1. To Eliot, a poet must be aware of the past and 'self-sacrifice' to this awareness and, once this awareness is achieved, all traces of the poet's personality will be removed from their creation because, with this awareness, the poet has become merely a medium for expression.
2. A concept created, possibly, by German writer and politician Walther Rathenau, to describe a force or entity that enters a system or situation from a position of lower status or power, disrupting the existing order.
3. Originally a Dravidian language, Kurukh is spoken primarily by people of the Oraon and other tribes in parts of eastern India.

RITWIK, BY RITWIK

'I don't see any reason to put cinema on a pedestal'

An interview with RITWIK GHATAK, conducted sometime in the 1960s

Why do you make films?

For the people. What else is there but people? The last word in all art is the people. I, in my own small way, try to do the same.

They say all art is mimesis of life. Do you agree that cinema is also an imitation of life?

There is nothing different about cinema. Like with all art, in cinema, too, we try to find something new, something deep. Cinema is a form of art. Therefore, it has to be responsible. Responsible to the people. This we cannot ignore.

If it imitates life, what life are we talking about: the social or the personal?

The personal is becoming less relevant now. It's the social that is becoming more and more significant. So art must make the social life of humans its accessory. Of course, there is the question of the art being liked; the artist is rendered irrelevant if that isn't the case. I feel that is a distortion of sorts in all art. If you understand that, you will understand what I have said so far.

'An artist is forever searching for something';
© NFDC – National Film Archive of India

Looking at the other forms of art—literature, paintings, dance, music—does cinema have a quality that sets it apart?

Nothing significant. The fact of attracting human beings and mesmerising them is true of all art and equal in all art. There's no need to assign any additional value to cinema in this regard. Human beings are human beings. They express their love in much the same way towards all art. I don't see any reason to put cinema on a pedestal. I don't know what else to say.

Along with changes in the social life of human beings, does cinema also change in terms of its form and content?

Content comes first. Rabindranath had said one must first bow at the altar of truth and only then beauty. Try to understand what he was saying. Form is nothing. It's just the shell. Take the films of Andrzej Wajda—made with so much labour and suffering, they are criticised for being impertinent. There is a need to penetrate the depths of the human mind. That's where content takes shape and where form charts its own path. But these are external factors. The main thing is philosophy. That is in short supply these days. After Luis Buñuel, [Kenji] Mizoguchi is no more, [Yasujirô] Ozu is no more. Only [Akira] Kurosawa has a free run. [Federico] Fellini has sold out. [Michelangelo] Antonioni doesn't have the mentality to go deep enough into these things. [Ingmar] Bergman is a knave. [Michael] Cacoyannis did try some good things, in films like *Elektra* (1962), but he also lost his way. The French Nouvelle Vague and the Polish and Czechoslovakian versions of Nouvelle Vague that followed pain me. The ones that adapted Jean-Paul Sartre's and Albert Camus's way of thinking were mostly infantile, childish. There was no depth to their work. Shirley Clarke has also been dishonest in films like *Connection* (1961) and so has Lindsay Anderson. They were not able to go deep into anything. All forms of art are constant, certain. If cinema is a form of art, then [Sergei] Eisenstein, [Vsevolod] Pudovkin, [D.W.] Griffith and [Charlie] Chaplin, in his earlier works, are the only ones standing tall, supremely powerful. The mischief film-makers are up to these days is not acceptable to me at all. Apart from Fellini's *La Dolce Vita* (1960) and everything Buñuel has made.

Are there any significant distinctions in the recent films made in the socialist countries of Europe and in other Western countries?

I don't think so. Film-makers from the socialist countries are imitating the gimmickry of the French. I despise that. Their society is nothing like they are portraying in these films. The Russian films, with the exception of a couple of film-makers, are idiotic. There is no need to waste time talking about them. I haven't watched films from Vietnam, I haven't watched films from Cuba, I haven't watched films from China. So I don't have a right to speak about cinema from these countries. If they have made films like educated and sophisticated people, then thank you to them.

In trying to paint a reflection of life, do the artists try to make us see the world the way they do?

An artist is forever searching for something. Maybe the artist reaches somewhere at the end of it, maybe they fail to. But both are right in their own ways. The artist tries. And at one point, the artist gives up trying. But the fact that the artist has raised a question, that is what touches people, makes them think. That is what the artist's success lies in.

But what if the audience doesn't accept the artist, or the artist's worldview? What should the artist do—stay firm in their convictions or think about their worldview based on what the audience tells them? Where does the independence of the artist end?

An artist must always remain firm in their convictions.

I asked you that because it is after your cinema that the era of subjective realism has begun to take shape in India.

Yes, I have heard that too, but such labelling has no meaning. Those are just labels, of no other use. Everyone is charting their own path. And this French 'New Wave' ... I think it's just a stunt.

This interview has been translated from the version published in Ritwik: Nijer Kothay, Nijer Lekhay (Ritwik: In his words, in his writings), *edited by Sanjay Mukhopadhyay and published by Bodhisattva Books in 2003. The interview has been published elsewhere too, but the editor of this anthology has regretfully not been able to confirm the name of the interviewer or the publication it first appeared in.*

Some thoughts on *Ajantrik*

RITWIK GHATAK

For twelve long years, I had thought about this story before I made it into a film. When it first came my way, quite by accident, I was a green boy, newly come to Calcutta and fresh from the university. *Ajantrik* caught my imagination and held it for ten days at a stretch—for more reasons than its pleasant rhyme with my name.

I thought about it for a long time in a vague and general sort of way. Never concretely. What struck me most was its philosophical implication. Here was a story which sought to establish a new relationship in our literature—the very significant and inevitable relationship between man and machine.

Our literature, in fact our culture itself (i.e. the culture of middle-class city-dwellers), has never cared very much for the machine age. The idea of the machine has always had an association of monstrosity for us. It devours all that is good, all that is contemplative and spiritual. It is something that is alien to the spirit of our culture—the spirit of ancient, venerable India. It stands for clash and clangour, for swift, destructive change, for fermenting discontent.

I am not a sociologist. I cannot explain the phenomenon. This apathy may be due to the fact that all change and the very introduction of the machine age was the handiwork of foreign overlords. It might have more comprehensive causes, encompassing all the pangs of Western civilisation.

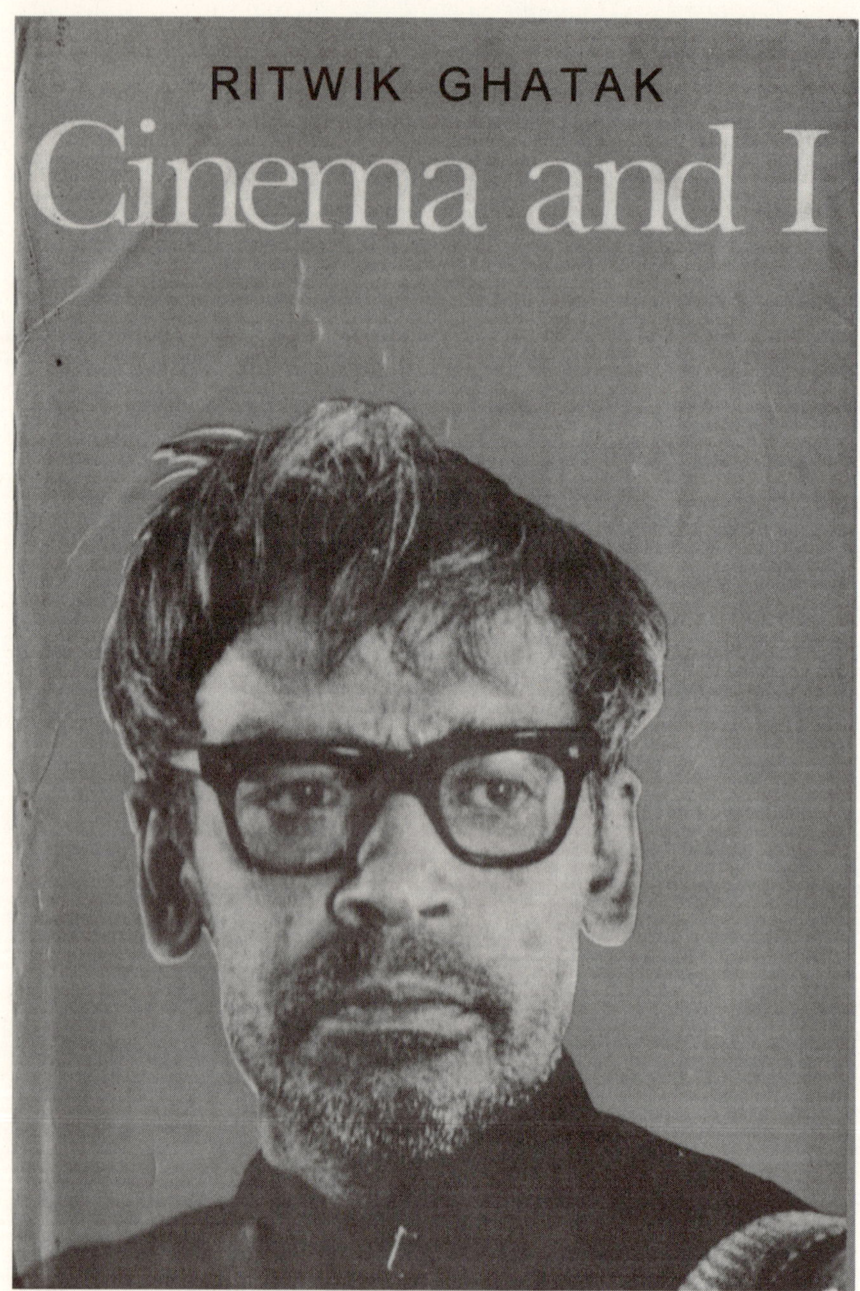

To many film-makers, this is a Bible of sorts

But the end product of all these causes seems to be an ideological streak which is doing immense harm in all practical spheres of life.

This attitude is hardly compatible with the objective truth as it obtains in present-day India. Or in our future, for that matter. With all our newly achieved technology, we have yet to find ways of integrating the future into our heritage—the order of the day is an emotional integration of this machine age.

And that is precisely what *Ajantrik*, the story, has achieved for the first time in our literature. It has achieved this in a unique, and in my opinion, a typically Indian way. It contains a quaint indigenous flavour in its plot structure, its characterisation, its very style of narration.

Also, it rings true. It rings true in every line of it. I have seen such men (I have had the doubtful pleasure of meeting Bimal himself in real life), and I have been able to believe in their emotions. Therein lies the story's greatest source of power.

I had a chance and made the film. It was fun all the way through—it is still fun while it is grossing exactly nothing at the box office.

There were other points of attraction for me.

Firstly, the story is laid out in a terrain that normal Bengali filmgoers hardly know. They have no emotional attachment to it. Try however I might, I could not peddle in nostalgic sentimentalism, which is the curse of many a fine worker in this country. I had to create new values, all within the span of the film itself. On the other hand, I could cash in on the novelty of the landscape. The different planes and levels are refreshingly unusual to the plainsmen of the Gangetic delta.

Secondly, the tribal people. They are the people who own the land where the story is laid out. Without them, the landscape would lose its charm and meaning. I cannot marshal my camera without integrating them into my composition.

Also, it is a silly story.

Only silly people can identify with a man who believes that godforsaken car has life.

Silly people like children, simple folk like peasants, animists like tribals.

To us, city folks, it is a story about a crazy man.

The machine especially repels us. Had it been a bullock or an elephant or some other animal object, it would not have been so difficult. We could imagine ourselves in love with a river or a stone. But a machine—there we draw the line.

But these people do not have that difficulty.

They are constantly in the process of assimilating anything new that comes their way. In all our folk art, the signs of such assimilation are manifest.

This process is even more marked among the tribal people of central India. And the tribe I chose—the Oraons—are very culture-minded and have this tendency in a pronounced manner. I had a nodding acquaintance with them, having been among them as a documentary film-maker for about five years. And I so often wondered at their vigorous imagination. They would fully understand Bimal, for they themselves are like him.

The Oraons have the same attitude to externals, and that is the emotional thesis of this story. I found an affinity between their pathetic fallacy and Bimal's. For this reason, they provided the ideal setting for this film. I could utilise their many significant customs. The different moods created by their high-flying bairakhis (flags) tilted at different angles and dangled at a different tempo is an expression of the most artistic temperament. I admit that these and many other things were too specialised in their meaning to have any general significance. But if I could go on integrating them into my pattern of things in a consistent manner, I could hope to arrive at a cumulative effect which would be a major contributing factor beyond just local colour.

Thirdly, the story has a ramshackle car as its central character. This very fact threw up so many plastic and dynamic potentialities. I could always fall back upon mechanical speed—what with opportunities of bringing in the time-honoured mechanism of the chase and hair-breadth escapes and breakdowns at judiciously chosen moments!

Fourthly, we had to work with the poorest possible materials, and that too, on a shoestring budget. This film threw before us a challenge at every step. Every shot taken was every shot achieved. This seemed to me to be really invigorating. It is a situation in which one curses oneself at every step and likes it.

All these considerations drove me to *Ajantrik*, and I jumped at the first opportunity to make it.

This essay was included in, among other publications, Ritwik Ghatak's Cinema and I, *published by Ritwik Memorial Trust, of which Ritaban Ghatak is the trustee. The piece has been lightly edited.*

Humanist film-making

RITWIK GHATAK

In all art forms, rasa is infused to varying levels. A man enjoys rasa depending on his ability to imbibe it.

Let us look at how this works in cinema. At an elementary level, it might be a story of laughter and tears, of the joys and the sorrows of life. If we go deeper, we find political and social implications. If we go even further, we find directions, depending on the philosophy and the consciousness of the artist. If one were to go beyond this too, the transcendent feeling one would then experience cannot be expressed in words. At that moment, one reaches the doorstep of something unknown, unknowable.

It is not possible for everybody to enjoy rasa at all these different levels. It should not be expected either. We all get satisfaction at the level at which we function. But truly great art touches all these different levels—in fact, this is the fundamental precondition of all great art.

This is all very similar to rituals. At the basic level, rituals are about worldly transaction with the gods; at a deeper level, the same thing becomes transcendental. Comparative mythology could immensely help us understand the nature of this intricate phenomenon. This is true not only of films, but of all art forms across every age. Comparative mythology illustrates certain rudiments of art appreciation, which are expounded in the experiments and research of neo-psychologists.

Take, for example, the idea of archetypes. The social collective unconsciousness was present even before man became complete. All the deepest feelings of mankind originate here. And some archetypes control man's reaction to various situations. The basis of most of man's spontaneous reactions lies here. And this archetype manifests as a symbol through images. It is all rather complicated, and difficult for me to explain fully, particularly in this short essay. But it can be made clear with the help of illustrations. The value of judgements in any human society are the manifestations of these mythical values. For example, pigs are used as a means for barter among the inhabitants of some Polynesian islands. This is because, in all their legends, the pig is a most sacred animal. The pig is the symbol of moon on earth to these people. And moon happens to be the very basis of their existence.

It may sound absurd, but it is not really. Is gold more precious than a pig? Gold is not of any particular use as a metal, even if it is more durable than a pig. But there are more durable and more easily available metals. The reason that special significance is attached to gold in European and Asian civilisations is that, in the myths, gold is the symbol of sun on earth. And sun is the life force of all civilisation.

At this stage, let me say a bit more about certain things regarding mythology. Myth, and therefore civilisation, is a poetic supranormal image conceived, like all poetry, in depth but susceptible to interpretation at various levels. The shallowest minds see it in the local scenery; the deepest minds in the foreground of the void. And mythology shows that the history of civilisation is the history of conflict between the two levels of consciousness—one is the consciousness of the activists, and the other is the consciousness of the thinkers. These thinkers are the poets, the artists, the shamans and medicine men, the sages and the visionaries. The two types of minds are therefore complementary. The strong-minded, representing the inert reactionaries, and the tender-minded, representing the living progressive impulse—one of these the attachment to the local and time-bound, and the other the impulse to the timeless universal. In human history, the two have faced each other in dialogue since the beginning, and the result has been progress and process from lesser to greater horizons, from simple to complex organisation to attain patterns of the artwork that is civilisation flowering in time.

'But Dada, I wanted to live'; © Ritwik Memorial Trust

The tender-minded are impatient and the archetype manifests before them in reason. Take, for example, the following archetype: the earliest example of artwork we get belongs to the Palaeolithic Age in the naked mother goddess from the Pyrenees mountains [The Venus of Lespugue] between Spain and France. This Great Mother is still haunting the consciousness of people in different parts of the world. She has two facets—one is benevolent in the form of Sophia; the other is malevolent in the images of Kali and Chandi. In our Puranas, the same goddess is conceived of in these two manifestations as Devisukta. And this archetype of mother goddess is deeply ingrained in our society. All the songs of Agamani and Bijoya, which are the mainstay of Bengali folklore, validate this point.

This introduction was necessary because these points are of immense significance in the process of film-making. A film must be significant to people across India, because only then can the final appreciation of it be made—this has been true of all art forms of the past. And only those artworks which passed this test survived the onslaught of time. Western intellectuals have shown with the illustration of Shakespeare how significant this notion of transcendence in the work of great artists is.

And that's where the ultimate success of the film *La Dolce Vita* lies. Federico Fellini had to confront the primordial archetype again and again while trying to shake the foundations of the Roman Catholic culture complex. It was spontaneous, and so moved you deeply, and the vibrations remained for long in your mind. The old Indir Thakrun in Satyajit Ray's *Pather Panchali* (1955) is the soul of rural Bengal because that particular force was generated in her image. That is why it is not possible to forget her character. Such a stature did the archetypal itinerant priest in the film *Nazarin* (Luis Buñuel, 1959) take on that, at times, Europeans would sing and dance as they returned from a viewing of the film—the priest seemed to be another Jesus Christ.

There are so many examples of this sort. Take, for example, the case of Charlie Chaplin. He is mythology incarnate for he is not the citizen of any country. The whole essence of life is filled in the hopeless, frail body of this man. The small man is the representative of all the deprivation and sufferings of a class from the day humanity became civilised. For that is when class distinction took shape.

I have tried to remember these things in my films. I have tried to penetrate the constellation of our national culture complex in all my films. As a result, I may have been misunderstood not only in Western countries but in my country too. Apart from my failings as a film-maker, there is something more to this. That is: our country, particularly the vocal section of it, has lost its roots. This is a bitter, blunt fact. In the light of that perspective, my failure is insignificant.

I only want to stress that, unless we try to fuse our traditions with science, it is impossible to build any national culture, forget films. We should not tinker any longer with film-making because an important creative role in film-making may soon emerge in this country. I am particularly sensitive to these developments because I involved myself with film-making from very early on.

Consider my film *Ajantrik*. The character of Bimal in it is archetypal. The mad Bulaki is his avowed extension, and the dancing Oraon tribal is his sublime extreme. Piara Singh is the strong-mind as opposed to tender-mind Bimal. The mud-throwing children are an extension of the image of Bimal and, at the same time, the symbol of cruelty.

I over-emphasise these elements to capture the whole structure properly. Tribal songs have been used judiciously, though their implications were not understood in this country. I have been castigated for this.

Again, take my film *Meghe Dhaka Tara*. The symbol of Uma is very clear here. Nita is the most favourite of the characters I have created. I have imagined her to be the symbol of the mother goddess Durga. She is born on the goddess Jagaddhatri's day of worship. She is united with the mountain—eternity—in death. When the first indications of her death come, we see some people singing the farewell songs of the goddess Menaka. Nita dreams of the enlightened future just before decay, through the memory of looking at the sunrise from the hilltop in her childhood. And the shopkeeper Bansi says, 'She is just a child. How can she withstand such terrible pressure?'

Let's also look at *Komal Gandhar*. To me, Shakuntala is symbolised as Bengal. There is a fascinating essay by Tagore ['Pracheen Shahitya'], where he draws an interesting comparison between Shakuntala [from Kalidasa's *Abhijnana Shakuntalam*] and Miranda [from William Shakespeare's *The Tempest*], which influenced me a lot. The main reason for the uncertainty, the decadence all around with which I am familiar, is the partition of Bengal. I do not think this just because I hail from Bengal. As I tried to master the traditions of all of Bengal, I knew that the union of the two Bengals was inevitable. I am not here to judge the political implications, but the cultural impact of this is of great value to me. So the melody of *Komal Gandhar* is that of union. I tried to approach this truth like the sparks of lightning—through stages, through images.

My latest film is yet to be screened, so discussion of it would not be meaningful. So I won't go into the main theme of the film. In the process of discussion, though, let me describe a scene from that film.

In her childhood, our heroine discovers a desolate airport in the deep teak forest on the banks of the river Subarnarekha. She is fascinated. Looking at the damaged aeroplanes, she remembers the stories of the American bombing, the sleeping towns of Burma, the desolate clubhouse that was full of noise and the bombing expeditions. She dances happily on that decrepit airfield. Suddenly, the ferocious image of Kali appears before her. Startled, she runs and climbs on to the lap of a person she finds nearby for shelter. Then she comes to know that the person in the garb of

Kali is nothing but a behrupiya who dresses like that only to earn some money. He had not wanted to scare the child, and only appeared before her by accident.

I somehow feel that all of civilisation is facing the archetypal image of that terrible mother today. The survival of all of civilisation depends on that confrontation. It is difficult for me to explain this in any greater detail.

Translated from the Bengali original, written in 1964, by Durgadas Mukhopadhyaya for a brochure released by the West Bengal Information Bureau for the 'Ritwik Retrospective' in New Delhi in 1981. This piece has been lightly edited for republication.

The film I want to make about Vietnam

RITWIK GHATAK

The idea of making a film about Vietnam is a particularly difficult—and intensely sacred—one for any film director today. Tossing off a casual remark on the subject without going deep into the matter, or before examining the complete information on Vietnam, is either insanity or travesty. It is this travesty that I have to commit now.

My knowledge of Vietnam runs only as far as newspapers, some photographs and analyses of the news in a few magazines go. Leave alone Vietnam, I haven't ever been anywhere in Southeast Asia. So, when it comes to the source of Vietnam's abundant spirit of life, I can only discuss it at my desk, I cannot capture its pulse. Still, somewhere, somehow, I have been given an indication that this is an event that will change the pages of history. In some way, it seems to me, Vietnam will profoundly change something for the world.

One more thing. To make a film, I have to be confined to Calcutta or to Bengal. Not only do I not think of this as a problem, but, on the contrary, it also signals the shining possibility of being a primary condition for creative art.

From the perspective of what little I have perceived of Vietnam, the battle there is also our battle. The same struggle is being waged here. Vietnam is the symbol of resistance against all kinds of oppression in today's world. Actually, terming it a symbol would be wrong; it is the most extended form of this resistance. The suffering and tears in our own country are extensions of the Vietnam War. American imperialists have not understood this, which is why Vietnam has stunned them.

Or, one might say, turned them into mad dogs.

I'm told that some film-makers in a country across the seas are planning films on Vietnam, and some have even made them. I'm not talking here about documentary journalists, who have presented with great power the visible war in Vietnam. I'm referring to those in a distant country, who are trying to participate in Vietnam on the strength of their brains alone. In my opinion, they are bound to fail. I have had the fortune of watching a film on Hiroshima made by someone from this class of directors. This is the film that has led me to such a conclusion.

I recall something else as well. A renowned French director has expressed a desire to make a film on Vietnam. Several years ago, he had been given a proposal to make a film on Napoleon's life. Not the Napoleon of the battlefield, he had said then, nor the wars themselves—what had appeared more meaningful and artistically inspiring to him was the couch on which Napoleon had sex with women. He would begin his film with this couch. I tremble at the very thought of what might ensue if Vietnam were to fall into the hands of such people.

For, given its involvement with many other things, Vietnam has also turned into something else that's lethal—fashionable. So-called intellectuals have begun to jump up and down about Vietnam. They will never be able to grasp Vietnam's tears of blood, and its resolve tempered in fire. Because, just like the American imperialists, they can never place their fingers on Vietnam's pulse. Like ikebana or terracotta horses, their study of Vietnam allows them to remain 'ultra-modern'. Even amidst all of this, they might manifest the terrifying tendency of being caught up in so-called human relations. May god bless them.

Now let me consider how I would move forward with my own film. These are, of course, entirely disorganised thoughts.

A Calcutta slum.

A hideously ugly room.

A mother, with her sick child beside her. A voice outside. The mother pours out some hooch from a pot in the corner and takes it out.

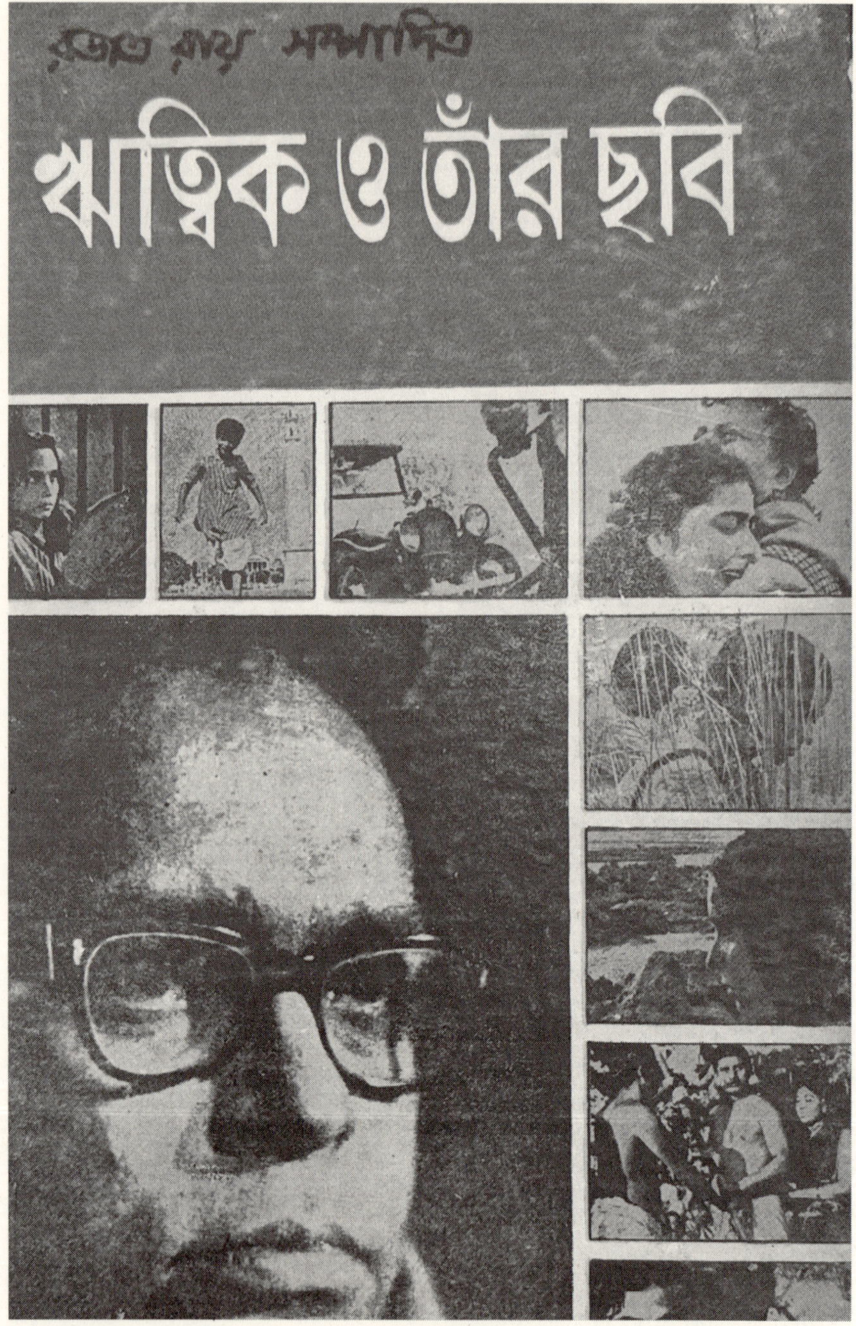

One of the first books to be written about Ritwik—*Ritwik and his Cinema*, edited by Rajat Roy

The sick child cries.

Outside, smoke rises from a freshly lit clay oven. The mother offers the bowl of hooch to a man.

A police whistle drowns the cries of the child. Several people run up and surround them.

Police whistles ... the child's crying ...

The sound of a rocket whistling upwards.

An American bomber plane. Split into two halves mid-air. About to plunge to the ground. (Seen in a still image, of course, for I always want to present the real war in Vietnam through stills. I will modulate these to the rhythms of living, moving images of the country.)

With this beginning, I want to show the helpless crimes of the impoverished in our country, which we normally avoid when we give the fighting spirit of the common people a stylish appearance for public presentation. I will reveal the entire picture of reality—the causal relationships between these so-called crimes, which are the lowest expression of the harsh realities of our fighting masses. The images of Vietnam will accompany them as explanation.

Then I will move to another episode, where I will depict the dreams of the downtrodden as just that—dreams. These segments will be based entirely on music and partly on dance. I will make no reference to reality here. As punctuation, there will be a succession of images of the brave girls and boys of Vietnam and of Algeria's National Liberation Front. As though they are determined to ensure that these dreams materialise. I will end this episode with a scene of musical joy and exuberance, with thousands of tender young children dancing. Their dancing and freedom fighters leaping over trenches will be choreographed to the same rhythm.

Now to the final episode. Here I will emphasise the presentation of the people as fighters. There will be full-throated recitations of Ho Chi Minh's poetry in translation, and scenes of the buoyant accomplishments of the combating and toiling masses will flow past our eyes. This ebullience is the elation of fulfilling the dreams presented in the previous episode.

Here I will try to capture that very pulse of life, which is a mystery to oppressors. The same survival spirit that sends roots into the earth and absorbs nutrition from it, the same survival spirit that is born in hard steel and the sweat of the body, the same survival spirit that exists in the depths of meditation—where there is profound peace—I will try to give it shape in the film.

I do not know if I will succeed, but I will try.

This is how I will end my film.

A young man who has been shot. Maybe a student, maybe a peasant. His agonised but elated screams will be borne to us, and he will collapse. Even in the face of death, he will clutch the earth with both his hands. My camera will go beyond his hands to his clotted blood—which the earth sucks in.

Another Vietnam is being born there. A Vietnam that is immortal.

This essay was originally published in Anandabazar Patrika *in 1968.*

Translated by Arunava Sinha.

Arunava Sinha translates classic, modern and contemporary fiction, non-fiction and poetry from Bengali and Hindi into English, and fiction and poetry from English and Hindi into Bengali. Over ninety-five of his translations have been published globally so far. He teaches at Ashoka University, where he is also the co-director of the Ashoka Centre for Translation, and is the books editor at Scroll.in.

Bengali cinema: Literary influence

RITWIK GHATAK

The Bengali novel is, in my opinion, in a moribund condition today. From among the thousands of books that have been published in the last twenty years, I cannot remember more than five or six that are worth mentioning. The rest have been written quite obviously with filming in view. They are notably conspicuous for their crassness and lack of sincerity.

The relationship between the cinema and the novel has now become a two-way affair. Literature is crammed with all kinds of cinema clichés and stock situations which authors think will endear them to film producers. And films are actually based on this stuff, thereby giving a further fillip to such writing.

The result: the growth of banality and vulgarity in literature and cinema. Both are boring and slow and packed with sentimental things. They harp endlessly on about certain family relations and complications which are non-existent in reality. They mouth the same kind of pedestrian morality. They strike poses which are patently false and even insulting to the intellect.

This was not the case with literature in the nineteenth century and the first half of the twentieth century. Authors then wrote because they had an urge to express some inwardly felt truth with honesty and sincerity. Bengal achieved at that time a literature of truly imposing stature. This was so up to the last war. The peddlers we see today were unknown at that time. There was dedication, passion for truth and beauty, and a sense of responsibility.

Naturally, when cinema came to Bengal, it was instantly under the influence of this great body of work. From the very beginning, cinema drew lavishly from the great novels and considered it an honour and a privilege to do so.

This gave Bengali cinema a goal and a direction. It was a positive gain.

Decay of Literature

However, literature soon started decaying. Yet, we clung to it. The more serious among us started looking to the past for exciting filmic material. All the great novels talked of a Bengal of at least forty years ago. The result was that we lost contact with present-day Bengal. The throbbing reality around us has been completely bypassed. Writers like Sarat Chatterjee [Sarat Chandra Chattopadhyay] became our guardian angels. And that tradition is still going strong.

Here we must take into account a cardinal factor—the question of audience. From its very birth, Bengali cinema has been a middle-class affair. To start with, the Bengali working class, as a class, is of very recent origin. And all Bengali films, even today, are patronised largely by the middle class.

This class indelibly imposed its philosophy and taste on cinema. If I may say so, weeping is one of the pleasures of people from the middle class. They like to have a good cry. They seem to derive some kind of pleasure from such crying. No one knows better than Sarat Chatterjee the sure-fire film formula that tugs at their heartstrings. These people want bold words, but always shrink from a really bold social situation. A family entanglement with, preferably, a female protagonist who suffers and eventually wins has a tremendous fascination for them.

So, our film-makers seek and film works of this sort. This goody-goody middle-class way of thinking still keeps our film-makers in shackles. Film-making is, by and large, merely photographed storytelling. The technique used is of the crudest kind. Any plastic possibility that the medium may have is not taken into account.

Of course, even in the olden days, there were some exceptions to formulaic film-making. The name of P.C. Barooah comes to mind. Here

Bari Theke Paliye was based on a book of the same name, written by Shibram Chakraborty

was a man who, in the late thirties, sometimes explored the potentialities of this plastic medium. His *Grihadaha* (1936) marks some of the earliest successful and significant transactions in films. In his *Uttarayan* (1941), he utilised the subjective camera to telling effect. Surrounded by mediocrity, he sometimes gave off sparks of pure cinema. In the ultimate analysis, however, he remained a product of his milieu.

The root cause of the poor state of cinema was its utter reliance on novels of varying quality. This is why, in my opinion, literature was an evil influence on Bengali cinema. This influence did not allow the medium of film to come of age. Our audiences were smugly happy in their ignorance and complacency.

This condition prevailed until some years ago. In the early 1950s came a break. Some groups of young intellectuals started considering cinema a serious art form. This way of thinking gathered momentum slowly and culminated in *Pather Panchali* (1955) and the emergence of Satyajit Ray. It is true that this film was also based on a famous novel. But, for the first time, the story was narrated in the filmic idiom. The language was sound. Artistic truth was upheld. The fundamental difference between two art forms was delineated.

From that time on, the trend towards serious film-making has been apparent in Bengali cinema, though the old school does carry on happily. Unfortunately, both schools lean heavily on literature.

Why unfortunate? Because, the serious film-makers, in their search for truly great works, had to turn to the past to find something worthy of serious attention. The contemporary was banished even from their work. But can cinema fulfil its function without looking at its surroundings? It cannot and has never been able to. Let us forget those celluloid storytellers, they are not film men; even the persons who know what cinema is, and what to do with it, are at a crossroads. On the one hand, they have to crawl back to an earlier era, an era which does not exist anymore, for truthful material. This makes their films remote from life as it is lived today. On the other hand, these men display a servility to literature, which is, to say the least, not filmic. How many great films are being made out of material from a different medium? It is original vision and expression that are wanted. And mighty few of our works belong to that category.

If we look around the world, we will see that modern cinema is largely born out of original material. We will also see that literature is on the decline. Cinema is increasingly becoming aware of its own power to express that which is inexpressible in any other medium.

When I consider all this, Bengali cinema presents a gloomy picture indeed. Yet, I find in our cinema a false sense of superiority, an unjustified pride. This attitude is eating at the very roots of the cinema in Bengal.

The Mission of Cinema

Cinema cannot but be engaged, committed, to be worthy of its mission. That, in the broad sense of these terms, is exactly what our cinema is not. It does not portray the burning reality around us.

What is the mission of cinema? I do not mean the approach of some film-makers operating both in Bengal and elsewhere, which is uninformed, foolish and sly. They pounce on and peddle long-winded words about big ideals and any recent national calamity, grafting this so-called purposeful talk on to age-old formula films. I mean the awareness, the sense of reaction of a truthful artist to the small things of life—literature today has abandoned this approach completely, and seems to have no intention of resuming it. Our cinema is toeing the line.

From the foregoing, let it not be thought that I reject out of hand all films and all literature being turned out today. There are happy instances, even today, of truthful films based on novels, and our literature is not all dead. But it is a question of proportions, to my mind. And the proportion is becoming alarming to me. Although the influence of literature on cinema brings many positive gains, these gains are being neutralised by other factors not so desirable.

It may be true that, considering the state of film-making in other parts of India, Bengal cinema presents coherent, consistent and logical fare, but that is not enough. Moreover, I consider cinema to be international, and, in that context, these shortcomings loom very large. We have to catch up with the best of world cinema.

There are heart-warming and welcome signs all around in Bengal. Large sections of Bengali audiences are sitting up and taking notice. They are being aroused. They are clamouring for the presentation of reality in cinema. Scores of film societies are springing up all over. They are organising audience thinking and reaction, and educating the intelligentsia in film appreciation.

Seeing this rapid growth, I am reminded of things as they were many years ago. College students used to join a literary circle and become poets. Today, they join a film society.

In Bengal, cinema has taken the place of literature to become the vanguard of culture. The youth, the student, the white-collar worker—they are all yearning for true cinema, committed cinema, pure cinema, from our film-makers. They want no more of those rehashed stories and novels which speak of days gone by.

They deserve more.

This essay was first published in Filmfare *in 1965, and later included in Ritwik Ghatak's* Cinema and I, *published by the Ritwik Memorial Trust, in 1987. It has been reproduced here with permission from the Trust, and has been lightly edited for republication.*

RITWIK AND I
PART TWO: THE AUTEURS

‘I am burning, everyone is burning ... the universe is burning’

KUMAR SHAHANI

This is Shahani’s second major essay on his mentor, Ritwik Ghatak: on his last film, the autobiographical Jukti, Tokko aar Goppo *(1974). That film had had a controversial reception politically, and more so for what was viewed as its somewhat self-indulgent autobiographical idiom. Ghatak died soon after it was made. It was additionally a matter of some irony that Ghatak’s first film,* Nagarik *(1952), long believed lost, was screened—after a gap of decades—more or less along with his last.*

After a generation has passed, Ritwik Ghatak’s first film is released—along with his autobiographical last. Yet, we should not be surprised. We have a habit of offering oblations to the dead while we starve the living. I remember him at a screening of *Komal Gandhar* at the Film Institute, the burning ash of his bidi falling on his kurta, watching his own film as if he had never seen it before. It had been taken off from Calcutta’s cinemas a few days after its release. He had tears in his eyes when a well-known Marathi film director, who, along with a couple of Ritwik’s favourite students, was watching the film, often turned around to express spontaneous appreciation. If Ritwik had a particular fault, it was that of arrogance.

So we were surprised by his childlike, helpless response when we told him that he should show this film to the whole wide world. We did not know then that he had felt deserted after *Komal Gandhar*, and his deep sense of waste, so sharply expressed in *Subarnarekha*, was being frenetically confirmed by his addiction to the bottle.

> Neelkantha Bagchi: For a bottle I will lie or steal, but for name or fame or position—I will never lie!
> Young man: You have practised that pose long enough to have become an adept!
> Neelkantha: *(Laughing)* You have caught me out!

But it was true of Ritwik. It is not a vain boast by a film-maker, narcissistically looking at himself. His commitment to truth, in and through the cinema, was total. It is not surprising, therefore, that even in his alcoholic condition, he is not self-indulgent when he presents himself. He himself is guilty, like his generation: a humbug whose childish demands never ceased.

With the suffering of Partition (into East and West Bengal), he also took on the guilt of the dismemberment of his 'mother'. He always wished to be fed: by the bottle, by his wife—by his Bengal. He tried to fight those who had violated and killed the unity of this mother-surrogate. In *Meghe Dhaka Tara*, the fertility principle suffers the same three-way split that Bengal society does: the cruel mother, the sensual daughter, and the preserving and nurturing heroine who dies in the process. The middle class itself is seen at the unsteady apex of an inverted triangle, a society divided three ways, which can find no equilibrium.

In *Jukti, Tokko aar Goppo*, the contact with the fertility principle is almost lost. The wife has rejected him, justifiably. The young girl, the future mother, is unabashedly asked: Are you the soul of Bengal, resurrected after the massacre of Bangladesh? Will she unite those who have already violated her selfish needs or narrow preoccupations? Will her desire for the young man, who resents her presence, bring forth children who—unlike Ritwik's generation—will not prostitute her? Perhaps; but he gives the girl no flesh and blood. And those who have no flesh and blood are dehumanised by that very condition.

No, Ritwik does not take a pessimist viewpoint. He only recognises the inevitability of violence. And, caught in that crossfire, it is not he alone

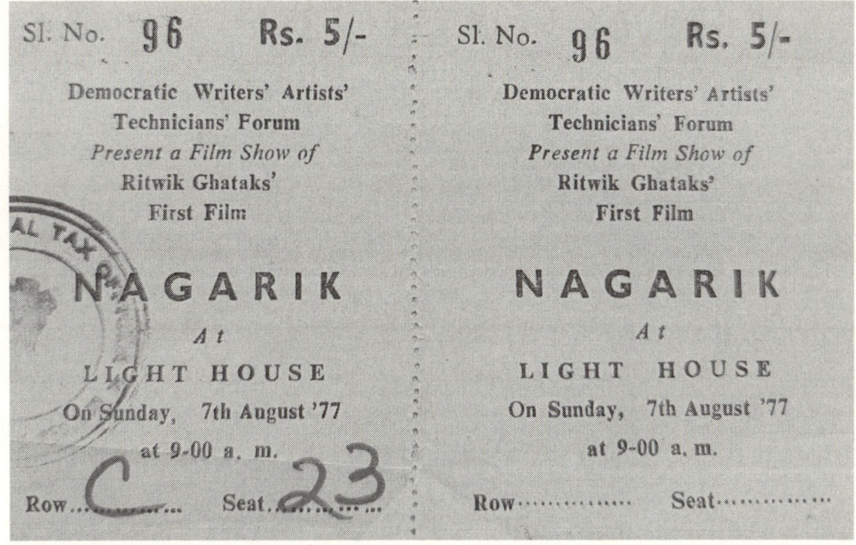

Sl. No. 96 Rs. 5/-

Democratic Writers' Artists'
Technicians' Forum
Present a Film Show of
Ritwik Ghataks'
First Film

NAGARIK

At

LIGHT HOUSE

On Sunday, 7th August '77
at 9-00 a. m.

Row C Seat 23

Sl. No. 96 Rs. 5/-

Democratic Writers' Artists'
Technicians' Forum
Present a Film Show of
Ritwik Ghataks'
First Film

NAGARIK

At

LIGHT HOUSE

On Sunday, 7th August '77
at 9-00 a. m.

Row.............. Seat..............

When *Nagarik* was finally released, twenty-five years after it was made

who dies unheroic, but also the young heroes whose moral courage he admires. But when, in his own way, he tries to deepen their humanisation and criticises himself, the answer is that 'You have practised that pose long enough to have become an adept'. Perhaps the soul of Bangladesh will now deliver a child of flesh and blood, with a purity which is not one-dimensional. Or will cruelty, violence, the recurrent dreams of youth, generation after generation, merely reproduce themselves? Ritwik seems to rejoice in the contemplation of the mere fact that life will go on—for if it moves on, it must be to something better—though the knowledge of that process frightens him.

Ritwik was world-weary, but could not forgive himself for that. After all, he was the most robust of film-makers that India has produced. Unlike most others, he was ruthless in the analysis and condemnation of the social decadence that he observed. The other cineastes, in search of mass acceptance, have often tended to caricature, either by way of slogan-raising or an appeal to indulgent humanism. The heroes and heroines of Ritwik's films, while their energies are sapped by a society which can sustain no growth, have inner resources that seem to assert themselves. In *Subarnarekha*, the young, slim slip of a girl is given, by way of a curious inversion of symbolisation (the sound of an anklet), a great strength. The apparently weak hero, the singer of *Meghe Dhaka Tara*, for whom the economy has no use, derives his strength from his disciplined pursuit. The cry of the nourishing woman Nita, even as she dies, asserts itself against the grand indifference of nature.

Ritwik's films are replete with semi-circular panoramics which show that nature is too great a container for individual sentiment. It is implied in the contradiction that, while characters often express their own feelings—and often even social failure—through the poetry of nature, the pathetic fallacy is an untruthful device. For this reason, one thing I cannot forgive in Ritwik's last film is the cliché-ridden sequence of his youthful love: 'I am in love, there's pleasure and there's pain … in my every limb the flute is playing …' Here alone is the glaring flaw within his own aesthetic. The technical flaws are understandable. He had told me that he was short of funds and vomiting blood when he made the film. Perhaps he was tired, that's all. Yet, in the scenes of confrontation with his wife and when the young woman of Bangladesh appears, he has shown his usual dynamism. The shot where he sits against the light falling from the window, the face emerging from the washed-out area as of a ghost, is dazzlingly expressive. His performance of a drunken man is, to my mind, unparalleled in world cinema.

In Indian cinema, the only other performance of such great simplicity and directness that I know is that of the saint-poet Tukaram (in the film of the same name), played by Vishnupant Pagnis. The great saint in his own time was also surely considered a deviant. Is it a commentary on our society—in the vein of Ritwik himself—that modern saints should be so driven to alcoholism or such other behaviour that they are emasculated before they can make a lasting impact? Sant Tukaram has lived through his songs and the legends about him amongst the people of Maharashtra. He has made a permanent dent in the rigid caste structure. In his own small way, Ritwik must have hoped to help make a global change. In all of the fifteen years that I knew him, every objective crisis brought to him a sense of euphoria.

The communist upbringing of his youth had taught him to act with a renewed vigour and hope whenever a crisis or breakdown occurred. But, like other poets, he had not the ability to organise. He chose instead to sing—or was that his form of action? At the time I met him, in the early 1960s, he had already rejected the mechanistic and somewhat alienated modes of some of his colleagues. He was extremely disenchanted with those of his colleagues who wanted to maintain a false unity and were not, implicitly, pained enough by the splintering of every form of social and cultural values and movement. His *Komal Gandhar*, interweaving the emotional break-up and confusion of the heroine with the splintering of Bengal and the communist theatre movement, was boycotted by those of his colleagues who had produced this very situation.

But in this social destruction, he continued to draw strength from the proto-materialism of the fertility cults. It is this tradition, secularised, that transforms the films by its complex structure—what may appear to the uninitiated to be mere melodrama. Moreover, by his extraordinary use of sound and the brutality of his narrative technique, the melodrama takes on an epic, rather than tragic, dimension. More and more, the episodes are fragmented and emotive signs, like the whiplash, become commentative signs. The ridiculous elements of the commercial cinema and theatre are here turned upside down and given sublime brutality. In nearly all of our commercial cinema, the audiences are made to enjoy the subterranean feelings of incest through an unspoken sexuality. In Ritwik's films, particularly *Subarnarekha*, incest is named as violation, destroying the very base of family entertainment.

It is these factors that make Ritwik's films a vitally generative force for the young. He does not hide behind a medieval or dead past, or a decorative Indianness. Nor is he content with the nineteenth-century critical tradition of the novel, moving from the romantic to the iconoclastic frenzies of a basically anarchist political genre. Very few of his contemporaries have avoided these pitfalls, whether they work in the cinema or other arts, or in the theoretical or cultural sphere. The conservatives have glorified the past in decorative and theological terms, and the moderns have rejected tradition and history to deprive even the contemporary of its meaning. The problems of underdevelopment have led them to civilise themselves through chauvinism or a totally alien reference system. It is as if they are ashamed of being themselves today, with their true history.

I hope that the young, who are beginning to return the love that Ritwik had for them, will neither be ashamed nor haughty about themselves or their society, but will meet the darkness around with Ritwik's bright agility.

I remember him on the days when he stalked down the Film Institute corridor and we addressed him as the tiger from Blake's poem. In *Jukti, Tokko aar Goppo* he seemed to remember it too—only, with a change of meaning: 'I am burning, everyone is burning … the universe is burning.'

Kumar Shahani, one of Ghatak's most celebrated students, was a film director and screenwriter whose best-known films are Maya Darpan *(1972),* Tarang *(1984),* Khayal Gatha *(1989) and* Kasba *(1990). A film theorist, Shahani also taught at the Film and Television Institute of Pune, where he had studied in the 1960s.*

Kumar Shahani, 'I am burning, everyone is burning … the universe is burning', in Kumar Shahani: The Shock of Desire and Other Essays *(edited and introduced by Ashish Rajadhyaksha), Tulika Books, Delhi, in association with The Raza Foundation, 2015, pp. 163–66. Reprinted with permission of the publisher.*

First published in Indian Cinema 1977 *(ed. Rani Burra), Directorate of Film Festivals, New Delhi, 1978.*

This piece has been lightly edited for house style.

The Royal Tiger of Bengal

ARUN KHOPKAR

Burns That Still Hurt

Roses bursting to life in a blazing fire. This is the image that comes to my mind when I think of Ritwikda's personality, his thoughts and his films. That fire burnt away even the tiniest trace of anything spurious, and the roses kept alive the tendermost feelings. The memory of his personality and his values grows stronger as the years go by.

Jukti, Tokko aar Goppo (abbreviated to JTG hereafter) was the last outburst of Ritwikda's creative genius. Like the authors of the Indian epics, Valmiki and Vyasa, he appeared in his own work. Neelakantha, named after a manifestation of Lord Shiva, is the central character of this film, played by Ritwikda. Shiva drank halahal, the deadly poison that was destroying all creation, and saved all forms of life. This poison turned Shiva's throat blue. Hence the name Neelakantha, the one with the blue throat.

JTG is a cracked mirror, reflecting the life and times of Ritwikda.

His was a fragmented personality. He was homeless by then, a perpetual wanderer like Ashwatthama, with the eternally bleeding wound of the partition of Bengal. His deep understanding of different cultures of the world made him a citizen of the world, and his deep love for Bengal made him a refugee of partitioned Bengal.

Ritwikda was more of a 'shramana', a wanderer, not accepting scriptural authority, than a 'grihastha', bound by domestic duties and rituals prescribed for a householder. Through his wanderings in *JTG*, he meets the people of Bengal from all strata of society. He reasons, debates, discusses and exchanges ideas and stories with them—hence the title of the film, *Reason, Debate and a Story*. The immediacy of the exchanges brings him viscerally to life, not only as a moving image on the screen, but in flesh and blood.

He meets young men and women of the Naxal movement. He has great compassion for them, and also has serious disagreements with them. The film ends with the armed young idealistic revolutionaries on one side and the gun-toting state mercenaries on the other. Our hero dies, calling for peace and compassion as he stumbles into their crossfire.

From the plot and characters of his films alone, it's difficult to see the depth, richness and power of his audio-visual expressive forms. The events and characters are part of the quotidian and mundane world. Yet, at decisive moments, they metamorphose into timeless and powerful archetypes. An ordinary, middle-class woman assumes the stature and power of a goddess. A simple folk tune, through Ritwikda's acoustic magic, becomes a haunting melody. The sound of boiling rice expresses the anguish in the heart of a mother deeply concerned with the future of her frivolous daughter. A whiplash expresses a protagonist's pangs of conscience, and the fading echoes of the dying heroine's cry are lost in the valleys of the Himalayas, indifferent to human suffering.

Ritwikda's complete control over visual images and sonic structures is easy to see in all his films. The heights to which he took the language of cinema and the emotional depths that he could fathom, too, is felt in all his films. There is a bipolar movement in his films. On the one hand, the visuals and sounds provide a rich experience of synesthesia, taking us to the deepest sensuous and emotional level; on the other, the cinematic form and intellectual content rise high with the flow of his narratives.

JTG is Ritwikda's swansong. As we hear its notes, lengthening and darkening shadows gather around the protagonist for his last hurrah. His screen death portends Ritwikda's material death. His last film's events and characters are drawn from the fairground of the life that he lived and observed. They are scattered and have no rising plot line. The film has no steady growth of character; the times and values themselves change rapidly.

The film has no well-defined grammar of cinema—in this anguished expression, there is no place for neat cinematic structures. The cries are so intense that you can't hear them even as a melodramatic melody. All you can hear is the cry of death. All is bleak, humanistic values are forgotten, and there is decay and ruin everywhere.

An Unforgettable Story

Ritwikda had made a short film called *Durbar Goti Padma* about Bangladesh's war of liberation. Whenever we asked him about any of his previous films, he would say, 'Don't ask me anything about them. The man who made them is dead. The man that you see here is a man who has seen the Padma river turn red with blood.'

He said: 'As we travelled in boats to shoot the film, the stench of bloated corpses floating around our boats was unbearable. At night, their limbs and even skulls thudded against each other, and at times against our boat. I will never stop hearing those thuds. How can I speak of art and cinema? In my youth, I saw the communal riots of the Partition, and now this pool of blood.'

In *JTG*, Ritwikda painted a picture of the Bengal of his times. So powerful was his vision and foresight that he ended up showing what all of India would be like in the years to come. On the one hand, decrepit and rotten. On the other, waiting for a new dawn and building upon its great traditions.

Ritwikda was born in what is now Bangladesh. Bengal's partition was based on the division of the land into two religious groups, the Hindus and the Muslims. The cracks in the cultural landscape have only widened ever since. But in his time, Ritwikda believed with all his heart that the cracks could be removed, Bengal would be united again, and that he would find these two half-seeds come together and give birth to new life.

Frank Lloyd Wright, the great architect, had said that, if a work of architecture possesses real greatness, it could be sensed even through its ruins. Ritwikda's last two films, *JTG* and *Titas Ekti Nodir Naam*, were such burnt structures. Despite the fire of self-destruction that raged within

Ritwik, during his initial FTII days; © NFDC – National Film Archive of India

him, the immense power of his vision and artistry are clearly visible in them. His earlier, more structured films prove his genius in one way; his last two films, full of symbolic characters and coincidences, and moving towards allegories, prove it in another way.

Glimpses of Great Power

Except for a couple of films, the characters of Ritwikda's films, their world, their circumstances and the events of their lives are all within the framework of the lower middle class. But his images, the sound effects, music and rhythms—there's something about them that goes beyond the realm of the familiar.

I had acted in Mani Kaul's *Ashadh Ka Ek Din* (1969). Everyone in Mani's unit was Ritwikda's student. In the bitter winter cold of Kasauli, our shooting location, we would gather around a bonfire at the end of the working shift and chat the night away. Many of the stories exchanged during these drinking sessions were about Ritwikda, his films, his teachings, his eccentric ways and his genius. Some were true, some apocryphal and some imaginary, but all vivid and memorable.

As time passed, this mosaic of stories gave form to Ritwikda's persona for me. A lot of these pieces were contradictory and continue to remain so. As I think about Ritwikda, or watch his films, the foundations of my memories begin to shake. *What am I watching, what are my memories of the film, what am I hearing, what is true, what is made up, what is myth and what is legend* ... it's impossible to decide.

I saw Ritwikda for the first time at the Film and Television Institute of India. The famous Prabhat Film Company's studios had stood at the very spot. Prabhat Film Company (or Prabhat Chitra or just Prabhat) was one of Indian cinema history's high peaks. *Sant Tukaram* (1936), a great favourite of Ritwikda's, was made here. It was the first Indian film to be feted overseas, and was adjudged one of the three best films in the world at the 1937 Venice Film Festival.

The FTII premises, spread over twenty-two acres then, were simple and down to earth, much like the films made there. No sparkle of new studios, though inconveniences were plenty. But everything about the place—the grounds, the trees, the living quarters—had the aura of having witnessed some of the greatest moments in the history of our cinema. Ritwikda fitted easily into this illustrious lineage and, in a sense, crowned it.

The Royal Bengal Tiger

The year was 1971, my first year as a student of the institute's direction course. One day, we heard that Ritwikda would be visiting the institute that evening, and would meet us and interact with us.

That morning, all of us gathered quite early. The first floor of the old studio had a row of make-up rooms that had been converted into guest rooms. We saw Ritwikda emerge from his room and walk down the passageway towards us. He was always dressed in white. He was wearing a dhoti, tied in the traditional Bengali style, with a knee-length kurta. Because of his lean frame and long limbs, he appeared taller than he was. He was ajanubahu (i.e. his arms reached his knees). Their long reach helped him slap anyone in his firing range if he were sufficiently provoked.

I saw Ritwikda's eyes from up close.
Tyger, Tyger, burning bright,

In the forests of the night;
What immortal hand or eye,
Could frame thy fearful symmetry?
In what distant deeps or skies.
Burnt the fire of thine eyes?
On what wings dare he aspire?
What the hand, dare seize the fire?[1]

It was this fire that gave him his creative power and also the power to destroy himself. Killer alcohol flowed through his veins like blood. It reduced him to ashes not long after he turned fifty.

He was indomitable. He didn't have hubris or arrogance, but had justifiable pride. He was aware of the historical value of his work, and so it pained him that his work was largely ignored. Along with being a man of exceptional creative powers, he could be humble and modest too. In his films, you can sense his childlike innocence and gentleness.

One day, he came to the class and, out of the blue, asked us, 'How many of you have ever loved a tree?' A couple of hands went up. He smiled sadly, and said, 'The rest of you can go home. You will never be artists.'

As I recall this story, the image of the giant tree in the first scene of *Meghe Dhaka Tara* comes to my mind. Under its vast canopy, you see a small figure, the heroine's brother, sitting with a tanpura and practising his singing. Nita, his sister, looks at him with admiration as she passes him. The whole scene is bathed in soft morning light. The vast canopy of the tree seems like an outstretched, gigantic hand, protecting all life underneath it.

As the film unfolds, Nita herself assumes the role of a canopy that supports and protects her entire family. She is both the strong, supportive vertical tree trunk and the horizontally spread immense protective canopy.

In a flash, I understood the connection between loving a tree and being an artist.

Oh Beethoven, My Friend ...

Our music teacher at FTII, Bhaskar Chandravarkar, loved Ritwikda deeply, and Ritwikda loved him back. Bhaskar was a disciple of Pandit Ravi Shankar, who was a disciple of Ustad Allauddin Khansaheb. Ritwikda was also a disciple of the Ustad, and thus they shared a common musical heritage.

Bhaskar used to tell us some remarkable stories about Ritwikda.

The students would gather around Ritwikda in his room till late at night. Bhaskar would occasionally be summoned and asked to play something on his sitar, which he would bring from the music room next door. This room also had a fine collection of long-playing records and an excellent stereo system.

Ritwikda loved listening to music with his students. Beethoven's ninth symphony was his great favourite. He would ask Bhaskar to play the LP of it. When it would reach the 'Ode to Joy' choral part, Ritwikda would say, sotto voce: 'My friend Beethoven, how divine is this! How did you create it!' If someone else had said this, it would have sounded absurd, presumptuous and downright ridiculous. But Ritwikda spoke from the heart. It was one genius paying homage to another; his excitement was infectious and it affected everyone present.

The remarkable thing about a true romantic is that he can leap from his own time to another in a trice. Through his imagination, he can overcome the barriers of time and space.

He was at home in many cultures, in all milieus. Ritwikda could traverse eras in minutes, go sit next to Kalidasa or clap his hands and applaud Sophocles or laugh loudly with Aristophanes, or travel to some Buddhist vihara and stand shoulder to shoulder with mendicants there or get lost in the magic of some ancient culture. His feelings, his experiences, his analytical thinking and his introspective nature, all combined to form his world. Though deeply rooted in history, he never allowed it to become a fetter in sensing what was timeless.

That Rascal of a Bergman ...

Ritwikda was never in awe of the reputation of an artist. He needed to test the greatness for himself. In fact, there would often be blazing rows with established names. He would unhesitatingly let fly a volley of crass, abusive words whenever he felt that it was well deserved.

One late evening, we met Ritwikda outside the main theatre of the FTII. We wanted him to watch *Silence,* an Ingmar Bergman film, with us and give his comments. The curator of the National Film Archives of India at the time, P.K. Nair, was also present. Ritwikda said, 'Nair, show them *Silence* by that rascal of a Bergman.'

It was almost midnight. A sinking man clutches at straws. Thinking on his feet, Nair said, 'If Bergman is a rascal, what's the point in showing his film?'

Ritwikda had started to walk towards the theatre. He stopped suddenly and dramatically turned back, looked over his left shoulder at Nair, raised his left eyebrow, and said, 'If I call him a rascal, that's between him and me. For these boys, he is a great artist.'

Ritwikda had never travelled abroad, so there was no chance he had ever met Bergman. But there was such conviction in his words that it went beyond fact; it spoke of a spiritual relationship between two geniuses.

The Sage and the Carpenter

Ritwikda visited us at FTII twice while I was there. In 1971, he spent two weeks. Then, in 1974, not long before he passed away, he was with us for another two weeks. On each visit, from the time he woke up to the time he went to sleep, he was with his students. I say students, but some of us were married, some even had children. To Ritwikda, though, we were all his 'children'.

Instead of using the conventional dichotomy of 'theory' and 'practice', Ritwikda on some days used to say that he was an architect of cinema and would deal with only concepts and ideas, so we shouldn't bother him with the nuts and bolts. On another day, he would say that he was only a carpenter and would have no truck with any abstract ideas. But each of these avatars brought its own enlightenment for us. It was his deepest conviction that architects and carpenters must share a common language.

Ritwikda loved the Greek arts, the sciences, the philosophies, and the dialectic between the concrete Aristotelian side and the idealist Platonic side. He admired the precision of the Pythagorean experiments of stringed instruments, which showed a practical and precise mind. He equally liked the Pythagorean speculation about the music of the spheres that connected the microcosm with the macrocosm.

He had great respect for the Greek tragedies, comedies and epics, as forms exploring and expressing some of the deepest truths about the human condition. He felt that the discussion in Aristotle's *Poetics* about lyrical, dramatic and epic verse was applicable to the arts of many civilisations, including our own. He made us see the relevance of our epics, myths, lyrics and dramatic verses with reference to not just Indian history, but also in a universal and timeless conceptual framework.

Ritwikda was thinking of making a contemporary film based on Kalidasa's *Kumarasambhavam*. In his film, Shankar and Parvati were to be a working-class couple, who lived not in the Himalayas but in a megacity, in a ten-foot-by-ten-foot room in a chawl. Listening to Ritwikda describing his concept for the film, we felt that we were witnesses to the first stage of an epic creation.

A Renaissance Man

When Ritwikda discussed the creative process, we realised how deep his knowledge of all forms of art was. With his experience as an actor, a writer, a director and a theorist, he had an insider's view of the theatre. Being involved with the Indian People's Theatre Association in his early years, he was close to some of its great artists, like Bijon Bhattacharya, Sombhu and Tripti Mitra, Utpal Dutt and others.

Ritwikda was equally knowledgeable about world literature. He had read a lot in Sanskrit, Bengali and English. He had read Greek, French, German and Russian literature in English translations. He wrote short stories, plays and screenplays, and was a great theorist of cinema and culture.

Music too. As I have mentioned earlier, he had learnt to play the sarod from Ustad Allauddin Khansaheb of the Maihar gharana. He was close to some of Khansaheb's students, like Ravi Shankar, Ustad Ali Akbar Khan and Bahadur Khan, among others. Khansaheb played many instruments, and knew their personalities as well as their idiosyncrasies. Inspired by him, Ritwikda grasped the very soul of music.

Tagore played a transformative role in the spread of art and culture in modern Bengal. His personality, his discovery of new forms of art, his worldview, his lifestyle and the institutions he created played a crucial role in the Bengal Renaissance. The arts of various countries lent their fragrance to the soil of Bengal. As early as 1922, Tagore had organised an exhibition

Supriya Choudhury in *Meghe Dhaka Tara*, the only Ritwik film that was considered a 'hit'; © NFDC – National Film Archive of India

of the Bauhaus artists in Calcutta, which included the works of Paul Klee, Johannes Itten, Wassily Kandinsky and Lyonel Feininger. Vasudhaiva Kutumbakam, or 'the world is one family', had become the motto of the times. It was a philosophy that inspired many great creations of Indian artists—a leading example is the mural made by the artist Benode Behari Mukherjee, installed on the wall of Santiniketan's Hindi Bhavan.

Benode Behari's mural narrates the history of saint literature through its key figures and their milieus. It brings to life the specific personalities of each saint. The faces, expressions, unique physical attributes, gaits, postures, attires, homes, the work implements are all drawn with loving attention to detail.

There are many similarities in the work of Benode Behari and Ritwikda—discernible at a deep level, but not easily seen at the surface level—which have to do with the way the two artists structured their images. Benode Behari worked with illusionist and realistic proportions of the human body but modified them to include spiritual and other-worldly dimensions as well. For example, the heights of the saints in his mural become indicators of their spiritual greatness. By such and other means, he achieved a synthesis between the pre-Renaissance artists, Baroque mannerists, the Renaissance realists and Far-Eastern scroll and landscape painters.

Ritwikda, working in a different medium, had to find his own solution to the problem of integrating different forms of perspective. To achieve that effect, he used a range of wide-angle lenses and created figures of great volume. His range included lenses with a focal length of 9.8mm, 12mm, 16mm, 24mm, 28mm and 32mm, the last of which he used only sparingly.

Lensing may seem like a technical issue, but great directors do not leave the choice of lenses to their cinematographers. It is an integral part of their vision of life and the form of their films.

Directors like Robert Bresson and Yasujirô Ozu restricted themselves to the 50mm lens all their lives. This lens creates images that are closest to the way the human eye normally sees the world. Broadly speaking, wide-angle lenses 'stretch' the space; objects further away decrease rapidly in size and seem to appear much further away. Also, the depth of field of wide-angle lenses is considerable. This means that the objects in the field of vision retain their clarity over a wide range of distances. This causes a baroque, exaggerated perspective. The object closest to the lens undergoes large distortion, but if the image is held for only a short while and introduced with a sudden cut, the distortion is barely noticeable. The image then feels like a monumental image from the rock-hewn cave sculptures of the Elephanta and Ellora temples.

Ritwikda used this range of wide-angle lenses as a musical scale. Images captured with a 9.8mm lens have very deep focus or even pan focus or universal focus, wherein the whole field of vision, i.e. foreground and background, stays in sharp focus. The image of an object close to the lens has the gravitas of a deep bass note. As you move through the whole range of lenses, step by step, the increasing focal lengths reduce the spatial tension and distortion. Each lens produces a 'note' of a specific volume and pitch, and the images, if rhythmically edited, can become lyrical, dramatic musical compositions in time and space.

The musicality of the visuals in Ritwikda's films carried them above a mere mechanical reproduction of the world around. The visuals created metric and rhythmic montage lines. His visual sensitivity responded to the tonal and even overtonal stimuli of the shots and created expressive and complex patterns.

Ritwikda's deep understanding of music made the soundtracks of his films memorable creations. Unlike the conventional division of the film sounds into voices, music and sound effects, Ritwikda strove to musicalise the entire soundtrack. Ordinary everyday sounds like the sound of a broken chappal, of boiling rice, etc., became expressive sonic figures in the rich tapestry of his soundtracks. In *Meghe Dhaka Tara*, when the heroine becomes aware of her imminent death and cries out to her brother that she wants to live, the sound reverberates and echoes over visuals of empty hills and valleys, indifferent to the tragedy of an individual.

Lyrical, Dramatic and Epic Forms

I have referred to Ritwikda's deep interest in the three forms—lyrical, dramatic and epic—of poetry discussed in Aristotle's *Poetics.* He saw this classification as applicable in principle to many artforms, including cinema.

According to Ritwikda, a lyrical form was something that referred to an event of a short duration, but had the potential of many emotional sympathetic vibrations, set in motion through similes, metaphors and other associative devices. Its soul was in its brevity.

The dramatic form was based essentially on conflict, often a single conflict of the main plot. Sometimes, it had subplots, too, but they were always secondary to the main conflict. The dramatic form was capable of handling a whole range of emotions, from extreme violence to serene peace. Bharat Muni's theory of the nine rasas, or flavours, gives a comprehensive list of these emotional states.

There may be many emotional flavours in a work in the dramatic form, be it a play, a story, a novel, a fresco or a musical composition, but the dominant ones are the tragic and the comic flavours, as the Greeks had recognised. It was this recognition that led to their annual festivals of the tragedies and the comedies.

Ritwikda used a specific dramatic form—the melodrama—in his films. The *Encyclopaedia Britannica* explains this form thus: 'Melodrama arose in the second half of the eighteenth century as a genre intermediate between play and opera. It combined spoken recitation with short pieces of accompanying music. Music and spoken dialogue typically alternated in such works, although the music was sometimes also used to accompany pantomime.' A combination of melody and drama then, and originally, a term that had no pejorative meaning attached to it. It was merely a lexical term for a specific dramatic form.

In the nineteenth century, the musical part of melodrama was either dropped completely or reduced noticeably. The term 'melodrama' came to assume a pejorative shade—sentimental, full of coincidences and unexpected, even improbable, turns of events. Ritwikda's use of melodrama was closer to its original meaning of 'melody and drama'. We will soon see how he took this form to epic dimensions.

The epic form deals with the lives of not just one set of characters at a given point of time in history, but has multiple narrative foci, which often include the history of several generations. It covers many aspects of life, like politics, wars, ethical issues, social mores, history, myths and even the aesthetic foundation of life.

Ritwikda's skill gave his melodramas the grandeur of epics. His lenses and camera angles created monumental images that approached mythic archetypes. In *Meghe Dhaka Tara*, he broke up the image of the Mother Goddess into three characters: Nita, the elder daughter, represents sacrificial suffering; Gita, the younger one, is the sensuous and frivolous character; the mother, in passively accepting Nita's sacrifice, becomes the destructive element.

Often, especially in Hollywood films, what is seen as 'epic' is just the piling up of many spectacular elements: large crowds of extras, dazzling sets and costumes and events sometimes bordering on the miraculous. This treatment of the epic form retains only its cadaver. But its soul, which resides in its ethical and edifying nature, is lost.

Though Ritwikda hardly ever attempted multicentric narratives, he often layered his stories through complex audio or visual devices, creating multiple cross-references. In *Meghe Dhaka Tara* and in *Subarnarekha*, the opening titles introduce many themes used later in the film. Some are drawn from either well-known folk tunes or from popular songs—often Rabindrasangeet, a large, syncretic body of musical compositions. He often uses the Wagnerian device of leitmotifs and their variations to create multiple cross-references. In *Subarnarekha*, he used the music of *La Dolce Vita*, from scenes dealing with the decadence of the middle class, to suggest the same kind of decadence in the characters of his own film.

In *Titas Ekti Nodir Naam*, Ritwikda alludes to the image of the Mahesh murti of the Elephanta Caves near Bombay. He framed the overlapping heads of three of his characters for a brief moment, using an extreme wide-angle lens. The effect is very similar to the image of the three-headed Mahesh, with all its grandeur. This is one of the most memorable images in his oeuvre, which momentarily lifts the film from its realistic symbolic plane to a monumental archetypal image, outside the frame of historic time.

As I have mentioned earlier, in the example from *Meghe Dhaka Tara*, of the split of the Great Mother image into three characters, Ritwikda's use of archetype is interwoven into the very narrative of the film. By using many such devices, he elevated the melodrama to the epic form.

Except for a couple of films, the characters of Ritwikda's films, their world, their circumstances and the events of their lives, all seem ordinary and contained within the framework of the petit bourgeois class of Bengal. But his images, the sound effects, music and rhythms—there's something about them that goes beyond the realm of the familiar.

In a Kavanagh poem, the poet sees two local groups involved in a fight. He is moved by the strong emotions expressed by the warring factions, but doubts if, with so many significant upheavals around the world, it is worth writing about such a trivial matter.

And then…

> *… Homer's ghost came whispering to my mind.*
> *He said: I made the Iliad from such*
> *A local row. Gods make their own importance.*[2]

Ajantrik: A Case Study

Ajantrik has been perhaps my favourite Ghatak film ever since I first saw it in 1966. Its picturesque landscapes, picaresque narrative, whimsical humour, comic flourish, unusual theme, emotional depth and philosophical significance are endearing to me. Fortunately, Ritwikda has written a lucid essay exploring the genesis of the film.[3]

He has, in fact, written extensively on cinema. During his lifetime, these writings were scattered in various journals, most of which had short lives. Fortunately, in 1987, eleven years after his death, a selection was published, under the title *Cinema and I*, by the Ritwik Memorial Trust. The book had a foreword by Satyajit Ray, full of deep appreciation of his illustrious fellow film-maker's contribution to world cinema.

Ritwikda's article on *Ajantrik* provides some rare insights into the nature of his creative process. After he read Subodh Ghosh's short story (which bears the same title), Ritwikda spent over a decade thinking about it. Once we see what he was trying to do, the twelve years he took to get to it seem fully justified.

The story has an unusual theme. It is about a man called Bimal, a taxi driver, madly in love with his old ramshackle taxi. He treats 'her' like his beloved and has lovingly named her Jagaddal.

In Indian culture, we have many stories about deep love between humans and manifestations of nature, be it a river, a tree or a mountain. We also have stories about love between a human and an animal, both in mythology and history. But I have never come across another example of love between man and machine. Such is not the case with cinema—even some of the classics of early cinema, especially of silent cinema, are about the symbiotic relationship between man and machine.

The very title of Sergei Eisenstein's *Battleship Potemkin* (1925) is the name of a machine. When the rebel battleship is surrounded by a hostile squadron, Eisenstein introduces a series of shots, which show the sailors, their faces full of anxiety, intercut with the rapid movement of the battleship's engine pistons, expressing the tension felt by the marines and the sympathetic beating of the battleship's heart.

How interesting it is to see this atheist and Marxist film-maker using a Romantic device like the pathetic fallacy, which attributes human emotions to an inanimate machine! Not only Eisenstein, but Friedrich Engels, one of the founders of Marxism, wrote with great admiration about the feelings that the Greeks had for their environment.

He writes: 'Hellas had the good fortune of seeing the nature of her landscape brought to consciousness in the religion of her inhabitants. Hellas is a land of pantheism ... each beautifully shaped individual feature lays claim to a particular god, each river will have the nymphs, each grove its dryads—and so arose the religion of the Hellenes.'[4]

Surprised? Well, though Marxism seems to be all about political economy, class struggle and class wars, isn't Utopian Socialism, dreaming of universal brotherhood or the harmonious relationship between the man, nature and machine, one of its sources and components?

A true revolutionary must always be a poet at heart, and capable of loving intensely, be he Engels, Gandhi, Chaplin or Mao. For only a poet can dream of a new and better world; all others will try and do a repair job. Does this list, throwing together as it does Mao and Gandhi, sound bizarre? Just give me a moment to explain why it is perfectly logical. Anyone who brings about radical change in the spiritual, conceptual or material condition of mankind and affects the lives of a large number of people is, in my opinion, a revolutionary. Of course, this is a personal selection; everyone is entitled to his list of revolutionaries.

Buster Keaton and Charlie Chaplin are great poets of cinema. They revolutionised the medium and made millions laugh (and shed tears too). *The General* (1926), Keaton's film, is also named after a machine, a locomotive. Johnnie Gray, the protagonist played by Keaton, is a train engineer. *The General* is one of two great loves of his life—the other is Annabelle, a young woman. His love for the locomotive seems to be greater than his love for the woman. Gray risks his own life as well as that of Annabelle for the sake of 'The General'.

In Alexander Dovzhenko's *Earth* (1930), this man–machine relationship is taken to a very intimate level. The tractor that Vasil, the protagonist of the film, brings to his farm runs out of water and there is no water nearby. Vasil urinates in the tractor and gets it going! Both urine and semen are ejected from the male organ. One interesting thing to note is that, when the protagonist is male, the machine is often seen as female.

Ajantrik unfolds in the Chotanagpur plateau region of Bihar (now Jharkhand), inhabited by the Oraons, a pastoral/agriculturist tribe with strong emotional ties to its environment. These are expressed in its beautiful rituals, a few of which are woven into the film. The loving picturisation of these rituals is not a mere decorative device, but intimately connected with the way the film-maker relates to his theme, in particular, and the world, in general.

The choice of *Ajantrik*'s location is apt. For one, on account of the film-maker's empathy for the Oraons' vision of the world, their love for nature and their ability to express it through rituals. Is not the setting of a truthful film a ritualistic and cinematic projection of the director's love for his theme, locale and characters? *Ajantrik*'s mise en scène uses the planes of the landscape, inclined at varied angles, as the treasure of visual possibilities offered to a film-maker. The choice of location makes it thematically significant and visually exciting.

The 'heroine' of the film, Jagaddal, is a taxi, an automobile. Automobiles have proved to be a marvellously suitable choice for cinema right from its early, silent days. With their unlimited possibilities for different kinds of movement—linear, circular, spiral, wavy, zigzagging, slow, fast, superfast—and their spectacular accidents, they have been one of the most popular sources of filmic thrills, excitement as well as humour.

D.W. Griffith, the great master of silent cinema, used the technique of chase sequences, which he had perfected, mainly with horses. The full comic potential of car chases was used by the masters of filmic comedy, like Mack Sennett and his *Keystone Cops* series, and the subsequent line of the great comedians that served a brief apprenticeship in his studio, viz. Chaplin, Keaton and Harold Lloyd.

Ritwikda exploited the visual potential of the automobile to portray the character of the heroine, and his fertile sonic imagination used the wide range of indescribable sounds that the taxi offered—from the resounding horn of happy times to her death rattle. After the heroine 'dies' and is sold as junk, the hero Bimal is shocked to hear the full blast of her horn, a sound he loved. Then he sees that a child had rescued the horn from the junk and was playing with it joyously. The death of the heroine and its 'resurrection' by a smiling child is truly a Chaplinesque moment, combining laughter with tears.

Very few films, Indian or otherwise, have such a rich soundtrack created from just one source: a dilapidated jalopy.

Ritwikda actually used this comic vein to make a very profound statement about Indian civilisation's attitude towards machines. As the machine age in India coincided with its subjugation by Britain, many nationalist leaders, especially the great Mahatma, were anti-machine. This is how Ritwida saw it:

> Our literature, in fact our culture itself (i.e. the culture of middle-class city-dwellers), has never cared very much for the machine age. The idea of the machine has always had an association of monstrosity for us. It devours all that is good, all that is contemplative and spiritual. It is something that is alien to the spirit of our culture—the spirit of ancient, venerable India. It stands for clash and clangour, for swift, destructive change, for fermenting discontent.
>
> … this apathy may be due to the fact that all change and the very introduction of the machine age was the handiwork of foreign overlords. It might have more comprehensive causes, encompassing all the pangs of Western civilization. But the end-product of all these causes seem to be an ideological streak which is doing immense harm in all practical spheres of life.
>
> This attitude is hardly compatible with the objective truth as it obtains in present-day India. Or in our future, for that matter. With all our newly achieved technology, we have yet to find ways of integrating the future into our heritage, what is the order of the day is an emotional integration of this machine age.
>
> And that is precisely what *Ajantrik*, the story, has achieved for the first time in our literature. It has achieved this in a unique, and in my opinion, a typically Indian way. It contains that quaint indigenous flavour in its plot structure, its characterisation, its very style of narration.
>
> Also, it rings true. It rings true in every line of it. I have seen such men (I have had the doubtful pleasure of meeting Bimal himself in real life) and have been able to believe in their emotions. There lies the greatest source of power of the story. I had a chance and made the film. It was fun all the way.[5]

Speaking of machine and cinema, let me remind you that one of the sharpest critiques of the dehumanising aspect of the machine age was provided by cinema's greatest clown, Chaplin, in *Modern Times*. Around the time Chaplin made *Modern Times*, he had just returned from his trip to Europe, deeply disturbed by what was happening to European civilisation after World War I. He thought deeply about it and discussed his ideas with many prominent men and women of his times, including H.G. Wells, George Bernard Shaw and others. He also met Gandhi.

Chaplin felt that the evil aspects of the machine were not inherent to machine itself but were historically conditioned. He tried to convince Gandhi about it. He describes this meeting in *My Autobiography* as follows:

> The packed room grew suddenly silent. And as the Mahatma's mask-like expression was one of waiting, I felt that all India was also waiting on my words. So I cleared my throat. 'Naturally I am in sympathy with India's aspirations and struggle for freedom,' I said. 'Nonetheless, I am somewhat confused by your abhorrence of machinery … After all, if machinery is used in the altruistic sense, it should help to release man from the bondage of slavery, and give him shorter hours of labour and time to improve his mind and enjoy life.'
>
> However, Gandhi was not convinced. 'I understand,' he said, speaking calmly, 'but before India can achieve those aims, she must first rid herself of English rule. Machinery in the past has made us dependent on England, and the only way we can rid ourselves of that dependence is to boycott all goods made by machinery. That is why we have made it the patriotic duty of every Indian to spin his own cotton and weave his own cloth. That is our form of attacking a very powerful nation like England.'[6]

Pantheism and Animism

Tagore and Ritwikda had an immense capacity to love, a love that was not restricted to human beings. Tagore's vision was pantheistic; he could see his creator as easily in a dewdrop as in a vast ocean or in the Milky Way.

Ritwikda's films are replete with meticulously depicted landscapes, using his trademark wide-angle lenses. They had both beauty and terror, culminating in *Titas Ekti Nodir Naam*, where the theme is the changing moods of a river and the wiping away of an entire inhabitation. *Titas Ekti Nodir Naam* is like Kali, who can take away life, and also like Gauri, the daughter of the Himalayas, who can give life and create civilisations.

Indian culture is syncretic, and includes even the pre-Vedic animistic practices and non-Aryan visions of the world. Ritwikda was a close friend of the great historian and scientist Damodar Dharmananda Kosambi, who was the first to explore these beliefs and practices for a materialist view of Indian history. Kosambi used to visit FTII and watch films with Ritwikda and his students.

Ritwikda was keenly aware of how Indian culture was and is infused with animism, and *Ajantrik*, an early film, acknowledges this. It is not only the hero's but also the director's capacity to love that turns this machine into a lover, with a range of emotional responses. When Bimal pays attention to a pretty woman who has been abandoned by her lover, she—the taxi—becomes obdurate and refuses to obey his commands.

Ajantrik is one of the finest depictions of animistic beliefs. The very title means 'non-mechanical'; it suggests that the 'anima', or soul, of the mechanical 'objects' makes them sentient 'subjects'.

It has been a long-held and oft-repeated cliché that cinema is a visual medium. Today's cinema, with its Dolby Atmos and similar technologies, is technically an audio-visual medium, but for great directors like Ritwikda, Alfred Hitchcock, Robert Bresson and others, sound was as important as the visuals even in the days of monophonic sound.

Ajantrik in the USSR

On 26 April 1986, the Chernobyl nuclear power plant reactor number four exploded. This horrific disaster brought out the fragility of human control over mechanical forces. The people of the Soviet Union had learnt the bitterest lesson of what could happen if we are not careful with that relationship, and human beings came face-to-face with the immense destructive possibilities of nuclear science. It was equally clear that Chernobyl wouldn't have happened had it not been for the arrogance of politicians and scientists. Hiroshima and Nagasaki weren't yet ancient history, but that had happened to the Japanese, not to 'us', the Soviet citizens.

Ajantrik was screened for the first time in the Soviet Union in 1986, thanks to the active support of Naum Kleiman, the then director of the Eisenstein Centre in Moscow. During my visit to Moscow as a Homi Bhabha Fellow at the time, Kleiman had organised for me to lecture under the auspices of the All-Union Advanced School of Filmmaking and Direction. It was against the backdrop of the Chernobyl disaster that I introduced *Ajantrik* in the USSR. Man had to decide if innocent people and natural forces were to be dominated by a handful of men. In light of that, *Ajantrik* brought an entirely new worldview to the tragedy. Seeing the rousing response to the film, I realised the universal appeal of Ritwikda's work.

A few important artists and thinkers of Moscow had attended the screening and took part in the discussion that followed. At that time, not many people knew Ritwikda outside India. When the film was over and the lights in the auditorium came on, there was pin-drop silence, perfect stillness. Then came the reaction of the audience, mesmerised by Ritwikda's genius. One question that was asked again and again: why was such a powerful film and its great director not known in the USSR? Many requested the host, Kleiman, to organise a retrospective of Ritwikda's work, some wanted to study him and write about him, some suggested that his work be shown commercially in the USSR. That experience showed me how the force of a work of art can, like a lighthouse, show us everything the eye can see, warn us about what it can't see.

This year, we are celebrating Ritwikda's birth centenary. He is now included in the best histories of cinema as a great director and pathfinder. These hundred years have not exhausted the rich harvest of his creative genius. Over and above his own films and writings, he is living through the works of many whom he inspired: directors like Mani Kaul, Kumar Shahani, John Abraham, Saeed Mirza and Kundan Shah; cinematographers like K.K. Mahajan; sound recordists like Narinder Singh. They all know that their art would not have been what it is without the impulse they received from the Prime Mover, Ritwik Ghatak.

Arun Vasant Khopkar is a film-maker, film historian, film teacher and independent scholar working on arts and culture.

Notes

1. From William Blake's 'The Tyger', https://www.poetryfoundation.org/poems/43687/the-tyger.
2. Patrick Kavanagh, 'Epic', *Collected Poems*, Penguin Modern Classics, 2005, p. 136.

3. The essay, 'Some thoughts on *Ajantrik*', is included in this anthology.
4. Friedrich Engels (signed: Friedrich Oswald), 'Landscapes', first published in *Telegraph für Deutschland*, Nos. 122–23, July/August 1840.
5. Ritwik Ghatak, *Cinema and I*, Ritwik Memorial Trust, 1987, p. 32.
6. Charles Chaplin, *My Autobiography*, Penguin Modern Classics, Kindle Edition.

Conventions were anathema to Ghatak

ADOOR GOPALAKRISHNAN

I joined the Film Institute in Pune in 1962. It was not yet the Film and Television Institute of India at the time. I belonged to the second batch of students. Next year, in 1963, Ritwik Ghatak joined as vice principal and professor of film direction. He continued in the position for a while.

I remember that, as a teacher, Ghatak talked extensively about his own works. The how and the why in them. And it was the most rewarding thing about his teaching for us, the students. He was a guru to me in the real sense of the word. I didn't meet him outside the classroom, but the uniqueness of his films and his scholarship and total commitment to cinema left an impression on me.

His favourite film-maker was Luis Buñuel and his favourite film was *Nazarin*. He seemed to hate Ingmar Bergman. He used to term Bergman's religiosity as 'fake'. Once, when he screened Satyajit Ray's film *Aparajito* in the classroom, Ghatak pointed out certain sequences and commented, 'Here is great cinema!'

Ghatak's deep knowledge of the Vedas and Indian culture and tradition found many an admirer among us. The best of Indian cinema, whether of Ray or Ghatak or Mrinal Sen, is invariably deeply rooted in our culture and life. A deep and proper understanding of our culture and life makes an artist's work genuine and worthwhile. If my work does not relate to

Subarnarekha: Young Sita waits for Abhiram at the airstrip;
© NFDC – National Film Archive of India

the life and culture of the people around me, what inspiration will I draw upon to create my art?

He elicited appreciation from Ray, as opposed to what was commonly believed and propagated. Ray once told me that Ghatak was someone who had cinema running through his veins. Not a small compliment from a person unfairly portrayed as an adversary. One could see that Ghatak's heart was throbbing with an unbridled passion for cinema, and he could induce in his students the same devotion and commitment, a rare phenomenon.

It was only natural that Ghatak was loved by people who appreciated the value of his work and his strong convictions, even though, at times, his opinions were of the extreme kind. People, the common lot, always identified him with his alcoholism. I was not a part of the small group at the institute that hung around him even in his living room. But, believe me, there was not a single instance of Ghatak coming to class in an inebriated state. In fact, I found it impressive that he always carried books in his hands when he came to take a class.

Ghatak's cinematic exercises were unique in their erratic charm, conceptual originality, untamed energy, incisive observation of everyday life and his obsessive preoccupation with the 'mother cult'. His originality lay in how he transformed melodrama into high art. He held extreme, even extremist, views on politics. He was an iconoclast in his approach to cinema as well. His use of visuals and sounds were totally unconventional. In fact, he carried a few practices from the theatre, where he had been passionately involved, and used them in ways alien to cinema at the time.

His use of sound and noise and music, to go with images, made Ghatak unique. Sound played a critical role in his film-making. It was given as much importance as visuals. His use of sound was not just meant to suggest the atmosphere of the place of action, but also to elicit a dramatic impact. His soundtracks were rich with created sounds, environmental sounds, music and dialogue. They enhanced the impact of the visual narration and the theme in general. He often composed his unique music himself, even though there were music directors at work in his films. As students, we relished the post-screening sessions and learnt how both visuals and sounds could be used innovatively and creatively. He tried to experiment with sounds and images as never before attempted by an Indian film-maker.

A lot of people talk about his unconventional camera positions too. A scene or a sequence can be 'pictured' strictly following a written script and carry forward an idea convincingly. But Ghatak handled the same scene in stark contrast to the commonplace way. He would fill it with urgency and feeling by using unfamiliar angles, lenses, lighting, compositions and, above all, using jump cuts when smooth transitions were the rule.

I must also mention *Madhumati*, which is an all-time classic in Indian cinema. It would seem to prove that Ghatak was capable of being a commercial success. The film had all the conventions of commercial Hindi cinema, but stood out for its innovative narration. Everything about the film is memorable. The story and, particularly, the twist at the end, the casting, the songs, the passionate romance, the locales—it was a great combination of two great film-makers, Ghatak and Bimal Roy, that did the magic.

All of us in the community feel sorry about Ghatak's untimely death, which, I have to say, appeared to be of his own volition. Conventions were anathema to Ghatak. He would cross the imaginary line—between the conventional and the unconventional—with such ease and audacity that everyone would be left in disbelief. He was a genius whom the world had neglected out of sheer ignorance and lack of care.

Adoor Gopalakrishnan is one of India's most celebrated film-makers, credited with introducing the new wave to Malayalam cinema with his debut feature, Swayamvaram, *in 1972. Feted at film festivals in India and abroad, he has been awarded some of India's highest civilian honours, as well as the Dadasaheb Phalke Award, the highest recognition in the field of cinema in India. He also served as the president of FTII from 1987 to 1989 and 1992 to 1995.*

An institution of cinematic passion

JAHNU BARUA

I hadn't heard of Ritwik Ghatak until I went to the Film and Television Institute of India in the early 1970s.

During my graduation days in Guwahati, I had attended discussions and seminars on cinema organised by Gauhati Cine Club (founded by Bhupen Hazarika, among others, in 1965) and had the opportunity to watch quite a few classic films, both Indian and from elsewhere. Some of these films were Bengali, but none of them were by Ghatak. No one spoke about him. I had no idea about his existence.

Then I went to FTII, and Ghatak was everywhere. It was like being introduced to an alien. He was a spirit, in a way. He wasn't there, but he was everywhere.

He was the vice principal at FTII in the early 1960s. Much before my time. I believe he was there for three years, and then he had to resign because of disciplinary reasons. But his ghost—the cinematic ghost—was always there. When I went to FTII, perhaps the first student from Assam at the institute, everyone seemed to be talking about him. But none of my classmates, bar a couple of people, knew much about him.

The first film of his that I watched was a short called *Rendezvous*, which he had made for the students when he was at the institute. I must say, I was mesmerised. I watched the film soon after joining FTII, and I still remember the images. That is the first time I realised that images were the main grammatical elements of the language of cinema. It was a film—and I don't want to overstate this only because I am writing about Ghatak—that made me realise the difference between an ordinary film-maker and a master film-maker. And this was just a short film, made for students. Later, of course, we got to see most of his other films.

Sometimes, you see the work of a film-maker and you admire the style or the presentation. This was the first time I wanted to know about the film-maker's personal life as well. But, at the time, nothing was available on him, and there was no internet. He wasn't around. No one had written much about him. There were a few articles available in the FTII library, but those were about his work and not about him. No one had written a book on him yet. If there was one, it was not easily available.

Then I read something about his childhood. I found out that he was the youngest son of a district magistrate. He had witnessed all the tragic events people who were born in the 1920s had: World War II, the Bengal Famine in 1943-44, the partition of Bengal ... But he was from a privileged background. His class meant that he didn't have to personally suffer during the famine like the common people. Then what made him react to all this so much?

He must have been affected deeply to devote his entire career to it. His reaction to these human tragedies, to my mind, was aggressive. He was so creative, he must have felt an urge to express himself, talk about the tragedies. He would probably have been suffocated if he didn't. In my reading, Ghatak was a film-maker who lived his life not as a satisfied creator, but as a victim of the human tragedies that he witnessed and experienced during his early years.

People who witness tragedies of such magnitude, if they are creative or are reactionaries or thinkers, these events become their strongest stimuli. For Ghatak, these human tragedies never left him in peace, they didn't let him breathe. They traumatised him, and made him restless. And eventually killed him.

Everything he did—the films, the plays, his scripts and screenplays, the articles and the poetry he wrote—were nothing but his creative expression. He had to get it out of his system. This extreme urge made him join platforms like the Indian People's Theatre Association and the Communist Party, and then move to a medium like cinema. But what

A rare photograph of Ritwik in his office at FTII;
© NFDC - National Film Archive of India

he could finally manage to express was just a small percentage of what he was dying to articulate all his life. From the outside, it felt like there was a constant fight against the evil within, he became so much a part of the tragedies that he was confined in them. He completed eight full-length films, as well as quite a few short films and documentaries, but many remained unfinished, and many remained in his mind—suffocated and unmade.

But for people like me, Ritwik Ghatak the failure, as he called himself, was a winner. He never compromised, no matter what he went through, ever, throughout his life and career. I am fortunate that I got to watch all his films except for the first one, *Nagarik*, which he made in the early 1950s. It was not allowed to be released. *Nagarik* released only after his death.

One can go on and on talking about this great creator, but I will limit myself to a few aspects that I feel are relevant to his beliefs as a fanatical humanist.

I have never thought of Ghatak as a leftist. I think of him as a humanist. And I adore him for it. Pick any of his films, and the humanist in him shines through. That was his greatness. He was a genius, and I don't say that lightly. The work he did, despite limited opportunities, and his own deterioration in terms of his health, is there for all to see. He created things no film-maker has done even to this day in India.

Ghatak made films during the celluloid era, like all of us before the digital era, and that too under such severe financial constraints. It's difficult to believe that he still managed to create what he did. It was possible because of the kind of passion that he had—for cinema, and for the subjects he worked with. I often mention this—the unflinching passion of Ritwik Ghatak—to my students and also to young film-makers. I say, and I sincerely believe what I say, that Ritwik Ghatak was not just a film-maker, but an institution of cinematic passion. It is the kind of passion I have always wanted to possess, though I would not want that passion to consume me the way it did Ghatak. I don't want to be obsessed the way he was; I don't want to be a slave to my feelings.

Ghatak was so obsessed with the subjects that were close to him that he could not detatch himself from them. I wish he could, and that he could engage himself in creating more, to talk about other aspects of humanity. The world would have gained more then, and I think his soul would have been happier. His unhappy soul, as one discovers at FTII, never left the world.

It was at FTII that I met him for the first and only time.

The meeting was a memorable one. This was 1971. He had left FTII long ago, but he had come to conduct a workshop for the senior students. He seemed to really enjoy his time with us, talking about cinema. And he was very sincere in what he said. He said what—it seemed—he truly believed. He had so much energy, it was incredible. And to think that he died within five years of that meeting. His health was already bad, but we couldn't tell that from the way he was, the way he talked about cinema.

He used a lot of Bengali swear words, and he used to shout a lot. But we were prepared for this because our seniors had warned us. And I realised that there were lessons even when he behaved a bit erratically. He used to dislike Ingmar Bergman. He felt that films must talk about real things. He felt that Bergman used exoticism to make his films beautiful. He had some special swear words for Bergman. He felt, and said, that when you make films the way Bergman did, you don't have any real connection with the subject. I felt then and I still feel that's true.

We had him for only one day, for just one workshop, and slowly we got comfortable with his behaviour. He would shout, abuse, 'Look at that!' He was just teaching. I still remember that day fondly.

I can also say, with all honesty, that the one thing I learnt from Ghatak, not just that day but from watching his films and reading his articles, is that you must love your people. I learnt from him that you can't go too far away from your roots as a film-maker. If you watch my films, you will see that I have tried to do that. I have spoken about subjects close to me. That comes back to me often—being connected to my roots.

He was a genius because of the way he thought about cinema and about people and about the world. If you see his films, he wasn't profound technically. Maybe that was also because of the constraints he worked with. You could see the struggles in his films. But the subjects—*Meghe Dhaka Tara*, *Subarnarekha*, *Komal Gandhar*—were chosen with care, and the films made with love. The one film that was very crudely made, *Ajantrik*, was so brilliant, and we see in it for the first time a director humanising a machine. I really admire that film. As a student of cinema, that film gave me a lot. It was an example of the humanist side to him too.

I followed everything he made until his death. He made *Titas Ekti Nodir Naam* and *Jukti, Tokko aar Goppo* after our meeting. He didn't deserve to go the way he did. He could have created so much. So much. But even the little he created is world-class.

There's so much to learn from Ghatak. Each and every student at FTII used to feel that. In every movement in his films, there is something unique. He used to live and breathe cinema. And he spent a lot of time thinking about cinema and reading and learning about cinema. You could *feel* him at FTII, like I said, and you will hear this from other students of the time too. You know what they say—people who die without all their desires fulfilled don't really go away. I think he stayed there, on campus, because his passion for cinema wasn't fulfilled. And also because he felt that, on that campus, he still had something to contribute. He felt hope there.

People need to know him as someone who created great things without being able to give his best. Don't go by what you hear about him. He could never find the space he needed. No one gave it to him. The government of West Bengal didn't release *Nagarik* till after his death. He needed help, and he didn't get it. I hope people properly understand him.

I use the words 'great' and 'genius' about Ghatak, and you might wonder why. But that's why his films are being talked about now; some of his films have been restored by people in the US and in England. People are discussing his films, writing dissertations about him and his films. He didn't know how to talk about himself, how to promote himself. He didn't care about the limelight. He wanted to create, and he couldn't do that. That's the really sad part. But he influenced so many film-makers. Even ones who never met him. Even me, I met him just once, and I vividly remember that day. That was his greatness. The energy and the passion, you could feel it.

When we were coming out of the studio that day, after the workshop, and we went to the FTII canteen, we kept talking about him. We talked about him for many days after that. And we are still talking about him now. Fifty years after his death.

Jahnu Barua is one of the modern masters among Indian film directors. His third film, Halodhia Choraye Baodhan Khai *(*The Catastrophe*, 1987) won the National Award for best film, and he won the best director National Award in 1995 for* Hkhagoroloi Bohu Door *(*It's a Long Way to the Sea*). He has gone on to make many seminal films, mainly in his native Assamese, and been awarded the Padma Bhushan, India's third-highest civilian award.*

Too much of a maverick to be successful

KETAN MEHTA

Ritwikda is one of the greatest film-makers India has ever produced. He had a great influence on many a film-maker in this country, especially those coming out of the Film and Television Institute of India in Poona, including Kumar Shahani, Mani Kaul, me and many stalwarts of our time. The main thing to learn from his oeuvre is how rooted it is in Indian culture and ethos, the traditions of our country.

The dramatic narrative that he used in his films is derived from Indian folk traditions with a direct line to Indian storytelling methods, and so they forge a direct emotional connect with audiences as a result. The fact that he was so rooted in all his films, whether *Meghe Dhaka Tara* or *Ajantrik* or *Subarnarekha* or *Komal Gandhar*, or any of the others, have touched film-makers and audiences alike.

Sometimes Ritwikda is pitted against the Satyajit Ray tradition of film-making, which was more directed towards the global audience, almost like a counterpoint. Ritwikda is painted as more Indian, a film-maker who was more committed and more directly in contact with the people of India and the ethos of India. Somewhere, his personality also influenced the way people perceived him, as much as the fact that he was a maverick, not caring about the establishment or the powers that be, and accepted norms of social behaviour. All of that contributed to the aura around Ritwikda.

I met him only once, when he had come to do a workshop over four days at the film institute. This was sometime in the early 1970s, well after he had retired from his position as vice principal. That brief interaction left a deep impact on me, as I have said in other platforms, and on my film-making too. The dramatic and charged emotional content of his films leaves an impression on anyone watching, shaking them up profoundly, making them question their very existence—that, I think, is a very strong element of Ritwikda's films.

He was a pathbreaker in many, many ways; deeply moving, profound, questioning and connecting directly to the Indian ethos and society at the time. He was an iconoclast, someone who challenged the social norms of his time and questioned the power structures. All these things have had an impact on my film-making, and I am very grateful to Ritwikda's films for guiding me through my cinematic journey. I owe a lot to his oeuvre.

The workshop wasn't a film-making course, really. It was more like an interaction with him. He was already unwell, and not active as a film-maker—though he would make a few more films after that before passing away in 1976—but I found his intensity very infectious. His passion for cinema was infectious, his passion for India and Indians was very infectious, and his empathy for all the young film-makers was enchanting. But it was his love for cinema that was, perhaps, my main takeaway from the workshop.

Of all the students who spent time at the film institute when Ritwikda was there, Mani Kaul and Kumar Shahani were the ones who were most deeply influenced by him. That's because they bought into his theories in a big way and spent a lot of time with him. Their connection to Ritwikda was more direct and more lasting than was the case with someone like me. I met him much later, but I have to say that while our interaction was very brief, it was very effective, for me at least. When it comes to the work of Mani and Kumar, if you are looking for traces of Ritwik Ghatak, it's in the form and not in the content. It's in the rootedness, the characterisations; not in the dramatic narrative, since neither Kumar nor Mani were into dramatic narrative at all. The social milieu, and the way to treat it and the way to respect it, those were directly derived from Ritwikda.

When I made my first film, *Bhavni Bhavai* (1981), there was most certainly that aspect, of making a film on a subject I was familiar with,

Anil Chatterjee (L), one of the more prominent actors of the time, acted in multiple Ritwik films; © NFDC - National Film Archive of India

something I knew and cared about. After I graduated from the film institute, I worked as a television producer for the Indian Space Research Organisation, with their experimental programme called SITE (Satellite Instructional Television Experiment), where we travelled to rural areas and were given the freedom to create content with the villagers and develop scripts with them and use them as actors, telecasting the production directly via satellite into the homes of the people in that particular district—Kheda in Gujarat in my case. It was quite an amazing experiment, where I worked with the people at the grassroots level, looking at their social issues, their problems, the dynamics of a changing society, and then trying to create meaningful content out of that interaction.

That was a keen learning curve for me, and during that time, we came across the caste riots in Gujarat (following the policy of reservation introduced in 1975; the most widespread riots took place in 1981), the violence against the people branded 'untouchables'. That had an impact on me—and was the germ for *Bhavni Bhavai*. The movie was based on a folk tale from Gujarat called *Achhutno Vesh*, which had been adapted for an old Bhavai (a popular folk theatre form in Gujarat). The story and narrative had been developed from a three- or four-page synopsis of the play that I had read, plus my own experiences. The narrative was split in two contemporary scenarios. The basti has been burnt down by the upper castes and these people, the untouchables, are migrating to the city. At night, an old man narrates a folk tale to the children. That folk tale is at the heart of *Bhavni Bhavai*.

For centuries, the untouchables in Gujarat were forced to wear two peculiar dehumanising appurtenances to identify them from a distance. They had to tie a broom around their backs to sweep their footprints as they walked, and a spittoon around their necks so they spat only into that. The story was about how these identifiers were finally removed. By the end of it, in some way, the movie was also a call to action.

The uniqueness was that there were two alternative climaxes. One was the traditional end to the folktale, and the other, proposed by someone from the crowd of the old man's listeners, who doesn't want to accept the status quo ending, and calls for a rebellious, revolutionary ending. The dramatic intensity of the narrative was somewhere influenced by the style of acting in Ritwikda's films. And basic social consciousness, of course. And yes, the same sort of ethos and logic holds true for *Mirch Masala* (1986) too.

Despite his greatness as a film-maker, Ritwikda wasn't successful in the conventional sense, and I think his personality was responsible for it. His iconoclastic, anti-establishment positioning, as well as the fact that he was a maverick, alcoholic film-maker, contributed to the lack of commercial success. He was clearly not interested in that sort of recognition, or in mass acceptance. His primary passion was communication. That was his strength. And that led to him not getting the sort of audience acknowledgement that he deserved. He was seen as a rebel at a time of great transition in India. It was post-Independence India where things were just about stabilising. The left-wing movements, Naxalism, were really spinning out of hand at the time. All of this too contributed to Ritwikda not receiving any accolades in his time.

Now, fifty years after his death, observers can still learn from his films. Firstly, his use of sound, which was phenomenal. The way he used sound effects and music was very effective. Secondly, the dramatic intensity of his narrative, which was very attractive. And thirdly, the characterisations:

earthy, rooted, connected to the local ethos and culture, and his empathy with his characters. In the end, it comes down to his passion, which is visible in his work. *Ajantrik* is a pathbreaking film, for instance, with Ritwikda using a car as a character. He was an innovator who was equally a passionate film-maker, and there is a lot to learn from that—even today.

Ketan Mehta, a graduate of the Film and Television Institute of India, is a maker of feature films—among them, Bhavni Bhavai *(1980),* Mirch Masala *(1985),* Maya Memsaab *(1993),* Toba Tek Singh *(1028)—as well as TV serials, like* Mr Yogi *(1988), and documentaries, with multiple awards at national and international film festivals.*

Let me call you, Ritwik Da

ARIN PAUL

Let Me Call You, Ritwik Da wasn't just an idea, it was a necessity. For me, Ritwik Ghatak is not just a film-maker; he is a voice that has whispered, screamed and wept in the back of my mind for as long as I can remember. His cinema is not just visual storytelling; it is poetry in motion, a cry of anguish, a hymn to the displaced, the longing for a home that exists only in memory.

But how do you capture the essence of someone like Ghatak? How do you pay tribute to a man who spoke in thunder and silence, who loved and fought with equal passion? I didn't want to make just another film. I didn't want to explain Ghatak—I wanted to feel him. I wanted the audience to feel him too.

And then I remembered John Abraham's poem—an ode to Ghatak, written with such raw emotion that it felt like a voice from beyond. John Abraham, who was Ghatak's student at the film institute in Pune, wrote this poem as a heartfelt tribute to his mentor. It's not a confrontation, it's an outpouring of love, respect and shared pain. Abraham, like Ghatak, was a maverick: fiercely independent, deeply passionate and, tragically, he too passed away young. His poem felt like a direct, emotional letter to Ghatak, one soul reaching out to another.

But *Let Me Call You, Ritwik Da* is not just about Abraham's words. It's about memory. About time. About the way voices echo across generations.

The film is a call across time, a bridge between the living and the lost. In the shadows, in the light, it felt like Ghatak was there, watching, listening.

Below is the poem.

Ritwik Ghatak,
in partition, not physically of willingness—the country departed
Out of his outer consciousness—cosmic consciousness
none of his mistakes,
Reactions—natural reactions—reflections
Ritwik Ghatak,
refugee, unborn, unwanted, unbearable
penetrative towards the Victorian hangover
of the Tagoreian corruption of thinking
Life was more important to him
than the words in praise of god,
the god of Victorian, Tagoreian thinking.
Hence, he was rejected from the Bengalian thinking
Ritwik Ghatak—the name doesn't suit
the hierarchic thinking of the Raynian Zamidarian thinking
Perhaps, the long echo of the forgotten factors
that becomes reminiscence of
the 'death of the salesman' or otherwise
the long columns and no more Chhabi Biswas,
Cardiac arrest is common.
The death of Ghatak is uncommon.
Nay, Ritwik Ghatak
I remember, a tall man
his hands moving around my shoulders,
catching me with the feeling of nearness,
rather than imperialism—
the man who stands before me questioning my manliness
loosening his hands to shake my hands in appreciation of manliness
recognizing each other—
abiding in each other
kicking on my ass and telling me
'Get up, awake, shoot.'
I remember, not with sentiments
with awakening proud, Ritwik Ghatak
Ritwik Daa,

let me call you Ritwik Daa,
I know that you are no more.
But I am, alive for you
Believe me. When the seventh seal is opened
I will use my camera as my gun
and I am sure the echo of the sound
will reverberate in your bones,
and feed back to me for my inspiration.
Thank you, Ritwik Daa,
I am thanking you
not with impotency and insipidity
Ritwik Daa,
I remember you,
when the words fail to criticize you,
Ritwik Daa,
eternally you are
in my brain
in my spirit and
in my Holy Ghost
Amen.

The reception to the film has been overwhelming in a way I didn't expect. People who love Ghatak's work have reached out with heartfelt messages, some of them also sharing their memories of discovering his films for the first time. What has been truly humbling is how the film has sparked conversations not just about Ghatak, but about John Abraham too—often remembered but not celebrated enough.

One comment from a viewer that stands out for me was, 'This isn't just a tribute to Ghatak. It's a voice calling out to him, and through him, to all of us.' That is exactly what I hoped to achieve. I didn't want to just praise Ghatak; I wanted to speak with him, to feel his presence, to share his pain and his passion.

But beyond praise, it has sparked curiosity about *The Ritwik Ghatak Experience*, my upcoming documentary. Some have asked me about the stories I have captured, the people I've spoken to and the hidden truths I've uncovered. In a way, this film has become the first chapter of a much larger story—a story that is still unfolding.

John Abraham, one of Ghatak's cherished students; © Venugopal Pillai (ISC)

The Ritwik Ghatak Experience is not just a documentary, it is a journey. It is a quest to capture the unsaid about Ghatak; his being, his soul, his fears, and above all, his love for people.

It is about the places he walked, the faces he captured, the voices he inspired. Since 2011, I have been chasing this dream—one memory at a time. I have collected stories, whispers and memories. The writer Shaktipada Rajguru spoke of how *Meghe Dhaka Tara* was initially planned in Hindi, with Waheeda Rehman playing Supriya Choudhury's role. Ramananda Sengupta, the cinematographer, spoke of *Nagarik*. Tapan Saha shared his memories as an assistant on *Jukti, Tokko aar Goppo*. Mahendra Kumar's stills, the lost dream of *Bedeni*, the visuals of *Cinema and I* being relaunched ... it's all there.

But this journey has been painful too. I lost Ghatak's daughter Samhita, who believed in this project. I lost Shantanu Ghosh, a dear friend who shared a dream with me—a feature film on Ghatak, half-written and now frozen in time. Yet, I haven't abandoned it. Someday, I will return to it. Someday, it will find life.

The Ritwik Ghatak Experience is about Ghatak's voice, but it is also about the voices he left behind. It is a promise to Samhitadi, to Shantanu, to myself, and more importantly, to Ghatak. It is a promise that one day, the world will see Ghatak not just as a film-maker, but as a soul who spoke for the lost, the forgotten, the broken and the dreamers.

Ritwik Ghatak and John Abraham were like two storms passing through the same sky. Ghatak was the elder, the mentor, a man who wore his pain like a second skin. His cinema was raw, unfiltered; it bled with the agony of displacement, the heartbreak of lost homes, the silent scream of the forgotten. He was a poet who painted his sorrow on celluloid. There was a fierce love in his work—a love for humanity, for the struggling, for the defeated who refused to be broken.

Abraham was his student, but never just a follower.

If Ghatak was a river—deep, vast and often turbulent—then Abraham was a wildfire, burning bright and fierce. He was a rebel, a dreamer, a film-maker who believed in the power of cinema to transform. But beneath his wild spirit was a tenderness, a deep respect for his mentor.

Their connection was not just one of teacher and student. It was a meeting of souls.

Abraham's poem is a tribute, a cry of love, a confession, a plea. It is a son calling out to a father, a disciple seeking the light of his master. That's what I felt.

A Personal Epilogue

Ritwikda,

Let me call you Ritwikda, too.

Are you listening?

I sometimes wonder if your voice still echoes in the wind, if your stories still drift like forgotten leaves. I never met you, but you have always been there—an unseen mentor, a distant voice that refuses to fade.

I have tried to capture your spirit, to tell your story; not because I want to preserve you, but because I want to remember you. To keep you alive. Because the world forgets too easily.

Sometimes, I wonder—do you see me? Do you smile at the irony of a film-maker chasing the shadow of another film-maker? Do you hear my voice calling out to yours?

Because you are not just a name, Ritwikda. You are a voice. And as long as your voice speaks, I will listen.

Arin Paul is the director of Let Me Call You, Ritwik Da, *a short film made in 2025 that, inspired by a poem by the film-maker John Abraham, pays tribute to Ritwik Ghatak.*

Bohurupee | The Polymorph

GOUTAM GHOSE

Ritwikda, to me, was a polymorph.

He appears suddenly at the old, abandoned airstrip dressed as a bohurupee in *Subarnarekha*. In *Jukti, Tokko aar Goppo*, he is Neelkantha, in wide-angle, pouring the alcohol from his bottle on to the lens of the camera.

Ritwikda observed the clashes of nation and nationhood, society, human life, and showcased it all in his cinema, his stories, his plays and in his thoughts, which he wasn't shy to share. Now, in his centenary year, Ritwikda is as relevant as he ever was, because he obsessed about the human search for identity, home and nation. The world today is rife with instances of forced migration. The Rohingyas' wail for help, the destruction of the homes and lives of thousands of people in Gaza; people everywhere looking for the corpses of those once closest to them; they are walking, as though in a silent procession, to find new lives and livelihoods.

He was born in Dhaka, and brought up on the banks of the river Padma in Rajshahi district in what is now Bangladesh. Ritwikda came from an educated and cultured family. His father, a district magistrate, had earned the title of 'Raibahadur' from the British. In his memoirs, Ritwikda has talked about a restless, whirlwind childhood. There was mischief, time spent with the fisherfolk and the boatmen; running away from home, reaching Kanpur when just fourteen years old, after which his elder brother brought him back and enrolled him in a school, hoping to give the young Ritwik a formal education and some discipline. He took it seriously enough, and also became interested in the arts.

Like many educated young Bengalis, Ritwikda also wrote poetry but realised soon enough that the form was not for him, '*amar kommo na*'. He turned to short stories instead. He had told me that he was most inspired by Maxim Gorky's semi-autobiographical trilogy *Three of Them*: 'It is not possible to be truly creative if one doesn't examine life in depth.'

In his youth, he was also initiated into Marxist philosophy and conflict, and dreamt of a socialist revolution. At the same time, he studied the Vedas and the Upanishads and the Puranas. A highly stimulated, thoughtful young man, he witnessed from up close the Great Famine of 1943, World War II, the last stages of the Independence Movement, the violent riots before and after the Partition and, of course, the division of our country itself. From a sense of social responsibility, young Ritwik started writing stories, but understood that it took literature a long time to reach the masses, if at all, and that far too many people were uneducated, even illiterate. Theatre was the easiest way to motivate people, he felt. It was a time when the Indian People's Theatre Association was on the rise. Bijon Bhattacharya's *Nabanna*, the playwright's reaction to the Great Famine, had created a stir. Ritwikda has written, '*Nabanna* changed my worldview completely.' He later acted in the play, when he was a member of IPTA, as it went to the most far-flung of villages in West Bengal. Many people, including Bijon Bhattacharya, Sombhu Mitra, Tripti Mitra and Kumar Roy, left IPTA at one point and started the Bohurupee theatre group in 1948, and Ritwikda acted in their plays too. He has written about a performance in Mymensinh, which was in Bangladesh after the Partition: 'When we performed, five hundred people watched us, excited, inspired, motivated.'

It was a heady time. Writers and cultural activists were carrying out anti-fascist protests, plays were being staged—sometimes in secret, since IPTA was affiliated to the Communist Party, which was banned at the time—and these were motivating people to rise, speak out. Ritwikda wrote a number of plays one after the other—*Jwala*, *Dalil*, *Sanko*—and these were all staged under the IPTA banner. Around that time, Ritwikda became interested in the lives and culture of the Adivasi communities and those of the most marginalised classes. 'We must conserve many things we have lost, which will catch the rotten and derelict middle-class society by the throat and shake them up.'

We see reflections of this worldview in many of Ritwikda's films.

How did he turn to cinema? Many scholars have written about it, as has his wife, Lokkhidi (Surama Ghatak), and Ritwikda has spoken about his 'excitement about the magic of cinema as a medium to reach the masses' in interviews too.

A lot has been written about this, what can I add? What I want to say is something that most people might not know, since Nemai Ghosh had told me this himself. Nemaida's *Chhinnamul* released in 1951—it was the first neorealist film made in India, with the Partition as its theme. Ritwikda acted in it. Nemaida had said that Ritwikda was very interested in all aspects of film-making, especially cinematography—he was particularly interested in the properties of each lens. 'In a way, Bhoba had become my assistant during the making of the film.'

Satyajit Ray had said, I recall, in the memorial service after Ritwikda's death, that there was no influence of Hollywood in Ritwikda's cinema. Hollywood—or English films in general—is all that came to India in the 1940s. Manikda (Ray) was deeply influenced by Hollywood films as a result, though he later watched Italian films, neorealist films, Soviet films, European films. Manikda was right—you couldn't see a trace of Hollywood in Ritwikda. His education came primarily from Soviet cinema, the films of, and essays on film theory by, Sergei Eisenstein and Vsevolod Pudovkin inspired him. We find the dialectics of montage in his cinema. Ritwikda had learnt about dialectics—argument, reason, logic—and dialectical and historical materialism from studying Marx, and he found signs of it in Eisenstein's cinema. We see the result of this in Ritwikda's cinema, especially in *Ajantrik*.

Besides Soviet cinema, we see the influence of Italian, French and Spanish cinema of the time in Ritwikda's work, and especially that of Luis Buñuel, of whom he was a great admirer. The influence of Buñuel and Federico Fellini is evident in Ritwikda's films from time to time.

But Eisenstein was his greatest inspiration. Let me quote Ritwikda from an interview: 'Sergei Eisenstein first caught hold of the damn thing and tried to teach us the rudiments of film-making. He found out what film

A polymorph in a polymorph's film, from *Subarnarekha*

is, what this damn camera thing does. He is the Kalidasa of the cinema, theoretician and creator. There are film-makers galore. There were, are and will be great and excellent film-makers all over the world, but they are just derivatives of Eisenstein. Eisenstein stands above all. Anywhere there is a film, the film-maker is only the child of Eisenstein. For he is the guardian, the father. He is Adam, the primaeval Adam of the cinema, the first man.' From this, you can see the respect he had for Eisenstein.

Ritwikda was moved not only by cinema as art, but also the history of visual art, which Eisenstein elaborated on to his students and in his essays. That aside, there was Buñuel.

And although he had nothing to do with Hollywood, Ritwikda was a big admirer of one American film, Orson Welles's *Citizen Kane*.

The same way Ritwikda explored conflicts in the lives and societies of the tribal and the marginalised communities in his cinema, he also brought into his films archetypes, parables and totems. Because he felt that he could get to the root of humanity and society if he trod that path. This, this symbolism, is a fascinating and vital ingredient in his cinema.

Ritwikda once quoted the American writer Joseph Campbell in one of his interviews: 'Myth—and therefore civilisation—is a poetic, supernormal image, conceived, like all poetry, in depth, but susceptible to interpretation on various levels. The shallowest minds see in it the image of the local scenery; the deepest, the foreground of the void.' This shook Ritwikda up.

When we speak about Ritwikda's cinema, we always speak about the Partition. But he wasn't all about the Partition. No! Like a sharp, pointed arrow, he told us, and the generations to come, 'They haven't seen the famine, they haven't seen the riots, they haven't seen the division of our country [in *Subarnarekha*].' But India wasn't partitioned. Bengal and Punjab were. The Partition and the outcomes of it hurt Ritwikda. That pain and divisiveness still remains; in fact, the chasms and the communalism and the fundamentalism have only increased, which might be why he said, '*Bhabo, bhabo, bhaba* practice *koro*' (Think, think, train yourself to think).'

But why do I call him a polymorph?

Once upon a time, Ritwikda used to have very many discussions on cinema with people like me. I met him for the first time in 1974. *Titas Ekti Nodir Naam* was done. He was waiting—as we all were—for the print to come to India from Bangladesh. He had started filming *Jukti, Tokko aar Goppo* already. Some of us friends would be at the shoot every other day, and we were very much a part of the post-production process—the dubbing, the mixing—at India Labs.

We used to chat, discuss films. He used to say, 'If you want to be a film-maker, you have to be a bohurupee.' In his work of course there was a vision, which led him to explore rootless people, their search for a homeland, but his vision was polymorphic. He saw things from multiple angles. He had told us, 'Polymorphic vision is very important in visual arts.'

He had given me a book, the mathematician Damodar Dharmananda Kosambi's *Myth and Reality: Studies in the Formation of Indian Culture*. Myth is but the mask of god, with many stories hidden behind it, many symbols. But what is its relevance to our lives, our realities? Kosambi had analysed it brilliantly.

I was most fortunate, needless to say, to be around Ritwikda. I had made *Hungry Autumn* in 1974. We had struggled a lot to make the film, and Mrinal Sen had helped us enormously—he helped us get a monetary loan from a bank.

It was completed, and we had a screening, also at India Labs, and many people had come to watch. Mrinalda was there, as were Ritwikda, Tarun Majumdar, Bhupen Hazarika, Harisadhan Dasgupta. When we left the screening room and were walking out, Ritwikda suddenly kicked me hard on my backside. I was obviously shocked. 'Ritwikda?!' Ritwikda was in a state of high excitement. '*Shala, phatiye diyechhish!* [You have shown them!] Here, we have so many great film-makers—tell him, tell him, tell him what he has achieved.'

This was Ritwikda and his affection. I still remember that kick. It was a kick of love.

Equally memorable was the screening of *Titas Ekti Nodir Naam*. Baby Islam, the cinematographer of the film, had brought the print. We were back at India Labs. Ritwikda hadn't seen the final cut himself. He had fallen ill while the post-production was on and had returned to India. So he was watching it for the first time too.

In this movie, he was back, talking about the same things: displacement, rootlessness, the search for a homeland. The river was drying up. The civilisation that had taken root on its banks would have to migrate, find a new river. But he was also saying that it was a cycle. The river would fill up again, crops would grow on its banks, people would return. 'Our lives are intertwined with nature, even though we don't care about nature anymore. This new corporate profit model doesn't care about people, it doesn't care about nature, it doesn't care about environmental disasters; it only cares about profit.' He put a finger in our eyes and showed us that with *Titas*.

We watched. Ritwikda was sitting there, shouting. 'Ayee, Baby, you have superimposed the wrong thing here! Oh, you can't do anything right!'

Babyda told him, 'Don't worry, you just need to come to Dhaka once and fix everything.' The laboratory was in Dhaka. I don't know if that ever happened.

It was a masterpiece; we were in a daze after watching it. But the real fun was before the screening. He had turned up wearing a pristine white, ironed kurta-pajama set, looking clean and tidy, which was rarely the case with him. We joked, 'Ritwikda, you are so dressed-up today, you are looking handsome.'

He laughed, 'Yes, Lokkhi is coming from Sainthia with the children.' They all came and watched the film with Ritwikda.

Jukti, Tokko aar Goppo was on the one hand a somewhat autobiographical film, a personal film; and on the other, a statement. It also had the familiar Ritwikda touch of mixing the real, the unreal and the surreal.

We had attended the shooting, and then we were at the dubbing. Ramesh Joshi—the editor who had worked on all of Ritwikda's films except *Titas Ekti Nodir Naam*, since that was made with technicians in Bangladesh—was in charge. But something was wrong. The film had not been shot with live sync, so everything had to be dubbed. We heard Ramesh Joshi say, 'Ritwikbabu, this is out of sync.' We wondered what could be done, since this wouldn't work. The lips are moving here, the voices are elsewhere.

What was the way out, my friend Jagannath Guha and I asked Ritwikda.

He said, quite casually, 'Have all of you read Eisenstein?'

We said we had, a little bit, it was tough to grasp, and so on.

Ritwikda was being mischievous, as he sometimes was. 'Eisenstein has written about synchronous and asynchronous sound,' he said, referring to *Sound and Image*, written by Eisenstein, Pudovkin and Grigori Aleksandrov.

We laughed. 'How is this possible? How can you make a film where the sync is off?'

'All right, all right. Ramesh, tell me where there is a problem, I'll fix it.'

That was also Ritwikda. He could be mischievous. And he would try to justify his mistakes with intellectual arguments. 'Asynchronous sound!' Rubbish!

I also remember, during the shoot, we met Tripti Mitra, who played Durga, and Shaonli Mitra, her daughter, who played Bangabala. It was such a pleasurable experience. There was also Utpal Dutt, who had played the role of Shatrujit. But he was busy shooting in Bombay for a Hindi film when the dubbing was happening.

So Ritwikda turned to Jagannath and said, 'Ayee, you dub for Utpal.'

Jagannath was having none of it. He said, 'How can I do that? Utpalda is my guru in the theatre, how can I dub for him?'

Ritwikda wasn't going to let him go. 'You have to do it. You do it, and when Utpal is back, he can redo it.'

The next scene is still fresh in my memory. We were at India Labs as usual. Jagannath started running. And Ritwikda gave him chase through the gullies of India Labs, shouting, 'Ayee, Joga, stop, come back right now!' Eventually Jagannath had to do it, and Utpalda redid it when he came back.

Like I had mentioned earlier, Ritwikda was almost oblivious to American cinema and its techniques, the narrative styles. Like long shot, mid-shot, close-up. Ritwikda didn't follow that.

Instead, he used mise en scène, which he had learnt in the theatre. Whether in *Nagarik*, which was his first film and quite raw, perhaps even amateurish, or in *Ajantrik*, which was a film of international class. But if you look at the angles in both—or all—his films, you'll see a lot of low-angle shots. He was a tall man, but his angles were low. He wanted to see his characters in that frame, not in separate cut shots. The style was evident in *Nagarik* itself.

As we see more of his work, we see how he shatters the imaginary lines of film-making. A long shot, and then an extreme close-up of the character's eyes. This was wrong grammar. But he didn't believe in that. To him, cinema was a continuous process, a creative process, and while the grammar of cinema had its place, it was also possible to twist and break it.

I have heard Adoor Gopalakrishnan, Kumar Shahani, Mani Kaul and others, who were his students at the film institute in Poona, talk about this. He would tell them, 'Learn the grammar of cinema but only to learn how to break it.'

He used to cite the example of *Ulysses*. When you read James Joyce's *Ulysses* the first time, you might find it impossible to comprehend. But if you keep reading it, you realise that James Joyce had internalised the grammar of the language so well that he could shatter it the way he did.

Ritwikda just thought differently. You look at his frames, his angles, they were all uniquely his own. And, though people say he was undisciplined and wayward, I think he was deeply committed to cinema, and never wavered from that commitment. People talk about the use of melodrama in his films. I find it quite odd when I hear that. There is no melodrama in his films. Ritwikda would approach an issue with his unique lens and attack certain notions. What people call melodrama in the formal sense, puts things in a box. I think Ritwikda used it not quite that same way, but for an effect. Which, to me, was not melodrama, but impact.

Let me try to explain. Think of the scene towards the end of *Subarnarekha*, where Iswar, looking for a woman to spend the night with, enters his sister Sita's quarters. What happens there can be categorised as melodrama. But to me it's shock therapy. The audience will be stunned. That's also the job of the director, to stun the audience into silence, shake them up. Ritwikda was very conscious of these things and did it very deliberately. Similarly, if you look at his use of sound, the sound montage, Ritwikda experimented with it a great deal. We see it in *Meghe Dhaka Tara* and *Komal Gandhar*, where an independent folk music track travels through the film, creating a parallel mood.

There are many moments which tell you that Ritwikda wasn't in this game to just tell a linear story. He wanted to exploit the power of cinema. The time and space of cinema is completely different from real time and real space. In cinema, you can manipulate time and space. You can tell a tale spanning thousands of years in two hours, and you can tell a two-hour story in two hours. This is the power of the language of cinema. He knew how to use this intelligently. He didn't just use myths and archetypes for the heck of using them.

I haven't watched *Ajantrik* in a long time, but one of the things that haunts me from that film is the manner in which Ritwikda captures how cruel children could be. The children attack Jagaddal and Bimal, because, to them, Bimal is a madman, worthy only of derision. Buñuel explores this with complete mastery in *Los Olvidados* (1950). Then we see the astounding use of Nino Rota's music—titled 'Patricia' from Fellini's *La Dolce Vita*—in *Subarnarekha*. In *La Dolce Vita*, the music accompanies an orgy. In *Subarnarekha*, it accompanies Sita's fall and ultimate destruction.

I know that Ritwikda has said that he wanted to make films to reach more and more people, but I think that, later, he made films because he needed to. If it reached people, so be it, but he knew that his films wouldn't achieve that. We achieved independence after a bloody partition but, after that, we weren't able to provide proper education to our people. What we call 'Bengal Renaissance' was an incomplete movement; unlike the European Renaissance, it never reached the working class. I feel that the work Ritwikda and others did at IPTA didn't work, in the sense that it didn't have a lasting impact. Our people, the common people, were never given a chance, the light never shone on them.

Ritwikda was pained by all of this, which we see a bit of in *Jukti, Tokko aar Goppo*.

'Civilisation never dies, it may change, but is eternal,' Ritwikda said. 'Where the paddy field is born on the dry river bed of *Titas*, there begins another civilisation.'

Goutam Ghose started making documentaries in 1973 while also active in Calcutta's group-theatre movement and as a photo journalist. In 1973, he made Hungry Autumn, *which won the main award at Oberhausen Film Festival. He has since made several significant feature films, including* Maa Bhoomi, Dakhal, Paar, Padma Nadir Majhi, Patang, Dekha, Moner Manush, Shankhachil *and* Raahgir, *and a short,* Shomoyer Smritimala, *as well as prominent documentary films like* Meeting a Milestone *(on Ustad Bismillah Khan),* Beyond the Himalayas, Land of Sand Dunes, Ray *(On Satyajit Ray),* Impermanence *(On HH Dalai Lama). Ghose has won sixteen National Awards as well as many international awards, like the Silver Balloon Award at Nantes Film Festival, the UNESCO Award at the Cannes Film Festival, Grand Prix at the Golden Semurg at Tashkent, UNESCO Award at Venice, Fipresci Awards, Red Cross Award at Verna Film Festival, The Golden Peacock at IFFI. He has also won the Best Director award at UKAIFF, London for* Raahgir. *Ghose is also the only Indian to win the coveted Vittorio De Sica Award in Italy, and was awarded the Knighthood of the Star of the Italian Solidarity in July 2006.*

SURAMA AND RITWIK

An evening with Surama Ghatak

AMRIT GANGAR

It is 1990 or thereabouts, and I am surrounded by the hustle of the evening traffic and the bustle at the local vegetable market as I navigate Chetla bazaar in south Calcutta, walking with Ajay De, an activist in the film society movement and a friend. He knows the way. We enter a simple middle-class tenement, where lives Surama Ghatak (née Bhattacharya), the late Ritwik Ghatak's wife. She lives in a modest apartment with her film-maker son Ritaban (Babu at home) and artist-daughter Suchismita (Bulbuli). I address Mrs Ghatak as Suramadi and try to trigger her memory of our meeting in Calcutta some years ago for the release of Ashish Rajadhyaksha's book on Ritwik Ghatak, *A Return to the Epic*, published by Screen Unit, a Bombay-based film society that I was heading at the time. It was released in Calcutta's Rabindra Sadan in the presence of Suramadi. Having placed me, Suramadi, who is nearing the age of retirement from her teaching job, welcomes us warmly. 'I very much like the book you published because it has been written by a non-Bengali and that provides a new perspective on Ritwik Ghatak,' Suramadi tells me in Bengali, and Ajay translates for me. My knowledge of Bengali is much too poor.

After that book, we had also organised a comprehensive retrospective of Ritwik Ghatak's films (including his documentary film *Amar Lenin*, the prints of which had come from Moscow), and on this occasion, we published another, quite different book, *Ritwik Ghatak: Arguments/Stories* (edited by Ashish Rajadhyaksha and Amrit Gangar).

In Indian cinema, Ghatak occupies a space as unique as Satyajit Ray does. The two respected each other. In the essay 'Film and I' (in the book *Cinema and I*, published by the Ritwik Memorial Trust in 1987), Ghatak writes about Ray in the context of *Pather Panchali*: 'Satyajit Ray and only Satyajit Ray in India, in his more inspired moments, can make us breathtakingly aware of truth, the individual, private truth. The Indir Thakuran sequences of that film remain to me the highest and noblest expression of art in the history of Indian cinema. Somehow, Satyajit has achieved a link with contemporary reality in these moments.'

Ray respected Ghatak for his Indianness, his deep understanding of and sensitivity to mythology. In his foreword to *Cinema and I*, Ray wrote, 'Ritwik had the misfortune to be largely ignored by the Bengali film public in his lifetime. Only one of his films, *Meghe Dhaka Tara*, had been well received. The rest had brief runs, and generally lukewarm reception from professional film critics. This is particularly unfortunate since Ritwik was one of the few truly original talents in the cinema this country has produced. Nearly all his films are marked by an intensity of feeling coupled with an imaginative grasp of the technique of film-making. As a creator of powerful images in an epic style he was virtually unsurpassed in Indian cinema.'

Ghatak was outspoken. He lived a stormy life. Failures kept chasing him. And he increasingly fell victim to alcohol. His heart was broken by the partition of Bengal, a pain he repeatedly articulated in his films. Ghatak's exploration of sound in his cinema was remarkably imaginative. He elevated the status of cinematographic narrative in cinema. Until the very end, he struggled as he engaged with his own creativity. In his film-making career and lifetime (1925–1976), he made only eight films. For one reason or another, several films of his remained incomplete.

During the shooting of *Titas Ekti Nodir Naam* in Bangladesh, Ghatak vomited blood and lost consciousness. On receiving the news, the Indian government (Indira Gandhi was prime minister then) sent a helicopter to fetch him to India. After recovering, he made *Jukti, Tokko aar Goppo*, which was almost an autobiography. In the film, Ghatak himself plays the lead role so transparently and with such truthfulness, it is as if he is not acting but becoming one with the character. *Nagarik* could not be released in his lifetime. In a scene from *Jukti, Tokko aar Goppo*, the wandering

Neelkantha Bagchi (Ghatak's character) meets a group of energetic young revolutionaries. During their dialogue, Bagchi tells them, 'I can lie or steal money for drinking, but I won't say a single lie for fame, for getting a position or to kill people.'

One young revolutionary retorts: 'This is a good dialogue. How many times have you used it for extracting money for drinking?' Bagchi laughs and tells the youth: 'You have caught me out.' Ghatak had completely immersed himself in the role. His disciple Kumar Shahani very poignantly compares this performance with that of Vishnupant Pagnis's in the film *Sant Tukaram* (1936) for his simplicity and directness.[1]

The sound of tea boiling in the kitchen brings back a memory of sound from *Meghe Dhaka Tara*. Suramadi brings in tea just as Ritaban joins us. Nowadays, he is busy retrieving and collecting his father's films and his writings, Suramadi tells us. There are many framed pictures in the room we are sitting in, particularly woodcuts from Santiniketan. They are the work of Bulbuli, who studied art in Santiniketan. From the bazaar outside, noises enter through the windows. The aggressive pushcarts, the vendors' shouts, the two-wheelers' honking, these strains mix with the flavour of the lemon tea, and in front of us emerges the image of Neelkantha Bagchi with a bottle in his jhola. We rewind our memory.

I request Suramadi to tell me about her husband's life. 'I don't possess the knowledge to have a critical view of Ritwik's films—that I must clarify at the beginning, that is your job. When I met him for the first time, our circumstances were difficult,' she begins.

'After being released from the prison in Shillong, I had gone to Calcutta for further studies. While in Calcutta, I joined the IPTA. At that time, some colleagues warned me that I should keep away from Ritwik Ghatak—among them, Utpal Dutt, Salil Choudhury, etc. because they were all Trotskyites. However, I was not interested in all that. Again, I went back to my hometown, Shillong, and when I returned to Calcutta, I came to know that Ritwik Ghatak was preparing for a play adapting Maxim Gorky's *Lower Depths*. The play in Bengali was titled *Neecher Mahal*. He was busy selecting people from different groups of the IPTA for participating in the play. He selected me too.[2]

'After that, he took up the play *Bisarjan*. One day, my aunt [maternal uncle's wife] and Nibumaashi [Nibedita Das] took me to see the rehearsal of

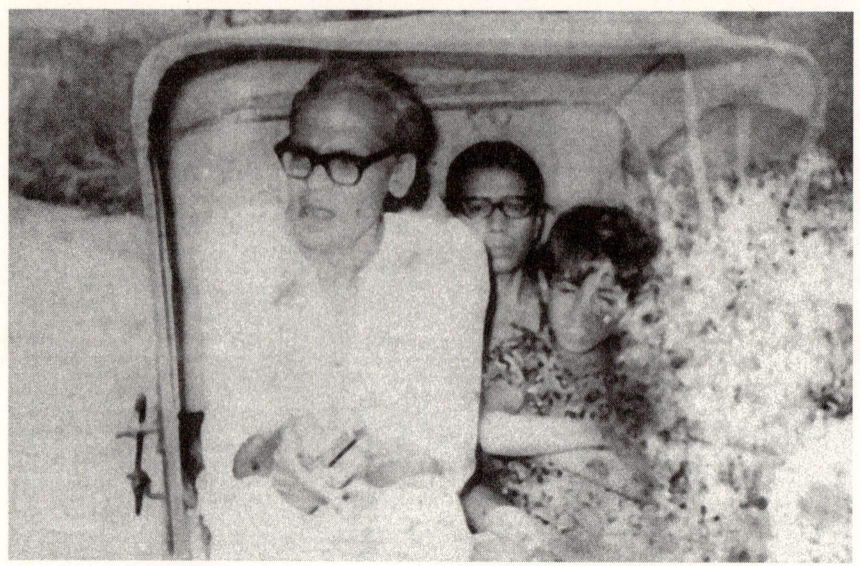

Ritwik and Surama with young Ritaban in a rickshaw;
© NFDC - National Film Archive of India

this play. In the play, the character of Aparna says, "*Boshe achhi bhora mone; dite chai, nite keu nai.* [I am sitting with a contented mind. I want to give something, but there is nobody to take it.]" Answering her, the character of Jayasingha says, "*Taai bote, taai bote! Srujaner aage debata jemon eka* ... [That's right, that's right! As god was alone before creation ...]"

'I liked those sentences. It piqued my interest. Producer Bhupati Nandy advised me to watch Ritwik's film *Nagarik*. I did. And then I went to Mumbai to participate in the IPTA's All-India Conference. There, Ritwik's play *Dalil* [*Document*] bagged the first prize. Ritwik was selected as the best director and the best actor. That was in 1953. But Ritwik was worried about *Nagarik*. He told me, "If *Nagarik* doesn't release, I will commit suicide."

'In order to boost his self-confidence, I showed him the diaries that I had kept during my imprisonment in Shillong. I also talked to him about my mother who had passed away in 1941. She was a very brilliant and bold woman. In his film *Komal Gandhar*, Ritwik imagines the character of Anasuya's mother based on the memories of my mother. The history of that time is scattered all over *Komal Gandhar*.

'When he was expelled from the party, once again I was advised to stay away from Ritwik.[3] Many charges were levelled against him. A committee was appointed to examine the charges. Ritwik had met only one of its members, Pramod Dasgupta, and submitted clarifications about all the charges against him. There were rumours floating around behind Ritwik's back. In the agenda of one of those meetings, even I was dragged in. Everybody opined that Ritwik would ruin my life. At that time, however, I was not obsessed with love for Ritwik, not at all [*laughs*]. But soon, I left the South Squad and joined the Calcutta Squad [of the IPTA].

'At that time, Ritwik was studying Stanislavsky's Group Acting. I advised him to form a Group Theatre. In 1957, he produced a play called *Sanko* [*Bridge*] based on the idea of Group Acting. I had also played a role in it. After that, he made two documentary films for the Bihar government: *Bihar ke Darshaniya Sthan* and *Oraon*. From Bihar, he would write letters to me. In my book *Ritwik*, I have listed all his letters to me. Soon after, we got married in Shillong and went to Mumbai. There he joined Filmistan Studios. But he could not stay long there because of the prevailing atmosphere.[4]

'During our stay in Mumbai, he wrote scripts for Bimal Roy's *Madhumati* and for Hrishikesh Mukherjee's *Musafir*. He also wrote the script for producer Hiten Chaudhury's film *Those Forgotten Ones*, but that was not made into a film. And then we returned to Calcutta. The time between *Ajantrik* and *Komal Gandhar* was optimistic for us. We were hoping better days would come. I was doing my MA and mothering two daughters. But *Komal Gandhar* failed at the box office. I was writing my exams then, but because my children were ill, I could write only four papers.

'After *Komal Gandhar*, Ritwik's life was filled with sorrow. His love for humanity, Indian history and mythology, and for Bengali culture, was so deep. His love was so intense that he could not bear the tragedy of *Komal Gandhar*'s failure. And then he made *Subarnarekha* in 1962. It could be released only three years after it was made. The Bengal Film Journalists' Association honoured this film with as many as eight awards. Between *Subarnarekha* and *Titas Ekti Nodir* Naam, there was a gap of eight years. But it is important to note two or three points.

'One: *Nagarik* could not be released during Ghatak's lifetime.[5] Two: The failure *of Komal Gandhar*. Three: After his death, I realised that human beings such as Manik Bandopadhyay, Michael Madhusudan Dutt, Pramathesh Barua were extraordinary creative artists who wanted to sacrifice their lives. But what is important is that they remained creative till the last moment of their lives. Ritwik was an extremely bright artist. In order to place him in an appropriate perspective, I will provide you with essential information.

'He began with writing short stories. Since theatre was a more powerful medium, he entered the field of theatre. And then cinema, because through films he could reach a greater mass of people. He would always say, "If I find a more powerful medium than cinema, I would plunge into it."'

We had invited Adoor Gopalakrishnan, the leading film-maker from Kerala, to release the book *A Return to the Epic*. Adoor had studied at the Film Institute of India (later Film and Television Institute of India) in Pune when Ghatak was vice principal. In his speech, Gopalakrishnan said, 'Ghatak was like fire; whoever went close to him got burnt. I had never gathered the courage to go near him.' But he also remembered, 'Whenever we saw him, he always carried a pile of books with him. He used to read a lot.'

The time Ghatak spent in Pune was happy. From there, he would often write to Surama. He would fondly talk about his students: Adoor Gopalakrishnan, Mani Kaul, Kumar Shahani, Rehana Sultana. Subhash Ghai, Asrani and Shatrughan Sinha were also there. In one of his letters (20 July 1965), he wrote, '*Amar Srimati, bhalobasha, bhalobasha, pranbhore bhalobasha. Aar kichhu apnake lekhar nei—namaskar, moshai, apnar ek matra, Ritwik.* [My dearest, love, love, love with all my heart. There's nothing more to write—salutations, sir, your one and only, Ritwik).' Sometimes, he would address Surama as 'Lokkhi' in his letters: '*Amar praaner Lokkhi.*' These letters are included in Surama Ghatak's book *Ritwik*.

I ask Suramadi about IPTA. Why did it split? Of course, there is a reference to the circumstances in the film *Komal Gandhar*. I had also read two volumes of *Marxist Cultural Movement in India*, edited by Sudhi Pradhan, by then. In these volumes, Pradhan had published some documents pertaining to the IPTA. But Suramadi had witnessed those days first-hand: 'I feel that period was significant in India's cultural history.' And then, after a long, thinking pause, she said, 'Besides IPTA, there were groups such as the Progressive Writers' Association. Those were great days. All that we have lost. Not only IPTA, but the Communist Party of India also split. Every leftist began to believe that only his ideology was correct, all others were wrong. Unfortunately, leaders were interested in themselves, not in people. At the global level, too, the Soviet Union broke down. East Europe got scattered.'

Titas could not be completed, right?

'No, it is a complete film. Ritaban has obtained its negatives also. He has also made new prints.'

What happened to the documentary film on the artist Ramkinkar Baij?

'We have also made prints of it. Now, Ritaban will edit it. That aside, *Bagalar Bangadarshan* is an incomplete film. Ritaban is busy completing that too. We have also published a volume of short stories written by Ritwik.'

Suramadi remembers that he was fond of classical music, and had many LPs in his collection. About Ghatak's working style, she says, 'I personally believe that he was very disciplined and methodical … He was completely absorbed in his work. While shooting *Ajantrik* in Ranchi, the producer Pramod-da [Pramod Lahiri] was very worried about how it would be completed. But without losing courage, Ritwik completed the shoot quietly. And then a letter was written to Prashanta Lahiri [Pramod's elder brother]. He arrived and paid everybody their dues. In only eighteen days, Ritwik had worked day and night and finished editing the film. He stayed in the laboratory for eighteen days. He also worked on the background score of the film. He himself wrote the tunes. All this work would not be possible if he wasn't disciplined.

'While *Meghe Dhaka Tara* was being shot, art director Robi Chatterjee got the news of his father's sad demise. Ritwik took on the responsibility of his work. He would stay in the studio all night and all day. There was a resource crunch. Ritwik himself was the film's producer. Friends such as Piyush Ganguly and Ajit Lahiri had tried to provide some financial help. But the help never came in. Ritwik borrowed about Rs 30,000 from here and there. He borrowed some money from my cousin, who was living in Shillong. A scene was shot there itself. All men and women working on the film had stayed in my father's house. Amidst many adversities Ritwik completed that work.[6]

'There were similar adversities during the making of *Subarnarekha* and *Komal Gandhar*, too. In order to raise some finances for *Subarnarekha*, Ritwik made an ad film called *Scissors* for the Imperial Tobacco Company. During this time, his intake of alcohol had increased substantially. Ritwik needed a competent and honest production manager who could take care of the money and management. But he could never get such a person. Often, people would cheat him. While scripting *Jukti* ..., he went to Shillong. At that time, I was working in Birbhum near Santiniketan. He came over there and did a script-reading session with me. He would work very hard on scriptwriting. There are two types of scripts for *Ajantrik*; *Komal Gandhar* had three; *Nagarik* had only one. He was very ill when *Titas* began.'

Did Ritwikda write poems, too?

'One or two. He began with short stories. When he was in a mental hospital, he had written a psychodrama called *Shei Meye* [That Girl]. Not only that, he also staged that play in the mental hospital. Doctors, hospital staffers and patients took part in it. In the mental hospital, he wrote the eighth "sarga" of *Kumarasambhava*. Among Ritwik's important plays are *Neecher Mahal*, *Sanko*, *Bisarjan*, *Dalil*, and also *Jwala* and *Jwalanta* are taken note of. He also translated the IPTA play *The Life of Galileo*. And adapted *HaJaBaRaLa* written by Satyajit Ray's father Sukumar.' (Sukumar Ray's nonsensical poems are well known. The best of those are to be found in his book *Abol Tabol*.)

Talking about Ghatak's family, Suramadi says, 'I never met my father-in-law. He was a district magistrate in East Bengal. He was said to be an excellent orator and a judge. He had nine children. In other words, Ritwik had eight siblings. The eldest was Manish Ghatak, who was a well-known writer of the Kallol group. His daughter Mahasweta Devi is also a well-known writer. Another brother, Sudheesh Ghatak, was a cameraman. He was head of the Films Division's Assam and Nagpur branches. He had also directed two or three films. Younger brother Lokesh was a naval officer. He was an artist, but an alcoholic. Among his sisters, one is a singer, another an artist and the third lives in Pondicherry, at the Aurobindo Ashram, with her daughter. The fourth one [Ghatak's twin] lives in Dhaka. The song "*Je rate mor duwarguli*" in *Meghe Dhaka Tara* is sung by Gita Ghatak. She played the role of Nita's sister in *Meghe Dhaka Tara*.'

Does Gita Ghatak belong to the Ghatak family?

'She is married to Anish, Mahasweta Devi's brother. Now Anish is also no more. His two brothers have also passed.'

What did your father do?

'My father, Kumud Ranjan Bhattacharya, worked as an accounts officer in the supply department in Shillong. For thirty-five long years, he was secretary of the Shillong-based Banga Sahitya Parishad. Besides being the commissioner of the Municipality, he was also chairman of Shillong College. He took deep interest in the working of the Ramakrishna Mission. He has also authored some books.'

How did you become a communist?

'During my student days, I came under the influence of the revolutionary leader Anjali Lahiri. All her sisters were members of the Communist Party. I was attracted to the philosophy of communism. I went underground for six months. And then I was arrested. Consequently, I was imprisoned for one year and eight months. In prison, I was locked up with insane women, hardened criminals, murderers and prostitutes.'

Was that during the British rule?

'No, all this happened in independent India. Our own government had sent us behind bars. And then the case was fought in the Supreme Court under habeas corpus. We were taken to Delhi. Our pleader was Sadhan Gupta, while Fakhruddin Ali Ahmed was on the government side. In the end, all the leaders were released, but ordinary comrades like us were left behind bars [*laughs*]. After returning from Delhi, I began writing a diary. It was released [as *Shillong Jailer Diary*] in 1952.'

Outside, drowning out the vendors' screams, an aeroplane whizzes past. Inside, Suramadi keeps unearthing the past. 'During the shooting of *Ajantrik*, I could not always accompany Ritwik. At that time, my daughter was a one-year-old. But I remember so well the scene of the Oraon adivasis' dance. It was an incredible scene. That scene of the shadows was shot by Sudheesh [Ghatak]. To shoot *Subarnarekha*, we stayed in Chakura for a month. The scenes of Sita and Abhiram, the song and the relics of an aeroplane on an abandoned airstrip, the following scenes of the behrupiya were all shot there.'

In *Subarnarekha*, Ghatak's 'melodramatic' form finds its zenith. All his life, he had endeavoured to transform 'melodrama' into the 'epic'. In a scene in a night club in *Subarnarekha*, we hear an excerpt of a musical note from Federico Fellini's Italian film, *La Dolce Vita*. Ghatak would effortlessly employ such cinematographic means to 'quote' another director. In this film, Fellini had whiplashed the worn-out European civilisation. In *Subarnarekha*, Ghatak, too, whiplashes the hollow bhadralok civilisation of Bengal. He showed us how the real and the imaginary reflect their unified resonances immersed in a sentimental and romantic 'modernism'. Ghatak's scrutiny is radical and rigorous. The search for the protective 'mother' results in a terrible, traumatic descent into prostitution. Ghatak's means for laying bare this trauma are myths, archetypes, music, symbols and coincidences. He kept every door open to explore ways to articulate his ideas. Ghatak could infuse theatricality into his cinematographic form.

He would say, '... *ami mone kori film-form or any other artform primarily ekta make-believe. Lok jaane she ekta golpo dekhchhe—lok jaane eta bastob noy. Amake coincidence use korte hoy, ami any amount of coincidence use korte bhoy paina aar melodrama ami konorokom bhoy paina. Melodrama hochchhe ekta birthright, eta ekta form.* [I believe the film-form, or any other artform, is primarily make-believe. People know they are watching a story—people know this is not real. I need to use coincidence; I am not scared of using any amount of coincidence or melodrama. Melodrama is a birthright, a form of art.]'

Ghatak has written several powerful essays. In India, very few film directors have written about film aesthetics like he has. Ritwik Ghatak is an 'event' in the history of Indian cinema. During his lifetime, not a single film of his could go to any foreign film festival. Today, there is a demand for his films in Europe. During his lifetime, Ghatak struggled to reach out to the wide audience he had so desired, and still didn't compromise at any stage. But the failures pushed him into a state of hopelessness. On 6 February 1976, he breathed his last in Calcutta. Now who will sing the songs of unity through cinema?[7]

Suramadi has already offered us another cup of lemon tea. It is quite late in the night, but the bazaar outside hasn't quietened. The city of Calcutta is looking at the void created by the absence of two great film-makers—Satyajit Ray and Ritwik Ghatak. Neelkantha Bagchi of *Jukti, Tokko aar Goppo* is no longer with us. Neither are those revolutionary young men and women and their reason, debate and a story. The only thing that survives is Nita's last heart-wrenching cry in *Meghe Dhaka Tara*, '*Dada, ami bachte chai …*'

Note: During our long conversation, Surama Ghatak spoke in Bengali, which was interpreted for me in English by Ajoy De. This 'dialogue' didn't acquire the conventional form of an interview. Hence there is no clear-cut Q&A. During our conversation, she becomes meanderingly meditative, and I, her listener. – AG

This piece was originally published in Bharatiya Vidya Bhavan's Navneet Samarpan, *a leading Gujarati monthly that is quite popular among middle-class Gujaratis in India and abroad, in December 1996. This English translation, by the author himself, is being published for the first time in this anthology.*

Amrit Gangar is a Mumbai-based film theorist, critic, author, curator, historian and cultural activist, who had held a week-long comprehensive retrospective ('Remembering Ritwik') of Ghatak's films in Mumbai in 1987. On this occasion, the book Arguments/Stories *was published. It was released by Ritwik Ghatak's disciple, Mani Kaul. Gangar, along with some Screen Unit colleagues, was in conversation on stage (on different days) with Ustad Bahadur Khan (music composer of* Subarnarekha *and* Titas Ekti Nodir Naam*) and the cinematographer Dilip Ranjan Mukherjee (*Komal Gandhar *and* Subarnarekha*). Gwalior gharana exponent Neela Bhagwat, the vocalist, sang khayals while paying tribute to Ritwik Ghatak. Gangar writes both in Gujarati and English, and some of his books have won awards. At present, he is engaged in writing a book on his theory of Cinema Prayoga.*

Notes

1 Directed by Vishnupant Govind Damle and Sheikh Fattelal and produced by the Prabhat Film Company, *Sant Tukaram*, the 1936 Marathi film, received a special jury mention at the Venice International Film Festival in 1937. Vishnupant Pagnis, who essayed the role of Tukaram in the film, was a last-minute casting decision for playing the lead role of the seventeenth-century saint-poet from Maharashtra.

2. Ritwik Ghatak had started rehearsing the play *Neecher Mahal* in 1954. Some dispute had taken place between Ghatak and IPTA's south squad about this play written by Umanath Bhattacharya. The lead cast of this play included Kali Bandopadhyay, Mumtaz Ahmed Khan, Umanah Bhattacharya, Amal Kar, etc. Kali Bandopadhyay had played the role of the father in Ghatak's first film *Nagarik*. Mumtaz Ahmed Khan played Sushant in this film.
   Ghatak had directed the Hindi play *Musafaron ke Liye* (written by Govind Mali), which was based on Gorky's *Lower Depths*. This play was first staged in Mumbai's Bharatiya Vidya Bhavan on 18–19 December 1956. Its lead cast included A.K. Hangal, Balraj Sahni and Biman Dalvi.

3. After the dispute over *Neecher Mahal*, Ritwik had to leave IPTA. After *Bisarjan*, the Communist Party of India had levelled many charges against Ritwik, and he was removed from the Party. (There is a difference of opinion about whether Ritwik Ghatak was a Party card-holder.)

4. During 1955-56, Ritwik Ghatak had worked in the Filmistan Studios only for three months as story and scenario writer. In his letter dated 10 April 1956, he made some suggestions to studio head Sasadhar Mukherjee to make the studios more creative.

5. Ritwik Ghatak's first film *Nagarik* (1952-53) could not be released during his lifetime. There was a general belief that the prints of the film had been destroyed, but after Gharak's death, technicians traced the film's positive prints, although they were in a seriously damaged condition. Very carefully, they made negative prints from those damaged positives and got it released for the first time in Calcutta in the month of August 1977. Thus *Nagarik* remained away from public attention for twenty-five years. Its director himself could not see the film released during his lifetime. For him, this was a tragic chapter of his life.

6. In this scene, Nita (Supriya Choudhury), who has been afflicted with tuberculosis and is emaciated physically could not hold herself back upon seeing her brother Shankar (Anil Chatterjee), and cries, sobbing, 'Dada, ami bachte chai ... [Brother, I want to live ...]'. Her heart wrenching cry

for survival is heard all across hills in a Shillong valley, it echoes in the brahmanda, the universe. Invoking the collective subconscious, the 360 degrees circular movement of the camera manifests the non-indifference of nature.

7. In his films, Ghatak deeply articulated his desire for a united Bengal. That desire kept manifesting in many ways through images and sounds. In *Komal Gandhar*, the event becomes three-fold: Anasuya's unsteady mind, the dilemma of the folk theatre movement and the anguish felt by partitioned Bengal. Through ancient marriage songs, Ghatak invokes the note of unity. As an archetype, the counterpoint of all these layers is lagna/marriage, in other words, unity. Ghatak immersed the inevitability of unity into the marriage songs. Rabindranath Tagore had once said, '*Naam rekhechhi Komal Gandhar mone mone.* [In my mind, I have named it Komal Gandhar.]' Bengal means Komal Gandhar. Poet Bishnu Dey amplified Tagore's note, Ritwik Ghataak picked it up as the inaugural note.

Madhumati, *Musafir* and disillusionment: The Bombay years

SHAMYA DASGUPTA

Pratiti Devi (Ritwik Ghatak's twin, Chhotopishi to my mother, and to all of us by extension) mentioned once that Ritwik owned a car at one point, possibly in the late 1950s. A car with a fancy name that she couldn't remember. If that was so, his time in Bombay working for Filmistan may have had a role in the temporary financial upswing for Ritwik and his family. Because, really, it was the only time he held a proper paying job. Of course, he spent some time at the Film and Television Institute of India, but that was in the 1960s. And, by all accounts, none of his films made him rich.

We are talking about 1955-56. *Nagarik* had been made, and its release scotched in 1952. He married Surama in mid-1955. The story of those years—Ritwik's time in the city he called 'rotten' and 'crude' and 'materialistic' and 'completely unsuited to any creative work'—is to be found in the letters he wrote to his wife, published by her in a book titled *Ritwik* (Anustup Prokashoni, 1996). In the letters, we find a young man, just around thirty, missing his wife (to-be, to start with) and his city and the avenues to channel his creativity; not being able to build with his wife the life they might have hoped for, but also a man full of hope. Hope that he would be able to do something useful while at Filmistan; hope that he would earn enough money to put some sort of life together for his family; and that it would be the start of better things for him as a creator.

'I just received a telegram from Salil Chowdhury, quite out of the blue. "Filmistan job almost fixed. Passage, hotel expense free. Start immediately!" We had a casual conversation around a year ago, and then this,' Ritwik writes in a letter dated 26 April 1955, in which he charts out his plans. 'I don't have the money to buy a plane ticket. If you can wire me the money, I can travel on the 2nd [of May] and return to Calcutta by the 5th, catch a flight to Shillong and get married, and join work by the 15th. You and I can stay in Bombay for a month or so.'

As is evident, at no point did Ritwik have any illusions about Filmistan or Bombay. He wanted to take up the job for the money. He was thirty. About to be married. Not many paisas to his name, and living rent-free in the house of a friend, Bhupati Nandy, who worked in the theatre and in cinema. He had made one full-length film that no one had seen—*Nagarik*—and Nandy was part of the group that had produced the film. In short, it was all looking rather bleak for Ritwik. And while alcohol hadn't made an appearance yet, it would soon. He would be expelled from the Communist Party of India by the end of the year.

'If the contract comes through, I will get a lump sum straightaway. We won't have any trouble setting up home. I can repay all debts and clear out of Bhupati's house. We won't have any worries; we can begin a new chapter.' But he wasn't counting his chickens yet. 'I am going by the assumption that I won't get the job.'

The job at Filmistan, as a writer, did come through. That's how we got *Musafir* and *Madhumati* (later tweaked and made in Bengali as *Rajkanya*). The couple first moved into Hrishikesh Mukherjee's house in Andheri. Bimal Roy's studio was close by. Salil Chowdhury lived not far away. Keshto Mukherjee, who had made his acting debut with *Nagarik* and would later do small roles in *Musafir*, *Ajantrik* and *Bari Theke Paliye*, 'stayed with us for a year as he was looking for work', Surama writes. What a fun time they must have all had. Ritwik had started writing for

Filmistan—or trying to write—and they shifted, not long after moving to Bombay, to a flat in Goregaon, close to where Filmistan was.

At some point, they must have gone back to Calcutta, possibly to drop Surama back. And, upon returning to Bombay, Ritwik writes on 30 June 1955, 'Salil tells me that Mukherjee [Sasadhar Mukherjee, the co-founder of Filmistan] was miffed that I didn't meet him while in Calcutta, and that I have become useless after getting married and he had made a mistake by giving me the job. Anyway, I met him [Mukherjee], told him some vague things and have joined work formally.'

Job in the bag, there was the question of work. And it started on the wrong foot. 'It doesn't look exciting at all. To be honest, there is no work. I just have to write some rubbish for the heck of it and go sit in the office from 10 a.m. to 5 p.m. I don't think I can do much here seeing Mukherjee's aversion towards me. I just have to grit my teeth and try to earn some money. I don't know how successful I will be, but there is nothing else to do here. Doing good work, trying to prove my creative ability or trying to find fame … all of it feels unattainable.'

This is all within a month-and-a-half of that first meeting with Mukherjee, remember. Ritwik appears to have given up already. And he wants to return to Calcutta.

'This life is not for us,' he writes, addressing Surama as Lokkhi, her name at home. 'To work for money, it's not something we have done before, and I feel filthy doing it now. If I can save up enough to repay the debts, which must be around a thousand rupees, and give Bhupati a hundred rupees a month for a year, I'll give this up. […] You must also try to find ways to earn something. I don't want to stay away from Calcutta. If, between us, we can earn three-four hundred rupees in Calcutta, we can have a grand life. I don't want to pay the price I must to make a name here.'

But things change soon after. He 'sells' a story, and he thinks up another one. The first will be a superhit film. The second will be a non-starter.

'Bimalda wants to buy my story immediately, and it will be the next Bimal Roy Productions film,' Ritwik writes on 5 July. In 1955, Bimal Roy Productions released *Naukari*, with Kishore Kumar in the lead role, and *Devdas*, starring Dilip Kumar, Vyjayanthimala, Suchitra Sen and Motilal. The company's next release, in 1958, was *Madhumati*.

'Bimalda has asked me to get started right away. He has promised to give me an advance of around 500 rupees in the next few days. I have found a small flat in Goregaon. If I get the advance, I will move there. Nothing is certain in this industry, so I won't know for sure about the money till I actually get it. But I am hopeful.'

Ritwik, despite never making a film himself that made money except *Meghe Dhaka Tara*, which is considered a success, might have been capable of churning out successful films. *Madhumati* is an example. *Musafir*, though not as big a hit as *Madhumati*, is another. Plus, as you would have read elsewhere in this anthology, he once told Habibur Rahman Khan, the producer of *Titas Ekti Nodir Naam*, 'I have wasted a lot of your money. I will write you a script, like I have done for others, and you make a commercial film with it. You will make a lot of money.' It was just a path he chose not to walk.

Here's Ritwik to Surama on the non-starter, about which he says, 'I really like the idea: an atomic scientist falls asleep and has a dream about the future of the world, of a time when the universal scientific community has taken shape. Of course, I will have to include some songs and dances and some drama and emotional scenes, basically everything a Bombay film needs. But still, I think I can be true to the logic of scientific advancement and social structures and psychological evolution while also making it interesting and fun. When I come back to Calcutta during Pujo, I will meet Dr Meghnad Saha [the astrophysicist] and ask him for help. And here, I can ask the bosses at the Nuclear Physics Laboratory for help too.'

He met Mukherjee with the story not long after. It was rejected.

The saga of good and bad continued for Ghatak over the coming months.

Differences with the Communist Party of India had reached a head. He could see the expulsion coming, as he writes in more than one letter. His health had taken a turn for the worse too—pneumonia had led to doctors asking him to get his life in order: 'Now, I need to eat, work, rest and sleep with some sort of routine and also have a tonic. That should set me right soon.'

Then, on 10 November—he was out of the party by then—we find, '[his eldest brother Manish Ghatak] has written to say that *Nagarik* has been nominated for a state award. After so much pain, will this be the start

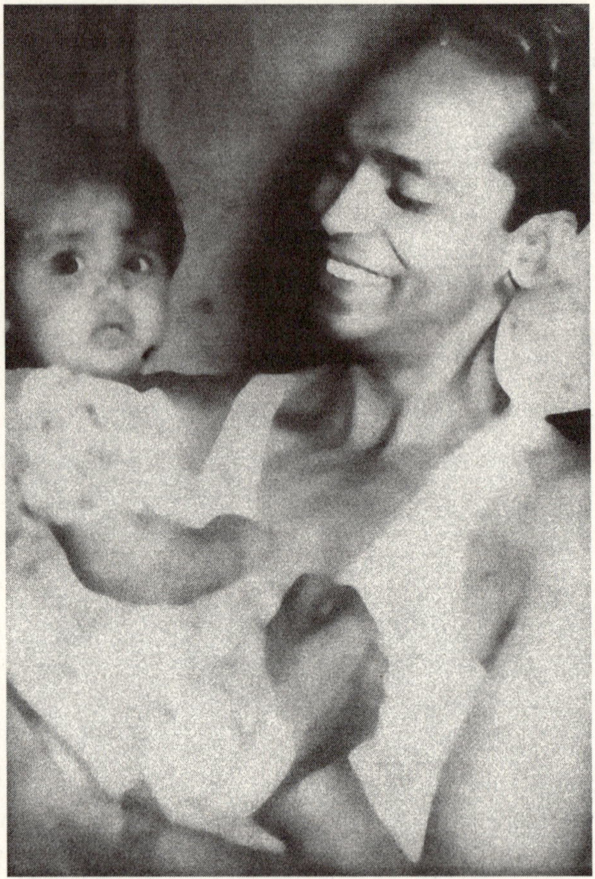

Ritwik with Tuntuni (Samhita), his first-born, in happy times;
© NFDC - National Film Archive of India

of my glory run?' But then, on 24 November, 'We got late submitting the documents for *Nagarik*, but he says that they have accepted it anyway. I don't know about the result of the competition yet.' It didn't win. He also writes that he had heard from the producers of *Nagarik* that they would be trying to give the film its much-delayed theatrical release. That didn't happen till after Ritwik's death.

The letters also recorded other tidbits that marked his days, such as this exciting sighting: '[Nikolai] Bulganin and [Nikita] Khrushchev just went past the studio towards Aarey Colony.' They were in Bombay at the time for a conference. 'This country will see its own communist revolution soon, because this ancient civilisation is being hollowed out from inside for years.'

But staying in Bombay, and being around commercially successful people, came with benefits. Ritwik writes on 16 December that Bimal Roy was going to produce a film in Bangla soon, and he had been asked to direct it. Not just that, both Radha Films and Aurora Films in Calcutta wanted Ritwik to direct films for them. 'I am happy at the thought of getting away from this city, but the financial problems we are bound to have if I work in Calcutta is a concern.'

As things turned out, Ritwik chose to leave the Filmistan job in 1956 itself. Less than a year after taking it up. The story and screenplay for *Madhumati* were done. *Musafir* (Hrishikesh Mukherjee's first film as director) was being written; it would be completed after Ritwik returned home. Ritwik was also one of the writers for a Filmistan movie called *Raja*. I am not sure what happened to this one. It's possible the film was never made. It's equally possible that it was released under a different title. Maybe Ritwik wasn't mentioned in the credits.

It appears, from Surama's notes, that Sasadhar Mukherjee had grown quite fond of Ritwik by this time—perhaps *Madhumati* helped. But it was around this time that Ritwik's mother died. He had also not got the increment he had expected at Filmistan. So he left. His resignation note to Mukherjee is most interesting and illuminating. It was written in English—unlike the letters, which were in Bangla—and Surama reproduced it in its entirety. An excerpt:

> You have a rare opportunity for a re-appraisal. You are a worshipper of facts, Sir. And what is more, you are also a manufacturer of facts. You know facts are not born, they are made. My request is to you, please create a corner where new facts can be made.
>
> Make a department for experimental film-making. Appoint persons with necessary flares [flairs], put all sorts of hurdles before them—a low budget, no stars, no good equipment, no fancy name in technicians, no massive sets, no legendary music director, and also, no colour. Just ideas. Let them get out of the studios and shoot out of doors, let them know that any story can be a great story with proper treatment, and also treatment mainly includes camera treatment. Let them see the world thru' of the camera, let them explore possibilities of the editing table, creative sound track, camera set-up.

The letter is long, and mostly stresses on the need to create space for experimental cinema. Eventually, he gets to the resignation: 'I, personally, do not feel like staying here if such a small corner is not made. I do not aspire after position or money but I must feel that I am living a worthy life. [...] I do not see any future in this smug complacency. This environment is fetter.'

Mukherjee was recuperating after a bout of ill-health at the time. Ritwik mentions that he had completed writing *Raja*, 'which [Mahesh] Kaul is not doing', as well as 'two stories for Sachin Sarkar about a dancer's life' and a story 'about a coalmine for [Rajinder Singh] Bedi'. These 'are awaiting your return'. This was the state of his projects as of 10 April 1956, the day he sent in the letter of resignation. Looking at Mukherjee's filmography, the 'small corner' was never made.

There is no record of what Mukherjee said in response to this letter, other than that he had asked Ritwik to meet him. We don't know from the letters if they did. Ritwik returned to Calcutta not long after, tried one last time to get *Nagarik* released, failed, and went back with Surama to Bombay, where the shooting of *Madhumati* had started. Apparently, Ritwik also wrote a script around this time for the producer Hiten Chaudhury (also the brother of Manish Ghatak's wife Dharitri Devi), but Surama mentions that the film never got made.

Soon after, *Ajantrik* and *Bari Theke Paliye* did get made and released. Both were produced by Pramod Lahiri. Both released in 1958. Then *Meghe Dhaka Tara*, *Komal Gandhar* and *Subarnarekha* between 1960 and 1965. Some documentary films were also started. Not all of them finished.

That phase, beginning with his Bombay years and lasting a decade, until 1965, was perhaps the most productive in Ritwik's short, stop-start career. He was in good health. Alcohol hadn't harmed him quite so much yet, though it would soon. It was a period where perhaps he wasn't as disillusioned as he would come to be. And it was a period where he did great work, some of the greatest our cinema has seen, even if not many people of his time had the opportunity to truly appreciate it.

I had written a less detailed version of the story, titled 'A bottle in one pocket, your childhood in the other—Ritwik Ghatak's Bombay-Poona years', *for* Cinemaazi *in 2019.*

Shamya Dasgupta is the editor of this anthology, the author of Don't Disturb the Dead: The Story of the Ramsay Brothers *(2017) and translator of Mahasweta Devi's* Mirror of the Darkest Night, *among other works.*

Acknowledgements

Won't you please, please, help me?

And they all did. Like heroes.

Veena Hariharan, associate professor at Jawaharlal Nehru University's School of Arts and Aesthetics and dear friend, connected me to everyone she could in the world of Ghatak academics and they sent in some magical essays.

Iyesha Geeth Abbas and her extremely committed-to-the-cause colleagues at National Film Archive of India were immensely helpful when it came to tracking down photographs and much else. Chandan Goswami and the Ritwik Smriti Granthagar at Nandan did much the same when it came to old books and other resources. Ritwik Memorial Trust, which owns most of whatever Ghatak left behind, was more than happy to let me use what I wanted for the anthology.

My sister Ina Puri opened doors I couldn't have. Arijit Sen and Sreyashi Dastidar, both more family than friends, helped with ideas, introductions, translations, the occasional review and suggestions, as did Prithviraj Guha, assistant professor of economics at Presidency University and dear friend.

Members of the extended Ghatak family—mashis Rina Chakraborty and Dhriti Bagchi in the main—helped with permissions and encouragement. Dhriti's husband, physicist Amitabha Bagchi, was to be a collaborator on the edits but unfortunately passed away in March 2025, but we had a number of exciting conversations prior to that. Aroma Dutta, another mashi, not only contributed a heartbreakingly beautiful essay but also made sure I could use chunks from the book her mother, Ghatak's twin Pratiti Devi, had written. Tathagata Bhattacharya said 'arre, what's to ask' when I called to check if I could translate his grandmother Mahasweta Devi's essay and transcribe/translate his father Nabarun Bhattacharya's lecture. Maitreesh Ghatak, Manishita Dass and Ananda Chakraborty wrote essays for the anthology despite their hectic schedules. Parambrata Chattopadhyay, busier than most people I know, contributed the thoughtful introduction to the book.

Not to forget the contributors, some of them friends now—if I may—even though we didn't know each other before this exercise began. Among them, Moinak Biswas, who sent two essays for inclusion in the anthology when I would have been thrilled with just one; Arun Khopkar, for the many conversations and the help with Bhaskar Chandravarkar's piece; Goutam Ghose, Jayant Kaikini and Jahnu Barua for the long chats they didn't owe me; Brinda Bose, Sumana Roy, Biswajit Chatterjee, Sanghita Sen, Erin O'Donnell and Paulomi Chakraborty for going the extra mile when it came to their essays.

It's perhaps unfair to just name these contributors and not the rest, who, apart from spending time, energy and thought on their pieces, also helped in ways small and big.

Film-makers Soumik Sen, Sanjiv Shah and Ramdas Kadavallur, the journalist Bedatri D. Choudhury, the academic and friend Rimli Bhattacharya, the researcher Abir Bhattacharya, and so many others I might be forgetting right now—much appreciation and gratitude.

Not to forget Soumitra Adhikary, whose illustrations have added so much colour in black and white to these pages.

And as always, Ajitha G.S.—wife, editor, mother to our Nimki—for all the ideas, suggestions and love, and of course the edits in her capacity as an editor and a publisher at Westland Books.

Also at Westland, the publisher Karthika V.K. (the second time she has been kind enough to collaborate with me) and the art director Saurabh Garge, and everyone else in this warm team.

This must end with a cliché, because, it really wouldn't have been possible for a sports journalist like myself to put together a volume such as this one without all these people and many others chipping in. It's all for Ritwik Ghatak.

Thank you, again, for joining us on this trip. And before I forget, *think, think, train yourself to think*.